Passion and Resurrection Narratives

Australian College of Theology Monograph Series

SERIES EDITOR GRAEME R. CHATFIELD

The ACT Monograph Series, generously supported by the Board of Directors of the Australian College of Theology, provides a forum for publishing quality research theses and studies by its graduates and affiliated college staff in the broad fields of Biblical Studies, Christian Thought and History, and Practical Theology with Wipf and Stock Publishers of Eugene, Oregon. The ACT selects the best of its doctoral and research masters theses as well as monographs that offer the academic community, scholars, church leaders and the wider community uniquely Australian and New Zealand perspectives on significant research topics and topics of current debate. The ACT also provides opportunity for contributors beyond its graduates and affiliated college staff to publish monographs which support the mission and values of the ACT.

Rev Dr Graeme Chatfield
Series Editor and Associate Dean

Passion and Resurrection Narratives

Post Nicene Latin Interpretations

ANDREW M. BAIN

WIPF & STOCK · Eugene, Oregon

PASSION AND RESURRECTION NARRATIVES
Post Nicene Latin Interpretations

Copyright © 2018 Andrew M. Bain. All rights reserved. Except for brief quotations in critical publications or reviews, no part of this book may be reproduced in any manner without prior written permission from the publisher. Write: Permissions, Wipf and Stock Publishers, 199 W. 8th Ave., Suite 3, Eugene, OR 97401.

Wipf & Stock
An Imprint of Wipf and Stock Publishers
199 W. 8th Ave., Suite 3
Eugene, OR 97401

www.wipfandstock.com

PAPERBACK ISBN: 978-1-5326-7433-4
HARDCOVER ISBN: 978-1-5326-7434-1
EBOOK ISBN: 978-1-5326-7435-8

Manufactured in the U.S.A.   NOVEMBER 8, 2018

Contents

Preface | ix
Abbreviations | xii
Major Primary Sources | xii
Journals | xiv

1 Introduction | 1
    The Approach of this Study | 2
    Key Primary Sources | 9
    Terminology | 19
    Overview of Scholarship | 26
    Key Questions | 37
    Note on Primary Texts Used | 39

2 Embodying the Text: Jerome's Commentariorum in Matheum | 41
    Scholarly Conclusions | 42
    Philological Interests | 49
    The Unity of the Text | 52
    Manner of Proceeding through the Text | 55
    Drawing Theology from the Text | 57
    Use of Allegory | 61
    Typology | 64
    Prophecy-Fulfillment | 64
    Practical Application to Audience | 66
    Polysemy and Monosemy | 70
    Conclusions | 72

3   Faith in Realities: Hilary's In Matthaeum and De Trinitate | 74
      Scholarly Conclusions | 75
        1. In Matthaeum | 81
          Manner of Proceeding through the Text | 81
          Realities Described by the Text | 85
          Telling Theological Stories | 88
          Monosemy | 91
          Typology | 92
          Practical Application of the Text | 97
          The Theme of Faith | 98
          Conclusions | 100
        2. De Trinitate | 101
          Manner of Proceeding through the Text | 102
          Monosemy | 104
          Manner of Argument | 105
          Hilary's Purpose: Theological Themes Practically Applied | 109
          Typology | 112
          Text, Theology, and Homiletics | 114
          Differences Between the In Matthaeum and De Trinitate | 116
          Conclusions | 117

4   Through the Eyes of the Evangelist: Ambrose's Expositio Evangelii Secundam Lucam | 119
      Scholarly Conclusions | 120
      Allegory | 127
      Literal Exposition and Manner of Proceeding through the Text | 129
      Typology | 132
      Prophecy-Fulfillment | 133
      Realities Behind the Text | 134
      Authorial Distinctives | 140
      Polysemy and Monosemy | 145
      Usage of Other Parts of Scripture | 147
      Audience | 150
      From Text to Theology | 156
      Conclusions | 162

5   Augustine and the Senses of Scripture: In Iohannis Evangelium and Sermones De Tempore | 164
       Scholarly Conclusions | 164
       Progressing through the Letter of the Text | 168
       Allegory? | 176
       Realities Behind the Text | 184
       Typology | 191
       Conclusions | 194

6   A Wide-Angle Lens: Distinguishing Features of Augustine's Exegesis | 196
       Wide-Ranging Interests | 196
       An Intuitive Love of Tangents | 197
       An Intuitive Love of Insightful Questions | 203
       An Intuitive Love for Examining Alternatives | 204
       Polysemy | 206
       Concern for Audience | 210
       The Workings of the Human Heart | 224
       From Text to Theology | 228
       Conclusions | 237

7   Conclusions: Interpretation Then and Now | 239

Bibliography | 253
       Primary Sources | 253
       Secondary Sources | 254

Preface

WHY STUDY THE BIBLICAL commentaries and sermons of late antiquity? This book is written out of the conviction that grasping how the church of a particular time and place read the Scriptures is key to understanding the Christianity of that milieu. By considering how the biblical accounts of the central events of the Christian faith—the crucifixion and resurrection of Christ—were interpreted, we might be able to grasp this with particular clarity and know something of the heart of Christianity in another time. The very familiarity of the Gospel descriptions of these events to Christians in all ages means that close examination of how they were read in one era can readily act as a mirror to the interpretative habits, theological tendencies, and pastoral concerns of any other time—including our own.

The late fourth and early fifth centuries are well known as times of great productivity in terms of Christian literature and theological reflection. For a long time, the commentaries, sermons, and other works of this period dealing directly and principally with the interpretation of Scripture received relatively little attention from modern readers, left in the shadow of the strong interest in theological and biographical matters. Over the past two decades, this has changed to a significant degree, as contemporary scholarship has increasingly recognized both the utility that the biblical works of the time hold for understanding the personalities, theology, and historical developments of the period, and their value in their own right as historical and theological documents. A very substantial proportion of the surviving output of the Christian authors of the period comes to us in the form of their writings on Scripture: in some cases, a majority of the material which is available to us (Hilary and Jerome being examples here), and in many others some of their longest works and a significant percentage of the total (as in the cases of Augustine and Ambrose). For most of the patristic authors, the reading and usually also the preaching of Scripture occupied a large part of their time, as an ever-present and central element of their ministry. For this reason, their works in this area are able to offer us insight into their daytoday work and a useful contrasting perspective to their other works which were more usually called forth by particular occasions or issues rather than by the grind of everyday ministry.

The Latin Christian writers of late antiquity are of particular interest for those who stand in the Western theological tradition rather than within the Eastern churches, due to their direct, substantial, and seminal influence upon that tradition. This is especially true of those Latin authors who were much revered by medieval Christianity and by much of the early modern period afterwards; Ambrose, Jerome, and above all Augustine are undoubtedly in the first rank of this category, with Hilary also figuring notably. All four of these authors lived and wrote within two generations of one another, and within the same broad context as wellknown clergy of the late Roman Empire. All four also wrote works on the canonical Gospels—all of which indiscriminately discuss material from across the four Gospel accounts, regardless of which Gospel they might ostensibly be commenting upon—making for a ready comparison of their methods.

Although interest in the biblical works of the patristic authors has grown considerably in recent years and has often deepened our understanding today of the exegetical and homiletical practices of the time, there is much to be gained by further exploration of the area. As we shall see, older paradigms for understanding patristic exegesis still exert a strong influence and are readily to be found in many contexts (among them the evangelical tradition of this author). Not only have the serious limits of these paradigms been increasingly apparent for some time, but as we shall see they are even less readily applicable to Latin authors than they are to Greek ones, and less relevant to patristic handling of New Testament texts than those drawn from the Old Testament. Through studying how four later Latin authors handled a focused yet critically important groups of biblical texts, this volume offers an in-depth analysis of patristic habits of reflection upon and application of Scripture, which seeks to identify alternative categories for describing the work of the Christian authors. It is hoped that the categories drawn out of the works in question will be more relevant to the Latin authors of late antiquity specifically, and of greater value than the alternatives in meaningfully distinguishing between the approaches of these authors.

Much of the work behind this volume began life as a PhD dissertation supervised by Professor John Moorhead at the University of Queensland. John was and remains a model to me in terms of reading, understanding, and teaching about late antiquity and the Christian literature it produced, and so I record my thanks to him here. My thinking about the period and its practices in relation to interpreting and applying Scripture has been developed through many interactions—most of them incidental—over the past decade with my colleagues at Queensland Theological College (QTC) as well as others within the Australian College of Theology (ACT) consortium, to whom I also owe thanks. I am also grateful to QTC for provision of study leave in late 2017, which assisted the completion of this project, as well as to Greta Morris for her assistance in the preparation of the manuscript. Lastly, thanks are due to my wife Robyn, for her encouragement to continue working on the question of how the late patristic authors interpreted and applied the biblical accounts of Christ's death and resurrection to real human lives.

Andrew M. Bain
Brisbane, 2018

Abbreviations

Major Primary Sources

Ambrose, *Lucam* — Ambrose, *Expositio evangelii secundam Lucam*. Edited by M. Adriaen). C[orpus] C[hristianorum] S[eries] L[atina] 14.

Ambrose, "Select Works" — Ambrose, "Select Works and Letters." In *Nicene and Post-Nicene Fathers: Second Series 10*. Translated by Henry De Romestin et al. New York: Christian Literature, 1896.

Augustine, *In Ioh.* — Augustine, *In Iohannis evangelium*. Edited by R. Willems. CCSL 34–36.

Augustine, *Serm.* — Augustine, *Sermones de tempore*. Edited by J.-P. Migne. P[atrologia] L[atina] 38.

Augustine, *Sermons* — Augustine, *Sermons. The Works of Saint Augustine: A Translation for the 21st Century*, III/6–7. Translated by Edmund Hill. New Rochelle, NY: Augustinian Heritage Institute, 1993.

Augustine, *Tractates* — Augustine, Tractates *on the Gospel of John, 55–111 and 112–24*. Translated by John W. Rettig. FOC 90, 92. Washington, DC: The Catholic University of America, 1994–95.

Augustine, *Liturgical*	Augustine, *Sermons on the Liturgical Seasons*. Translated by Mary S. Muldowney. *FOC* 38, 59. New York: The Fathers of the Church, 1958–59.
Hilary, *Comm. Matt.*	*Commentary on Matthew*. Translated by Daniel H. Williams. *FOC* 125. Washington, DC: The Catholic University of America, 2012.
Hilary, *Matt.*	Hilary, *In Matthaeum*. Edited by J. Doignon. Tome 2, Les Éditions du Cerf, Paris, 1979.
Hilary, *Select Works*	Hilary, *Select Works, Nicene and Post-Nicene Fathers: Second Series* 9. Translated by Edward W. Watson and Leighton Pullan. New York: Charles Scribner's Sons, 1899.
Hilary, *The Trinity*	Hilary, *The Trinity*. Translated by Stephen McKenna. *FOC* 25. New York: The Fathers of the Church, 1954.
Hilary, *Trinitate*	Hilary, *De Trinitate*. Edited by P. Smulders. *CCSL*, 62–62A.
Jerome, *Math.*	Jerome, *Commentariorum in Matheum*. Edited by D. Hurst and M. Adriaen. *CCSL* 77.

Note: I have followed this publisher's practice of spelling the Latin title of the work as "Matheum" throughout, rather than any of the other variants that are in use (e.g. "Matthaei," "Matthaeum").

Jerome, *Matt.*	Jerome, *Commentary on Matthew*. Translated by Thomas P. Scheck. *FOC* 117. Washington, DC: The Catholic University of America, 2008.

Journals

Aug	*Augustinianum*
AugSt	*Augustinian Studies*
CHB	*The Cambridge History of the Bible*
FOC	*The Fathers of the Church: A New Translation*
JECS	*Journal of Early Christian Studies*
JTS	*Journal of Theological Studies*
RAug	*Recherches Augustiniennes*
REAug	*Revue des études augustiniennes*
SP	*Studia Patristica*
ThR	*Theologische Realenzyklopädie*
VChr	*Vigiliae Christianae*

Abbreviations of biblical books follow those used by the Society of Biblical Literature.

I

Introduction

THE STUDY OF THE later Latin Fathers' exegetical works could benefit from a modest broadening of its focus, and consideration of these ancient authors' writings from some less familiar angles. Traditionally, scholarship has tended to describe these interpreters, alongside their Greek counterparts, by placing them somewhere along a continuum whose ends are labelled "literal" and "allegorical." The biblical works of the major later Latin Fathers (and of some less well-known figures) have also been thoroughly analyzed in terms of the influences acting upon them. While scholarship over the past two decades or more has explored their exegetical works in terms of a wider range of categories, this process has tended to be piecemeal, with many major works continuing to give the greatest place to concepts such as allegory, literalism, and the senses of Scripture.[1] What is needed are some additional categories within which the exegetical works of these Fathers can be analyzed, distinguished, and discussed. Ideally, these will be categories which are both demonstrably present within the deliberate practices and methods of the ancient authors themselves, as well as being of value to modern readers in understanding those same authors and using their methods and exegeses to prompt reflection on our own practices of biblical interpretation, today. This study attempts

---

1. A parallel and related tendency has been for many standard accounts to continue to draw a strong and definite distinction between Alexandrian and Antiochene approaches to exegesis, with the latter being focused on "literal" and "historical" methods of reading: Young, "Traditions of Exegesis," 735–6 observes as recently as 2013 that this tendency is still quite common, even though scholarship has provided many reasons for moving beyond the distinction in its traditional form.

to provide such a group of additional categories, while downplaying to some extent the relative usefulness of the senses of Scripture and their associated concepts for providing meaningful distinctions between the different exegetical approaches of the later Latin Fathers. However, before moving into the body of the work, several preliminary issues must be discussed. Firstly, the approach and methodology employed in this study will be outlined, and the authors and texts studied shall be introduced. Secondly, several key terms used will be defined. Thirdly, the modern study of patristic exegesis in the Latin West shall be summarized, with particular reference to trends and patterns in the treatment of the authors and texts under consideration here. Lastly, we shall consider relevant technical matters such as texts used and the translation philosophy employed.

The Approach of this Study

This study attempts to gain an understanding of the character of fourth–and fifth-century Latin biblical interpretation by examining selections from four major Fathers who wrote between the mid-fourth century and the early fifth century: Hilary, Ambrose, Jerome, and Augustine. Taken together, the biblical works of these four authors include well over 50 percent of the corpus of surviving Latin exegetical material written between Nicaea and the fall of the Western Empire. The commentators chosen were also influential figures and exegetes, in their own time and afterwards.[2] Hilary (ca. 315–367), bishop of Poitiers in Gaul, was the first major Latin theologian to emerge in the post-Nicene period. While relatively few of his works were purely exegetical by design, he is constantly using Scripture in order to serve his purposes, as shall be seen in chapter 3. Ambrose (339–397), bishop of Milan, was the major ecclesio-political figure of the Latin West in the 370s and 380s. As bishop of what was sometimes the imperial capital, his works on Scripture had substantial influence, and were instrumental in introducing the riches of Eastern

---

2. Further details of the life and times of the four authors chosen and of their influence can be found by consulting the following: Kelly, *Jerome*; Rebenich, *Jerome*, 1–59; Moorhead, *Ambrose*; McLynn, *Ambrose*; Pasini, *Ambrose of Milan*; Brown, *Augustine of Hippo: A Biography*; Chadwick, *Augustine*; Hollingworth, *Saint Augustine of Hippo* (on Augustine's intellectual development). In the absence of a good recent biography in English on Hilary, basic details plus a bibliographical survey can be found by consulting "Hilary of Poitiers," in *The Oxford Dictionary of the Christian Church*, 769–70.

scholarship to the West. Jerome (ca. 347–419/20), a native of Stridon in modern-day Croatia and subsequently a long-term resident of Bethlehem, was regarded by many in his own day, and many more since, as the leading exegete of the Latin West. A prolific commentator on the Bible, his works were highly regarded among his contemporaries for their being based on his presumed mastery of the Greek and Hebrew Scriptures. Lastly, Augustine (354–430), bishop of Hippo Regius in Roman Africa (modern-day Algeria) cannot be ignored in any study such as this. One of the most important theological figures in the history of Western Christianity, he has also left a substantial body of exegetical works to posterity.

The body of the exegetical works of these four major Latin authors is too substantial to be considered in its entirety in any meaningful depth. This book therefore takes a case-study approach, focusing on how each of the four chosen Fathers interprets the crucifixion and resurrection accounts within the Gospels.[3] There are several advantages of choosing this particular area. Firstly, the Gospels, taken together, are one of the few instances where major commentaries from several Latin Fathers of the period are extant. Developing a study that is representative of the methods of later Latin exegesis as a whole would not be possible from surviving commentaries on most other books of the Bible: the Gospels and the Psalms in fact represent the only case where the works of four major figures are available.[4] Secondly, the Gospels have been an important and well-known part of Scripture in every era of ecclesiastical history, and such a case study as this is therefore likely to be of greater interest to modern students of Scripture and scholars interested in biblical interpretation in other periods than most of the alternatives. Thirdly, the final chapters of the Gospels are of substantial importance to several major theological themes, such as the atonement, the resurrection and its consequences, and the nature of Christ. As a result, most commentators on these passages, both ancient and modern, tend to discuss such matters

---

3. In terms of its scope, this study includes the events associated with Christ's suffering which immediately precede his actual crucifixion, commencing with Christ's appearance before Pilate in Matt 27:11, Mark 15:1, Luke 23:1, and John 18:28. It also makes reference to certain events prior to this which our commentators associate closely with Christ's impending death and resurrection, most notably the scenes in the Garden of Gethsemane (Matt 26:36–46) and on the Mount of Olives (Luke 22:39–45).

4. In the case of the Psalms, direct comparison is difficult because the various Psalms commented upon by the different Fathers do not overlap as much as might be desired. For example, Hilary and Ambrose only comment upon Pss 1 and 118 (119 in the English Bible) in common.

through their exposition of the text. Analysis of how commentators use the text to explore such theological themes is easier in this case study than considering the interpretation of other parts of the Gospels, due to the wealth of available material. It also yields interesting results, as shall become apparent in the chapters that follow. Lastly, although the four Fathers under consideration are not all commenting on the same Gospel, comparisons between them are relatively easy when it comes to the final chapters of the Gospels. This is because at this point in their discussions of the Gospels, all four commentators tend strongly towards reading all of the evangelists in harmony as they interpret them, rather than rigorously sticking to the particular Gospel text that is their chosen passage. Biblical commentators in the early church tended to harmonize the Gospels rather than note their various distinctive contributions, and in this case study, the practice is even more apparent than in general. For example, Ambrose devotes about as much attention to the Johannine text as he does to the Gospel of Luke that he is preaching on.

At this point some of the limitations of what follows in this book should be noted. Firstly, it must be remembered that differences in exegetical style and method, whether cast in the traditional terms of the senses of Scripture or described using alternative categories, are to a large extent a product of various background factors which operate to influence the work of any given exegete. The case studies examined here have been written by four different men, with different characters, capabilities, backgrounds, failings, and foibles. Observations and conclusions regarding differences in their exegetical methods therefore tell us something about the personalities and capabilities of those concerned. Indeed, one of the aims of this study is to provide biographical students of the lives, times, and personalities of four major Christian figures of late antiquity with additional raw material to work with, by describing how they differ in their approaches to one particular activity, that of biblical exegesis. That said, this study is primarily concerned with identifying features in the work of the Fathers which can usefully be applied to distinguish between their exegetical methods. Naturally, these differences do tell us something about the personalities and backgrounds of the relevant Fathers. However, as this is a study of comparative exegesis and not of a biographical nature, it does not attempt to provide a detailed elaboration of what its conclusions about exegetical method might have to add to study into the personalities in question themselves.

A related issue, but one which touches more directly on our conclusions themselves, is the fact that the works in question differ in terms of aim, mode of composition and delivery, and intended audience. This raises the question—if the aims, audiences, and genres employed by the authors under study did not differ in the same manner, would the conclusions of this project be different? It needs to be acknowledged at the outset that several of the distinctions drawn between patristic writers by this study are indeed likely to be influenced by such factors. That said, it is proposed that some significant conclusions can still be drawn even when this is taken into account. As we shall see in the case of Hilary in chapter 3, two works produced at different times in the author's life, with different purposes and different formats (one a commentary, the other a doctrinal treatise), certainly are contrasting pieces in several respects. However, they also do share certain notable characteristics and tendencies in common, which allow useful conclusions to be drawn.

Furthermore, some of the results which are obtained through this study are rather surprising in light of the potential influence of such factors as aim, genre, and intended audience. For example, one might expect Hilary's and Jerome's commentaries on Matthew, probably written for select audiences, to be less interested in practical application than the sermons of Ambrose and Augustine, which were designed to be preached to public congregations. However, as we shall see, the results in this matter are not quite what might be expected. This also suggests that definite conclusions can be drawn about exegetical differences in spite of the influence of other factors. All of the authors under consideration, whatever their particular audiences or aims or modes of composition, share the broad goal of interpreting Scripture for the good of other Christians. All of them, therefore, need to take up a certain hermeneutical stance with respect to the question of how they and their audience are to derive meaning from Scripture, irrespective of their genre and context. It is this question that is the primary concern of this project—a matter in which, to be sure, factors such as the immediate audience and occasion do play a part, but in which we might still expect some degree of consistency from any given interpreter even as such factors change.

A significant disadvantage with the choice of exegetical works on the Gospels for a case study is that, being commentaries on New Testament texts, they are less likely than works on the Old Testament to find frequent occasion to use "spiritual" interpretations.[5] New Testament commentaries, the argument might go, will tend to be more literal than "spiritual," including less varied usage of the full range of the senses of Scripture than ones on the Old Testament. Attempting to prove that too much has been made of the senses would therefore be an easier task from the cases that have been chosen.

It should be acknowledged that this is the principal limitation of the proposal offered in this book. However, against this limitation must be weighed the advantages listed above in choosing to compare different exegetical approaches to the Gospels rather than some other part of Scripture. In addition, there are two other considerations which somewhat mitigate the force of this objection to our project. The first is that the assumption that exegesis of New Testament texts will necessarily entail a more restricted use of the non-literal senses is not entirely true. The final events of Jesus' time on earth are rich in allusions to and quotations from the Old Testament, and these provide ample opportunities for the exegete to develop his response to the text in a "spiritual" direction if that is the intention. The closing chapters of the Gospels are also replete with potentially symbolic material which readily lends itself to allegorical interpretation. When taken alongside the density of the literal narrative, it is apparent that a commentator could easily spend all of a lengthy exposition on either the literal or allegorical senses alone—or almost any combination of proportions of each—if he so chose. Augustine's sermon on the 153 fishes is a well-known example of some relevance here! It is true that the patristic exegete may more often feel compelled (or at least tempted) to resort to allegory when studying the Old Testament than when studying the New, since the former more often contains passages which are very difficult to interpret from a Christian standpoint. However, the point remains that the Gospels also contain many obscurities and details whose inclusion in the text can be much more easily accounted for through resort to the spiritual sense than adherence to the literal throughout.

Furthermore, to the extent that this is more often true of the Old Testament than of the New, does this not suggest that exegesis of it is in fact more constrained in terms of which senses of Scripture the commentator may use? Often when dealing with the Old Testament and in seeking

---

5. Particularly since some scholars are of the belief that "spiritual" interpretation is primarily directed at establishing a unity between the Old and New Testaments, e.g. Lubac, *Medieval Exegesis*, 1:226–9.

to relate it to the gospel, the patristic interpreter finds himself forced into a choice between working very hard to make the literal sense of a difficult passage "work," or utilizing allegory. These were the only tools available to the patristic exegete. When studying the New Testament, however, he has greater freedom of choice in the tools which he may use for his work, and so we can see more clearly whether such categories really are all or most of the story when it comes to describing patristic exegesis. This is because it will be more apparent whether in fact there are other things operating behind the senses of Scripture which in Old Testament interpretation are obscured by the more obvious need to deliberately move between the different senses of Scripture. In examining patristic exegesis of the New Testament, we are not necessarily considering a "biased" sample, but on the contrary, have the opportunity to observe what interpretative strategies are chosen by the Fathers when they have relatively fewer constraints placed on their choice by the nature of the biblical text in view. Choosing Gospel texts for a case study is therefore not so much choosing an exception as an illuminating choice, because the interpreters here have more freedom to move.

Moreover, to the extent that the Latin Fathers might in fact pay more attention to the senses of Scripture in their works on the Old Testament than when commenting on the New, what does this actually suggest? Certainly not the frequently-held assumption which this project seeks to question, namely that the senses are the most important universally applicable categories for patristic exegesis, but in fact that they are only of partial relevance because they are less helpful in explaining some parts of it, such as that part concerned with the New Testament as is claimed here. This in turn suggests that scholars ought to look for other categories which might have a wider application across Latin exegesis, or at the very least be of significant aid in describing those portions of it where discussion of the senses appears to leave some things unexplained. In addition, a conclusion that the framework of the senses is only one of several useful ways of describing exegesis of the New Testament (and one which is not particularly helpful in identifying the substantial differences in the exegetical styles of commentators), does not represent merely an aberration or a minor exception to a generally applicable rule. For why should patristic exegesis of the Old Testament be regarded as normative, and that of the New an exceptional case rather than a significant part of the whole?

The contention of this project is that while our four authors did indeed have considerable conscious regard for how they should interpret their texts from the standpoint of the various senses of Scripture, they appear to have made deliberate choices in other areas which are also worthy of significant attention. Furthermore, this study seeks to illustrate how the four major figures appear to have come to relatively similar conclusions about how to use the senses of Scripture, but comparatively different ones in other areas. This study will therefore suggest that the latter may be of greater use than the former in describing and differentiating between the exegetical styles of various Latin Fathers. The choice of New Testament texts for this study is not an evasion of the importance of the senses in patristic exegesis of much of the Old Testament, so much as a selection which is designed to more effectively highlight that the senses are not necessarily as central or helpful as some scholars can suppose, as well as providing a context in which other interpretive descriptors can be more clearly seen.

In considering whether the choice of portions of the works of our authors on the Gospels might represent an unhelpful bias into this study, a second mitigating factor should also be noted. This is that the works chosen, far from being eccentric or minor examples of exegesis, represent major pieces by the authors in question, and have been regarded as such by many others since they were first composed. Hilary's *In Matthaeum* is one of only two significant exegetical writings from his pen which are currently extant,[6] as well as being the earliest surviving continuous Latin Gospel commentary,[7] and his *De Trinitate* is his best-known non-exegetical work.[8] Ambrose's *Expositio evangelii secundam Lucam* is the longest of that author's surviving writings, and the following description of it is typical: "Ambrose's biblical exegesis is most clearly expressed in his commentary on Luke, the major commentary we have from his pen."[9] In the case of Jerome's *In Matheum*, it is easier to make the case that this work represents a relatively small and possibly idiosyncratic portion of his exegetical output, owing to his voluminous output on the Old Testament. However, the fact remains that this work is Jerome's largest on the New Testament and is at least comparable in size with most of his

---

6. Simonetti, "Exegesis, Patristic," 309.

7. Driscoll, "The Transfiguration in Hilary of Poitiers' Commentary on Matthew," 395.

8. Altaner, *Patrology*, 423.

9. Hall, *Reading Scripture with the Church Fathers*, 108.

individual Old Testament commentaries, as well as being popular and influential throughout the Middle Ages.[10] Lastly, Augustine's *In Iohannis evangelium* ranks alongside his *Commentary on the Psalms* as one of the most substantial examples of his exegetical work, and has been particularly influential down through the centuries.[11] The suggestion that the case studies chosen here are exceptions to a rule might well be partly true; however, they are all rather substantial and important exceptions, which might bring into question the general applicability and usefulness of the rule itself. That said, it should be borne in mind that case studies taken from works by the same authors on the Old Testament might be expected to support a more substantial role for the senses of Scripture framework than this project does.

Key Primary Sources

Regarding the works chosen for study here, we shall not consider them in exact chronological sequence. Instead, they are studied in order of increasing complexity, moving from Jerome, through Hilary, then Ambrose, to Augustine. This is done to make clear the issues at stake, because Jerome and Hilary provide two extremes among the types of biblical interpretation found in the period, while Ambrose and Augustine represent more nuanced positions somewhere between these two extremes. It is easier to delineate the interpretative strategies of Jerome, and—to a lesser extent—Hilary, than those of Ambrose and Augustine. By taking such an approach as this, it is hoped that the unique interpretative approaches of each will be made clearer than they might be otherwise, and that appropriate categories for distinguishing between them will also emerge—from their works themselves, and in comparison to their own contemporaries—in the most helpful fashion possible.

The study therefore begins with Jerome's *Commentariorum in Matheum* (Commentary on Matthew). This work was dictated by the

---

10. Rusch, *The Later Latin Fathers*, 84.

11. One scholar recently made the following comment on it: "the *In Ioannis euangelium tractatus CXXIV* and the *In epistulam Iohannis*... like the *En. In Ps.*, have been of extraordinary importance to the Middle Ages, the sixteenth-century Reformation movements, and beyond": Van Oort, "Biblical Interpretation in the Patristic Era, A 'Handbook of Patristic Exegesis' and some other recent books and related projects," 94. See also Norris, "Augustine and the Close of the Ancient Period of Interpretation," in *A History of Biblical Interpretation*, 1: *The Ancient Period*, 386.

author to a secretary in March 398, for Eusebius of Cremona, who was also charged to give a copy of the commentary to Principia, a friend of Marcella who was one of Jerome's principal companions in Bethlehem.[12] The work was therefore intended to be a written commentary for the benefit, in the first instance, of Jerome's circle of wealthy, educated Roman friends. Eusebius had requested that Jerome prepare a commentary for him before his impending return to Rome. It was therefore completed hurriedly, in the space of two weeks, while Jerome was recovering from a protracted illness.[13] Little is known about Eusebius's intentions, and therefore what factors may have influenced Jerome's work.[14] That he had the luxury of being able to travel to Bethlehem from Rome to visit Jerome for scholarly purposes would appear to suggest that he was at least moderately wealthy and reasonably well educated.

By the time he wrote the commentary, Jerome had been resident in the Latin monastic community which he had founded at Bethlehem for some thirteen years. Although by this stage the Origenist controversy had broken and Jerome had begun at least partially to disassociate himself from Origen's works,[15] scholars have long recognized in this commentary significant borrowings from Origen,[16] as well as occasional fragments from Jerome's Greek-speaking contemporaries, Apollinarius of Laodicea, Theodore of Heraclea, Theophilus of Antioch, and (most significantly) Didymus of Alexandria.[17] However, these are not instances

---

12. Jerome, *Math.*, Praefatio, 7–8, 104–8. The commentary was produced at around the same time as Jerome's translations of Proverbs, Ecclesiastes, and the Song of Songs from Hebrew; cf. Williams, *The Monk and the Book*, 217.

13. Jerome, *Math.*, Praefatio, 7–8.

14. Jerome had met Eusebius while still in Rome; Eusebius made several journeys between Bethlehem and the West, in order to raise money for the Bethlehem community, which he became the leader of following Jerome's death. Kelly, *Jerome*, 222. Cf. Madigan, "Christus Nesciens?," 1–23.

15. Brown, *Vir Trilinguis*, 159.

16. E.g. Brown, *Vir Trilinguis*, 160. Jerome's library at Bethlehem appears to have contained a large number of Origen's works, together with a substantial number of other examples of Alexandrian exegesis, most notably for our purposes including Didymus's works on the Gospels of Matthew and John (Jerome had also spent several weeks learning from Didymus in person during his travels after his departure from Rome and his settling in Bethlehem); see Williams, *The Monk and the Book*, 117–9, chapter 4.

17. Courcelle, *Late Latin Writers and Their Greek Sources*, 102–23 discusses the influences on Jerome's exegesis in convincing detail; cf. Kelly, *Jerome*, 223 and Campenhausen, *Fathers*, 163 for briefer summaries of the relevant material. Jerome's familiarity

of plagiarism; Jerome acknowledges his debt to Origen and several others in the preface,[18] and elsewhere defends his practice of giving his readers the best material available in other writers: "They say that I made excerpts from Origen's works, and that it is illegitimate to touch the writings of the old masters in such a way. People think that they gravely insult me by this. For myself, however, I see in this the highest praise. It is my express desire to follow an example of which I am convinced that it will please all men of discernment and you too."[19] However, it should be stressed that Jerome's commentary is by no means merely a Latin compendium of previous Greek works.[20] At the very least, it is shaped by a variety of influences from other quarters, and on the other side of the coin Jerome did not have access to large parts of the Greek exegetical and theological tradition. He appears to have no direct familiarity with any Greek writers between Origen and Eusebius of Caesarea, and only rarely refers to Greek authors prior to Origen. His commentary also draws upon Jewish works occasionally,[21] is acquainted with Hilary's commentary on Matthew,[22] and in style and method owes much to various pagan Latin writers.[23]

Chapter 3 deals with Hilary's commentary on Matthew, the *In Matthaeum*. This work, unlike Jerome's which relied heavily on the Greek Scriptures, was based solely on the Latin,[24] although it is uncertain which Old Latin version he relied upon.[25] It probably dates from 354, and is

---

with some commentators in preparing with his commentary is undoubted, as he refers to Apollinarius, Origen, Theodorus, Theophilus, and Didymus in the prologue to the commentary: *Math.*, Praefatio, 92–97.

18. Jerome, *Math.*, Praefatio, 92–97. Cf. Brown, *Vir Trilinguis*, 156.

19. Jerome, *In Michaea*, 2. In *Commentarii in prophetas minores*, CCSL 76:226–30; cf. Williams, *The Monk and the Book*, chapter 3.

20. A point also made in relation to his commentaries on the Minor Prophets by Canellis, "L'*In Zachariam* de Jérôme et la Tradition Alexandrine," 153–62.

21. E.g. Jerome, *Math.*, 22–23. Cf. Brown, *Vir Trilinguis*, 191.

22. Burns, *Christology*, 36; Williams, *The Monk and the Book*, 277–9. Cf. Jerome, *De viris illustribus*, 100 (PL 23:701A).

23. Particularly Terence, Cicero, the Elder and Younger Seneca, Quintillian, and Virgil. McDermott, "Saint Jerome and Pagan Greek Literature," 372–82. What Kamesar says of Jerome's approach to the commentary genre more broadly, is essentially true of his work on Matthew: "His notions of the form a commentary should take were determined by two principal sources: the Latin secular tradition and the Greek Christian tradition." Kamesar, "Jerome," 670.

24. Because he probably could not read Greek at the time that he wrote the commentary: Burns, *Christology*, 43–44.

25. Newlands, *Hilary*, 54 and Amersfoort, "Some Influences of the Diatessaron of

the oldest extant commentary on a whole book of the Bible from the Latin tradition.[26] It is also the earliest of Hilary's surviving works, and was written before he was exiled to the Greek East.[27] As it was only during his exile that Hilary came into substantial contact with the writings of Origen, it is distinct from some of his later exegetical works, which are heavily dependent upon the works of the Alexandrian.[28] Unfortunately, the opening and concluding sections of the work are missing, with the result that most of Hilary's comments on the resurrection are not available, and that the portions of the remaining work relevant to this enquiry are quite brief. The complete lack of references in the commentary to a particular setting or audience, together with its stylistic features, has led the majority of scholars to conclude that it did not originate as a preached series, but as a written work.[29] The *In Matthaeum* appears to assume considerable knowledge of the Scriptures and of the Christian faith on the part of its readers, and hardly ever uses apologetic motifs, while on the other hand it does address contemporary heresies within the church,[30] suggesting that it was probably produced for a Christian audience. However, little is known beyond that. The lack of references to any potential recipients, together with the loss of the prologue and an absence of useful data in Hilary's later works, means that little can be said about its occasion, purpose, or intended audience.

More can be said concerning probable influences on Hilary's exegesis. The major studies on Hilary by Wille, Newlands, and Doignon have all searched for direct borrowings in the commentary from other

---

Tatian on the Gospel Text of Hilary of Poitiers," 200–205. He does not consistently use any one version in particular (although the "Irish" version is the most frequently quoted), and occasionally even combines quotes from more than one version—possibly because he was quoting from memory.

26. Rusch, *Fathers*, 12; On the matter of dating, the more extended treatment of Newlands, *Hilary*, 41–43 concludes that the work must have been written between 353 and 355, most likely in 354. Burns, *Christology*, 14 notes that most modern scholars believe that the work was written between 353 and 356.

27. Newlands, *Hilary*, 1.

28. Simonetti, *Biblical Interpretation*, 69; Driscoll, "Transfiguration," 395.

29. Newlands, *Hilary*, 43.

30. That Hilary in the commentary opposes those who would undermine the divinity of Christ in some way is clear, however the identity of those he opposes (specifically whether they were "Arians," "Photinians," or something else) is debated. For a recent overview of the evidence and arguments in favor of the Photinian option, see Beckwith, "Photinian Opponents in Hilary of Poitier's *Commentarium in Matthaeum*," 611–27.

patristic authors, especially Origen, and found none.[31] No certain evidence of indirect influence from the Greek Fathers has been found within the work, either.[32] His apparent interest in at least some aspects of the Arian controversy in this early work can be more plausibly accounted for by assuming that the commentary was written with an eye on Latin Arians, rather than on Greek exegesis.[33] However, Hilary's indirect dependence on earlier Latin authors is apparent, particularly Tertullian, and to a lesser extent Novatian and Cyprian.[34] His method shows traces of possible influence from Irenaeus.[35]

Chapter 3 also considers Hilary's exegesis of the final chapters of the Gospels within his *De Trinitate*. In this treatise, Hilary spends a large amount of time engaged in interpretation of the Gospel narratives. Indeed, book 10 is dedicated to examining the passion and crucifixion narratives (mostly in John), in order to determine what they say about the issues that Hilary is concerned with in the work. The usefulness of supplementing analysis of Hilary's exegesis in *In Matthaeum* with that of *De Trinitate* is twofold. Firstly, the brevity of the relevant material in the former work means that it is worthwhile to confirm the conclusions drawn from it through examination of another work. Secondly, the fact that Hilary's exegetical career divides neatly into two portions—before and after his exile to the East—makes supplementing the earlier material from Matthew with later material from *De Trinitate* all the more interesting and valuable.

The work itself was written several years after the *In Matthaeum*, after Hilary had been directly exposed to the exegetical practices of the

---

31. Newlands, *Hilary*, 11–18; Wille, *Studien zum Matthauskommentar des Hilarius von Poitiers*, 11–15; Doignon, *Hilaire de Poitiers avant l'Exile*, 170–8.

32. Contrary to Brennecke, "Hilarius von Poitiers," 315–22 which suggests that there was strong Greek influence. Doignon, "Deux approches de la Resurrection dans l'exégèse d'Hilaire de Poitiers," 9, however, briefly outlines evidence for one possible instance. Simonetti, "Note sul commento a Matteo di Ilario di Poitiers," 35–64 also leaves open the possibility of some indirect influence.

33. Burns, *Christology*, 85–87.

34. Newlands, *Hilary*, 36–39; Doignon, *Hilaire*, 180–90 convincingly argues for Hilary's strong dependence on Tertullian but discounts the influence of other Latin authors; Burns, *Christology*, 44–46 supports Doignon's conclusions with regards to Origen and Tertullian, but also mounts a good case for the influence of other Latin authors such as Novatian and Cyprian, as well as the indirect influence of Cicero and other pagan authors on his style.

35. Newlands, *Hilary*, 70.

Greek East during his exile there.[36] As such, it bears more definite traces of influence from Greek Fathers[37], particularly Origen.[38] However, the work still contains marks of strong usage of earlier Latin writers.[39] Apparently intended for wide dissemination among educated Christians in the West—which indeed it did achieve in time—much of it was written in direct refutation of Arian ideas.[40]

Chapter 4 turns to consider Ambrose's *Expositio evangelii secundum Lucam* (Exposition on Luke). The longest of his writings, it is also his only extant work on a book of the New Testament. It was most probably produced in 389 (and certainly sometime between 388 and 392), after Ambrose had been in bishop of Milan for some fifteen years, and is therefore an example of his mature thought.[41] All ten books of the work, except for book three, were originally delivered as sermons, preached to his cathedral congregation.[42] Ambrose spoke from memory, with reference to both the old Latin scriptural text that was set for the day in the Milanese lectionary, and to the Greek text.[43] The congregation to which he would normally have addressed his sermons would have been large (his cathedral could house up to three thousand people, and was full

---

36. When he was in exile in Asia Minor from 356–59, the majority of it probably written sometime in the first two years of his exile. Newlands, *Hilary*, 10, 101.

37. Simonetti, *Interpretation*, 89.

38. Newlands, *Hilary*, 110.

39. Jacobs, "The Western Roots of the Christology of St Hilary of Poitiers," 198–203. In this respect it is like Hilary's commentary on the Psalms, also produced after his exile, which displays a deliberate integration of practices he has picked up in the Greek East alongside a strong continuing influence from Latin exegesis, theology, and grammatical and rhetorical traditions which were evident in Hilary's exegesis prior to his exile: Burns, *A Model for the Christian Life: Hilary of Poitier's Commentary on the Psalms*, 11–14.

40. While doubts have previously existed as to whether the opponents in view were actually the Arians who followed beliefs condemned at the Council of Nicaea, the leading scholars are now agreed that they were. See Newlands, *Hilary*, 10; Doignon, "L'exégèse d'Hilaire de Poitiers," 508–20.

41. Guinot, "L'exégèse ambrosienne des apparitions pascales (Lc. 24)," 145–72 gives an up-to-date summary of the state of debate on dating of the work. A dissenting opinion is given by Nautin, "Hieronymus," 306.

42. All of the sections under consideration here were preached. Ramsey, *Ambrose*, 59.

43. Paredi, *Saint Ambrose*, 259; Satterlee, *Ambrose of Milan's Method of Mystagogical Preaching*, 103; Muncey, *The New Testament Text of St Ambrose*, xxiv, suggests that the Milan church used a late version of the Old Latin Bible, that bore close similarity to the Vulgate at points.

most Sundays), and included senior officers of the Empire, sometimes members of the imperial family, wealthy merchants, and landowners resident in the city, plus a significant number of the poor and needy.[44]

The work is thought to be heavily dependent on Origen's *Homilies on Luke*, although less so in the concluding sections that are the subject of this study.[45] Indeed, Jerome, who was apparently familiar with Ambrose's work on Luke, accused him of plagiarizing Origen's homilies.[46] Corsato believes that there may also have been some influence from later Alexandrian exegetes.[47] In the past, Ambrose has been believed to have been influenced by Hilary's *In Matthaeum* in his exegesis on Luke—certainly this was the view of the Maurist editor—however, whether this influence extended beyond occasional indirect borrowings is unclear amongst modern scholars.[48] In method and style, the work also bears marks of general influence in style and occasionally method from Basil, Didymus, Philo, Hippolytus, Virgil, Cicero, and several neo-Platonist authors.[49] In short, Ambrose's exegesis shows that he was well-versed in pagan classical literature as well as the work of several major eastern interpreters of the Bible.

Chapter 5 examines Augustine's *In Iohannis evangelium* (Tractates on John). Of the 124 tractates, the first fifty-four have long appeared to scholars to be distinct from the last seventy.[50] The latter group, which contain all of the tractates relevant to our purposes, were most likely

---

44. See Satterlee, *Ambrose of Milan's Method of Mystagogical Preaching*, 116–20. for further details.

45. Lenox-Conyngham, "Review of: *La Expositio euangelii secundum Lucam di sant' Ambrogio*," 780–2; Puech, and Hadot, "L'Entretien d'Origène avec Heraclide et le commentaire de Saint Ambrose sur l'Évangile de Saint Luc," 234; Guinot, "L'exégèse," 146–56; Corsato, *La Expositio euangelii secundum Lucam di sant'Ambrogio*, 286 argues that the major source for Ambrose from Origen was not his homilies on Luke, but a commentary on Luke, of which only fragments survive.

46. Jerome, *De uiris illustribus*, 124. Cf. Adkin, "Jerome on Ambrose," 5–14.

47. Corsato, *Expositio*, 287.

48. Cf. Corsato, *Expositio*, 183 who comments briefly on this, and one of the most recent contributions to this discussion, Bellifemine, "Due ipotesti ilariani nell'*Expositio evangelii secundum Lucam* di Ambrogio," 31–52.

49. Corsato, *Expositio*, 179–85. Swift, "Ambrose," 42.

50. However, the differences between the two blocks should not be overstated, and the 124 tractates still do form something of a single and coherent whole for Augustine: Milweski, "Augustine's 124 Tractates on the Gospel of John," 71–75.

produced during the period 419–421, or certainly close to this time.[51] They therefore belong to the final major phase of Augustine's works, after the defeat of Donatism, and when Pelagianism loomed as the major threat on his horizon.[52] They were either preached to Augustine's cathedral congregation at Hippo, or dictated to a secretary or a small audience for others to preach in the cathedral, as well as for distribution to be preached elsewhere in Roman Africa in the case of at least some of the later tractates.[53] If the final seventy tractates began their life as sermons which were preached "live," then it appears that unlike most of Augustine's other sermons which were preached extempore, tractates 55–124 appear to have been prepared or practiced to some extent beforehand.[54] The congregation to which they would have been addressed, while not as cosmopolitan or wealthy on average as that which faced Ambrose in Milan, would not have been entirely rustic in its composition. Hippo in Augustine's day was still a significant Mediterranean seaport, second only within Roman Africa to Carthage. It also contained a substantial number of wealthy citizens, the majority of whom lived in the immediate

---

51. The dating of the final seventy tractates has been disputed for several decades, with a dating around this time being the most persuasive to the majority of scholars. See Berrouard, "L'exégèse de saint Augustin predicateur du quatrième Evangile," 311–38. For an overview of the debate on their dating, see Milweski, "Augustine's 124 Tractates in the Gospel of John," 65–69, 76.

52. Doyle, "Augustine's Sermonic Method," 213–38.

53. Berrouard, "Augustin," 313 and "Les Tractatus LV–CXXIV dictée à partir de Novembre 419," 14, in contrast to Altaner, *Patrology*, 512, thinks that preaching to a secretary is more likely, but is still not certain. Doyle, "Method," 217 suggests that he probably preached them to a small audience of junior clergy, who then in turn preached on Augustine's behalf. Houghton, *Augustine's Text of John*, 107, leans towards the view that the later tractates began their life having been dictated for publication rather than preached, primarily on the basis of Augustine's comments in Ep. 23A*.3 where he mentions dictating and sending six homilies on unspecified latter parts of John (with potentially more to come) to Carthage for publication. However, it is difficult to determine the matter conclusively, given the brevity of Augustine's comment and its lack of further specific detail: cf. Milweski, "Augustine's 124 Tractates on the Gospel of John," 75–77. We might conclude by observing with Milewski that in the final analysis it is largely irrelevant whether the sermons were initially preached to a congregation or dictated to a secretary in order to be preached on subsequent occasions, given that in either case Augustine produced the sermons at the same point in his life and theological development, with the intention of them being preached.

54. Wright, "The Manuscripts of St. Augustine's *Tractatus in Euangelium Iohannis*," 55–143.

neighborhood of Augustine's cathedral.⁵⁵ The *In Iohannis evangelium* is heavily dependent on the Vulgate tradition and overall is quite closely aligned with it, although Augustine does quote relatively often from or refer to the Old Latin version, most likely quoting it from memory.⁵⁶ By this stage in his career, he appears to have gained sufficient knowledge of Greek to be able to refer to the Greek text occasionally.⁵⁷

Although Augustine apparently was familiar with Ambrose's work on Luke by the time he produced his work on John, there appears to be no significant direct connection between the two works.⁵⁸ The main impact of Ambrose and Jerome's works on Augustine's *In Iohannis evangelium* was not direct, but rather in mediating the whole tradition of Greek exegesis to Augustine, which the Bishop of Hippo had no direct familiarity with.⁵⁹ He was familiar with Hilary's *De Trinitate*, and may have occasionally borrowed ideas from it in preparing the *In Iohannis evangelium*, with the same relatively small level of influence also probably having been exercised by the works of Cyprian and Ambrosiaster over the *In Iohannis evangelium* at points.⁶⁰ At the more general level, scholars have found echoes of the style and methods of the neo-Platonists, Roman orators, Stoics, and Cynics, most likely a reflection of his educational background and early religious experiences.⁶¹

As was the case with Hilary, in considering Augustine's exegetical method, it is appropriate to undertake a second case study, on the

---

55. Cf. Brown, *Augustine*, 183–5. While many of the church-going folk of Hippo would have attended the Donatist cathedral instead of Augustine's, it appears unlikely that this would have left Augustine's congregation denuded of the wealthy and powerful: most scholars believe that North African Donatism was, on average, either poorer or on a par with Catholicism: see Brown, *Augustine*, 212.

56. Houghton's analysis summarized in *Augustine's Text of John*, 118 leads to this conclusion. For an influential earlier and somewhat contrasting perspective, see: Bonnardière, "Did Augustine Use Jerome's Vulgate?," 245–51, which argues that Augustine does make occasional use of Jerome's Vulgate from around 420 onwards, i.e. possibly but most likely not in preparing the tractates.

57. Pope, "St. Augustine's Tractatus in Iohannem: A Neglected Classic," 161–72.

58. Rollero, *La "Expositio evangelii secundum Lucam,"* 4.

59. Rollero, *La "Expositio evangelii secundum Lucam,"* 139.

60. Kilmartin, "Augustine's Tractate 27," 166.

61. Lawless, "Augustine's Use of Rhetoric in His Interpretation of John 21:19–23," 53–66; Doyle, "Method," 225–38; Mohrmann, "Saint Augustin Prédicateur," 83–96; Muller, "Iohannis euangelium tractatus CXXIV, In," 724.

Sermones de tempore (Sermons on the Liturgical Seasons).⁶² On this occasion, however, this decision is not due to a lack of material, but rather to abundance thereof. Although the *In Iohannis evangelium* is the longest of all the works considered here, it still forms only a small portion of Augustine's output. It will therefore be helpful to supplement this material with a second source, to test whether the conclusions reached in chapter 5 are borne out when set against another part of Augustine's exegetical corpus. Furthermore, the considerable diversity present within Augustine's writings means that it is unwise to let any conclusions reached about his exegesis rest only on one part of his works produced within a single period of his life.

Not all of the sermons within the corpus of the *Sermones de tempore* are concerned with the relevant Gospel passages, and so this study will concentrate on twenty-three sermons, most of which deal with the resurrection and post-resurrection accounts rather than the crucifixion narratives.⁶³ Although dating for most of these sermons is uncertain, it appears that, taken together, they cover the bulk of Augustine's episcopal career.⁶⁴ Most of the sermons were probably preached to the cathedral congregation at Hippo, and a small number possibly delivered in the metropolitan cathedral in Carthage, where Augustine would have preached to a congregation that would have included a proportionately greater number of senior officials and wealthy merchants than at Hippo.⁶⁵ Compared with the *In Iohannis evangelium*, the *Sermones* appear to be less scholarly and carefully prepared. This is in large measure due to the fact that in preparing these, and most of his other sermons outside of

62. Kremen, *The Imagination of the Resurrection*, 62–65 argues that the perspective of the *Sermons* is similar to that of other key texts that also deal with the crucifixion and resurrection accounts, notably parts of the *Enchiridion* and *The City of God*.

63. Sermons 218 (On the Passion), 219, 231–9, 242–53 (on various Easter-related Gospel passages). Notably, Sanlon, *Augustine's Theory of Preaching*, 141–3, observes that Augustine's preaching practice in relation to the Easter Vigil (incorporating the majority of the sermons considered here) is consistent with his approach to preaching elsewhere in his corpus. This suggests that these sermons are not an atypical outlier that is unrepresentative of Augustine's practice: and is therefore a suitable choice for consideration alongside the *In Iohannis evangelium*.

64. It appears as if the majority of those under study here were delivered between 400 and 420; cf. the table listing various scholarly proposals for dating of each of the *Sermones*, supplied by Rotelle, in Augustine, *Sermons*, 138–63, and the introductory remarks made by M. Pellegrino, 21–24.

65. Rusch, *Fathers*, 138. Cf. Muldowney, Introduction to: Augustine, *Sermons on the Liturgical Seasons*, xiii and xvii.

the *In Iohannis evangelium*, it was not Augustine's practice to write out his sermons beforehand; he usually just meditated on his chosen passage for a time prior to preaching alongside relying upon his extensive memorization of large portions of Scripture.[66] Scholars have identified a similar range of influences within the *Sermones* as within the *In Iohannis evangelium*. His work shows strong signs of indirect influence from various pagan Latin authors, neo-Platonists, and Stoics.[67] Although he was familiar with various parts of their work on the Gospel texts on which he preached, Augustine was not much influenced by Ambrose or Jerome.[68]

Terminology

Before proceeding to survey the conclusions of contemporary scholarship on later Latin exegesis, it is necessary to define briefly several terms arising from patristic usage that occur in the literature and which are of some importance for this study. Frequent reference is made to various senses of Scripture, and the cognate forms of interpretation that attempt to uncover the meaning of each of these senses. It should be noted that contemporary textual criticism would take issue with the neatness with which these categories are often drawn, and more to our purpose here, some scholars in the patristic field have also recently sought to emphasize that the usage of the Fathers themselves of these concepts is more complex than has traditionally been recognized.[69] However, it needs to be recalled that this complexity has been recognized for some time, and was something that the most seminal of twentieth-century thinkers on patristic use of the senses was certainly conscious of some fifty years

---

66. Bonner, "Augustine as Biblical Scholar," 557; Labriolle, *History and Literature of Latin Christianity: From Tertullian to Boethius*, 419; Moorhead, "Hearers and Readers of Christian Latin Texts in Late Antiquity," 490–1.

67. Harrison, *Beauty and Revelation in the Thought of Saint Augustine*, 69–70; Teske, "Spirituals and Spiritual Interpretation in Augustine," 65; O'Meara, "Augustine and Neo-Platonism," 96–101; Barnard, "To Allegorise or Not to Allegorise?," 1–10.

68. Rollero, *Lucam*, 138.

69. Most particularly, note should be made of the work of Young, *Biblical Exegesis and the Formation of Christian Culture*, especially 116–9. She argues that the usage of these categories by certain pre-Nicene Fathers is not univocal, identifying five different uses of the literal sense, seven of the allegorical and four types of typology. However, Young's work does not bear directly upon this enterprise, being mainly concerned with Greek exegesis (and making no reference to any of our authors except for Augustine).

ago.[70] However, a recognition in some quarters of this complexity has not prevented very widespread and general use of the relevant terminology both in older and more recent publications. Much of this usage, either out of ignorance or a desire to make helpful simplifying assumptions about patristic exegesis, has tended to adopt straightforward, commonly accepted working definitions of the major terms. This study is essentially an historiographical examination of the usage of the senses of Scripture by modern scholars rather than an attempt to precisely define patristic usage of the relevant terminology. For this reason, and because there is a fair degree of uniformity in modern scholarly application of the terminology, this study will therefore proceed by identifying and utilizing such commonly accepted modern usages of the relevant terms. For the purposes of this exercise, such an approach is preferable to engaging in the murkier business of seeking to systematically establish widely applicable definitions from the patristic sources themselves. In any case, this study seeks to downplay the importance of the senses of Scripture not by quibbling over definitions as such, but by suggesting that the commonly understood and applied framework of the senses is not quite as helpful as certain alternative frameworks for distinguishing between the exegetical approaches of the later Latin Fathers. We shall therefore begin here by presenting traditionally accepted working definitions of the most common terms used.

The most basic of these is the "literal" sense which follows the letter ("littera"), sometimes also known as the "historical," based on history ("historia"). This sense approximates to what in common parlance is called the "plain meaning," or the grammatico-historical exegesis of modern scholarship, minus some of the technical apparatus which attends to the latter.[71] To quote the words of some of our chosen authors, the literal

---

70. See the recent treatment of the scholarly context of Henri de Lubac's work in: Hughes, "The Fourfold Sense," 451–62.

71. Some scholars would want to be more precise and add that it is the meaning that would have been plain (without recourse to the spiritual sense—see below) to an ancient reader familiar with the grammatical and rhetorical conventions of the day, e.g. Ayres, Review of C. Kannengeisser, *Handbook of Patristic Exegesis*, 532–6. However, exactly what would have been "plain" to such a hypothetical reader is the subject of considerable conjecture and not at all well clarified by scholarship as it stands. It is therefore considered most helpful here if we continue with the above working definition, as the kind of operational principle adopted for ease by much of the ongoing discussion of the Fathers' exegesis, as we shall see below.

sense according to Ambrose is "the simple history of the truth,"[72] and for Augustine, "the truth of the story as a faithful record of historical fact,"[73] in which words "are used to designate those things on account of which they were instituted . . . we mean *bos* [ox] when we mean an animal of a herd."[74] The literal sense or meaning, however, should be distinguished from the literalistic. That is to say, the literal sense admits that in some passages, the plain or natural meaning contains some symbolism and metaphors, and its truth does not necessarily exist in its being read as literal truth. An example is the parables that are found in the Gospels. The truth-claim implicit in these narratives lies not in any suggestion that they are all real stories about real things that happened to real people, but in what they obliquely direct their hearers to do. It should also be noted that recent patristic scholarship warns us against always equating the literal sense with the conscious intention of the human authors of Scripture. Sometimes, in the view of the Fathers, the literal sense might refer to what the text plainly says to Christians, but which the original author may not have been cognizant of.[75]

The allegorical sense or meaning is that which seeks significance in the text by treating its literal data as though it holds symbolic importance. To quote Ambrose, "There is allegory when one thing is being accomplished, but another is being indicated."[76] The details recorded by the text are closely examined in order to discover the truth that lies beneath or beyond them, hidden by symbolism, metaphor, and code. Augustine famously describes Ambrose's preaching as seeking to do this in the following excerpt: "he would remove the veil of mystery and expose the spiritual meaning of things which taken literally would have seemed to teach perverse things."[77] Allegorical interpretation—or literal for that matter—therefore rests on certain assumptions about the kind

---

72. Ambrose, *Lucam*, VII, 73.

73. Augustine, *De civitate dei*, XIII, 21 (PL 41:0395). Translation from Augustine, *The City of God*, 535.

74. Augustine, *De doctrina christiana. De vera religione*, 2.10.15 (PL 34:0042). Translation from Augustine, *On Christian Doctrine*, 43.

75. Cf. Scalise, "Sensus," 45, 64–65.

76. Ambrose, *De Abraham*, 4.28 (PL 14:0432 C). Edwards, "Figurative Readings," 715, gives a modern summary which echoes this closely in discussing the common understanding of *allegoria* in antiquity: it was used "of texts which were believed to 'say one thing and mean another.'"

77. Augustine, *Confessiones*, 6.4.6 (PL 32:0722).

of literature that Scripture is; in this case, that the Bible's divine truth is not always plainly apparent, but is presented on two levels, the literal and spiritual, the latter being discovered through an appropriate identification of its codes and symbols. As Augustine explains, "while all can read it [Scripture] straightforwardly, it also has a deeper meaning in which its great secrets are concealed."[78] Allegory is often equated or closely associated with "anagoge" or with the idea of "tropes" in modern literary criticism,[79] although in this work we will avoid such conceptions in favor of Latin patristic usage as exemplified by the quotations given above. The allegorical sense is frequently referred to by the Fathers as the "spiritual," and contrasted with the "letter," the literal sense. This distinction was often set forth by those who preferred the allegorical sense with reference to 2 Corinthians 3:6b, "for the letter kills, but the Spirit gives life."[80] As Jerome puts it, "we ought to climb from the letter to the spirit, from earthly to heavenly things."[81] The allegorical or spiritual sense is sometimes also known as the "mystical," owing to its relatively esoteric character, or in the writings of some Fathers, is referred to by terms such as "anagoge" and "tropologia" in preference to "allegoria."[82] It should be noted that "anagoge," "tropologia," and their cognates in later, medieval usage came to refer primarily to two other senses of Scripture (which can be described loosely as "eschatological" and "moral" respectively) which were regarded as distinct from the allegorical, but still described as "spiritual." Thus, a definite distinction was made between the terms "allegorical" and "spiritual," the latter being broader than and incorporating the former. This delineation is not well-established in the patristic era, which normally still uses them interchangeably, as de Lubac notes.[83] While it might be possible to find these terms used in this way in the earlier Latin period, they were most often used as rough substitutes for the spiritual sense, i.e. to describe allegory.[84] To avoid confusion, this study

---

78. Augustine, *Confessiones*, 6.5.8 (PL 32:0723).

79. E.g. Cuddon, The *Penguin Dictionary of Literary Terms and Literary Theory*, 22–23, 35.

80. Sometimes use of the allegorical sense is justified with reference to other verses that draw a distinction between spirit and letter, such as Rom 2:29 and 7:6.

81. Jerome, *In Amos*, 1 (PL 25:1000B).

82. Such as Jerome: Kannengeisser, *Handbook*, 1105.

83. Lubac, *Medieval*, 2:1 and 9.

84. Lubac, *Medieval*, 2:129 and 180 shows how Jerome used such terms relatively indiscriminately to refer to the spiritual sense in general and argues that they only

therefore uses "allegorical" and "spiritual" interchangeably to describe the non-literal sense, and avoids use of "anagoge" and "tropology" except in quotations and where the context makes clear what is intended.

Also worthy of note is the term "typology." It has most frequently been used to describe the tendency of some patristic writers to draw significant historical-theological connections between earlier and later parts of Scripture (usually between the two Testaments), such as when Augustine says that "all things that were said . . . in all the writing of the Law, were a shadow of those to come,"[85] or Ambrose's comment that "you see that the whole series of the old law was a type of the one to come."[86] The place of typology in discussions of patristic literature has been the subject of considerable debate for several decades.[87] For some time, it was seen by most scholars as wholly distinct from and in opposition to allegory, because although it was regarded as being like allegory in its attribution of a symbolic meaning other than the literal one to a word or passage in Scripture, it is concerned with "linkages between events, persons, or things within the historical framework of revelation."[88] Allegory, on the other hand, was regarded as being an arbitrary, ahistorical imposition of secondary symbolic meanings on the text without reference to its context in salvation-history. In summary, typology was regarded as historical in orientation; allegory, literary. However, while such views are still relatively common, the majority of scholars today treat the relationship of typology and allegory differently, or at least emphasize that the patristic authors' understanding is more complex and nuanced than presented by more traditional accounts in modern scholarship. Not uncommonly, typology is regarded as a subset or form of allegory, with allegory itself referring to any case where there is more than one meaning (surface/obvious meanings versus hidden/deeper), and typology to examples within this genre which posit a historical connection between the obvious and hidden meanings.[89] Some examples from the Fathers' writings support this position by virtue of the fact that they apply the terminology of allegory to typological relationships, as in the following comment from

began to be used systematically in the West to describe different things from the time of Cassian onwards.

85. Augustine, *In Ioh.*, 28.9.
86. Ambrose, *Lucam*, II, 56.
87. Cf. Louth, "Typology," 727–9.
88. Woolcombe, *Essays on Typology*, 40.
89. E.g. Cuddon, *Dictionary*, 20–22.

Augustine: "What shall I say of the Apostle Paul, who intimates that even the very history of the Exodus was an allegory of the people to come?"[90] In the specific case of patristic scholarship, many modern commentators, beginning with de Lubac, have questioned the practice of opposing allegory and typology as mutually exclusive concepts on the grounds that there is no clear distinction between them in the writings of the Fathers.[91] The suggestion is that to the extent that patristic authors speak about a particular "typus" or "figura" as highlighting a historical relationship between two parts of the biblical account or between something in the biblical account and something in the church, such readings were for the Fathers instances of the letter pointing to the deeper, or more important "spiritual" meaning.[92] As Edwards puts it, "the Latin 'figura' renders the Greek noun 'trope' hence why 'tropological' is used as a synonym for 'figurative' . . . typology describes the trope (more often, the tropological operation) whereby characters and episodes in the Old Testament are made to foreshadow the work of Christ or a mystery of the church."[93]

For this reason, this study does not propose to devote extensive attention to considering the extent to which the authors studied use typology, or to distinguishing precisely which instances in their exegesis might be described as "typological" as opposed to "allegorical." However, it does not avoid the matter of typology altogether, and for each of the Fathers considered a shorter section on typology is included, normally alongside discussion of the authors' treatment of prophecy-fulfillment within the New Testament texts. This is because even today, "most scholars with any sympathy for patristic exegesis accept some kind of distinction between allegory (or for some, typology), as discerning patterns in God's saving activity, and allegory as a kind of play on words."[94] That is to say, in some patristic works there is evidenced a habit of drawing connections of a determined, historical nature between earlier and later parts of Scripture, and also between specific events in Scripture and historical realities in the

---

90. Augustine, *De utilitate credendi*, III, 8 (PL 42:0068–0069).

91. E.g. Lubac, *Medieval*, 2:19, 95, and 134. In de Lubac's case, the distinction between allegory and typology, with the latter being concerned about historical connections between the Old and New Testaments, is also attacked because he believes that truly Christian allegory *is* properly concerned with describing the relationship between the Testaments.

92. Lubac, *Medieval*, 1:251–3.

93. Edwards, "Figurative Readings," 716.

94. Louth, "Typology," 729.

life of the church. While this is closely related to the practice of allegorical exegesis, it is also connected to the tendency of many authors to stress how certain events and practices in the New Testament "fulfill" earlier biblical events or prophecies.[95] The phenomena of prophecy-fulfillment and spiritual exegesis of a typological kind are similar in that they both rest on assumptions about unique historical relationships. For this reason, they are treated together in the chapters that follow. They differ in that prophecy-fulfillment normally involves the latest of the relevant biblical texts explicitly referring or even drawing attention to the note of fulfillment, whereas in the case of typology the historical connection is normally implicit, even if it might still be relatively obvious.

It should also be stressed that typology is of a different order to other kinds of "spiritual" exegesis, which, even if they are concerned with relating Old and New Testament realities, do not do so in a way that presupposes a unique or special historical relationship between the two things so joined. For example, every aspect of every Psalm may be read allegorically as symbolizing a New Testament truth, but not necessarily as being in a fixed historical relationship with a particular element of New Testament history. All instances of the first category can be called "allegorical," but only those in the second, which is a smaller subset of the first, are typological. Typology therefore differs from other kinds of spiritual interpretation in that it presupposes a unique relationship between signifier (the type) and the thing signified (the fulfillment).[96] Whereas an allegorical signifier could potentially be a symbol for an infinite number of hidden "things," a type normally has only one ultimate fulfillment, and a limited number (if any) of secondary fulfillments.[97] A corollary of this is the fact that while every detail of any Old Testament text can potentially be assigned an allegorical meaning, the same is not true for typological

---

95. Nassif, "School," 453.

96. It should also be stressed that typological connections need not be messianic, but could refer to other historical connections within biblical history, or spiritual illuminations connected to past or future events in the mind of a biblical character or author. In the past, patristic scholarship tended to speak of typology only in terms of explicitly messianic historical connections within Scripture, as the Antiochenes (those assumed to be the champions of a typological approach) were thought to only highlight these kinds of connections using the terminology associated with typology. However, more recently it has been recognized that this was not the case. Cf. Nassif, "The 'Spiritual Exegesis' of Scripture: The School of Antioch Revisited," 437–70.

97. Goldsworthy, According to Plan, 85–87.

meanings, which presuppose a historical link between phenomena.[98] As we shall see, typology can take a number of forms in patristic exegesis, variously describing special historical relationships between Old and New Testament realities (classical typology), several similar or connected New Testament realities, and biblical events which prefigure practices and features in the life of the church. Clearly, even though typology is appropriately seen as a form of spiritual exegesis, it also stands in relationship to other facets of patristic interpretation which do not necessarily fall within the ambit of "allegory," such as prophecy-fulfillment in the case of classical typology, and the practical application of the text to the audience in the case of connections between biblical history and the church.

Lastly, reference is made in all chapters to the related terms "monosemy" and "polysemy." These terms are used here to define whether the reader of a text believes that the text contains, or can admit, several meanings or only one.[99] Monosemy assumes that only one valid meaning exists in the text, or that the reader is justified in seeking only one meaning from it. Polysemy, on the other hand, allows and even seeks after multiple meanings.

Overview of Scholarship

The study of Latin patristic exegesis as a whole has been dominated by the idea of the senses of Scripture, along with its associated concepts such as the spiritual and literal meanings. From 1950 until the 1970s, this dominance was almost total, thanks in part to the immense influence of Henri de Lubac's monumental *Exégèse Médiévale*,[100] which regarded the framework of the senses of Scripture as foundational to understanding

---

98. Irvine, *The Making of Textual Culture*, 264.

99. There are a range of terms which might be used to refer to the possibility of multiple meanings in the text, for example "polyvalence" or "plurisignation" (Cuddon, *Dictionary*, 677). To maintain consistency, I have used "polysemy" and its opposite, "monosemy," throughout and in so doing have followed the usage of several well-known authors in the field of later Latin exegesis, e.g. Margerie, *An Introduction to the History of Exegesis*, 3; *St. Augustine*, 34 and 35; and Markus, *Signs and Meanings*, 19.

100. Lubac, *Exégèse médiévale* (4 vols.). For a recent overview of developments in the field over the past half-century and of the pivotal role assumed by de Lubac's work in them, see: Kannengeisser, *Handbook*, 228–51. Subsequent and previous references to the first two volumes of de Lubac's work are to the English translation, for ease of access, hereafter abbreviated as Lubac, *Medieval*, in distinction from the French original, Lubac, *Exégèse*.

patristic exegesis as well as that of medieval interpreters which developed from it. De Lubac's work is essentially a defense of allegorical interpretation vis-à-vis the claims and criticisms of modern "scientific" exegesis,[101] as the means by which patristic and medieval authors read the Bible as a unified whole,[102] and understood the relation of all of its component texts in light of the revelation of Christ.[103] De Lubac therefore rejects any suggestion that allegorical interpretation should be viewed merely as an excuse for premodern minds to engage in uncontrolled flights of exegetical fancy unconnected to the literal/historical dimension of the scriptural record.[104] He also strongly denounces claims that early Christian use of allegory amounted to an artificial intrusion of "foreign," pagan literary methods into a Bible which knew nothing of such methods.[105] De Lubac believes that the kind of allegory practiced by the best of the patristic and medieval exegetes was an activity which arose from the thought-structures of Scripture itself[106] (in that he considers Christian theology to be properly composed of four dimensions—historical, spiritual, moral or tropological, and anagogical or eschatological, which correspond to the classic sense-framework of medieval exegesis),[107] was directed to appropriate Christian ends, and was quite distinct from pagan allegorism.[108]

It should be noted that de Lubac is not greatly concerned over differences between various authors regarding how many in number the senses of Scripture are, and what the names or scope of each of these senses might be.[109] For him, there are ultimately only two senses of Scripture that really matter, both in historical usage and the shape of theology

101. Lubac, *Medieval*, 2:18 and 72.
102. Lubac, *Medieval*, 1:126.
103. Lubac, *Medieval*, 1:40–48.
104. Lubac, *Medieval*, 1:266.
105. Lubac, *Medieval*, 1:229 and 2:4. Beryl Smalley is particularly in de Lubac's sights in this regard.
106. Lubac, *Medieval*, 2:9 and 59. Naturally, de Lubac begins here by noting, along with many of his sources, the pivotal Pauline supports for allegory, Gal 4 and 1 Cor 10. However, he advances on a broader front than this, arguing that spiritual interpretation of one kind or another is at the foundation of how the New Testament in general interprets the Old in terms of Christ. He thus sees those passages which other interpreters might categorize as "typological" as being allegorical—for de Lubac, the distinction between typology and allegory is not sustainable.
107. Lubac, *Medieval*, 1:74.
108. Lubac, *Medieval*, 2:11–18.
109. Lubac, *Medieval*, 1:90–96.

itself: the letter and the spirit, which were present in Christian exegesis from its beginnings in the New Testament.[110] What interests him in terms of later developments is not so much the enumeration of various other subdivisions, as what these different subdivisions have to say about the relationship between the senses, and consequently, about the structure of Christian theology.[111] On this point, de Lubac's concern is to stress that the study of the spiritual sense must always follow on from that of the letter, so as to be foundational for all other exegesis and theology, particularly moral and eschatological reflection.[112] He spends a large part of his work tracing the historical pedigree of this preferred ordering of the senses, alongside those of its competitors and variations.[113] Thanks to the depth and detail with which he makes his case, multiplying primary citations to an imposing degree, de Lubac's final product has been revered and treated as an encyclopedic resource by students of patristic and medieval exegesis ever since. His study is single-mindedly focused on the question of how the senses of Scripture developed through time and the theological assumptions carried by different manifestations of the letter-spirit framework. Therefore, it is not surprising that one important effect of de Lubac's labors was a perpetuation for some years after the publication of his *Exégèse Médiévale* of the tendency of scholars to ask questions of patristic exegesis that were similarly focused around this framework—to the detriment of other angles of investigation.

The supreme objectives of de Lubac's work are essentially theological—he wishes to rehabilitate spiritual interpretation and resist the claims of modern scientific exegesis in order to affirm a more holistic view of both the Bible itself and the task of interpretation (one that incorporates both "literal," historical-critical approaches alongside a "spiritual" reading in the light of the gospel). Ultimately, he aims at establishing a structure for all theology that follows the pattern of the four senses of Scripture. In contrast, this study is primarily historical, and therefore does not seek to directly contest any of these theological objectives. Indeed, it must be reiterated here that de Lubac's use of the senses of Scripture is theologically illuminating, and from a historical point of view more subtle and better researched that most of what has been produced in the field since.

110. Lubac, *Medieval*, 1:225, 267; 2:1, 25.

111. Lubac, *Medieval*, 1: 90.

112. Lubac, *Medieval*, 1:94 and 225.

113. Lubac, *Medieval*, 1, chapters 2, 3, and 4 are all largely taken up with this enterprise. See particularly 1:82–105, 137–54.

Rather, our point of departure from de Lubac is a less direct one, namely, that he studies the exegetical work of the Fathers exclusively through the framework of the senses of Scripture. The only questions he asks of the corpus concern the development and ideal shape of this framework: does this author place tropology after allegory or the historical sense?[114] What were the influences acting upon this Father's particular formulation and use of the senses?[115] Does this author use a two, three, or fourfold form of the framework?[116] What were various exegetes trying to express theologically through their use of the senses?[117] What is the character and meaning of each of the four senses?[118] Naturally, de Lubac might reasonably be expected to have replied to such a charge that he has asked only these kinds of questions because they are most pertinent to establishing his theological claims. However, in doing so at the length that he does, particularly in a work entitled "Medieval Exegesis," he risks giving the strong impression that a thorough understanding of the usage of the senses of Scripture will provide readers with all that they need to know about medieval exegesis—and about the patristic exegesis which he sees as so intimately connected to these later developments. Furthermore, his singleminded concentration on the senses, when allied to the great influence exercised by such a substantial and scholarly work, has had the effect of stressing the centrality of the senses to later scholars who do not necessarily share his theological objectives and instead are seeking to describe the historical landscape. This study seeks to establish that there are other illuminating questions which we can ask of patristic exegesis that are not necessarily tied into the norms of "scientific exegesis" and "critical scholarship" which de Lubac detests so much.

Although de Lubac's work has received more criticism over the past thirty years than previously, the same basic framework still occupies the most influential place in much of the scholarship in the field. His central contention, that "the Christian tradition understands that Scripture has two meanings. The most general name for these two meanings is

---

114. Lubac, *Medieval*, 1:94–115; 142–8, 152–5.

115. Lubac, *Medieval*, 1:117–32, 161–77.

116. Lubac, *Medieval*, 1:82–94.

117. Lubac, *Medieval*, 1:94–105, 148–53.

118. This question in particular is of serious interest to de Lubac, occupying almost two hundred pages plus footnotes: chapters 7–10 (vol. 2) each focus on one of the four senses and explore their nature through their historical development across a wide range of authors.

the literal meaning and the spiritual (pneumatic) meaning,"[119] the latter developing over time into three clearly defined subcomponents, is still quoted approvingly as the foundation for study of patristic as well as medieval exegesis by a reviewer as late as 1999.[120] For example, as recently as 2002, Kannengeisser, citing many other scholars in support, argued that the senses of Scripture are "A Key for the Future of Patristics," and that de Lubac's work in particular is still of vital importance.[121]

The major reference works, while not going as far as de Lubac, in most cases still operate within the same paradigm. The entry under "hermeneutics" in the *Oxford Companion to Christian Thought* gives a typical account of the development of patristic exegesis:

> 2 Cor 3:6 ("the letter kills but the spirit gives life") became a hermeneutical rule, establishing the fundamental distinction between the literal sense, given in the very letter of the text, and the spiritual sense, hidden behind or beyond the latter. Patristic hermeneutics elaborated this distinction into various theories of the senses of Scripture, the most thoroughgoing being those of Origen in the East and Augustine in the West . . . The Middle Ages set about systematising the patristic heritage, translating it into a fourfold scheme of the senses of Scripture. This first appears in Cassian (5th century) and remains the guiding principle for centuries of biblical exegesis.[122]

The entry under "exegesis" in the *Oxford Dictionary of the Christian Church* affirms the same approach, discussing all exegesis between the rise of Gnosticism and the advent of the Reformation exclusively in terms of the allegorical and literal senses of Scripture, and observing that "[t]he most important exegetes among the W. Fathers were St Jerome and St Augustine, who sought to combine the two kinds of exegesis, though the former emphasized the literal, the latter the allegorical sense."[123] That is to say, while some exegetes may not fit neatly into the categories that have been constructed, this can be explained by classifying them as some kind of hybrid type. Simonetti's article, "Exegesis, Patristic" in the

---

119. Lubac, *Medieval*, 1:225.

120. Cunningham, "Review of Medieval Exegesis by Henri de Lubac," 29.

121. Kannengeisser, "A Key for the Future of Patristics: The 'Senses' of Scripture," 102, 106. Cf. Barnard, "Allegorise," 6–10.

122. Bühler, "Hermeneutics," 295.

123. "Exegesis," in Cross and Livingstone, *The Oxford Dictionary of the Christian Church*, 585.

Encyclopaedia of the Early Church briefly evaluates the exegesis of all four of our subjects here with reference in each case solely to how "allegorical" or "literal" their approach can be considered.[124] Kelly's chapter on the Latin Fathers in *The Church's Use of the Bible Past and Present* breaks the mold a little, arguing that there were two types of exegesis in the West—imported Alexandrianism, and an indigenous Latin tradition that was very similar to the Antiochene school in its methods, although relatively independent of it.[125] However, he is still heavily reliant on the other part of the traditional framework, the concept of the senses of Scripture.[126]

More substantial treatments of the history of exegesis, including many well-known volumes published in recent years, take the same approach. McKim's *Handbook of Biblical Interpreters* describes the development of exegesis in the East in terms of Antioch and Alexandria, and then suggests that this schema, and the influence of the Eastern exegetes it embodied, was what decisively shaped exegesis in the West.[127] Likewise, Bray's chapter in *Biblical Interpretation Past and Present* on patristic exegesis dwells heavily on the Antiochene-Alexandrian distinction, and stresses that this axis came to define the major fault lines of exegesis in the West, too, since Western exegesis was not just influenced by, but born out of that of the East.[128] Kannengeisser, in his more recent *Handbook of Patristic Exegesis*, the most substantial work in the field of the past decade, retains the old apparatus of the senses of Scripture at the center of his ambitious enterprise, even if he does, like many more recent serious scholars in the field, recognize at least that the Alexandria-Antioch axis is less directly relevant to some Latin exegesis than others have assumed.[129] After the introductory background sections, he arranges his initial, or-

---

124. Simonetti, "Exegesis," 311. These conclusions are made, as we might expect in a short reference article, in the context of explicit references to only a small number of the works of our four authors—but among this small number is included Jerome and Hilary's works on Matthew, Ambrose's on Luke, and Augustine's on John.

125. Kelly, "The Bible and the Latin Fathers," 41–55. Jerome and Ambrosiaster are listed as later representatives of this Latin tradition, while Hilary and Ambrose are described as classic cases of the "imported Alexandrianism."

126. Kelly, "Bible," 41–43.

127. McKim, *Handbook*, 5–10.

128. Bray, *Biblical Interpretation Past and Present*, 77–111; see especially 90 and 107.

129. Kannengeisser, *Handbook*, 2, 998 and 1045. This work was not well received by a significant number of its reviewers. Oort, "Interpretation," 80–94 provides a lengthier sample than most of the kinds of criticisms which it has received.

ganizing chapter on patristic hermeneutics into two basic sections, the first being "The Literal Meaning of Scripture," and the second, "Spiritual Exegesis."[130]

In this respect, Kannengeisser's work is typical of much scholarship produced in the past decade: recognizing that some of the old generalizations in terms of the senses of Scripture do not fit as well as we once thought they did, but still operating largely within the same paradigm. Another recent treatment of later patristic exegesis, that of Lössl, also illustrates this tendency. Lössl's thesis is that in the late fourth and early fifth centuries, there was a shift among some writers towards a more literal, source-based kind of exegesis at the expense of the preceding emphasis on allegory.[131] While this may be true, and to some extent accords with one of the conclusions of this study, that all of the four writers being examined are fundamentally literal rather than allegorical in their approach, the fact remains that Lössl is still operating within the same paradigm. All that is achieved by such works in terms of our perceptions of patristic exegesis is merely a shifting of the balance in terms of how allegorical or literal certain works or authors are regarded to be. This kind of scholarship, while operating within the old framework, effectively undermines it by helping us to recognize that the letter-spirit picture is not quite as clear as we might like it to be, and that it will as often suggest points of commonality between patristic exegetes as it does points of distinction. This is because most broad-scale or dictionary-level treatments, as seen above, rely on the senses of Scripture primarily as a means of distinguishing between exegetes. Hall introduces his chapter on the exegesis of the four great Western doctors with the following paragraph:

> The four Latin doctors represent an exegetical tradition noted for its variety and richness. Latin exegetes such as Jerome and Ambrose mirror the Alexandrian tradition's reliance on allegory in making sense of biblical texts. Jerome . . . was initially attracted to the allegorical method of Origen, although later he severely criticized it. Ambrose . . . taught the allegorical interpretative methodology to Augustine. Augustine, in turn, interpreted Scripture in both a literal and allegorical fashion. Gregory

---

130. Kannengeisser, *Handbook*, 1, 167–205 and 206–58 respectively; c.f. 173 and 206. Additional detail on how Kannengeisser applies the framework of the senses to the particular authors and works under study here in volume two of his *Handbook* is given in the introductory sections of each of the relevant chapters.

131. Lössl, "A Shift in Patristic Exegesis," 157–75.

the Great . . . is similar to Ambrose in his love for discerning a deeper allegorical meaning in the text of Scripture. While all four Latin doctors used the allegorical method of interpretation at least to some degree, their exegetical tradition is not easy to categorize, as we shall see in this chapter.[132]

One of the major questions posed by this study is, if the exegesis of the later Latin Fathers is so difficult to categorize in terms of their use of allegory, then why continue to use this conceptual structure as the primary means of categorization?

However, a number of scholars have in recent years questioned the dominant paradigm, or at least have focused on other factors as means of distinguishing between the exegetical methods of the patristic writers, particularly focusing attention on the influence of grammatical and rhetorical training and conventions, as well as that of contextual factors on the development of different paradigms of interpretation among the Fathers apart from the "senses."[133] Vessey's evaluation of Augustine's exegesis has led him to make some interesting comparisons with that of Jerome: "Augustine's paradigm of scriptural interpretation involves conference between two or more Christians in a spirit of charity. He developed this view in reaction to Jerome, who advocated an ascetic and professional practice of scriptural interpretation."[134] However, Vessey's work is relatively brief, and does not take his conclusions about possible comparisons between the Latin Fathers much further than this. It is also based on Augustine's *On Christian Doctrine*, *Confessions*, and his correspondence with Jerome: not on a study of any of Augustine's exegetical works themselves.

Young's *Biblical Exegesis and the Formation of Christian Culture* makes a more direct attack on the traditional framework, or at least Simonetti's rendering of it. She dismisses as inaccurate the historical pedigree whereby Origen is believed to have thoroughly established the threefold view of Scripture, which Cassian later developed into the fourfold scheme that the medievals used.[135] Young then stresses that categories such as allegorical and literal have limits to their usefulness for describing patristic exegesis owing in part to their highly variegated character within

---

132. Hall, *Reading Scripture with the Church Fathers*, 102.
133. C.f. Ayres, "Review," 533.
134. Vessey, "Conference and Confession," 175–213, particularly 175.
135. Young, *Exegesis*, 186.

that corpus,[136] and proposes some alternative categories, albeit without working them out in detail.[137] In the words of one of her reviewers, Young "refuses to reduce patristic exegesis to a fight between Alexandria and Antioch or between allegory and typology," and stressing that "[w]hile these terms . . . did figure prominently in the minds of many early Christian interpreters, they hardly constitute a preoccupation."[138] These comments might also serve as a rough summary of some of the key claims of this book. Unfortunately for our purposes here, her work is mostly interested in the Greek Fathers. None of the works of Jerome, Ambrose, or Hilary are referred to at any stage, and Augustine only makes an appearance in chapter 12, at the end of the book.[139] However, Young's study is still worthy of note here, as some of the new categories that she proposes are similar to those that emerge from the selected exegetical works in the following chapters as being useful for distinguishing between different interpretative strategies. In particular, her identification of the paraenetic impact of the text—how the commentator uses it to provide ethical and moral guidance—as a notable factor parallels this study's stress on the importance of practical application.[140] Young also suggests that attention should be paid to how the exegete uses philological data in the text, a point which will assume particular relevance when we examine Jerome's work.[141]

Having surveyed the perspective of contemporary scholarship on the Latin Fathers' exegesis as a whole, some indication now needs to be given of the state of the same on the particular authors and works under study. A more detailed examination of the work that has been done on the exegesis of each of our four authors is given at the start of each chapter; what follows here is an indicative summary. In all four cases, the vast

---

136. Young, *Exegesis*, 191.

137. Young, *Exegesis*, 202–12.

138. O'Keefe, Review of Young, *Biblical Exegesis and the Formation of Christian Culture*, 311.

139. Even this chapter is only of oblique relevance to this study, as she does not consider either the *In Iohannis evangelium* or the *Sermones*. Much of her analysis is concerned with Augustine's formal theories of exegesis, as laid out in the *Confessiones* (Young, *Exegesis*, 266–70) and *De Doctrina Christiana* (270?). The only case study of an actual example of his exegesis occurs at 282–4, which briefly examines how Augustine handles Psalm 30.

140. Young, *Exegesis*, 203.

141. Young, *Exegesis*, 206.

majority of scholarship adheres to the framework that has been identified as prevailing across patristic studies in general.

Relatively little work exists specifically on Jerome's exegesis of Matthew, but that which does conforms to the dominant paradigm with very few exceptions. This is certainly true of the two major modern studies of his exegesis that include his *In Matheum* within their purview. The first, Brown's *Vir Trilinguis*, discusses the work almost exclusively in terms of the distinction between allegorical and literal.[142] The second, Penna's *Principe e carattere dell esegesi di S. Girolamo*, places Jerome's exegesis firmly within the Alexandrian-Antiochene framework.[143]

The same conclusion obtains from a survey of the scholarship on Hilary's exegesis. Doignon, arguably the leading student of Hilary's works, regards the senses of Scripture as an essential framework for understanding Hilary's exegesis.[144] Others have followed his lead.[145] Simonetti's article on the *In Matthaeum* concludes that "Hilary has a strong preoccupation with the mutually supportive relationship between the literal and allegorical senses."[146] Simonetti's approach is therefore to consider "whether he always prefers the profound and allegorical, and to what extent does the literal sense express itself."[147] Another well-known Jerome student, J. N. D. Kelly, summarizes the commentary in similar terms, suggesting that Hilary "employed it [allegorical exegesis] lavishly in his Commentary on Matthew."[148] Driscoll also believes that grasping Hilary's use of spiritual interpretation is the key to understanding his exegesis: "A

142. Brown, *Vir Trilinguis*, 138–156.

143. Penna, *Principe e carattere dell esegesi di S. Girolamo*, 161–7. See especially 167.

144. Doignon, "L'exégèse," particularly 511–2.

145. Burns's monograph on Hilary, *Christology*, also devotes substantial attention to Hilary's use of the two senses. See particularly 51–55.

146. Simonetti, "Note," 38: "Ilario, dal canto suo, è convinto che anche la semplice conoscenza del significato letterale della parola del Signore sia utile, anzi necessaria per progredire spiritualmente." Indeed, the entire first half of this lengthy article is devoted to Hilary's use of allegorical and literal interpretation, with some occasional attention to his recognition of types: Simonetti, "Note," 37–50.

147. Simonetti, "Note," 40: "Se passiamo ad esaminare come questi principi siano stati tradotti in pratica dall'autore, ci accorgiamo subito come egli non abbia ritenuto opportune applicare sistematicamente il principio secondo cui l'esegeta deve giungere sempre al significato più profondo, allegorico, celato sotto il senso letterale dell'espressione evangelica."

148. Kelly, "Bible," 45. Froehlich, *Biblical Interpretation in the Early Church*, 23, argues similarly with respect to some of Hilary's other works.

coherent system of scriptural interpretation is operative throughout the commentary, a system which serves Hilary's basic concern to uncover the spiritual meaning in the text."[149]

A substantially greater volume of material has been written on Ambrose's exegesis than on that of either Jerome or Hilary, resulting in a more sophisticated level of analysis. However, the same framework dominates study of his work that prevails over that of the first two interpreters.[150] Corsato's detailed study of the *Expositio evangelii secundum Lucam* is heavily dependent on the threefold distinction between literal/historical, moral, and allegorical/mystical senses; indeed it is the sole focus of part one of the book.[151] He concludes that for Ambrose, "Historical, moral, and mystical—these represent the three means of comprehending Scripture."[152] Graumann's book on the *Expositio*, although strongly critical of Corsato on many points of detail, operates within the same framework. For him, allegory is also one of the major means by which the text is interpreted in terms of doctrines about Christ.[153] Shorter treatments tend to approach the *Expositio* similarly. Ramsey summarizes the work in the following terms: "Ambrose discusses the literal sense of Luke, and as often as possible, then passes on to its moral and mystical senses."[154] Simonetti's conclusion is framed in the same way: "his *Expositio in Lucam* (which also makes room for literal interpretation) shows his preference for allegory. Ambrose normally distinguishes between the literal, moral and mystical (spiritual) senses, but like Origen, gives greatest importance to the last."[155]

Little is different in the scholarship on Augustine's exegesis. Thus, we find Bray discussing his work within the same familiar framework: "Augustine generally tackled problems from a literalistic point of view,

---

149. Driscoll, "Transfiguration," 395.

150. In addition to the examples referred to below others could also be added, for example the chapter on Ambrose's exegesis in Pasini's biography, the majority of which is devoted to an analysis of Ambrose's practice in relation to the senses of Scripture: Pasini, *Ambrose of Milan*, chapter 15.

151. Corsato, *Expositio*, part 1, 13–64, especially 25–30. Part two is also dominated by the same themes: 70–175.

152. Corsato, *Expositio*, part 2, 282: "Storico, morale e mistico—queste rappresentano i tre il modo di capire le sacre Scrittura."

153. Graumann, *Christus Interpres: Die Einheit von Auslegung und Verkündigung in der Lukaserklärung des Ambrosius von Mailand*. See especially chapter 4.

154. Ramsey, *Ambrose*, 59.

155. Simonetti, *Interpretation*, 89.

though he also frequently lapsed into allegory."[156] Smalley's opinion is similar: "In his exegesis St. Augustine tries to steer a middle course between literal and allegorical exposition."[157] This view, that Augustine fell somewhere in-between the two dominant approaches, is often used to account for the fact that he does not neatly sit within either, when this latter point perhaps ought to alert readers to the fact that there may be better ways of categorizing his work within his historical context. Others are less equivocal, such as Carroll, who claims that it was "[o]n allegory that his [Augustine's interpretation] rested."[158] Weissman's overview of the *In Iohannis*, after noting their occasion, date, background, and theological themes, discusses his hermeneutic solely in terms of how he relates the literal and spiritual senses.[159] Although fewer studies have been published on Augustine's exegesis in the *Sermones de tempore* than on the *In Iohannis*, the same approach tends to have been advanced there, also.[160]

Key Questions

Some of the statements quoted or summarized above are doubtless valid; what is significant is that the categories employed seem to fill the role of a kind of default position, with the result that other tools of analysis and classification receive relatively less attention than they deserve. This study argues that the dominant paradigm, the framework of the senses of Scripture and its related categories such as "allegorical" and "literal," in and of itself is unable to provide as full a description of the exegesis of the later Latin Fathers as many scholars tend to assume it can. For each source that is considered, the issue of the respective role of allegorical and literal interpretations is addressed, along with the place of typology. Through consideration of these matters, we do learn a considerable amount about the exegetical practices of the Fathers under examination. We discover

---

156. Bray, *Interpretation*, 93. At this point, he is referring to the *In Iohannis evangelium*.

157. Smalley, *The Study of the Bible in the Middle Ages*, 24. See also Jeanrond, *Theological Hermeneutics: Development and Significance*, 22.

158. Carroll, *Preaching the Word: Message of the Fathers of the Church*, 11:192. See also Cameron, "The Christological Substructure of Augustine's Figurative Exegesis," 75.

159. Weismann, "Introducción a la Lectura e Interpretación de los *Tractatus in Iohannis Evangelium* de San Augustín," 51–69.

160. E.g. Carroll, *Preaching*, 189.

that the senses of Scripture framework does occupy an important place in the thinking of each of them, and that it is possible to describe the extent to which they are relatively "allegorical" or "literal" in approach. We shall also discover that a study of some of the Fathers' use of allegory in particular is very helpful in clearly identifying some of the other, additional traits of their exegesis that our study in this book will go on to describe. The aim of this project is not to dispute any of these things. Its contention is not that the Fathers were not cognizant of the senses of Scripture, nor that the exercise of seeking to place them at some point on the literal-allegorical spectrum is either impossible or of no value in describing the exegesis of any of them individually. It is simply that the conclusions which we might draw about their various usages of allegorism and literalism do not successfully distinguish between their different approaches because at this point they are relatively similar. By contrast, in terms of other categories identified by this project, their methods are relatively different.

However, this study does not only seek to achieve a moderate devaluation of the usefulness of the senses of Scripture framework. It also aims to identify some additional, workable categories that can be used in a complementary fashion alongside this framework. The new categories that are proposed arise from an examination of what perspective each exegete took in approaching the text, and what his aims in expounding it appear to have been. A particularly important concept is that of the interpreter's "lens" or primary focus: is he chiefly interested in examining the text itself, the realities that lie behind the text which are depicted in it, the intentions of the biblical author who stands before the text, or a hybrid of these three alternatives? Several other issues feature in all of the chapters and form the basis of other proposed categories for describing later Latin exegesis. These include the extent and function of doctrinal and practical-moral matters within each exposition, the degree of attention that is drawn to typological connections and prophecy-fulfillment, and whether a polysemic or monosemic approach is preferred. In addition, the question of how the exposition proceeds is examined in each case study: does it move forward in an ordered, logical fashion, or with greater randomness and eclecticism? This issue is examined at two levels. Firstly, at the broad level, how the exegete moves through the passage: does he do so in the order presented by the text, or more randomly? Secondly, at a more detailed level, how he arranges the comments that he makes on the chosen verse,[161] and whether his observations are an eclectic collection held together by few connections and common themes, or are connected to one another in a predictable and obvious manner. Examination of all of these features within each case study does appear to produce several categories which are of use in the study of later Latin exegesis.

Note on Primary Texts Used

A note on the texts used: For the *Expositio evangelii secundum Lucam*, the *In Iohannis evangelium*, Hilary's *De Trinitate*, and Jerome's *Commentariorum in Matheum* I have used the texts provided in the *Corpus Christianorum Series Latina*. However, for Hilary's *In Matthaeum*, I have followed the preference of most scholars for Doignon's edition.[162] Given that Augustine's *Sermones de tempore* are not available in the *Corpus Christianorum*, I have used Migne's *Patrologia Latina* edition for this text. In order to assist readers who may not be able to access the Latin documents, when providing I have in the majority of cases made reference to reliable English translations where these have been available, rather than to the Latin editions. Such translations are currently available for both of the Augustine texts, both of the Hilary texts, and Jerome's *Commentariorum in Matheum*.[163] For Ambrose's *Expositio evangelii secundum Lucam*, and at points for the other texts where this has best served the purpose at hand and drawn out most clearly key aspects of the text, I have supplied my own translations of the Latin texts wherever these have been quoted.[164] In

---

161. Of course, the notion of "verses" was unknown to patristic commentators on the Gospels. However, it is retained here as the term most commonly employed in contemporary usage to refer to brief, distinct units of biblical text.

162. Hilary, *Matt*. Cf. Burns, *Christology*, 14.

163. Generally, I have preferred more modern translations, for example those from the Fathers of the Church series, to earlier ones such as the Nicene and Post-Nicene Fathers series. For the major works under consideration in this study, the following have been used: Augustine, *Tractates on the Gospel of John, 55–111 and 112–24*; Augustine, *Sermons, The Works of Saint Augustine: A Translation for the 21st Century*, III/6–7; Augustine, *Sermons on the Liturgical Seasons*; Hilary, *The Trinity*; Hilary, *Select Works, Nicene and Post-Nicene Fathers: Second Series*, 9; Hilary, *Commentary on Matthew*; Jerome, *Commentary on Matthew*.

164. Where biblical texts have been included, my normal practice has been to translate the Latin text as quoted by the author in question rather than to insert a translation from a modern version of the Bible. Wherever I have utilized one of the English translations listed in the previous footnote in quoting a primary source, I have normally incorporated the translator's rendering of any biblical verses which are

doing so I have followed Jerome's own dictum, that the translator should attempt to render "sense for sense and not word-for-word."[165]

---

embedded in the patristic text.

165. Jerome, *Epistola*, 57.5 (*PL* 22:0571).

2

Embodying the Text
Jerome's *Commentariorum in Matheum*

As arguably the leading exegete of the Latin West,[1] and also the most straightforwardly assessed of the examples under consideration, it is appropriate that Jerome be the starting point of this study. In examining the final sections of Jerome's *Commentariorum in Matheum*, this study will proceed by first noting the conclusions generally drawn by existing scholarship on Jerome's exegetical works, then examine Jerome's interest in philological features and in the unity of the text before him. The question of how Jerome moves through the text from verse to verse in his exposition will then be considered, followed by his manner of treating doctrinal matters, and the extent to which he uses allegory, typology, and the fulfillment of prophecy to make points in his exposition. The chapter concludes with an investigation of the extent to which Jerome draws practical applications from his exegesis, whether he focuses on one practical theme or many, and whether he prefers a monosemic or polysemic approach to the text. As well as the more specific conclusions that are drawn from each of these enquiries, one common theme continues to appear in virtually every case: whatever aspect of Jerome's exegesis might be under study, it is his single-minded preoccupation with the scriptural text that comes to the fore.

---

1. Sparks, "Jerome as Biblical Scholar," 510–40; Altaner, *Patrology*, 262; Hartmann, "St. Jerome as an Exegete," 35–83.

Scholarly Conclusions

Five modern book-length works of some significance for this study have been written on Jerome's exegesis. The first, Penna's *Principe e carattere dell esegesi di S. Girolamo*,[2] does not consider Jerome's use of textual criticism or the influence of his life and historical background on his exegesis.[3] The book's analysis is located solely within the paradigm of the senses of Scripture, starting with the question of how many senses of Scripture he uses,[4] then considering the literal sense,[5] the spiritual sense,[6] and which types Jerome tends to draw attention to,[7] before examining how Jerome relates the literal and spiritual senses to one another.[8] The exegetical theory of Jerome is then analyzed, and summarized as essentially being a form of the Antiochene approach.[9] The second major study, Pierre Jay's *L'Exégèse de saint Jérôme d'après son Commentaire sur Isaïe*, only addresses Jerome's commentary on Isaiah, and within that focuses primarily on whether Jerome used two or three senses of Scripture in this work.[10] Although Jay examines other parts of Jerome's exegetical corpus, with some reference to the *In Matheum*, in two articles, these are squarely in the same mold. The first is primarily concerned with the extent to which Jerome was allegorical and literal, and influenced by Alexandrian or Antiochene models.[11] The second is devoted to examining how closely Jerome's theory and practice regarding the senses of Scripture match up.[12]

The third and fourth works, Adam Kamesar's *Jerome, Greek Scholarship, and the Hebrew Bible*,[13] and C. T. R. Hayward's *Jerome's Hebrew*

---

2. Pontificio Instituto Biblico, Rome, 1950.
3. Penna, *Girolamo*, 11
4. Penna, *Girolamo*, 4–58.
5. Penna, *Girolamo*, 59–92.
6. Penna, *Girolamo*, 93–124.
7. Penna, *Girolamo*, 125–46.
8. Penna, *Girolamo*, 147–60.
9. Penna, *Girolamo*, 161–7. See especially 167.
10. Études augustiniennes, Paris, 1985. See also Lardet's enthusiastic and more recent discussion of Jay's work: "Jerome exégète: une cohérence insoupçonnée," 300–307.
11. Jay, "Jérôme et la pratique de l'exégèse," 524–41.
12. Jay, "Saint Jérôme et la triple sens de l'écriture," 214–27.
13. Clarendon Press, Oxford, 1993.

Questions on Genesis,[14] both deal specifically with Jerome's *Quaestiones Hebraicae in Genesim*, the latter being a translation with an introduction and commentary. Neither of these books gives much attention to the matter of the senses of Scripture. However, this is not because they provide alternative frameworks for describing Jerome's exegesis so much as that they are concerned with quite different matters. Kamesar's thesis is that Jerome's aim in writing the *Quaestiones Hebraicae in Genesim* was to establish the centrality and priority of the Hebrew text of the Old Testament and to defend his philological system of Hebrew-Latin translation.[15] Hayward argues instead that Jerome's aim in writing this work was the broader one of justifying his dealings with Judaism and the Jews, which he seeks to accomplish by demonstrating that Jewish understanding of the Scriptures is often correct.[16] Much of Hayward's detailed commentary therefore is, as might be expected, concerned with Jerome's treatment of the Hebrew text, the LXX, and Jewish and other sources for his commentary rather than with systematically identifying distinguishing features of Jerome's exegetical practice.[17] The efforts of both Kamesar and Hayward, though of considerable value to scholars interested in other aspects of Jerome's work, are therefore of such a character that they offer little that can be readily utilized in the project at hand.

The fifth major work on Jerome's exegesis, Dennis Brown's *Vir Trilinguis*, is more comprehensive than any other study of Jerome's exegesis to date, but it does not vary much in its conclusions from the standard view which has been taken of Jerome's exegesis for decades, and which is described below. It discusses his work at length in terms of the distinction between allegorical and literal.[18] Additionally, much of Brown's work is

---

14. Clarendon Press, Oxford, 1995.

15. Kamesar, *Jerome*, 193–4.

16. Hayward, *Hebrew Questions*, 14. Note that Cameron's more recent article "The Rabbinic Vulgate?," 117–30 disagrees with the conclusions of Kamesar and Hayward on this point: according to Cameron, Jerome's usage of Jewish learning is normally limited to utilizing its philological material rather than exegetical resources.

17. Hayward, *Hebrew Questions*, 88–245.

18. Brown, *Vir Trilinguis*, 138–56. Little has changed in Brown's more recent work, for example Brown, "Jerome and the Vulgate." This chapter is mostly taken up with discussion of the influences on Jerome's exegesis (summed up in the concluding section on page 371 as "Antiochene" and "Alexandrian"), and the extent to which his exegesis reads for the literal or allegorical senses: see particularly the section entitled "Literal and Allegorical Understanding," 368–71, in addition to the material on pp. 366–68 which surveys his Old Testament commentaries and described them in terms

concerned with studying the history of exegesis as it developed before Jerome's time, in order to examine the antecedents to and influences on his exegesis. His other interest is in Jerome's use of translations, texts, and specific terms within his exegesis. Brown does not devote much attention to Jerome's exegesis in relation to that of his contemporaries, or to how he uses his exegesis to, say, discuss a doctrine or apply it to his audience, matters which are the primary concern of this study. In summary, he advances little that is of use in effectively distinguishing Jerome from other Latin exegetes of the period.

A large number of journal articles and chapters within book-length works have been written on Jerome's exegesis. Most of these works either briefly consider a specific feature of Jerome's exegesis, or give general summaries of Jerome's exegesis on a broad scale, based on a survey of a small number of examples. The vast majority of articles on Jerome's exegesis concern his major commentaries on the Old Testament, particularly on the Prophets. Until recently, English scholarship in particular paid relatively little attention to Jerome's exegetical works. This is partly due to the fact that much of the work on Jerome generally has been undertaken for many decades by French scholars, but also because what English scholarship there is has tended to be more concerned with Jerome's work as a translator, or general matters of his life and times.

That said, what scholarship there is takes a similar approach to that found in the five book-length works discussed above, which this study argues can only assist up to a certain point in defining Jerome's exegesis against that of his contemporaries. Jerome's work is frequently defined in terms of the senses of Scripture, allegory, literalism, and the Alexandrian-Antiochene distinction. This is true of both earlier and more recent assessments of Jerome's exegesis. Hartmann's 1952 article on Jerome's exegetical works describes them in terms of the influences that acted upon him, which are all categorized, without exception, as either Antiochene or Alexandrian.[19] He defines Antiochene and Alexandrian in terms of paying attention to the literal and mystical meanings respectively.[20] The commonplace acknowledgment of Jerome's movement away from the allegorizing exegesis of his early years as a commentator towards an approach which was essentially grammatico-historical, with occasional ref-

---

of these two categories.

19. Hartmann, "Jerome," 47–67.
20. Hartmann, "Jerome," 51.

erences to allegorical methods, receives a mention in many of the short summaries of Jerome's work that are extant. Typical is Altaner's statement that "[i]n his earlier works he followed the allegorical exegesis of Scripture, but under the influence of his philological activities he increasingly appreciated the historico-grammatical sense of the words of Scripture, without, however, abandoning the Alexandrian method entirely."[21] De Lubac, on the other hand, regarded Jerome's work as fundamentally allegorical and Origenistic throughout his career,[22] despite occasional appearances to the contrary:

> Saint Jerome, who had formed, in his enthusiasm, the plan to translate into Latin the entire works of Origen, imitated the great Alexandrian both in his scientific zeal and in his abundant, nay superabundant, practice of allegorical exegesis . . . he remained faithful to allegorism to the end, both to its most controversial features and to its best grounded principles . . . from time to time he confined himself to literal explication, but that was in self-defense: as soon as he had the liberty to do so, he "fell back" into allegory.[23]

Weisen's 1964 treatment also argues that Jerome was thoroughly Origenistic and should be read as an exegete who applied not two or even three senses of Scripture, but the four later popularized by John Cassian.[24]

While recent scholarship may avoid such readings of later developments into Jerome's writings and sometimes gives greater recognition to the role of the Latin grammatical tradition of literary criticism than earlier works did,[25] the general framework within which his exegesis is discussed has not changed. Kannengeisser is careful to not read the four medieval senses of Scripture into Jerome's writings anachronistically, but still believes that, "[i]n reality, his exegetical practice is normally set in the traditional framework of the two great senses of Scripture: the lit-

---

21. Altaner, *Patrology*, 473. Similar statements can be found in Campenhausen, *Fathers*, 165, and Kieffer, "Jerome: His Exegesis and Hermeneutics," 676.

22. A view still put in print and applied specifically to the *In Matheum* as recently as 2003 by Brown, "Jerome," 369.

23. Lubac, *Medieval*, 2:213.

24. Weisen, *St Jerome as a Satirist*, 95. Several years earlier, de Lubac also had suggested that Jerome followed Origen in his approach to the senses of Scripture—but like Origen and unlike Cassian, evidenced a strong preference for three, not four senses: *Medieval*, 1:90–95.

25. E.g. Williams, *The Monk and the Book*, 86–87.

eral sense and the spiritual interpretation . . . [and] [t]o the literal sense Jerome accords a particular attention."[26] Dockery's analysis sets out to prove that Jerome was the mediator of a modified Antiochene literalism to the West.[27] The modification spoken of is due to his exposure to Alexandrian and Jewish methods.[28] While more accepting than earlier scholars that Jerome cannot be neatly placed in either the Alexandrian or the Antiochene school, his work is still described in terms of how it fits with respect to these two broad approaches, and their different emphases on the spiritual and literal senses.[29] Dennis Brown's 1998 discussion similarly argues that the primary background to Jerome's exegesis is differing attitudes to allegorism in the East among Jews, Alexandria, and Antioch.[30] Brown goes on to describe Jerome's exegesis—including the *In Matheum*—almost entirely with reference to the senses of Scripture and his use of Antiochene, Jewish, and Alexandrian methods.[31] Graves likewise argues that "the exegetical method of the Latin Doctor can be broken down into a mixture between two main tendencies in interpretation: the allegorical/spiritual on the one hand, and the literal/historical/Hebraic on the other."[32] In her 2006 study, Williams devotes the greater part of two chapters to discussion of Jerome's exegesis with a focus on his commentaries on the Prophets, and while a number of other important aspects of Jerome's interpretative practices are discussed, the primary focus remains on the senses of Scripture, particularly the distinction between the literal/historical ("according to the Hebrews") and the spiritual/allegorical readings which Jerome provides. This distinction not only predominates Williams's analysis quantitatively speaking but is also the framework within which Jerome's exegesis is considered as a whole: "Jerome deploys all of the many resources at his command, both textual and interpretative, according to a clear, twofold division. He presents, at least in theory, a double commentary. Two versions of the text under exegesis, two methods of interpretation, and two exegetical traditions appear in

---

26. Kannengeisser, *Handbook*, 1104.
27. Dockery, *Biblical Interpretation Then and Now*, 132.
28. Dockery, *Biblical Interpretation Then and Now*, 132.
29. Dockery, *Biblical Interpretation Then and Now*, 135.
30. Brown, in McKim, *Handbook*, 44.
31. Brown, in McKim, *Handbook*, 42–46, especially 45 on the *In Matheum*.
32. Graves, "Judaizing Christian Interpretations," 146.

parallel."³³ In the introduction to his relatively recent (2008) translation of Jerome's commentary, Scheck devotes virtually the entire subsection on "Jerome's Exegetical Method" to a discussion of Jerome's use of the senses of Scripture, and specifically a defense of his use of allegorical interpretation within his work.³⁴ Writing in 2013 regarding Jerome's biblical scholarship more generally, Kamesar observes that Jerome follows the practice of the Alexandrian exegetes in systematically distinguishing between literal and allegorical exegeses of the biblical text, with this established pattern in Jerome's case shaped by his use of Jewish interpreters as his key source for the former and Greek Christian interpreters as central to the latter.³⁵

Within this framework, several aspects of Jerome's exegesis are frequently commented upon, on which there exists a strong degree of scholarly consensus. The compliment most usually paid to him by students of his work in connection with his "Antiochene" tendencies is that he was particularly learned in matters of philology and textual criticism. His familiarity with the original biblical languages and dexterity in gleaning points of interest from the text in these languages has often been observed over many years, as his readily applied knowledge of the historical and geographical context of the text and the events that lie behind it. For example, Sparks claims that "[t]he outstanding characteristic of Jerome's commentaries is learning—secular, sacred, philological, textual, historical, exegetical, all mixed together . . . phrases like 'the Jews think' or 'the Hebrews say' are not uncommon."³⁶ Simonetti's conclusion is similar: "On the whole, Jerome's exegetical work is more impressive for its philological rigour and the abundance of materials used than for coherence of method or originality of interpretation."³⁷

On the reverse side of the coin, the criticisms most frequently made of Jerome are that he was inconsistent and unsystematic, that he was unoriginal, or simply dull and boring, as Smalley says, "he was too hurried to be consistent or systematic."³⁸ Campenhausen puts it more eloquently,

33. Williams, *The Monk and the Book*, 92–93.

34. Scheck, "Introduction," 24–30.

35. Kamesar, "Jerome," 673.

36. Sparks, "Jerome," 539. Similar sentiments are also expressed more recently by Williams, *The Monk and the Book*, 51 and 92, as well as in somewhat more nuanced form by Rebenich, *Jerome*, 52–56 and 59.

37. Simonetti, *Interpretation*, 103.

38. Smalley, *Bible*, 21.

observing that "[h]is explanations of the Bible fluctuated between dull philology and unauthoritative edification."[39] Also frequently commented on is the fact that sloppiness in his exegesis illustrates his hurried method of composition, that his commentaries on the Bible were "unique for his time in their knowledge of the older exegetical literature and their historical and archaeological scholarship, [and] have mostly been composed too quickly and superficially."[40]

Another observation commonly made on Jerome's exegesis is the frequently expressed view that he was largely disinterested and lacked ability in handling matters of any theological substance. For example, Kelly, speaking on Jerome's commentaries on various New Testament epistles, comments that "[w]hat is chiefly disappointing, especially in expounding Galatians and Ephesians, is Jerome's failure to understand, much less present adequately, the profound theological issues with which these letters are concerned."[41] He later suggests that in Jerome's exegesis there is "everywhere a striving to find the doctrines of current orthodoxy in the text."[42]

To summarize, existing scholarship still tends to describe Jerome's work using the senses of Scripture, allegory, literalism, and the Alexandrian-Antiochene distinction. Within this paradigm, Jerome is regarded essentially as a literalist. His philological orientation is typically highlighted, alongside his relative disinterest or expertise in exploring complex theological matters. The analysis of Jerome's exegesis which follows in this chapter does not suggest that this view is substantially accurate with respect to the portion of his exegesis of Matthew which is under study here. It accepts that a crucial element of Jerome's exegesis is its literal orientation, an orientation which Jerome probably consciously aimed at when commencing the *In Matheum* in particular.[43] However, it does suggest that some modifications and additions to the accepted view of his exegesis are helpful. In particular, it appears, in the context of this case study, as if scholarship has tended to overplay Jerome's avoidance of complex theological matters. In addition, his strongly philological orientation, when considered alongside a number of other features of Je-

39. Campenhausen, *Fathers*, 167.
40. Altaner, *Patrology*, 470.
41. Kelly, *Jerome*, 143.
42. Kelly, *Jerome*, 224.
43. Jerome, *Math.*, Praefatio, 104–8, notes that his reader had requested a historical exposition.

rome's exegesis described below, is best viewed as an indication of where Jerome's vision is focused as he interprets the text rather than of where he sits on the allegorical-literal spectrum—although there certainly is still some truth to observations on the latter. The primary thesis of this chapter is that Jerome's exegesis is most helpfully understood when his prominent philological orientation is examined together with his manner of proceeding through the biblical passage at hand, his view of the unity of the text, his use of allegory, typology, prophecy-fulfillment, and the extent to which he engages in practical application and polysemy. These features of his exegesis will therefore now be examined in turn, in order to gain a fuller picture of the character of Jerome's exegesis than it is possible to gain through applying the traditional framework alone.

Philological Interests

As is the case in his other exegetical works, in his exposition of the crucifixion and resurrection narratives Jerome seldom strays far from the text. Features, details, and ideas intrinsic to the text drive his exposition, rather than doctrinal or personal concerns.[44] In this regard, several characteristics distinctive of Jerome's exegesis generally are in view. A number of these can be summarized as a concern with philological matters. Minor or incidental features of the text, even individual words can often determine the direction of his exegesis for an extended period. On occasions, such details can receive considerable attention, while other features of the verse in question are ignored altogether.

The study of individual words in Latin, Greek, or Hebrew can assume pivotal importance in Jerome's exegesis. For example, Jerome's discussion of Matthew 27:33, "And they came to the place that is called Golgotha, which is the place of the skull," centers around the related meanings of "Golgotha" and "Calvary" (*Calvariae*) as "the place of the condemned" and "the place of the skull" respectively.[45] In his analysis of the verse, Jerome is only exercised by the question of how these two place-names, brought together by the text, might conjointly indicate a meaningful interpretation of the verse. Jerome sees two possibilities. Firstly, building

---

44. While this is true when Jerome is compared with other late patristic commentators, it should be stressed that relative to the earlier classical authors, Jerome does not pay that much attention to detail and form rather than content: Hiemann, "The Polemical Application of Scripture in St. Jerome," 309–16.

45. Jerome, *Math.*, IV, 1656–80.

on the popular belief that "the place of the skull" is called thus because Adam, the "first man," was buried there, Jerome muses whether the key to the verse might be a symmetry between "Golgotha" as the place of Adam's burial and "Calvary" as the place of Christ's execution—a belief given apparently additional impetus because "Calvary" is more literally rendered "the place of the decapitated."[46] However, Jerome believes this option to be untenable because he believes that Adam was buried at Hebron.[47] He therefore proposes as correct his second possibility, that Christ was crucified in "the place of condemnation" of criminals and "the place of the skull" (i.e. the place of the dead) to highlight that Christ died "like a sinner among the sinners for the benefit of all," "having been made sin for us on the cross."[48] According to Jerome, the text's remark on the two place-names therefore helpfully underlines that Christ was executed as one under condemnation for sin and its ultimate result, death.

Similarly, Jerome often highlights individual words or short phrases to create linkages to other passages or ideas.[49] For example, when commenting on the fact that in Matthew 27:39 those passing by were reviling Jesus as he hung on the cross, Jerome notes that "they were unwilling to walk in the way of the Scriptures. Those who were now shaking their heads at him had previously also shaken their feet against him—the same feet that had stumbled on the rock."[50] Here, Jerome refers in turn to the "walk in the way of the Law" formula of Exodus 18:20, to those who shake their heads at the Lord's anointed in Psalm 109:25, the stamping of the feet of the wicked in Ezekiel 25:6, and finally to Christ as the rock referred to by Isaiah 8:14 (quoted in 1 Peter 2:8 and Romans 9:33). His ability to seamlessly pick up on a string of successive, similar words and phrases from all over Scripture is testimony to how he is driven along

---

46. Scheck reflects this in his translation of the relevant text: Jerome, *Commentary*, 315–6.

47. An opinion that he gives in a little more detail when commenting on Genesis 22:2 in *Liber Hebraicarum Quaestionum in Genesim* (PL 23:0972B). Jerome believes that the meaning of the older name for Hebron referred to in Joshua 14:15 and 15:13 (Kiriath Arba, named after "the forefather of Anak") suggests that Adam was buried there, a view which accords nicely with the position of Hebron as the burial place of Abraham, Isaac, and Jacob even if it does remove the useful geographic connection between the deaths of the old and new Adam. The alternative view, that Adam was buried at Calvary, had been held by Jerome at an earlier time: *Ep.*, 46.3 (PL 22:0485).

48. Jerome, *Math.*, IV, 1668–71 (translations mine).

49. Hall, *Reading*, 115.

50. Jerome, *Math.*, IV, 1718–22 (translation mine).

by the words of the biblical text. The same aspect of his exegesis is in view when he engages in a wordplay upon the mention of the "light" ("lumen") of the sun having been hidden at Jesus' death: "And it seems to me that this darkness should have made the light of the world ["lumen mundi"] all the more clearer, since he, and not the sun, is the greater light ... and that you should not hide in the darkness, impiously cursing your light."[51] Here, Jerome uses the appearance of the word "light" to make a point about belief and unbelief through reference to John 1:4 and 3:19.[52] Jerome handles Matthew 28:4-5 similarly; within these verses he is concerned only with the etymology and uses of the repeated phrase "be afraid."[53] Likewise, Jerome's exposition of Matthew 28:9 weaves the words of the evangelist in amongst his own.[54]

Also relevant at this point is his delight in turning to the original biblical languages, typically as the final arbiter of the meaning of a verse in question.[55] When discussing Matthew 27:46, "And about the ninth hour, Jesus cried with a great voice saying, 'Eli Eli lema sabacthani,' that is: 'my God my God, why have you forsaken me?'" Jerome does not merely refer to the Greek, but to the Hebrew text of Psalm 22:1 which is quoted in Matthew.[56] Several details which follow in the Hebrew version of the Psalm are decisive for Jerome, who uses their presence here to stress that this Psalm is to be directly applied to Christ, rather than to an earlier royal figure in the history of Israel.[57] At least with reference

51. Jerome, *Math.*, IV, 1762-5, on Matt 27:45.

52. Jerome and his contemporaries studied and preached on the Bible in a culture which was considerably more oral than that of many more modern readers of the Bible, with oral reading and memorization of texts being very common. As such, the sounds of words, and similarities in sounds between relatively unrelated words, could possibly lead to exegetical connections being made between various passages which might seem surprising to modern readers. Cf. Moorhead, "Hearers and Readers of Christian Latin Texts in Late Antiquity," 479-99.

53. Jerome, *Math.*, IV, 1939-44.

54. Jerome, *Math.*, IV, 1961-4. Note Jerome's repeated use of "worshipped," "touched," and his reference to "the rest of those who were seeking the living amongst the dead"—all words or phrases from the verse or its immediate context.

55. This has long been recognized by scholarship and was popularized by the work of Courcelle. See esp. *Writers*, 51-58.

56. Jerome, *Matt.*, IV, 1768-74. In relation to quotations of the Old Testament within the New Testament and Jerome's citation practices in relation to these, see Kato, "Jerome's Understanding of Old Testament Quotations in the New Testament," 289-315.

57. Cf. his discussion of Ps 21:1 (22:1 in English Bibles: in the Latin Bible used by

to some biblical texts, Jerome appears to consider that the application of Hebrew language knowledge assists with reading the New Testament as well as the Old, because human authors of the New Testament such as Matthew and Paul were conversant with the Hebrew Bible and used their knowledge of it in ways that Jerome assumed to be similar to his own exegetical methods.[58] However, one must be careful not to place too much emphasis on Jerome's use of the original biblical languages.[59] For example, in the portion under study here, there are only two discussions of the Hebrew (in his comments on 27:46 and 27:47 respectively).[60] The Hebrew references demonstrate his background as an experienced Old Testament scholar as much as they do his interest in philological matters: any thorough exegete with a good knowledge of Hebrew would refer to the original context of an Old Testament quotation if a relevant point could thus be made, as is the case with both of the Hebrew references.[61] Jerome's use of the original languages therefore cannot be regarded as a central feature of his exegesis of Matthew; at best, it merely supports the overall impression that one gains of his being interested in details of the text.

The Unity of the Text

Furthermore, Jerome is not interested merely with the philological characteristics of the text in their own right, separately from their biblical context, but also in them as part of the unified narrative of the Gospel, and in terms of how they contribute to the story of Scripture as a whole.[62] Thus, when dealing with Matthew 28:2b, where the presence of the angels at the tomb of Jesus is described, Jerome does not just take the term "angels" and examine its etymology or its uses in other, unrelated biblical contexts. Rather, he starts with the more precise idea of angels appearing

---

Jerome, Psalms 9 and 10 in the English Bible are joined together as Psalm 9) in Jerome, *Commentarioli in psalmos* (*CCSL* 72:98).

58. Williams, *The Monk and the Book*, 51.

59. Note also that even though Jerome did make use of Jewish philological expertise in his exegesis on the Hebrew, his use of Jewish exegesis itself was very limited and highly cautious: Cameron, "The Rabbinic Vulgate?," 117–30.

60. Jerome, *Math.*, IV, 1682–3 is the other Hebrew reference.

61. On the extent of Jerome's Hebrew proficiency, see Newman, "How Should We Measure Jerome's Hebrew Competence?," 131–40.

62. Old, *The Reading and Preaching of the Scriptures*, 2:337.

to Gospel characters, and notes their function and importance within the narrative, in order to suggest that angels are present at many of the key points in the Gospel story:

> Gabriel came to Mary, the angel spoke with Joseph, the same were sent to the shepherds, and from angels was afterwards heard the chorus: "Glory to God in the highest and peace over the earth; good will to all men," when He [Christ] was tempted when He was alone, and immediately after His victory [against Satan's temptations] angels served Him. Now also an angel came to watch the tomb of the Lord and pointed to His conquering glory in a shining white garment, and in addition, when the Lord was rising to the sky, two angels on the Mount of Olives were perceived promising the apostles the second coming of the Saviour.[63]

His stress on the narrative unity of the text is also underscored by his tendency on occasions to gather together and summarize key points within the Gospel story "so far." Thus, when discussing Jesus' statement in Matthew 28:18 that "All authority in heaven and on earth is given to me" he observes that "[a]uthority has been given to him who a little earlier was crucified, who was buried in the tomb, who lay there dead, who afterward was resurrected."[64] All of these preceding events that have been recorded are regarded by Jerome as important background to Jesus' receiving of authority, not just the one that occurred most recently, or merely the very fact that Jesus has been given all authority. Jerome believes that the Gospel account is a unified whole, and as such, the broader context of individual words within the flow of the narrative should receive proper attention.[65]

When he discusses Matthew 27:34, he moves more broadly within the Bible. In this case, he uses the reference to the soldiers giving Jesus bitter wine to drink on the cross to jump to the indictment of Israel as having turned into an alien vineyard, filled with those who do bitter deeds in Jeremiah 2:19–21.[66] Jerome's vast knowledge of the Bible and

---

63. Jerome, *Math.*, IV, 1927–35 (translation mine).

64. Jerome, *Matt.*, IV, 1995–7.

65. See also Jerome's discussion of Matt 27:53–54, at Jerome, *Math.*, IV, 1837–44. Cf. Eliot, "Exegetical Genres in the Patristic Era," 793, who suggests that Jerome's exegetical approach in general is driven partly by a concern for context in relation to details in the text, along with an interest in producing a "flowing commentary."

66. Jerome, *Math.*, IV, 1687–94.

the allied biblical sciences allows him to make many such connections elsewhere in his exegesis.⁶⁷

Jerome's consciousness of the unity of the text, and his faith in it as an accurate record of events able to convey divine truth, is further underlined by his concern to reconcile apparent differences between the various Gospel narratives.⁶⁸ One example is his discussion of the reference to the two thieves in Matthew 27:44, which differs from Luke's account in that it does not mention the fact that one thief expressed faith in Jesus, but only that both were maligning him: "Here, through a figure of speech termed syllepsis, both thieves instead of only one, are described as having mocked Jesus. According to Luke, however, after one thief blasphemed, the other professed faith and rebuked the first. There is no discrepancy between the evangelists, but that initially, both thieves blasphemed, but later . . . one of them believed in Jesus, recanting his earlier denial by subsequently confessing."⁶⁹

In this case, Jerome deals with the apparent discrepancy by suggesting that the two evangelists are referring to the behavior of the two thieves at different points in the day.⁷⁰ Likewise, a similar explanation is found when Jerome, commenting on Matthew 27:32, where Simon of Cyrene is recorded as being ordered to carry the cross, is concerned to allay any fears of a discrepancy with John's Gospel, where Simon is not mentioned, and Jesus is recorded as carrying the cross himself: "So that we may not think that in this place John's Gospel is contradictory [to Matthew's] . . . understand that when they were going out of the garrison, Jesus carried the cross, and that afterwards Simon did so, whom they impressed the cross upon."⁷¹ Interestingly, Jerome uniformly resolves such difficulties without any reference to the human authors of the various biblical books, and to their different purposes and perspectives—a point at which his approach is starkly distinct from that of Ambrose. In the first

---

67. C.f. Hartmann, "Jerome," 69.

68. Another example of this can be found at: Jerome, *Math.*, IV, 1910–94.

69. Jerome, *Math.*, IV, 1740–5 (translation mine). "Syllepsis" refers to a figure of speech in which a verb (or an adjective) is applied to two nouns, though appropriate to only one of them.

70. On Jerome's use of the Lukan reference contrite bandit, see Courtray, "La Figure des Deux Larrons chez Jérôme," 105–16, who argues that this example of a last-minute conversion is used by Jerome across his writings (following earlier exegetes, particularly Origen) as an exemplum of faith, harking back to the heroic age of the persecutions.

71. Jerome, *Math.*, IV, 1657–62 (translation mine).

example, he does, however, note the presence of an unusual grammatical device in the construction of the text (but without making an explicit, Ambrosian, connection between this and the conscious workings of the author), and at this point underlines for us his concern above all with the form of the text.

It is therefore to be concluded that although philological concerns assume a prominent place in Jerome's exposition, they are only one part of a broader agenda on his part. It is more appropriate to describe Jerome's work in more general terms, as "embodying" the text in his own exposition, rather than as being driven only by philological matters and the details of the text, and recognizing that evidence of the latter can be subsumed within the former statement. This is to say he makes the text, its concerns and manner of argument, as well as its language, his own. Generally speaking, his commentary is a simple and direct exposition of the plain meaning of the text,[72] operating within the logical structures that are provided for him by the narrative, which seldom strays far from the text itself. Regarding the latter characteristic in particular, at least, Jerome's approach is similar to that of Antiochene exegesis, with its emphasis on attention to the *akolouthia* or logical ordering of the text.[73]

Jerome's manner of proceeding through his chosen passage further highlights his focus on the text. However, it also brings to our attention another feature of his exegesis, the eclecticism of the comments that he actually does make on the text. That is to say, while Jerome is very disciplined in that he remains closely tied to his text, the comments that he makes within this framework tend to have a random rather than a thorough character to them. We shall examine the latter feature first.

Manner of Proceeding through the Text

Jerome proceeds in an orderly fashion from one verse to the next, seldom spending an inordinate amount of time on discussing any one sentence or phrase.[74] However, this does not mean that he discusses every verse. The *In Matheum* often skips over verses or treats them scantily.[75] In the

---

72. Carroll, *Preaching*, 164.

73. Edwards, "Figurative Readings," 729.

74. A feature observed of his other commentaries, too: Jay, "Exégèse," 531; Kannengeisser, *Handbook*, 1102.

75. Kelly, *Jerome*, 223.

selection under study, Jerome avoids discussion in chapter 27 of verses 40-41, 43, 49, 56, 58, 62-63, 65-66, and in chapter 28 of verses 3, 7, and 11-15. That is to say, out of the fifty-four verses within the passage, Jerome does not even mention nineteen: while he does attend to the majority of the passage, a substantial portion of it receives no comment.

Furthermore, Jerome's treatment of some verses is partial; he tends to note some details while ignoring others, for little apparent reason. For example, at 27:55, all that he notes about the women accompanying Jesus to the tomb is the practical point that Paul said that teachers were allowed to have women accompany them, to care for their needs.[76] The motives behind their actions and their devotion are not noted, and the facts observed by the verse itself that they had accompanied Jesus from Galilee and had followed him for a long time are ignored. The discussion that follows in 27:57, on Joseph of Arimathea, gives a similar impression.[77] Jerome chooses to explore the fact that Joseph is called a rich man, but none of the other details that are mentioned about him, such as his going to Pilate, possible motivations for his action, or his being from Arimathea and what significance that might entail.[78] In both these examples, it is not clear that Jerome has a particularly strong reason for commenting on some details and not on others. Neither the theme of Christian teachers being allowed to be accompanied by women who support them, nor that of wealth and poverty are discussed in what immediately precedes or follows Jerome's commentary on these verses. Neither theme is common elsewhere in his exegesis in this commentary.[79] In this regard, Jerome's exegesis is distinct from that of Ambrose and Augustine, in their more thorough scrutiny of the details of the narrative and tendency to skip over fewer verses, and yet like that of Augustine in the random character of its choices about what to say on a particular verse. Jerome's work is like that of Hilary, who also tends to pass over some verses. However, as will become apparent in chapter 3, Hilary is more intentional and less random than Jerome in terms of which details he chooses to address,

---

76. Jerome, *Math.*, IV, 1847-61.

77. Jerome, *Math.*, IV, 1864-72.

78. C.f. the other points made about Joseph by Hilary, *Matt.*, 33.8, and Ambrose, *Lucam*, X, 140.

79. The first theme is not mentioned anywhere else, while the second occurs only occasionally in the commentary, almost always when it is raised by the text itself, as at Jerome, *Math.*, I, 810-7, on Matt 6:19-21.

since he is more focused on elucidating what he believes to be the main point and flow of the passage.

Drawing Theology from the Text

For the vast majority of the verses in the selection under study here that Jerome does discuss, the comments that he makes on any particular details which receive his attention are direct and straightforward. His interest in philological features such as the meanings of particular words might conceivably allow him to either develop allegories or additional literal readings of the text.[80] However, it is the latter which predominates over the former practice in Jerome's work: his observations are usually quite down to earth, and firmly established on the literal sense. That said, on several occasions he also discusses the spiritual realities that lie behind the mundane facts. This is rarely pure allegorizing, and most often a reference to or an explanation of the theological reasons and factors operating behind the historical details of the narrative.[81] An example of this is his commentary on Matthew 28:19, "Go therefore, teach all nations, baptizing them in the name of the Father, and of the Son and of the Holy Spirit": "First they teach all nations, then they dip in water those who have been taught. For it is not possible that the body receives the sacrament of Baptism unless the soul first receives the truth of the faith."[82] Likewise he makes a direct and simple theological point from Matthew 27:51, "And the curtain of the Temple was torn in two parts, from top to bottom," noting that "[t]he curtain of the Temple was torn and all the mysteries of the

---

80. Hall, *Readings*, 114.

81. The terms "theology" and "theological" can take on a variety of meanings. In many contexts they are broadly applied to all matters which pertain to the study of God and Christian truth (including exegesis). In others, such as among many of our secondary sources, they are used more narrowly, to describe particular Christian themes, issues, and truths which result from reflection and debate: "theological views," "theological statements," and "theological themes." This second usage, which is employed throughout this book, does not include biblical exegesis but is a rough synonym with "doctrinal." That said, its semantic range is a little broader than that of "doctrinal," in that it is concerned with more than just systematic statement and debate concerning that which ought to be believed. In the context of a project such as this, it also incorporates reference to such areas as broad biblical themes, patterns, or ideas which are not adequately described by the label "doctrinal," as well as Christian reflection upon praxis. Cf. Hastings, "Theology," 700–702.

82. Jerome, *Matt.*, IV, 2001–4.

Law that were previously woven together were made known and passed to the Gentile people."[83] More often than not, he relates such statements about the "spiritual" background directly to the narrative itself. For example, consider his exposition of Matthew 27:42, "Let him come down now from the Cross, and we will believe in him": "But it seems to me that demons are guiding this. For immediately when the Lord was crucified, they sensed the power of the cross and understood that their strength was broken. They do this that he might come down from the cross. But the Lord knows the plots of his adversaries and remains on the gibbet in order to destroy the Devil."[84]

At one point, when commenting on Matthew 27:38, "At that time they crucified two thieves with Him, one on the right and one on the left," Jerome makes a theological statement on the basis of an incidental detail, in this case an earlier observation that Calvary was the burial place of Adam: "If Golgotha is the grave of Adam and not the place of condemnation . . . why were two thieves crucified in the place?"[85] The implication is that the thieves were crucified alongside Jesus so as to emphasize that Jesus stood condemned. However, although an obscure preconception of Jerome's is used in the discussion, it should be noted that the theological point (that Jesus stood condemned) is made primarily from the literal history given in the text, namely, that two thieves were crucified alongside Jesus.

As can be seen from the foregoing examples, Jerome does show significant interest in explaining the theological background to the narrative in this exposition, although he does not demonstrate nearly the same penchant as Augustine, for example, for digressing onto matters of theological interest. Jerome's comments on theological matters are typically brief,[86] and almost always rooted in the text, such as his sole statement on the verse, "And with a great shout, Jesus gave up His spirit," where he says that "to be able to give up His spirit is a mark of His divine authority."[87] However, on occasions he does demonstrate a degree

---

83. Jerome, *Matt.*, IV, 1799-80. Interestingly, Jerome adds in one of his letters (120.8) that the now lost Gospel according to the Hebrews speaks of a cleavage in the masonry of the temple porch, which might have left the most holy place open to view.

84. Jerome, *Matt.*, IV, 1732-6.

85. Jerome, *Math.*, IV, 1713-6 (translation mine).

86. Kannengeisser, *Handbook*, 1109.

87. Jerome, *Math.*, IV, 1795-6, on Matt 27:50 (translation mine). See also IV, 1834-44, on Matt 27:54.

of theological sophistication and originality not often found in his other commentaries,[88] all the more notable as the *In Matheum* was completed very rapidly. Particularly noteworthy is his discussion of Matthew 28:2, "And behold, the rock was split open; for an angel of the Lord descended from the sky and rolled away the stone and was sitting on it; moreover his appearance was bright and his garment was like snow":

> Our Lord, who is at the one time Son of God and Son of Man, possessing both the nature of deity and of flesh, sometimes expresses His greatness, and at others His humility. In this present place, on the one hand there is the man who was crucified, who was buried, who was shut away through burial, who was held by the great stone placed against the tomb. However, on the other hand, this entrance [into death] declared Him to be the Son of God: the sun hidden by the darkness which was falling over the earth, the veil cut in half, the rocks split open, and the fact that He was attended by angels.[89]

In this passage, Jerome begins with what was a commonplace doctrinal point after the "Arian" controversy, namely, that Jesus is both fully divine and fully human, and that different incidents in the Gospel narratives point to one or the other of these two aspects of his nature.[90] However, he does not simply say that the cross points to his humanity and the resurrection to his deity. The manner of his death, and the signs which accompanied it, also point to his deity. It should also be noted that Jerome's discussion of this point is thoroughly embedded in the Matthean text. In discussing the link between Christ's death and his deity, he does not merely present a random selection of Old and New Testament passages, but refers to the sequence of signs as presented in the segment of Matthew he has just commented on.[91] It is therefore apparent that it is the text that is driving Jerome's exegesis forward, and not his theology. While the latter may have a significant place in his exegesis, it is the former that occupies the central position.

Some sophistication in theological matters is also apparent in Jerome's exposition of the rising of many holy people upon Jesus' death, where he comments that "[j]ust as the dead Lazarus was resurrected, so

---

88. Sparks, "Jerome," 537–9.

89. Jerome, *Math.*, IV, 1919–27 (translation mine).

90. Cf. Keiffer, "Jerome," 676.

91. Similar to the sequence of angelic appearances Jerome lists at *Math.*, IV, 1928–31, on Matt 28:2.

also many bodies of the saints were resurrected. Thus they showed the Lord rising again. And yet though the tombs were opened, they were not resurrected before the Lord was resurrected. Thus he was the firstborn of the resurrection from the dead."[92] In this passage, Jerome identifies a possible criticism of the biblical witness: that Jesus cannot accurately be described as the firstborn from the dead if others have already risen. In his answer, Jerome exercises a modicum of theological nous in emphasizing that their rising is consequent upon and subsequent to Christ's death, and is merely a sign of the greater resurrection to come two days later. Again, however, it is Jerome's interest in the text, in this case in defending its veracity, that is the driving force behind his exposition at this point, rather than any deep, abiding interest in theological issues.

Although Jerome does demonstrate significant interest and sophistication in handling theological matters, it must be admitted that there are occasions where this is not the case. The most obvious example here comes at the conclusion of the *In Matheum*, in his exposition of Jesus' post-resurrection statement, "And behold I am with you for ever, even until the end of the age," where Jerome comments that "Even to the end of the world itself he promises to be present, not ignorant of the day on which he knows he will be with the apostles."[93] Jerome's comment that Jesus "was not ignorant of the day" appears to be directly at odds with Jesus' own statement about his return, recorded only a few chapters earlier in Matthew 24:36: "No one knows about that day or hour, not even the angels in heaven, nor the Son, but only the Father." In this case, Jerome, without defending or explaining his position, makes a statement which seems more like an imposition of his own views on a particular area of Christology, than making a doctrinal point as an extension of his exposition of the text.[94] However, it should be noted that in this case, Jerome's view that Christ had perfect knowledge of all matters while on earth is consistent with his stated views elsewhere in his exposition. Specifically, in his discussion of the taunts of the crowds in Matthew 27:42 as part of a secretive demonic plot, he comments that "the Lord knows the plots of his adversaries and remains on the gibbet in order to destroy the Devil."[95] Thus, even where his theological views may be poorly considered, his

---

92. Jerome, *Matt.*, IV, 1817-22, on Matt 27:52-3.

93. Jerome, *Math.*, IV, 2019-21 (translation mine).

94. Cummings, "Jerome," 282, argues that Jerome frequently imposes his own views on the biblical texts in this manner.

95. Jerome, *Matt.*, IV, 1735-6.

dealing with such issues in his exposition of the crucifixion and resurrection narratives is thoroughly consistent.

The fact that Jerome has at least a little interest and originality in handling doctrinal matters in his comments on the crucifixion and resurrection narratives differs somewhat from the popular stereotype of his work among scholars.[96] As was noted at the beginning of this chapter, scholarship tends to regard Jerome as a commentator who had difficulty thinking coherently on such matters, let alone showing a real and perceptive interest in deep theological themes. He has also frequently been accused of attempting to read basic doctrine crudely into the text, rather than allowing theological truths to emerge from his exegetical labor. Indeed, Kelly, in his brief remarks on Jerome's work on Matthew states that "[e]verywhere one senses a striving to discover the doctrines of current orthodoxy in the text."[97] However, the foregoing analysis has demonstrated such comment, while containing a substantial element of truth, is a little overstated in its criticism of Jerome's handling of theological themes in his commentary, and inadequate in its failure to recognize that Jerome's theological observations typically arise directly from the text.

Use of Allegory

Given the tendency of many scholars, identified in the introductory section of this chapter, to interpret Jerome's exegesis in terms of the extent to which he uses allegorical methods, some examination of this question in the context of the commentary needs to be performed. To begin with, it can be observed that Jerome very rarely gives only an allegorical interpretation of the verse at hand, or gives that interpretation the primary place. This may seem surprising, since the Origenist controversy had only recently broken when Jerome dictated the *In Matheum*, and he had not yet disowned his erstwhile role model's exegetical works.[98] Even on the two occasions where Jerome engages in full-scale allegory, he also gives the

---

96. E.g. Dockery, *Interpretation*, 135; Smalley, *Bible*, 21.

97. Kelly, *Jerome*, 224.

98. But see Brown, *Vir Trilinguis*, 128, who argues that Jerome's respect for the literary sense is present in all of his works, even early in his career when he tended to allegorize more than later.

plain meaning of the text alongside his allegorizing.[99] Thus, he gives the following interpretation of Matthew 27:60:

> "And he buried Him in a new tomb which had been carved into the rock, and rolled a large stone to the mouth of the tomb, and went away." His body was placed in a new tomb lest it be imagined after the resurrection that one of the other interred bodies had arisen. The new tomb, however, may also signify Mary's virginal womb. The stone placed against the door, a great stone, shows that it was not possible for the tomb to be opened without the help of many persons.[100]

In this case, although he attributes an allegorical meaning to the verse, he does not move away from the text for long, and hastens to add a more basic comment on the verse. This comment would appear to be in line with the concerns of the text at hand. As Jerome himself notes afterwards, the presence of the large stone taken together with the reference to the guard at the tomb in verse 64 seems to be emphasizing the power of the resurrection.[101]

The other point at which Jerome allegorizes is in his exposition of Matthew 27:39, "Moreover those passing by reviled him and shook their heads": "Those who were reviling as they passed by his way . . . in actual fact they were not wishing to walk in the way of the Scriptures. Those who now were shaking their heads had before shaken their feet [in disgust] and they were not standing on the rock. Moreover the same people now spoke insults because they [the Pharisees] had procured false witnesses."[102] In this excerpt, allegorical connections are made between, firstly walking by the way of the cross and not walking in the way of the Scriptures, and secondly, between what the non-believers had previously done with their feet literally (shaken them) and what they were figuratively not doing with their feet (standing on Christ, the Rock). How-

---

99. The only other point at which Jerome might be considered to be engaging in allegorical interpretation is a brief allusion to the angel's shining white garment pointing to Christ's resurrection in his commentary on Matt 28:2 (Jerome, *Math.*, IV, 1932-3). However, this observation is left unexplored in the midst of a long passage of more direct commentary. Also, it should be noted that even the example considered in this paragraph isn't purely allegorical in every respect—it may be argued that the connection which Jerome makes between Mary's womb and the new tomb contains an element of typological-historical logic.

100. Jerome, *Math.*, IV, 1881-8 (translation mine).

101. Jerome, *Math.*, IV, 1896-1902.

102. Jerome, *Math.*, IV, 1718-22 (translation mine).

ever, it should be noted that Jerome's figurative statements here are not allegories disconnected from the plain meaning of the passage, but rather are natural elaborations upon the theme of the verse as read literally.[103] The plain meaning of the verse is that many of those who saw Jesus on the cross rejected him; Jerome's figurative comments essentially restate this underlying idea. Furthermore, he goes on to give a simple, naturalistic explanation as to why people were mocking Jesus in his statement about the procurement of false witnesses.

It should be noted here that Jerome's use of allegory in the work under study here is at variance with a view that has sometimes been presented by scholars on the matter, namely that Jerome's allegories are an artificial intrusion into the text, rather than a natural outworking of his exegetical conclusions drawn from the text, as for example Simonetti suggests: "too often allegory appears unexpectedly and without any cogent reason."[104] More significantly for the purposes of this study, it is to be concluded that allegory occupies only a small place in Jerome's exegesis, and that in the *In Matheum*, Jerome has been faithful to his promise to Eusebius of Cremona in the preface to produce an essentially historical exposition.[105] This is significant for two reasons. First of all, this conclusion does little to distinguish Jerome's exegesis in any substantial way from that of his contemporaries—as shall be seen in the subsequent chapters, all of the writers under study here are to be regarded as essentially literal, while still regarding the use of allegory as useful on occasions. Secondly, the fact that there are any number of other features in Jerome's exegesis that are more prominent than Jerome's use—or non-use—of allegory suggests that conclusions regarding his use of allegory say little about the character of Jerome's exegesis on its own terms.[106] While it is true, if one is

---

103. The consensus is that this is typical of his allegorizing in his Old Testament commentaries, too. Cf. Kannengeisser, *Handbook*, 1108; Graves, "Judaizing Christian Interpretations," 147–50; also, several decades earlier: Lubac, *Medieval*, 2, 47 and 52. Jerome seems to suggest elsewhere that he believes the allegorical sense ought to be founded upon the literal: *Ep.*, 129.6 (*PL* 22:1105).

104. Simonetti, *Interpretation*, 102.

105. Jerome, *Math.*, Praefatio, 104–8.

106. In this connection, we may observe further regarding Jerome's preface to his commentary that his comments to Eusebius on his having produced a largely historical commentary are of a brief and passing character (no more than three sentences within the entire preface), in the context of much more substantial and deliberate discussion of various other matters within the preface around the details of Matthew's life, context, and written work.

interested in the question of which sense he prefers, that Jerome's exegesis is based on the literal sense, a far more important feature that his slight use of allegory and his preference for the literal sense both highlight is his firm adherence to exegesis of the text before him.

Typology

In any case, Jerome applies typological logic to the passage or sentence at hand more frequently than he does other kinds of non-literal exegesis. Most of the time in the *In Matheum*, this does not appear in the form of "classic" typology (where an Old Testament character or event prefigures an element of the Gospel narrative), but in Jerome suggesting that aspects of the narrative are best seen as prefiguring and setting a pattern for the Christian and the life of the church. Such instances as these are therefore to be seen more as tied to Jerome's method of drawing practical applications from the text, discussed further below, than as instances of a special kind of "spiritual" exegesis. Thus, for example, Jerome sees the fact that Simon of Cyrene carried the cross in Matthew 27:32 as a pattern for the Gentile church: "Afterwards they placed the Cross on Simon, who carried it. Indeed in like manner, the nations who acknowledge the Cross of Jesus obediently carry the disgrace of the Saviour."[107] Jerome uses similar logic when discussing Matthew 27:46b, "They bound my hands and my feet," although in this case applies Jesus' servitude not to believers at large, but to the individual Christian, that "you also might know 'the form of a servant,' having seen the stumbling block of the Cross."[108] This tendency to see events in the Gospel more as prefiguring events in the life of the church rather than as echoes of Old Testament occurrences is a habit which we shall meet again in Hilary's exegesis, and which distinguishes the work of these two exegetes from that of Ambrose and Augustine.

Prophecy-Fulfillment

Related to Jerome's use of typology, and a major feature of his exposition, is his repeated emphasis on the prophecy-fulfillment theme. In this respect, his approach closely follows that of the text which he is expounding, given that Matthew's Gospel is peppered with comments noting

---

107. Jerome, *Math.*, IV, 1663–5 (translation mine).
108. Jerome, *Math.*, IV, 1777–9 (translation mine).

that various events that it described occurred so as to fulfill prophetic expectations, such as the repeated refrain, "This was to fulfil what was spoken through Isaiah the prophet . . ." (e.g. in his commentary on 9:14 and 11:17)[109] and "Then what had been spoken through Jeremiah the prophet was fulfilled" (4:17).[110] On some occasions, Jerome simply notes the prophetic fulfillment, before moving on. For example, Jerome makes an even shorter statement than John's Gospel in linking the casting of lots for Jesus' clothing described in Matthew 27:35 with Psalm 22:18: "This too had been prophesied in the same Psalm: 'they divided my garments among themselves and cast lots for my clothing.'"[111] At other points, he is a little more elaborate, as when discussing the darkening of the earth at Christ's death in Matthew 27:45, he emphasizes that the event fulfills two distinct Old Testament references (Isaiah 13:10 and Amos 8:9).[112] However, Jerome does not just refer to fulfillment of prophecies as evidence of the reliability and unity of Scripture, or out of his obvious strong interest in the Old Testament. He also believes that there is a necessary historical link between the two elements, prophecy and fulfillment. Thus, when discussing Matthew 27:64, which describes Jesus' burial in the tomb, he argues that "That he had to be placed in a tomb is a testimony of the prophet who says: 'He dwelt in a deep cave of very strong rock' . . . and at once, after two little verses, follows: 'you will see the King in glory.'" Note Jerome's statement that "He *had* to be placed in a tomb."[113] He emphasizes that there is a causal, historical, link between the prophecy and the fulfillment; because the Old Testament reference is believed to point to Christ, however obscurely, subsequent history had to see Jesus laid in a rock tomb.[114] This strong emphasis on the fulfillment of prophecy on Jerome's

---

109. Jerome, *Math.*, I, 1310 and II, 166.

110. Jerome, *Math.*, I, 400. See also Jerome's comments on Matt 13:14 (II, 116–120), 13:35 (II, 949–52), 21:4 (III, 1195–97), 22:41–46 (IV, 11–34), 26:31 (IV, 1187–95), 27:9 (IV, 1520–31).

111. Jerome, *Matt.*, IV, 1696–8, and similarly when discussing the previous verse (Matt 27:34) on the offering of cheap wine to Jesus on the cross, IV, 1690–1.

112. Jerome, *Math.*, IV, 1760–2.

113. Jerome, *Matt.*, IV, 1904–5. "Quod autem in sepulchro ponendus esset prophetae testimonium." The citation is from Isa 33:16–17.

114. This emphasis of Jerome's on a historical-literal link between Old Testament prophecy and its New Testament fulfillment differs from the claim of Graves that for Jerome, the literal fulfillment of Old Testament prophecy usually took place in the time of the Old Testament, with only non-literal fulfillment taking place in the New Testament era or afterwards: Graves, "Judaizing Christian Interpretations," 150.

part places his work alongside that of Augustine, and in opposition to the relative disinterest of Hilary and Ambrose in such matters.

Practical Application to Audience

One point at which Jerome's exposition of the final chapters of Matthew's Gospel differs from his major Old Testament commentaries is in his practical application of material to his audience.[115] The main point to note is that in the *In Matheum*, Jerome is much more inclined to apply his exposition to his audience in a practical sense. At first sight, this is rather surprising, as the *In Matheum* is not a series of sermons delivered in the monastery chapel and taken down by a monk, in which case Jerome might reasonably be expected to address repeatedly the audience before his eyes. However, this work was produced instead for the benefit of a scholarly reader, located in a distant land, to be read at a later date.[116] Given that this was the occasion of its composition, it is surprising that it contains such a substantial amount of practical material. A possible explanation for this is that Jerome produced the commentary at great speed, dictating to a secretary, with little opportunity for self-correction or reflection. His mind driven by adrenalin, much as in the pulpit, he would have drawn applications from the material as he "preached" to the secretary, and these would have been noted down as he moved through the passage.

Jerome's points of application are firmly rooted in the text before him. That is, they tend to be based directly upon on Jerome's observations on the literal facts present in the text. Sometimes, they are simple applications from a brief note about the text, for example the following comments on the verse, "And having taken the body of Jesus, he wrapped it in clean linen," where Jerome notes that "The ambition of the rich is condemned through the simple burial of the Lord. They are unable to be without their wealth, even among tombs."[117] He uses the attentiveness

---

115. Cf. Sparks, "Jerome," 539.

116. As discussed in the introductory chapter, we know little of Jerome's relationship to Eusebius, and whether this may have had any bearing on Jerome's practical applications. Cf. Rusch, *Fathers*, 84.

117. Jerome, *Matt.*, IV, 1874–5, on Matt 27:59.

of the onlookers at the cross similarly, in this case as a model for the believer, who ought also to contemplate the cross.[118]

In his commentary on Matthew 27:55, "The women who had accompanied Jesus from Galilee were waiting on him for a long time," the application is made from a simple observation about the text, although more narrowly directed:

> It was according to the ancient custom of the Jews that women were to provide food and clothes for their teachers. Paul himself refers to this custom . . . "Do we not have authority to take around with us sisters and other women, just like the other apostles do?" [1 Corinthians 9:5] Moreover they were supplying the Lord with their support . . . so that a model might be presented concerning teachers, that they should be satisfied with food and clothing provided by their disciples.[119]

In making this point of application, Jerome draws a typological link between Christ as teacher and subsequent Christian teachers, and makes a point of contemporary relevance from this link. Interestingly, it would appear as though Jerome may have been obliquely defending his own practice of depending upon his prominent female followers for support of his and the monastery's earthly needs. Perhaps even Jerome's retaining of the first person "we" in the quotation from Paul is a deliberate choice on his part. The words of Jesus recorded in the text have a potency that makes them relevant today. Thus, when he is discussing belief in the resurrection in his commentary on Matthew 28:4–5, he exhorts his readers as follows: "The rest of you who seek Jesus crucified, listen, because He has risen and fulfilled his promises."[120]

In his efforts at application to his audience, does Jerome consistently zero in on a particular theme that he believes arises from the text as a whole, as we shall see Hilary do in the following chapter, or does he simply draw isolated practical conclusions as seems to fit the occasion? Certainly, in the material under study, a recurring point of application for Jerome is his stress on the related themes of belief and unbelief.[121] The point that people should respond to Jesus with belief, rather than

---

118. Jerome, *Math.*, IV, 1699–71, on Matt 27:36.
119. Jerome, *Math.*, IV, 1747–56 (translation mine).
120. Jerome, *Math.*, IV, 1943–4 (translation mine).
121. In addition to the comments noted here, see also his comments on Matt 27:48, 27:51–52 and 28:20, at Jerome, *Math.*, IV, 1789–94, 1807–14, and 2016–22 respectively.

opposition and unbelief, is first explicitly made when he discusses Pilate's well-known answer to the Jews regarding the sign placed over Jesus' head in Matthew 27:37, commenting that "[t]he seditious clamour of these faithless people is the critical factor: nothing else caused his execution except the fact that he was the king of the Jews . . . also, Pilate, not really intending this meaning, answered that 'What is written is written' . . . the whole multitude of the [Jewish] race ought to have answered: 'Jesus is the king of the Jews, believe and confess that this one is Lord.'"[122]

Like many commentators before and since, Jerome plays upon the fact that the notice is unintentionally correct, although it is added as an insult, and suggests that his readers, unlike most of the onlookers should not only recognize this, but actively acknowledge it. He attacks unbelief more bluntly in his exposition of the taunt, "Come down now from the Cross, and we will believe in you," of Matthew 27:42: "Lying promises! Which is greater: to come down from the Cross while as yet living, or to rise from the tomb while dead? He rose, and you did not believe. Therefore, even if he had come down from the Cross, you would not have believed."[123] In commenting on Matthew 28:5 and 6, the same theme of belief and unbelief is present, although not applied as directly as in the preceding examples:

> "Do not be afraid." These [guards] he says, were afraid; those who persevere in this dread remain unbelieving; the rest of you who seek Jesus crucified, listen, because He will rise and accomplish His promises. "Come and see where He lay"—if you do not believe my words, you may believe the tomb; "go and announce to His disciples that He has risen and is gone ahead of you to Galilee"—He is in that region where previously there had been doubt and uncertainty, but also some faithful followers.[124]

Similarly, attentiveness to the fact that a guard was placed at the tomb serves to "advance our faith. For the more [the tomb] is guarded, so much more is the power of the resurrection shown."[125]

Certainly, this theme is the most common of Jerome's practical applications, but it by no means gives unity to the *In Matheum* as a whole. Many verses pass without even a passing reference to belief or unbelief,

---

122. Jerome, *Math.*, IV, 1705–11 (translation mine).
123. Jerome, *Math.*, IV, 1728–33, on Matt 27:42 (translation mine).
124. Jerome, *Math.*, IV, 1941–9 (translation mine).
125. Jerome, *Matt.*, IV, 1899–900, on 27:64.

and Jerome draws a wide range of other practical conclusions from his exegesis. He urges perseverance in the Christian life when discussing the patience of the women outside Jesus' tomb in Matthew 27:61, devotion to good deeds in 27:36 when observing the behavior of various characters before the cross, and condemns striving after riches on account of the simplicity of Jesus' burial in 27:59.[126] All Christians are to be encouraged at the fact that all of Jesus' promises will be fulfilled, taking the angelic announcement of the resurrection in 28:5 as evidence for this.[127] The command given within the Great Commission of 28:20 to teach converts concerning all that Jesus has said is highlighted as making it incumbent on every Christian teacher to have diligence in teaching and doing *all* that Jesus has commanded them to.[128] Most importantly of all, Jesus submission to humiliation and death is presented as an example of humble submission for all Christians to follow.[129] It must therefore be concluded that Jerome's practical application has an occasional character to it, and is not united by any one particular theme. As with all of the other matters that he discusses in the course of his exposition, it is driven by whatever detail of the text before him strikes Jerome as being worthy of comment. In this light, the relatively common appearance of the belief-unbelief motif is more probably due to its preponderance within the Gospel account itself, whose text Jerome is studiously devoted to, than to any desire on Jerome's part to highlight it in particular.

In terms of the place of application within the *In Matheum*, it must therefore be concluded that practical matters, although referred to more frequently than in some of Jerome's other commentaries, are not what hold the work together. Jerome applies the text to his audience in an incidental manner, as and when the text itself—specifically, the very text that is immediately before Jerome at that very moment—raises such matters in his mind. Jerome's principal aim is to discuss his text, not to push a particular homiletical agenda. This is reinforced by the fact that most of his practical comments, although derived directly from the text, are largely incidental to its broad direction, and to the flow of Jerome's exposition. Hence, his observation that the darkness covering the land at Jesus' death (Matthew 27:45) should have reminded those present that Christ is the

---

126. Jerome, *Math.*, IV, 1890-4, 1699-1701 and 1874-80 respectively.
127. Jerome, *Math.*, IV, 1941-4.
128. Jerome, *Math.*, IV, 2016-21.
129. Jerome, *Math.*, IV, 1768-74, on Matt 27:46.

light of the world follows immediately on from his arguments that the event could not have been an eclipse. No connection is made between these two comments, and having made his point, Jerome moves on to discuss something unrelated.[130] Jerome's note on Christian perseverance when discussing Matthew 27:61 is equally incidental in character.[131] In this case, Jerome's practical advice is squeezed into the same sentence as its basis in the text (the perseverance of the women outside Jesus' tomb) and the reason for the women's action. All three ideas are hastily sandwiched together in association with the verse that occasioned their birth in Jerome's mind, before the exegete skips over the next three verses to discuss the—unrelated—reasons behind why the Jewish leaders wanted a guard at the tomb. Again, it is Jerome's random interest in particular features of the text before him that is the driving force behind his exposition. Practical application, although having a significant place, is of relatively subordinate importance within Jerome's intentions.

Polysemy and Monosemy

In speaking of Jerome's intentions, another relevant question concerns the extent to which he regards the text as having multiple meanings, or only one meaning. Jerome's practice in his commentary is difficult to pin down, owing to the rushed character of his exegesis of the text, which means that his comments on particular verses are often so brief as to only allow room for only a single meaning to be presented. Certainly, he does not present clearly distinguished, multiple meanings with the frequency that Augustine does. Nowhere in the section under study is he guilty of the criticism leveled at his exegesis by De Labroille, that he has "an annoying tendency to pile up opinions which have been given at an earlier date on any particular Scriptural difficulty, instead of making his own selection and putting it forward."[132] On the few occasions where Jerome does present more than one possible meaning, he does in fact choose between them, albeit so briefly that he doesn't bother to justify his choice,

---

130. Jerome, *Math.*, IV, 1781–6.

131. Jerome, *Math.*, IV, 1890–3.

132. De Labroille, "Saint Ambrose et l'exégèse allegorique," 361. This is not to say that he is unaware of different perspectives and opinions among interpreters, on the contrary, he is more familiar than most of his contemporaries with the history of biblical interpretation: cf. Old, *The Reading and Preaching of the Scriptures*, 336.

instead proceeding to unpack swiftly his preferred interpretation.[133] Furthermore, Jerome does not at any point advance distinct literal, allegorical, or typological interpretations of the same part of the text and cannot therefore be regarded as polysemic in the fullest sense of the word.

Jerome does, however, on a significant number of occasions exhibit partially polysemic tendencies. On a significant number of occasions, he advances several comments on a passage that are quite distinct and disconnected from one another. Thus, for Jerome, the tearing of the temple curtain in two at Jesus' death is a symbol of the end of the old covenant, of the Jew-Gentile distinction, and of the temple's cultic role.[134] That the body of Jesus was wrapped in clean linen symbolizes both his purity, and the simplicity of his burial—a virtue which Jerome states that his followers should also strive for while they are still alive.[135] The darkness that comes over the land during Jesus' crucifixion both underlines that Jesus is the true light of the world, and also gives occasion for Jerome to stress that it really was a miracle, and not merely an eclipse.[136]

It should be noted that in these examples, the distinction between the various meanings advanced by Jerome does not lie in any consistent application of the senses of Scripture.[137] While the two meanings given in the final case could be described as allegorical and literal respectively, this is not true of the meanings advanced in the first two. None of the three meanings attributed to the tearing of the temple curtain is literal; all three are spiritual—and more specifically, all three are allegorical rather than moral or tropological. The two meanings associated with Jesus' burial clothes are allegorical and literal-issuing-in-moral respectively. Jerome's polysemy cannot therefore be described as consistent or founded on any systematic usage of categories such as "allegorical" and "literal." Furthermore, in none of these cases does Jerome suggest that he is distinguishing the various meanings in this manner.

---

133. E.g. Jerome, *Math.*, IV, 1864–73, on Matt 27:57. See also his strong dismissal of the popular interpretation of Matt 27:33 which claims that Christ was executed in the same place where Adam was buried: Jerome, *Math.*, IV, 1671–8.

134. Jerome, *Math.*, IV, 1799–1805, on Matt 27:51.

135. Jerome, *Math.*, IV, 1874–1889, on Matt 27:59.

136. Jerome, *Math.*, IV, 1751–9, on Matt 27:45. A further example occurs at IV, 1730–6, on Matt 27:42.

137. This is in contrast to the generalizing claims made by Williams, *The Monk and the Book*, 91–93, regarding the relationship between the literal sense and allegorical readings in Jerome's exegesis.

Conclusions

It can therefore be concluded in the context of the present case study that the categories "literal" and "allegorical," together with the framework of the senses of Scripture of which they form a part, are of limited value in gaining a clear understanding of the contours of Jerome's exegesis. While Jerome's exegesis can be described as predominantly "literal," he still does make some use of allegory, and, more importantly, there are several other categories available that give a fuller description of the character of his commentary. As we shall see, these alternatives are more helpful in assisting with attempts to articulate the differences between his Gospel exegesis and that of his contemporaries. The most important of these is his all-pervading concern with the text of Scripture itself, with its philological characteristics, with the unity of the Gospel narrative and indeed of the whole Bible itself. This characteristic of his work is further buttressed by his love of word studies, his confident referencing of the original languages behind the text, and his concern to reconcile apparent differences between the Gospel texts. Secondly, the random, eclectic manner in which he decides which textual features to comment on, and what to say about each of them, is often prominent. Thirdly, the fact that doctrinal matters or particular theological themes are not the primary driver of his exegesis is a point which distinguishes his work from that of others, as shall be seen in subsequent chapters, even though it is a feature which has been overstated by some scholars. His peculiar manner of using typological logic to point forward to contemporary events is also notable, as is his related willingness to point out instances of prophecy-fulfillment. Fifthly, the significant but not central role of practical application in his work, particularly his tendency to touch on a wide range of practical issues in his exposition, is also an important area in which his work, as we shall see, differs from that of others. Lastly, his preference for a polysemic approach to reading Scripture, while not a prominent feature of his exegesis in its own right due to the fact that it isn't an overly pronounced characteristic, is also of interest, since it is another means of differentiating between Jerome's work and that of others. The distinctiveness of these aspects of Jerome's exegesis will become more noticeable as the works of his contemporaries are considered. This is particularly true of the following chapter, since the works of Hilary in particular are almost diametrically opposed to those of Jerome on the majority of the indices that have just been listed, including those which are most integral to the character of Jerome's exegesis.

3

Faith in Realities
Hilary's In Matthaeum and De Trinitate

As INDICATED IN THE introduction, this chapter will examine the exegetical methods employed in two of Hilary's works, the *In Matthaeum* and the *De Trinitate*. We shall proceed by treating the two works separately, firstly the *In Matthaeum* and then the *De Trinitate*. In the context of the commentary, Hilary's manner of proceeding through the biblical text will be discussed first, followed by analysis of whether Hilary's primary focus is on the text or the events that lie behind it. The theological themes that Hilary develops in the course of the commentary are considered next, then the questions of whether he prefers monosemy or polysemy, and how he uses allegory and typology. The discussion concludes with an investigation of Hilary's manner of developing practical applications from the text, and his particular interest in the theme of faith. *De Trinitate* is treated similarly: Hilary's method of moving from sentence to sentence within the text is treated first, followed by his method of argumentation, the extent and manner of his use of allegory and typology, the question of whether the text or the events behind it drive his exposition, and his approach to practical application and the theme of faith. However, it will first be necessary to survey the body of scholarship on Hilary's exegesis.

Scholarly Conclusions

Up to a point, students of Hilary's exegesis tend to analyze it in the same framework of the senses of Scripture that has been commonly applied to the other three writers considered here. Certainly, this is the case for most overview treatments and reference-level commentaries. The *Theologische Realenzklopädie's* entry on Hilary states that the commentary on Matthew shows "the influence of Greek theology . . . and moves back and forth between allegorical and typological."[1] Kannengeisser in the *Handbook of Biblical Interpreters* claims that Hilary, "[i]n search of the deeper meaning of the main episodes of the Gospel narrative, found it by stressing their symbolic significance,"[2] while the new *Handbook of Patristic Exegesis* has little to add beyond comments backing up the assertion that it is "allegorical in focus."[3] Bray's volume on the history of exegesis suggests that Hilary was "attracted by Alexandrian methods."[4] However, we might assume that the *In Matthaeum* at least is not included within this general assessment even though it is one of Hilary's two major extant exegetical works alongside his *Commentary on the Psalms* (and therefore a significant exception to such a generalization), on the grounds that it was written before Hilary directly encountered Alexandrian methods during his exile in the East. A few scholars do recognize that it is a different case in this regard, although they usually still see the *In Matthaeum* substantially as an allegorical commentary, occupied with drawing symbolic truths from the text.[5] Some, however, do not treat it as an exception. Kelly regards Hilary, together with Ambrose and Hippolytus, as leading examples of an imported Alexandrian approach to exegesis. He argues that Hilary "employed it lavishly even in his Commentary on Matthew."[6] Burns recent study of Hilary's *Commentary on the Psalms* sums up his

---

1. Brennecke, "Hilarius," 317: "da keine Einflüsse griechischer Theologie . . . der Text wird unter bewußten Auslassungen allegorisch und typologische heilsgeschichtlich ausgelegt." The *Encyclopedia of Early Christianity* and the *Oxford Dictionary of the Christian Church* do not comment directly on the *In Matthaeum*, or the exegetical aspects of *De Trinitate*.

2. McKim, *Handbook*, 10.

3. Balás and Bingham, "Patristic Exegesis of the Books of the Bible," 336.

4. Bray, *Interpretation*, 107.

5. Of Western origin rather than Alexandrian in its methods. E.g. Kannengeisser, *Handbook*, 2:998.

6. Kelly, "Fathers," 45. Froehlich, *Interpretation*, 23 argues similarly with respect to some of Hilary's other works.

exegetical method in both of his major commentaries as being consistent, in the following terms:

> Hilary clearly retains confidence in the principles that guided his early exegetical writing in the *In Mathaeum*. He continues to rely on two levels of meaning in the biblical text, and retains the same range of terms . . . He recognizes two levels of interpretation: the obvious sense that is designated as historical, literal or corporeal; and the deeper, more internal or spiritual sense. Hilary respects the historical level but defends the importance of the deeper level . . . This appeal to two levels of meaning is certainly consistent with the principles of his earlier exegesis on Matthew and it is also compatible with the basic approaches of Origen.[7]

Altaner's older but influential work describes Hilary as "the first eminent exegete of the West, to which he introduced important ideas of Eastern theology."[8] Furthermore, his *In Matthaeum* "aims towards penetrating to the 'deeper' allegorical sense, the 'interior significantia,'"[9] a view of the *In Matthaeum* also propagated by Smalley[10] and de Lubac.[11] Likewise, Hilary's exegesis of Scripture in the *De Trinitate* is said by Jacob to utilize allegory in order to reorient the biblical text towards the problems of a new age in the Trinitarian debates.[12]

Some of the specialist works on Hilary's *In Matthaeum* take a similar line. In particular, Simonetti's article is heavily interested in understanding it in terms of the two senses: "Hilary . . . has a strong preoccupation with the mutually supportive relationship between the literal signification and the allegorical meaning."[13] He aims to "examine the principal question . . . of what systematic principles of exegesis are

---

7. Burns, *A Model for the Christian Life: Hilary of Poitier's Commentary on the Psalms*, 77–78.

8. Altaner, *Patrology*, 423.

9. Altaner, *Patrology*, 423.

10. Smalley, *Bible*, 89, whose cursory comments on Hilary's work on Matthew extend only to the statement that Hilary, before being exiled in Asia, wrote a commentary on Matthew "which was predominantly allegorical but not specifically in the style of Origen."

11. Lubac, *Medieval*, 2:96.

12. Jacob, "The Reception of the Origenist Tradition in Latin Exegesis," 689.

13. Simonetti, "Note," 38. See footnote 83 in chapter 1 for Italian original. Indeed, the entire first half of this lengthy article is devoted to Hilary's use of allegorical and literal interpretation, with some occasional attention to his recognition of types, 37–50.

applied ... [considering] whether he always prefers the profound and allegorical, and to what extent does the literal sense express itself."[14] Much of the latter half of the article is preoccupied with the equally traditional question of Origenistic influence on the commentary.[15] Simonetti concludes that there was probably substantial indirect influence, but little direct impact, if any, and that the two commentaries are quite different. However, this very difference is seen in terms of the framework of the senses of Scripture, in that Origen's work is consistently allegorical, while Hilary, although primarily interested in drawing out the spiritual meaning, will sometimes just discuss the literal interpretation without giving an allegorical one.[16]

Of the major studies undertaken on Hilary's exegesis, Doignon's corpus of writings on Hilary's works is the most focused around the traditional senses of Scripture distinction. He argues that fundamental to the exegetical approach of Hilary is the idea that simple, carnal things express hidden mysteries.[17] Furthermore, he suggests that Hilary's exegesis in "[t]he *In Matthaeum* reflects the classical opposition between the true (the 'ratio spiritalis') and the imitation (the 'corporalia')."[18] In this regard, Hilary's ideas, at least in the later *De Trinitate* and *In Psalmos*, are supposed to follow Origen's views closely.[19] This understanding is a classic attempt to cast Hilary's work within the frameworks that apply to Greek thought and exegesis.[20] By contrast, Doignon's article "L'exégèse d'Hilaire de Poitiers" examines the exegetical work of Hilary in the light of earlier Latin commentators.[21] However, even here, where Hilary is recognized as

---

14. Simonetti, "Note," 40; Cf. footnote 84 in chapter 1 for Italian original.

15. Simonetti, "Note," 61–64. Cf. Lubac, *Medieval*, 1:154.

16. Simonetti, "Note," 63–64. See also Simonetti, "Hilary of Poitiers and the Arian Crisis in the West: Polemicists and Heretics," 49.

17. Doignon, "La connexion du spirituel et du charnel dans la méthodologie exégétique d'Hilaire de Poitiers," 259–66.

18. Doignon, "La connexion du spirituel et du charnel dans la méthodologie exégétique d'Hilaire de Poitiers," 265: "de l'In Matthaeum, par cets mots, qui reflètent l'opposition classique entre la vérité (ici la *ratio spiritualis*) et l'imitation (ici les *corporalia*)."

19. Doignon, "La connexion du spirituel et du charnel dans la méthodologie exégétique d'Hilaire de Poitiers," 266.

20. A view reiterated, for example by Jacob, "Reception," 682.

21. In Fontaine and Pietri, *Le monde latin antique et la Bible*, 508–20. Similar to his earlier work, *Hilary de Poitiers avant l'Exile*.

being substantially influenced by Latin rhetorical traditions, the distinction between the senses of Scripture is still central.[22]

Newlands, in his book on Hilary places less emphasis on this issue, if only because its primary focus is elsewhere, namely, on how Hilary develops his theology from biblical texts in a number of works, including the *De Trinitate* and *In Matthaeum*. He argues that Hilary uses his exegesis to put forward his theology of Christ, particularly Christ as the means of understanding the shift from *lex* to *fides*.[23] "For Hilary, the primary issues in the text are theological rather than hermeneutical."[24] The *De Trinitate*, written while Hilary was in the East, "involves the use of argument from and exegesis of the Bible in the exposition of doctrine, corresponding roughly to modern systematic theology."[25] However, Newlands does give some consideration to the issues of the senses of Scripture, even though his purpose is to show how Hilary's theology emerges from his exegesis, and essentially argues that Hilary sees two senses—the hidden, usually described in terms such as "typus," "prefiguration," "interior," *sacramentum* and *mysterium*, and the literal.[26] For Hilary, allegorical and typological meanings both fall under this category; he doesn't distinguish between these two and is usually more typological.[27] According to Newlands, a key distinction between Hilary's approach in *De Trinitate* and *In Matthaeum* is that he uses much less allegorical interpretation in the former.[28] Newlands recognizes that the commentary "reveals no direct borrowing by Hilary,"[29] although he notes that "[e]choes of the western tradition of Tertullian, Novatian, of Cyprian and Irenaeus have long been noted, but detailed evidence is lacking."[30]

The work of Burns, like that of Newlands, is not primarily a study in exegesis, but, as the title implies, in his Christology. However, being solely concerned with the commentary on Matthew, and with how Hilary uses the genre of commentary to advance his christological views, it does

22. Doignon, "L'exégèse," particularly 511–2.
23. Newlands, *Hilary*, 82.
24. Newlands, *Hilary*, 77.
25. Newlands, *Hilary*, 10.
26. Newlands, *Hilary*, 2–73.
27. Newlands, *Hilary*, 71, 74.
28. Newlands, *Hilary*, 103, 106, 108.
29. Newlands, *Hilary*, 11.
30. Newlands, *Hilary*, 11. Detailed discussion of possible influences on Hilary follows, 35–43 and 92–98.

bear some relevance to this study. For Burns, the key question is whether Hilary, in the *In Matthaeum*, is seeking to address the Arians and the same doctrinal issues that he is concerned with after he goes to the East, or not. His conclusion is that the *In Matthaeum* is not directed at the Arians, but that outlines of the Christology that Hilary was subsequently to develop in response to the Arian challenge are already present in this work.[31] Burns argues that when Hilary composed the *In Matthaeum*, he had little familiarity with the eastern Trinitarian and christological debates, or even with Greek exegesis. Instead, he suggests that, prior to Hilary's exile, he was dominated by Latin influences, most notably Tertullian, and to a lesser extent Novatian and various secular Latin authors whom he had probably been exposed to in his education.[32] Burns is primarily interested in exploring how Hilary uses the commentary as a vehicle to advance his christological views, concluding that "christology exercises a formative influence on many aspects of the work."[33] However, Burns also devotes substantial attention to Hilary's use of the two senses.[34] Where he does so, his view is that the commentary is heavily allegorical: together with Origen's work on Matthew, it is the only patristic work on Matthew that examines the Gospel according to the spiritual or inner sense.[35] For this view to be confirmed, it should therefore follow that Hilary's commentary is substantially more allegorical than Jerome's, which as will be seen is not the case. The allegorical sense is referred to as the "typica ratio," "caelestis intelligentia," or "sermo spiritalis." In the commentary, Hilary uses the term "allegorical" only once and the term "literal" never.[36] Burns only gives three references to these terms from the earlier parts of the commentary.

Burns's view that the Latin tradition that preceded Hilary was a significant influence on his exegesis, particularly in his work before his exile, most notably in the commentary on Matthew, is echoed in a number

---

31. Burns, *Christology*, 11. Scholarship since Burns produced his book has tended to support his position. Cf. Williams, "Defining Orthodoxy in Hilary of Poitiers' *Commentariorum In Matthaeum*," 151–71.

32. Burns, *Christology*, 21–22. In contrast to Doignon, "Connexion," 266, who as seen above argues for Origen's work having had a substantial influence on the preexilic *In Matthaeum*.

33. Burns, *Christology*, 113.

34. Particularly, 51–55 in Burns, *Christology*.

35. Burns, *Christology*, 45.

36. Hilary, *Matt.*, 51.1

of shorter studies. For example, Tevel suggests that Hilary's interpretation of the parable of the Workers in the Vineyard is relatively novel, and certainly not particularly dependent on Greek models such as Origen.[37] Rusch likewise comments that "his exegesis [on Matthew] shows a virtual absence of any Eastern influence."[38] A smaller number of scholars has gone further and claimed that even in *De Trinitate*, written after Hilary had experienced the Greek traditions more directly, he makes heavy use of interpretations of Gospel texts that he received from his Western predecessors.[39] However, recognizing the possible importance of native Latin exegetical traditions does not necessarily mean that scholars will also consider the work apart from the framework of the senses of Scripture, as Driscoll's comments illustrate:

> It is the oldest Gospel commentary which has come down to us in the Latin tradition and was written before Hilary's exile to the East . . . as such it is a privileged piece of testimony to a sophisticated Latin exegetical tradition before that tradition came into sustained contact with the exegetical traditions of the East. A coherent system of scriptural interpretation is operative throughout the commentary, a system which serves Hilary's basic concern to uncover the spiritual meaning in the text.[40]

Existing scholarship on Hilary's exegesis can therefore be summarized as being quite conscious of the role played by Latin traditions in his work, particularly in the *In Matthaeum*, and yet still heavily dependent on the idea of the senses of Scripture for providing descriptions of his work. As this chapter will suggest, Hilary's own intentions in interpreting the Gospel texts are a world away from being organized and defined by this idea. Furthermore, although there is a greater willingness to recognize other factors as important to Hilary's exegesis than in the case of the other writers considered here, the majority of the varied observations made on Hilary's exegesis that do not make reference to the senses of Scripture also tend to be inaccurate, at least with respect to the two case studies considered here. This will become apparent as we examine Hilary's exegesis in light of the comments made by scholars on various elements of it below.

---

37. Tevel, "The Labourers in the Vineyard," 356–80.

38. Rusch, *Fathers*, 13.

39. E.g. Jacobs, "Western Roots," 198–203, who argues this from a brief survey of selected evidence.

40. Driscoll, "Matthew," 395.

1. *In Matthaeum*

Manner of Proceeding through the Text

In the *In Matthaeum*, Hilary moves through the passages of the Gospel roughly in order, noting some things and ignoring others. He is primarily interested in the basic events that the text of the Gospel describes and the theological themes that they point to, as will be seen later. His aim is not to note everything, or to be driven in his exegesis from one detail or arcane textual concern to the next.[41] In this respect, his exegesis is quite different from that of Jerome or of Origen.[42] However, this is not to say that Hilary's exposition proceeds with little regard for the text. In fact, he moves through the text by discussing each of the major events that it describes in turn, seldom straying from these events for very long, either into more obscure details of the text or into doctrinal and philosophical matters. The sequence of his exposition rarely strays away from the order of events found in the passage.[43] Hilary's method in this regard can be understood through an overview of his exposition of the final chapters of the Gospel of Matthew, commencing with the account of Christ before Pilate in Matthew 27:11–26.

In commenting on the Pilate-Christ pericope, Hilary gives a brief exposition, in order, of each of the major elements of the dialogue.[44] The only elements that he ignores are some aspects of the interaction between Pilate and the crowd (the repeated refrain "Crucify!" in verse 22 and Pilate's question, in verse 23, as to what crime Christ had committed), and the handing over of Christ to be flogged in verse 26b. He discusses all of the verses in the text in the same order as in the narrative, apart from Pilate's offer to free either Christ or Barabbas (vv. 15–18) and the demand of the priests and the crowd that Barabbas be set free instead (vv. 20–21).

41. To some extent, this contrasts a little with Hilary's later commentary on the Psalms, which tends to cover every line and every phrase of the Psalm under consideration: Burns, *A Model for the Christian Life: Hilary of Poitiers' Commentary on the Psalms*, 15.

42. See Driscoll, "Matthew," 401 for comments on the distinction between Hilary's and Origen's exegesis; his point may be extended to distinguish between Hilary and Jerome.

43. As is the case in his other major extant commentary, also, on the Psalms: Burns, *A Model for the Christian Life: Hilary of Poitiers' Commentary on the Psalms*, 79.

44. Hilary, *Matt.*, 33.1.

Hilary deals with these two items together with the passing reference to the release of Barabbas (v. 26) at the end of the section.[45] However, this is hardly evidence of disorder in Hilary's method: in this case, his practice appears to be a sensible manner of dispensing with three related details that are of relatively minor importance within the passage as a whole.

Hilary then follows the text in moving on to the soldiers' mocking of Christ (Matthew 27–31).[46] He devotes some attention to every detail in this episode, except for the fact that these events are recorded as occurring in the Praetorium and involved the governor's soldiers (v. 27), and that Christ's clothes were stripped from him (v. 28a). He then discusses the crucifixion itself (Matthew 27:32–44).[47] All elements of the episode receive some attention, except for the insults made by the priests and Pharisees in verses 41–44, and the sign above Christ's head on the cross (v. 37). The former is a surprising omission, given that the comments made here are pregnant with material that could support Hilary's chief theological and homiletical purpose of promoting faith in Christ, discussed below, by serving as negative counterexamples of the proper response to Christ.[48] His avoidance of discussion of the sign is an even more surprising omission for the same reason, since what is written on the sign is ironically true, and potentially of use as a statement of faith.[49]

The discussion of the death of Christ (Matthew 27:45–56) that then follows discusses the vast majority of the events described in the text in turn.[50] The only elements which Hilary passes over in silence are the misunderstanding of the bystanders in verse 47 that Christ was calling Elijah, the appearance of those that had been raised in Jerusalem in verse 53b, the terror of the guards in verse 54, and the fact that the women were watching over Jesus (vv. 55–56). In moving on to examine the account of the burial of Christ (Matthew 27:57–66), Hilary comments on most of the major elements of this episode.[51] He only digresses to discuss the identity of Joseph and his place among the apostles, and only passes over the fact that the two women sat opposite the tomb (v. 61), and the reason

---

45. Hilary, *Matt.*, 33.2.

46. Hilary, *Matt.*, 33.3.

47. Hilary, *Matt.*, 33.5.

48. Hilary does, however, give a brief exposition of some of the insults in *Tractatus super Psalmos*, 69.3 (CCSL 61:6–26).

49. Ambrose, for example does discuss it, in *Lucam*, X, 115–6.

50. Hilary, *Matt.*, 33.6–7.

51. Hilary, *Matt.*, 33.8.

given by the priests and Pharisees as to why a guard should be placed at the tomb in verses 63–64.

In his short exposition of the resurrection,[52] Hilary briefly digresses to discuss the significance of the fact that women were the first to see Christ. In the section 28:1–15, the elements that he makes no reference to are the guards being terrified (v. 4), the angel's statement about Jesus having gone to Galilee and injunction to go and tell the disciples (v. 7), the women's joy and the fact that they ran to tell the others (v. 8), and some details of the fabrication of the story by the chief priests and guards (e.g. the fact that their story has continued to circulate among the Jews in v. 15b). However, the angel's words to the women about Christ having risen and gone to Galilee are alluded to when reference is made to Christ's own words in verse 10 to the same effect. In this case, Hilary groups these two obviously related elements of the narrative together for convenience, just as he did in the case of the references to Barabbas in 27:11–26.[53]

It is more difficult to draw definite conclusions about Hilary's omissions in the case of the resurrection account than it is for other parts of the Gospel commentary, as the final section of the commentary is missing. It is possible that Hilary further discussed aspects of the resurrection account in this missing section. However, it is unlikely that he added much of significance in terms of commentary on the text up to and including the last verse that he comments on in the text that remains to us, 28:15. As has been seen from the foregoing, Hilary is very consistent in discussing the events described in the Gospel in the order in which they were given.[54] He seldom jumps back to return to discussion of something found a few verses previously, unless there is a clear link in the text itself with what he is currently examining, in which regard, as will be seen in chapter 5, he differs substantially from Augustine's practice. Given that the portion of the commentary which remains ends with a discussion of the guards' report, it is highly improbable that the resurrection account prior to this (vv. 1–10) received much attention from Hilary in the missing conclusion to the commentary, as such treatment would be out of character with Hilary's exegetical method throughout the *In Matthaeum*. Rather, it is more likely that, in addition to exposition of the remaining verses of the Gospel (the Great Commission of vv. 16–20),

---

52. Hilary, *Matt.*, 33.9.
53. Hilary, *Matt.*, 33.2.
54. Also noted by Newlands, *Hilary*, 10.

some further discussion of the guards' report could have been included, as what remains of the commentary may end part of the way through Hilary's exposition of this section of the Gospel narrative.

From this overview of Hilary's exposition, it can be seen that Hilary's method is one that follows the order of the text closely, and proceeds by examining each of the major events which it describes in turn.[55] Beyond that, Hilary discusses some details, while passing over others.[56] Within the text itself, no explanation is apparent of his rationale for commenting on some details of the narrative and not on others. The explanation of Newlands and Burns is that some elements of the text are not commented on by Hilary because they are "absolutus": their meaning is so apparent that it requires no further interpretation.[57] While some of Hilary's omissions, such as the fact that the guards were terrified at the appearance of the angel, can be plausibly explained in this way, it is unlikely that Hilary neglected to make any reference to several other more poignant elements of the narrative purely because he thought their meaning needed no further discussion. This is particularly true of Hilary's unwillingness to discuss the cry of the crowd, "Come down from the Cross, and we will believe in you!," and the sign above Christ's head. Given that Hilary thought it appropriate to comment at least briefly on the significance of most other elements of the text under study, and that these two elements receive extended discussion from other commentators such as Jerome,[58] it is difficult to believe that he wrote nothing because he felt that he could not develop the meaning of these details further.

As to the material that Hilary does discuss (which includes the bulk of the text under study), Hilary is quite consistent in the amount of attention that he gives to each element of the narrative. Most features of the account which attract his attention are given a sentence or two of comment, before he moves on. In fact, there is very little that he does discuss at length. In terms of the crucifixion and resurrection accounts, the only real exception is his discussion of Christ's taking on the sins of the world, raised by the account of Christ's death.[59] Even this passage can only be considered as a brief discussion when seen alongside the lengthy rumina-

---

55. Driscoll, "Matthew," 400; Burns, *Christology*, 49.
56. Simonetti, "Hilary," 49.
57. Newlands, *Hilary*, 51; Burns, *Christology*, 48.
58. Jerome, *Math.*, IV, 1724–36, on Matt 27:42.
59. Hilary, *Matt.*, 33.6, on Matt 45:50.

tions of other commentators of the period, such as Augustine. He seldom digresses to themes which are not directly raised in the passage at hand, or is drawn away from exegesis of Matthew to discussion of other, related biblical passages. At the two points at which he might be seen to digress, a reference to John's Gospel (19:30), and a discussion of the role of Joseph of Arimathea (who buries Christ in Matthew 27:57–60) among the disciples, he quickly moves back to the concerns of the Gospel itself.[60] The reference to John's Gospel is seamlessly integrated with the flow of his argument, which remains rooted in the Gospel of Matthew throughout.

Thus, it can be said that Hilary, like Jerome and, as will be seen, unlike Augustine, is a commentator who is in constant communion with the text before him and who is not easily distracted from the Gospel account to other more distant concerns.[61] However, Hilary is not bound to the text in the same way that Jerome is.[62] As has been described above, Hilary is not concerned to explain every detail in the text itself. He is not driven by the text and its features (as Jerome is) so much as the events that the text describes. For Hilary, the events described in the Gospel progress and tell out the "real" story, which is an account of theological themes.[63] Almost all of the brief remarks of which Hilary's commentary is made up are statements imparting theological meaning to the events at hand. Typically, he proceeds by noting an event in the account, succinctly stating the theological significance of the event, before noting another event, and continuing on in the same manner.

Realities Described by the Text

An important point to note here is that Hilary does not proceed by making brief comments on the theological significance of points *in* the text, but comments on the realities described *by* the text.[64] By this it is meant that he is not so much interested in philological details in the text itself, as in the real phenomena described by the text, such as characters, events,

---

60. Hilary, *Matt.*, 33.6 and 33.7 respectively.

61. Driscoll, "Matthew," 400, makes the same observation, but draws rather different conclusions from it, as are noted below.

62. Newlands, *Hilary*, 54.

63. This contention is related to one of the fundamental characteristics of Hilary's exegesis identified by Doignon, that corporeal things signify the incorporeal: "Connexion," 261.

64. Driscoll, "Matthew," 403.

contexts, and conversations. Augustine, who as we shall see has the same preference, expresses a similar idea through his distinction between *res* and *signum*. Although signs are things in and of themselves, Augustine argues in *De Doctrina Christiana* that we should not consider signs for what they are but rather for their value in signifying something else.[65] This is particularly true of those signs whose whole use is in signifying, most notably *verba*.[66] Thus, if we were to try and put it in the terminology of the day, we might say that Hilary or Augustine are more interested in gleaning theological significance from the *res* (real things and events) to which various *signa* (philological data) point to than from a study of the *signa* in their own right, largely detached from the *res*. That said, care should be taken in advancing a full equivalence between Augustine's use of these concepts, and the distinction between the text itself and the phenomena described by the text. For example, some of the things described here as "realities behind the text" (such as at least some conversations or statements quoted from characters in the text), would be placed by Augustine in the category of *signum* rather than *res*.[67]

The point which we seek to establish here is that nowhere in the segment of his work under study here does Hilary make theological statements from grammatical features of the text, and only once does he argue from a word study, when he gives the meaning of the name "Barabbas."[68] Unlike Jerome, he does not use any other etymological devices.[69] Although he is heavily focused around Matthew's account of the events he is studying, he shows no interest in the peculiarities of Matthew's style or perspective, and what these things might say about the theological matters which are his primary concern. As will be seen in chapter 4, this is a major difference between Hilary's approach and that of Ambrose.

This tendency to make points from the realities behind the text is most clearly seen in his manner of attributing symbolical meanings to things. Hilary's clear preference, when he does use allegory, is to apply it to give meanings to the events and objects of the Gospel rather than to

---

65. Augustine, *Doctrina*, 2.1.1.

66. Augustine, *Doctrina*, 1.2.2.

67. E.g. Hilary, *Matt.*, 2.6.7.

68. Hilary, *Matt.*, 33.2, on Matt 27:16–17. Presumably, he only does so because of its strongly poignant significance: "son of the Father." Ambrose makes a similar connection: *Lucam*, X, 102.

69. Newlands, *Hilary*, 44.

words and phrases. His interest is not verbal.[70] For example, when discussing the soldiers' mocking of Christ (Matthew 27:27–31), he begins by stating that the color of the garments which were placed on Christ point out that he took on the infirmities of the saints, and also points to the martyrs, and the heroes of the Old Testament. He then moves on to use the pricking thorns and the cane to point out doctrinal truths by observing, "He also is crowned with thorns, that is, the sins of the pagans who pierced him. In this way glory could be derived from pernicious and worthless things that encircled the head of God. For the points of the thorns are the sins from which the crown of Christ's victory is woven."[71] Similarly, when he refers to the thieves crucified on either side of Christ (Matthew 27:38) as symbols of all the human races present at Christ's death, it is to be noted that they are *real* representatives of humanity, pointing in a sacramental way to the Lord's passion.[72] They are not merely symbols that point to Christ in an obscure or abstract way: "And thus on the tree the salvation and the life of all people is suspended. Two thieves are crucified, to His right and to His left, who show that all of mankind is universally called to by the mystery of the Lord's passion. But because of the difference between believers and unbelievers, a distinction between all those to His right and all to His left is established, for the one of the two who is placed on the right is saved by justifying faith."[73]

This preference of Hilary to concentrate on the events of the biblical narrative in interpretation has been well expressed by another scholar, who noted that "his interpretation is always very much the interpretation of *gesta*, of the historical phenomenon."[74] T. F. Torrance similarly observes of Hilary's allegorization that "[h]e makes a distinction between the mere hearing of words and understanding of sentences, and an ap-

---

70. Interestingly, Origen distinguishes between words and realities in the case of believing in Christ: he insists that "believing in his name is a different thing from believing in him ... We must, therefore, cleave to him rather than to his name." Translation from: Origen, *Commentary on John*, 10, 28, in *Ante-Nicene Fathers*, 9.

71. Hilary, *Comm. Matt.*, 33.3. Cf. his similar manner of discussing royal imagery in the context of Ps 2: Hilary, *Psalmos*, 2, 6.

72. A point not made by Jerome in his discussion of this verse: *Math.*, IV 1712–6 (Matt 27:38). Augustine's only interest in the verse is in its fulfillment of prophecy, an idea that holds much less interest for Hilary, as shall be seen below: Augustine, *In Ioh.*, 117.3.

73. Hilary, *Matt.*, 33.5 (translation mine).

74. Rousseau, "The Exegete as Historian: Hilary of Poitiers' Commentary on Matthew," 113.

prehension of the realities they indicate, and so insists that the inner meaning must not be detached from the facts or the events which they narrate."[75] However, Torrance merely notes this as a distinction between Hilary's exegesis and that of the East,[76] whereas, as this study suggests, he could have also added that it is a feature which also distinguishes his work from that of other Latin authors also, such as Jerome. However, this is a less substantial underestimation of the importance of the distinction between text and the realities behind it than that evident years ago in de Lubac's work, which noted the theoretical existence of such a distinction, only to use his observation, backed by many references, to stress that an emphasis on the realities is a universal characteristic of all Latin exegesis—a universal characteristic for which even such a master of citations as de Lubac could not find references in certain significant Latin authors, most notably Jerome.[77]

Telling Theological Stories

However, Hilary does not merely use the realities described by the Gospel narrative to point out theological truths. He goes further than that. For Hilary, the events of the Gospel reflect the theological story which is unfolding in parallel to the story of the events.[78] Thus, when great fissures open up in the ground at Christ's death, Hilary tells us that this is "because the bonds of death were loosed."[79] Similarly, the supernatural events surrounding Christ's resurrection are seen to reflect what is happening in the spiritual realms, such as the "earthquake early on the Sunday morning which declares the power of the Lord's resurrection as the sting of death is defeated. Hades is shaken with alarm at the resurrection of the Lord of the powers of heaven."[80] The creation is seen by Hilary to be an actor which responds to God's script, a point illustrated by his observation that during the crucifixion "it is night when it should be day-time: for three hours of the day, for precisely this many hours it

---

75. Torrance, *Divine Meaning: Studies in Patristic Hermeneutics*, 392.

76. Torrance, *Divine Meaning: Studies in Patristic Hermeneutics*. Cf. 395 and 397.

77. Lubac, *Medieval*, 2, 83–85.

78. Although he does not make this point, Newlands, *Hilary*, 54 observes that a key feature of the commentary is that it is essentially an analysis of the theological themes of the Gospel, rather than of the text, line by line.

79. Hilary, *Comm. Matt.*, 33.7, on Matt 27:51–2.

80. Hilary, *Matt.*, 33.9, on Matt 28:2 (translation mine).

is dark, and by this the whole creation declares its astonishment at the mystery of the divine work."[81] One of his comments made on the death of Christ also illustrates this: "The earth is shaken: for it could not hold *this* One among the dead."[82] Here, it is the greatness of the divine nature that is both the explanation and the significant doctrinal conclusion to be drawn from the event given in the Gospel. By contrast, the only point that Ambrose makes about the great signs accompanying Jesus' death is regarding the "darkening" of the earth, which reminds us of the fact that the eyes of the faithless are darkened. Ambrose also uses the narrative to point to a theological truth, but not to the theological story behind the narrative.[83]

For Hilary, it is the theological story told by the events of the Gospel that is central to his understanding of the text. For this reason, he frequently places the historical events of the account and theological remarks closely side by side, even in the same sentence. However, it must be emphasized that Hilary does not regard the Gospel text as a framework upon which he can hang theological ideas as he pleases. His exegesis is therefore not heterogenous.[84] Rather, he allows the text to direct which theological themes he raises at particular points. This is because he believes that the events of the Gospel narrative tell *the* story, rather than merely enabling him to tell *his* story.[85] This can be seen in the example of Hilary's observation on Matthew 27:32 that "they placed the wood [i.e. the cross] of his passion on a certain man from Cyrene. The Jews were unworthy to carry the cross of Christ, so it was left to the faith of the pagans, both to take the cross and to suffer together with him."[86] In this example, the taking of the cross by Simon is seen to signal a shift in the theological narrative away from the Jews and towards the opportunity for the Gentiles to come to the knowledge of God through the cross over the succeeding sentences in Hilary's exposition.[87]

---

81. Hilary, *Matt.*, 33.6, on Matt 27:45 (translation mine).

82. Hilary, *Matt.*, on Matt 27:51 (translation mine).

83. Ambrose, *Lucam*, X, 128.

84. Simonetti, "Note," 50 argues this with particular reference to his use of allegory.

85. Relatedly, Driscoll, "Matthew," argues that "meaning is believed to be embedded in this order" (of events), 401.

86. Hilary, *Comm. Matt.*, 33.4.

87. Hilary, *Matt.*, 33.5, on Matt 27:37–40. Compare with Jerome's account of the same episode: Jerome, *Math.*, IV, 1655-65.

In general, Hilary, as he progresses through the text, raises theological themes that one might expect him to raise at various points in the Gospel. There are very few places at which he surprises by responding to an event in the account with a theological point that bears only a distant relation to the concerns of the text itself. Thus, when discussing Christ's humiliation at the hands of the soldiers (Matthew 27:27–31), he points out Christ's assumption of our infirmities, his solidarity with the martyrs, and his bearing of the sins of the world.[88] At the cross, he discusses the contrasting responses of faith and unbelief that people present at the event and since have made to the Christ's passion, and the causes of these responses.[89] The major theological point made in response to Christ's death is that he was separated from God because he bore the sins of the world.[90] All of the theological themes drawn from the miraculous events that followed Christ's death serve to emphasize the greatness of the one who had died, and the cosmic significance of the event.[91] In dealing with the resurrection account and the guards' report (Matthew 28:1–15), the glory of Christ receives repeated notice (the terms "gloria" and "honor" are mentioned four times).[92]

Hilary is consistent not only in avoiding digression from the text, but in following its guidance in determining what theological points he will note and stress. He uses the Gospel account to progress the theological narrative that he believes the Gospel itself was written to tell. This characteristic of Hilary's exegesis stands in contradiction to Newlands's statement on the commentary, that "[d]ue to his focus on one theme, Hilary loses many of the individual emphases of the Gospel."[93] Certainly, as will be seen below, Hilary does place strong emphasis on one theme, but follows the individual emphases of the Gospel closely and therefore cannot be said to lose more than a few of them.

---

88. Hilary, *Matt.*, 33.3.
89. Hilary, *Matt.*, 33.5, on Matt 27:38–9.
90. Hilary, *Matt.*, on Matt 27:46.
91. Hilary, *Matt.*, on Matt 27:51–3.
92. Hilary, *Matt.*, 33.8.
93. Newlands, *Hilary*, 91.

Monosemy

This understanding of Hilary's exegetical method is reinforced by Hilary's strong tendency to monosemy, that is, belief that the text has a single meaning. At no point in the expositionary segment under study does Hilary even entertain meanings alternative to the one he gives, or discuss the relative merits of various positions on the passage (as Jerome sometimes does), let alone present two or more meanings/points of significance of the passage alongside one another (as is Augustine's practice).[94] The only exception to this is his use of typology, discussed below, but this is a special case where the two meanings are closely linked by both history and theology, and one meaning serves to point out the other. Without exception, he proceeds by noting the event, and then stating its singular meaning or significance without equivocation, before moving on to the next point in the account. At no point does he justify the meanings that he gives or provide explanations as to why he has chosen one possible interpretation over others that may have been extant at the time as "the" meaning. This reflects the fact that his work is not intended to be a critical examination of technical issues or doctrinal possibilities. Instead, Hilary's focus is on the realities described in the Gospel and the narrative of theological truths which those realities indicate when examined in order, rather than on the vagaries of the text with its range of alternative meanings derived from its potentially infinite store of etymologies, literary features, and critical issues. His exegesis is not so much an exercise in using the multiple possibilities present in the text to discuss matters which he believes are relevant, as an attempt to point out simply and directly the theological story which the events of the Gospel tell.

However, it must be emphasized that Hilary's concern to use the narrative to tell a theological story does not mean that his exegesis is largely concerned with discussing particular theological matters in their own right. As noted above, he seldom digresses to discuss doctrinal issues, and constantly turns back to the events of the narrative. This contrasts strongly with the practice of Augustine, who often makes a series of apparently random digressions before returning to the text several pages later. Furthermore, his pattern is not to use a series of events in the narrative to develop a particular theological idea of interest, but to mention a different theological concept with each reference to the text. He does

---

94. Of related interest is the fact that Smalley, *Bible*, 20, argues that Hilary (like Ambrose) did not regard allegory as an instrument of speculation.

not refer frequently to the text in order to justify his theological ideas, but rather to point out what the theological concerns of the account are. Thus, his exposition is not so much exegesis for the sake of theology, as an exegesis of the theological significance of the events of the Gospel. As will be seen when Hilary's homiletical concerns are examined, his purpose is certainly not to explore theological themes for his readers. This central feature of Hilary's exegesis is further illustrated by the use that he makes of typological connections.

Typology

Typology is a central feature of Hilary's exegesis, as a number of scholars have recognized.[95] In the vast majority of cases where Hilary uses symbolism to make a connection between an event in the narrative and the theological point that he believes to be the meaning of that event, he interprets typologically rather than by using other, less historically-grounded forms of spiritual exegesis.[96] An example of Hilary's use of typology in his commentary is his exposition of the fact that women were the first to see the Lord after his resurrection in Matthew 28:9, which he sees as significant in the light of the primal sin of Genesis 3: "Now the customary pattern, which had been from the beginning, is reversed. Whereas death had its beginning from the female sex, the same sex was the first to bring the tidings of the glory, the sighting, the benefit, and the news of the resurrection."[97] In this case, an event in the text is given

---

95. E.g. Kelly, "Bible," 48, and Simonetti, "Note," 50–54. Cf. Newlands, *Hilary*, 71 who also discusses the relationship between allegory and typology in Hilary. However, note that the typology spoken of by these authors and in the pages that follow is distinct from the broader "typological exegesis" discussed by Williams, "Introduction," in Hilary, *Matthew*, 18–21. Williams correctly observes that Hilary does not use the Latin term for "allegory" but instead at least in some places employs a range of phrases to refer to the allegorical or spiritual sense, including the term "typica." Therefore Williams (with some terminological justification) incorporates all usage Hilary might make in the commentary of non-literal exegesis that is not "simple" under the heading of "typological exegesis," while noting that much of what Hilary does do in this regard is typological in the sense discussed elsewhere in this work and indeed in Paul's usage.

96. Rusch, *Fathers*, 13 also notes Hilary's typological inclinations in the commentary, albeit only with a passing reference.

97. Hilary, *Comm. Matt.*, 33.8. This typological connection was popular amongst the Fathers, e.g. Ambrose, *Lucam*, X, 156, on John 20:14–17. Jerome, *Math.*, IV, 1890–4 (on Matt 27:61), by contrast, does not make it, but says instead that the women were the first to see Christ arise on the grounds of their being the most devoted to him

theological significance by making a connection between it and another event at an earlier stage of the theological narrative of biblical history.

However, Hilary's use of typological logic is not usually in as traditional a form as with this example. He highlights cases which come in the form Old Testament type—New Testament fulfillment/antitype sparingly, and in general refers to the Old Testament less frequently than the other writers under study here. This is particularly surprising, given that the Gospel of Matthew is particularly rich in Old Testament references, and itself makes habitual use of concepts such as the prophecy-fulfillment motif.[98] This characteristic of the Gospel led other commentators, such as Jerome, to strongly and frequently emphasize issues of Old Testament—New Testament continuity. However, it should be remembered that Jerome achieves this through frequently observing instances of prophecy-fulfillment; like Hilary, he uses traditional typology sparingly. Hilary has relatively little interest in noting Old Testament prefigurings or prophecies of the material before him, let alone digressing onto such matters at length. Instead, he tends to look forwards rather than backwards when making historical connections within sacred history. His preference is for making historical connections between events in the narrative and phenomena elsewhere in the New Testament or in the Christian life.

Even within the small portion of the *In Matthaeum* under study, there are several instances where Hilary makes a historical connection between an event in the Gospel and another point in the New Testament. One example is his view that the resurrection of the holy on Good Friday, discussed above, is a pointer to Christ's own resurrection.[99] Another is

---

through his death and burial.

98. During a later phase of his ministry, after his exile, Hilary does appear in the commentary genre to utilize traditional Old Testament–New Testament typologies more frequently; cf. Burns, *A Model for the Christian Life: Hilary of Poitiers' Commentary on the Psalms*, 80.

99. Hilary, *Matt.*, 33.8, with reference to Matt 27:52. A point also made by Jerome, *Math.*, IV, 1819–31, on Matt 27:52–3. However, Jerome makes the point by more philological means, by playing upon the repeated use of the terms "dead" and "rise" in the relevant passages. Interestingly, Ambrose, in *De excessu fratris Satyri*, II, 83 instead makes the point that the rising to life of the bodies of the holy points forward to our own resurrection, which has been purchased by Christ's death: "when he gave up the ghost, in order to show that He died for our resurrection, worked out the course of the resurrection; for so soon as 'He cried again with a loud voice ... and the tombs were opened, and many bodies of the saints which slept arose' ... If these things happened when He gave up the ghost, why should we think them incredible when He shall

the sealing up of Christ's tomb, which is seen as an action that points forward to Christ's resurrection: "Due to a fear that the body might be stolen, a guard was placed at the tomb which was sealed. These [actions] are testimonies to their stupidity and unbelief, since the fact that they chose to seal up His tomb shows that they recognized in advance that He would be raised from the tomb of death."[100] Jerome, when commenting on the same verse, also suggests that the stone points forward to Christ's resurrection, but for him the main point is more textually focused, namely, that the presence of the stone supports the veracity of the account of the resurrection.[101]

However, the most frequent form in which Hilary uses typological logic is not typology within the New Testament, but in making historical connections between events in the Gospel and contemporary Christian realities. Again, his practice in this regard echoes that of Jerome. He looks forward from the Gospel, rather than backwards, a practice which, strictly speaking, cannot be described as typological.[102] As Simonetti explains,

> Hilary tends to gather together the spiritual significance of the Gospel of Matthew in a rather more organic and homogenous manner and interprets the deeds and words of the life of Jesus in the light of the consequences which derive from them. He thus perceives in them the prefiguration of the hostility of the Jews toward the church, the abolition of the old economy and the preaching of the gospel to the pagans. Although these motives are indeed already present in the Gospel, Hilary systematically gives prominence to them even when the Gospel text contains something quite different.[103]

For example, the mocking worship of Christ by the soldiers is taken to prefigure the more genuine worship that he has since received.[104] A more complex example is found when "finally Pilate washed his hands and then declared himself before the Jewish people to be innocent of the Lord's blood. For each day, while the Jews take on themselves and their descendants the responsibility for spilling the blood of the Lord, the Gentiles

---

return to judgement?" Translation from: Ambrose, "Select Works," 10, 187.

100. Hilary, *Matt.*, 33.8, on Matt 27:64 (translation mine).
101. Jerome, *Math.*, IV, 1896–1907.
102. Doignon, "Hilaire," 511 notes this tendency in other parts of the commentary.
103. Simonetti, "Hilary," 49.
104. Hilary, *Matt.*, 33.3, on Matt 27:29.

by washing themselves, daily pass into a confession of the faith."[105] In this case, one event does not simply prefigure others, but the connection between an event in the Gospel (Pilate's action and the crowd's self-condemning words) and a contemporary event (the Gentiles' confession of faith) points out a contemporary theological reality (the ongoing guilt of the Jews versus the removal of guilt from believing Gentiles who confess faith in Christ).[106]

Hilary's preference is to relate the events and theological narrative of the Gospel to contemporary realities in his own time, rather than to discuss theological issues in their own right. This is clearly illustrated by his comments on the crowd's preference for Barabbas over Christ (Matthew 27:21), in which "already is the mystery of their future unbelief shown here: instead of Christ they preferred the 'son of the father,' namely, the Antichrist, who is the man of sin and the son of the devil. Incited by their leaders, the Jews chose the one who is reserved for damnation rather than the Author of their salvation."[107] In this example, Hilary makes passing reference to the fact that Christ's resurrection marks him out as the author of life. However, he does not choose to elaborate at all on any of the major abstract doctrinal themes that this observation might raise, such as the nature of Christ, the effects of his resurrection, the relationship between his condemnation/death and his resurrection, or the idea of Christ as the sustainer of all creation and life (as in Colossians 1). Instead, for Hilary the main idea here is the fact that the preference of the crowd for Barabbas over Christ points to the contemporary reality of faithlessness (either of the Jews or people in general) that effectively prefers the Devil to Christ.[108]

In contrast to the practice of other Gospel commentators, particularly in the Greek East, Hilary does not use the Gospel text to discuss classical christological themes as such. When he does comment on Christ himself, it is seldom in the form of an ontological or philosophical statement about Christ's nature. Instead, he prefers to make more downto-earth statements about Christ's function or attitude or the appropriate response of onlookers, such as the following comment on the resurrection, with its emphasis on Christ's submission to the Father: "His

105. Hilary, *Matt.*, 33.1, on Matt 27:24 (translation mine).
106. Hilary makes the same point in *Tractatus Mysteriorum*, 1.7.
107. Hilary, *Comm. Matt.*, 33.2.
108. Other instances of where Hilary sees events in the Gospel as prefiguring realities in the gospel age of the church can be found at Hilary, *Matt.*, 1.6, 8.5, 15.12.

Resurrection is indicated beforehand, so that His service of the Father's will might be declared by His resurrection."[109] Hilary's comments on Christ's death in the light of the cynical comments of some of the Jewish onlookers—"Here is the one who would destroy the Temple of God and in three days rebuild it"—also illustrate this: "What pardon will there be for these when, after three days, they see the rebuilding of the Temple of God in his bodily resurrection?"[110] In this example, Hilary begins with a classical statement of the greatness of Christ, but does not move on to discuss, say, the greatness of the divine nature, preferring to look forward to Christ's resurrection and the grace it brings.

Hilary's tendency to look forwards from the events of the Gospel can at times add an eschatological element to the commentary.[111] Consider, for example, his comments on the soldiers' dressing of Christ in a scarlet robe (Matthew 27:28), where Hilary observes that Christ "is covered with the scarlet blood of all the martyrs destined to reign with Him."[112] Here, the sufferings of Christ are seen to prefigure the sufferings that his followers would endure, with an emphasis on the eschatological reality that the martyrs shall reign with Christ. By contrast, Ambrose notes the reference to the scarlet cloak, but keeps its significance firmly in the present of the Gospel account, in its representation of Christ's priestly office.[113] In Hilary's discussion of the clean linen shroud in which Christ was buried (Matthew 27:59), he looks forward eschatologically from the burial of Christ to the all-inclusive nature of the church. For Joseph of Arimathea "wrapped the Lord's body in a clean linen shroud; in this same linen we find every kind of animal coming down to Peter from heaven. It is not impossible to understand from this common element that the church is buried together with Christ under the name of this linen shroud."[114]

---

109. Hilary, *Matt.*, 33.8, on Matt 28:2 (translation mine).

110. Hilary, *Comm. Matt.*, 33.5, on Matt 27:40.

111. Driscoll, "Matthew," 407 notes the eschatological connection between Christ's glory and his passion in Hilary's work.

112. Hilary, *Matt.*, 33.3 (translation mine). In the *Tractatus Mysteriorum*, 2.9, Hilary also mentions the color of the robe in connection with a characteristic of the church. The scarlet color of the robe is reminiscent of the blood of the Passover lamb of Exod 12:7 as well as pointing forward to the blood of Christ that will shortly be shed. Just as the Passover lamb only protected those who were inside the house marked with its blood, so too the blood of Christ only subsequently preserves those who are within the church.

113. Ambrose, *Lucam*, X, 118.

114. Hilary, *Matt.*, 33.7 (translation mine).

Practical Application of the Text

More significantly, though, Hilary's concern to connect the events of the Gospel with the life of the contemporary church gives his exegesis a strongly homiletical flavor. At first sight, this may seem a surprising comment to make about the *In Matthaeum*, given that in the section under study here, Hilary never addresses his reader(s), or makes a direct practical application of the text.[115] Furthermore, being a written commentary, there is no opportunity for interaction with a congregation. However, Hilary is clearly concerned to connect the events of the Gospel with practical matters, very often through brief and straightforward remarks, the latter feature being notable given that the commentary genre was directed at a more advanced and well-educated audience.[116] Thus, in response to the guards' acceptance of money in payment for lying about the resurrection (Matthew 28:11–15), he makes the succinct comment that "he whose praise is in money—he is denied glory."[117] Another example is his comment on Christ's being mistreated by the soldiers, that "He assumed all of the weaknesses of our body."[118] He is not interested only in how the events of the Gospel prefigure contemporary realities of a cosmic scale, such as the continuing unbelief of the Jews or the nature of the church, but also in how they can encourage the individual Christian. Hilary's exegesis of the burial of Christ illustrates this further:

> "For according to the teaching of the apostles, the body of the Lord is placed in a new and empty place of rest cut out of stone, indeed roughly cut, and also new and devoid of doubt before God's entry. And so that nobody besides Him may enter into our hearts, the stone is rolled against the door; furthermore, in order that nothing unclean would enter into us once the knowledge of the divine author had been placed in us, nobody apart from Him was carried in afterwards."[119]

---

115. Indeed, in the entire work, Hilary makes no reference to or for whom he was writing. The prologue, which may have provided some information, has been lost. Cf. Newlands, *Hilary*, 43–44.

116. Eliot, "Exegetical Genres in the Patristic Era," 784.

117. Hilary, *Matt.*, 33.8 (translation mine).

118. Hilary, *Comm. Matt.*, 33.3, on Matt 27:27–30.

119. Hilary, *Matt.*, 33.7, on Matt 27:64 (translation mine). By contrast, Jerome and Ambrose both simply note the reason why the stone is referred to in the narrative and leave the reader to draw any encouragement implied by this for themselves. Ambrose, *Lucam*, X, 136; Jerome, *Math.*, IV, 1896–1907.

Here Hilary encourages his readers, by stating that the stone against the door represents God's guarantee that no one apart from Christ can enter into the hearts of Christians, once Christ has entered in.

In the example just considered, Hilary uses the events of the narrative to make a theological point, which he develops in a practical direction. This rapidly flowing movement from event to theology to homiletic concern is common in Hilary's exegesis, and emphasizes the fact that Hilary is not concerned merely to tell the theological story of the Gospel for its own sake, but for the sake of contemporary Christians. Thus, when Hilary discusses major doctrinal themes in his exposition, he does not only relate them closely to events in the narrative, but also to believers. For example, when discussing the sponge filled with wine vinegar offered to Christ immediately before his death, Hilary makes a statement on the classic theme of Christ's taking on the sin of the world: "he received the corporeal sins of pagans, sins that corrupt eternally. He transferred those sins of ours to himself and to the communion of his immortality."[120] Yet it is a statement which links the theological idea with contemporary Christians, as he does not merely state the concept on the cosmic scale, but also stresses what Christ's work accomplished regarding "those sins of *ours*."[121]

The Theme of Faith

In fact, the theme which receives the most attention in Hilary's exposition of Matthew is an eminently practical one: faith. He repeatedly stresses the faith of God's people, usually in contrast to unbelief or unfaithfulness and very frequently in relation to justification.[122] Consider, for example, his comment on the thieves crucified with Christ: "And so it was that the salvation and life of all was hung on the tree of life. To his left and right, two thieves were crucified, showing that the whole human race everywhere is called to by the sacrament of the Lord's passion. But because there is a difference between believers and unbelievers, there is an overall division between those on the right and those on the left. The

---

120. Hilary, *Comm. Matt.*, 33.6, on Matt 27:34.

121. Emphasis mine. Whereas Jerome, *Math.*, IV, 1685–94 refers the reference in an entirely different, and less practically relevant direction, backwards to the corruption of Israel's "wine" (devotion) in the Old Testament.

122. A fact commented on by others, e.g. Williams, "Introduction," in Hilary, *Comm. Matt.*, 30–33.

thief placed to the right was saved by the justification of faith."[123] Here, Hilary gives a common allegorical interpretation of the significance of the two thieves (as representatives of those on the right and wrong sides of God's ledger, described in Matthew 25:31-46), but with an emphasis on salvific faith. The two groups are characterized not by, say, righteousness and unrighteousness, but by faith and unbelief, with the thief on the right being saved by faith. In this way, the two thieves for Hilary sum up the soteriological drama which engulfs all of humanity throughout human history, in which the call to faith in the Lord on the cross is issued to all, but with two diametrically opposed outcomes occurring both in the Gospel narrative and in the human race as a whole.[124]

At some points, Hilary draws a more specific contrast between Gentile faith and Jewish unfaithfulness, as in his discussion of the Jewish crowd's acceptance of Christ's bloodguilt in Matthew 27:25.[125] Here, he observes that "each day, while the Jews take on themselves and their descendants the responsibility for spilling the blood of the Lord, the Gentiles by washing themselves, daily pass into a confession of the faith."[126] Hilary similarly develops this idea shortly afterwards in his comment on the crowd's preference for Barabbas as summarizing the ongoing unbelief of the Jews.[127] Hilary regards the present confession of faith of the church as accomplishing God's purposes ("each day . . . the Gentiles by washing themselves, daily pass into a confession of the faith"), and in his comment "that afterwards in the confession of the Church on earth, the diversity of clean and unclean things has brought together."[128]

Hilary stresses that the events of the Gospel themselves are objects of faith. He often connects them with the faith-experience of believers: "No less do the two thieves heap insults on him for his sufferings, which shows how the scandal of the cross will be for all believers."[129] The events of the Gospel call those who witness them (and by implication those who read of them) to faith, as in the case of Pilate's wife in Matthew

123. Hilary, *Comm. Matt.*, 33.5, on Matt 27:38.

124. Cf. Beckwith, *Hilary of Poitiers on the Trinity*, 185-6.

125. Burns, *Christology*, 48 also notes that Jew-Gentile contrasts are a recurring theme in the commentary.

126. Hilary, *Matt.*, 33.1 (translation mine).

127. Hilary, *Matt.*, 33.2, on Matt 27:21.

128. On Joseph of Arimathea's manner of burying Christ in Matt 27:57-60; Hilary, *Matt.*, 33.7 (translation mine).

129. Hilary, *Comm. Matt.*, 33.5, on Matt 27:44.

27:19, where "in this woman there is an image of the Gentile people, who already believing, calls her husband and the unbelieving people to faith in Christ."[130]

Thus, the primary thrust of Hilary's homiletical focus in the *In Matthaeum* is to encourage rather than lambaste, and to encourage towards faith in particular. Unlike some other students of Hilary's *In Matthaeum*, Tevel, in his brief case study on the parable of the Laborers in the Vineyard, does recognize that Hilary is not interested just in writing a "theological commentary," but has a practical purpose for the work.[131] Also quite accurate is Rusch's statement that "the work is a pastoral exercise rather than a polemic against Arianism,"[132] reinforced by the fact that there is no explicitly anti-Arian polemic in the material under study.[133] Its main aim is to promote faith in Christ, not to establish orthodoxy or attack heresy.

Conclusions

By examining the concluding sections of Hilary's *In Matthaeum*, it becomes apparent that Hilary's objective in writing the commentary was not to deal with complex textual, doctrinal, or philosophical issues that arise from the text. Rather, his chief concern was to illuminate the single, theologically purposeful account that he believed the events of the narrative told. As a result, Hilary's exegesis has a highly consistent character, which seldom digresses far from the "natural sense" of the text. Even his allegories usually develop theological themes that flow naturally from the text. He generally concentrates on themes that are raised by the events of the Gospel themselves, although he unites the themes he raises by relating them all to his focused homiletical concerns. His aim in interpreting in this way was to encourage and exhort his contemporaries by pointing them to important practical-theological matters raised by the events of the Gospel itself. In particular, he believed that the events of the Gospel were there to point to the need for faith in Christ, and to

---

130. Hilary, *Matt.*, 33.1 (translation mine). Cf. 33.7, on the sealing up of Christ's tomb in Matt 27:62–6, which Hilary regards as an unwitting act of faith in the resurrection.

131. Tevel, "Vineyard," 360.

132. Rusch, *Fathers*, 13. C.f. Kannengeisser, *Handbook*, 999.

133. Perhaps because it was written in 353–55 before Hilary visited the Greek East; Cf. Newlands, *Christology*, 43.

the condemnation of the faithless. Hilary accomplished this purpose by using a form of typological logic to link the events of the Gospel with other events in the New Testament that explicated their meaning, and with contemporary realities.

Considered in the light of the above, the views of some scholars on the nature and purpose of the *In Matthaeum* require some modification. Driscoll's study, although one of the most insightful English works on the *In Matthaeum*, appears wide of the mark in its conclusion that "Hilary's basic concern [is] to uncover the spiritual meaning in the text."[134] One of Newlands's main points in his work on the *In Matthaeum* is that the entire commentary is centered around the contrast between law and gospel; Jew and Gentile. While the distinction between the unbelieving Jews and faithful Gentiles is clearly a significant subtheme, Newlands's claim that "the commentary contains no other themes"[135] is something of an overstatement. If one theme was to be identified from the foregoing analysis as "the" theme of the commentary, it would be the practical theme of faith identified above, which is supported by *several* other ideas, such as the one identified by Newlands. Although probably representing the most detailed English work written on the *In Matthaeum* in recent years, Newlands's conclusions appear open to question at other points as well. Of particular importance here is the assertion that the work is "not primarily of a homiletic nature."[136]

2. De Trinitate

In *De Trinitate*, Hilary spends a large amount of time engaged in interpretation of the Gospel narratives. Book ten of this work is dedicated to examining the passion and crucifixion narratives (mostly in John), in order to determine what they say about the issues that Hilary is concerned with. A study of *De Trinitate* reveals that most of the major features of Hilary's exegesis identified above through analysis of part of the *In Matthaeum* are also present in his handling of Scripture in this work. As will be seen, there are some obvious points of dissimilarity, due to the fact that one work is a commentary, and the other a treatise written with a specific, anti-Arian purpose in mind. For example, Hilary's homiletical

---

134. Driscoll, "Matthew," 395.
135. Newlands, *Hilary*, 46.
136. Newlands, *Hilary*, 44.

concerns are more explicit and polemical in form. He also applies a wider range of exegetical tools in his interpretation of Scripture, probably due to the fact that *De Trinitate* was written several years after the *In Matthaeum*, after Hilary had been directly exposed to the practices of the Greek East.[137] However, more striking than these differences are the points of similarity across both works, specifically, the concern with the events of the Gospels rather than textual features, the tendency to monosemy, the use of typological logic, the faithfulness to the concerns/themes of the Gospel narratives, and above all the tendency to apply theological themes and ideas to contemporary realities, especially the issue of believing faith.

Hilary constantly refers to Scripture in the course of his argument in *De Trinitate*. Indeed, the work itself is largely a study of biblical references quoted in the Arian-Nicene debate, which aims to show that the orthodox interpretation of the Bible (and the Gospels in particular) is the only correct one on the issue at hand, namely the divinity of Christ.[138] He seldom deals at any length with the philosophical or technical doctrinal issues that occupied many of his contemporaries who wrote works on the same topic.[139] However, due to the nature of the work, he does discuss individual theological topics at considerably greater length than in the *In Matthaeum*.

Manner of Proceeding through the Text

As is the case in the *In Matthaeum*, Hilary seldom dwells on a single verse for a long period, but quickly moves from one part of Scripture to the next. However, this is not an eclectic process. He does not jump randomly and rapidly from one verse to another, his argument only held together by the thin threads of a common abstract philosophical idea, which as we will see can sometimes be the case with Augustine. Instead, he groups verses together that refer to the same basic doctrines, the same heretical claims, or the same phases in Christ's life in order to develop his argument. The work as a whole is structured in this way. Thus, for example, book three deals with references that support the orthodox

137. Probably when he was in exile in Asia Minor. Cf. Newlands, *Hilary*, 10, 101.

138. See Newlands, *Hilary*, 105 where it is pointed out that Hilary is not interested in the full range of issues encompassed within the title "*De Trinitate*," but almost exclusively with this christological point.

139. See, for example, Hilary's dismissive comments on the value of philosophical reflection for the theological task in *Trinitate*, 10.64.

interpretation of the words "I am in the Father, and the Father in me," book eight with biblical statements that refer to the unity of God, book nine with passages where Christ appears to distinguish himself from God, and book ten with relevant references from the passion narratives. Hilary maintains the same practice on a smaller scale within each book, as can be seen through an overview of the themes discussed in book ten.

After an introductory passage, in which he comments on the ways of the heretics and states his purpose,[140] Hilary deals in turn with verses, groups of verses, or implications drawn from events surrounding the passion that the Arians used for their purposes. He begins with a critique of the Arian contention that Christ feared his suffering and death.[141] He then moves on to a defense of the key orthodox contention that Christ was God come down from heaven in human form, centered around John 3:13, "No one has ascended into heaven except Him who has descended from heaven: the Son of Man who is in heaven."[142] This leads into a discussion of the question of the nature of Christ's body, specifically, in what sense he experienced pain, suffering, and fear during his passion, and the related issue of the exact meaning of those passages that refer to Christ taking on the form of a servant and the sinful flesh of man.[143] He then deals with Christ's prayer "remove this cup from me" (Matthew 26:39), which he returns to at greater length afterwards.[144] In between, he deals in turn with several other references located nearby in the passion narratives which appear to emphasize Christ's humanity at the expense of his deity, specifically, the exclamation in Matthew 27:46, "My God, My God, why have you forsaken me?," the dishonorable nature of his execution, the statement "into thy hands I commend my spirit" (Luke 23:46), and the words of Matthew 26:38, "My soul is sorrowful even unto death."[145] He then contrasts Christ's behavior in the garden of Gethsemane with that of the disciples, before briefly considering some relevant references in the Old Testament.[146] The suffering of Christ is then considered in the light of his resurrection, after which Hilary turns aside to make extended

---

140. Hilary, *Trinitate*, 10.1–9.
141. Hilary, *Trinitate*, 10.10–15.
142. Hilary, *Trinitate*, 10.16–19.
143. Hilary, *Trinitate*, 10.20–24 and 10.25–29 respectively.
144. Hilary, *Trinitate*, 10.30 and then 10.37–39.
145. Hilary, *Trinitate*, 10.31, 10.33, 10.34, and 10.36 respectively.
146. Hilary, *Trinitate*, 10.40–44 and 10.45–47.

and highly rhetorical comment on the ideas of the heretics, the nature of the faith, and of the divine mystery.[147] The fact that Christ wept in Luke 19:41 is then considered,[148] before an examination of John 10:17, "I lay down my life that I may take it up again," and an extended discussion of issues that arise from it.[149] He concludes with a survey of Pauline texts on the passion.[150]

Monosemy

Hilary typically proceeds by taking a relevant biblical reference, perhaps noting the interpretation that it is given by his opponents, and showing that its correct meaning supports the orthodox case.[151] As is the case in the *In Matthaeum*, Hilary only envisages one correct meaning for the text at hand. He never explicitly argues in favor of monosemy, but a theme that runs through the whole work is the contrast between the true meaning of the text, perceived by faith, and the blaspheming interpretations of the heretics.[152] Consider part of his attack on the interpretative abilities of his opponents in book one, where he complains that "Because they are ignorant . . . they attempt by a distortion of the sense and meaning to maintain that God was created rather than born . . . [by contrast] we shall explain the true meaning and intention of this testimony from Wisdom Itself."[153] Here, Hilary makes the assumption that there is a single meaning of the text that is of divine origin, which can only be understood in the light of the Gospel. For Hilary, there is no concept of multiple allegorical meanings of the text that are valid provided that they are in accord with the faith (as there is for Augustine). Instead, he proceeds not by noting a range of edifying meanings, but by providing simple explanations for the events of the Gospels, and assuming that there is only one (obvious) explanation in each case. Thus, when discussing the reason for Christ's sadness in the garden of Gethsemane (Matthew 26:36–46), he assumes

147. Hilary, *Trinitate*, 10.48–50, then 10.51–54.
148. Hilary, *Trinitate*, 10.55–56.
149. Hilary, *Trinitate*, 10.57–63.
150. Hilary, *Trinitate*, 10.64–71.
151. Interestingly, Simonetti, *Interpretation*, 124, argues that in the Arian controversy, the doctrinal position of different exegetes cannot be systematically linked to one or another mode of interpretation.
152. Torrance, *Meaning*, 418.
153. Hilary, *The Trinity*, 1.35.

that there is only one (true) cause, after dismissing the proposed reasons given by the Arians: "Are the reason for the sadness and the prayer for the removal of the cup still obscure?"[154] In the case of *De Trinitate*, Hilary's close adherence to the practice of monosemy has the advantage of supporting his polemical and anti-heretical intentions within the work: in assuming that there is only a single true meaning of the text, and in advocating for this meaning in relation to texts which support his account of Christ, Hilary strongly implies that alternative readings (such as those proposed by his opponents) are incorrect and to be discarded.[155]

Manner of Argument

Hilary in *De Trinitate* demonstrates that his meaning is the correct one in several ways. One of the most common tools he uses is the juxtaposition of the verse in question with another relevant biblical reference that illuminates the meaning of the first verse. This is what he does in dealing with the cry of Christ, "God, my God, why have you forsaken me?" (Matthew 27:46), by observing that "perhaps it is your opinion that, after the humiliation of the cross, the Father withdrew His help from [Him], whence arose the complaint about the loneliness of His weakness. If the contempt, the weakness, and the cross of Christ therefore are a disgrace in your eyes, you should not be unmindful of the saying: 'Nevertheless, I say to you, hereafter you shall see the Son of Man sitting at the right hand of the Power and coming with the clouds of heaven.'"[156] Here, Hilary spells out in a declamatory style his opponents' supposed understanding of the verse, and uses another reference from the same Gospel to illustrate that in spite of his apparent dereliction at this point in time, Christ would come again with glory, and that his cross should be seen in this light. Similarly, he deals with the argument demonstrated in Mark 14:36, "Father, all things are possible for you: remove this cup from me," that Christ's (non-divine) will failed by simply asking, "might you not have refuted for yourself this dull impiety by your own reading of the words, 'Put down your sword: shall I not drink the cup which My Father has given Me?'"[157] Likewise, in response to what he regards as improper

---

154. Hilary, *The Trinity*, 10.37.
155. Cf. Beckwith, *Hilary of Poitiers on the Trinity*, 188–92.
156. Hilary, *The Trinity*, 10.31, quoting Matt 26:64.
157. Hilary, *Select Works*, 10.30, quoting John 18:11.

use of Christ's statement in Matthew 26:38, "My soul is sorrowful unto death," he enquires of his audience, "why do you not recall what He said when Judas departed in order to betray Him: 'Now is the Son of Man glorified'? If the passion was to glorify Him, how did the fear of the passion render Him so sorrowful? Unless, perhaps, He was so unreasonable as to be afraid of suffering that which would glorify Him who suffers?"[158] It is noteworthy that in most cases of such juxtaposition, the two verses that Hilary uses are quoted from the same Gospel, and often refer to an event in the narrative that is situated close to the first event. This tendency illustrates the fact that even in the context of a doctrinal treatise, Hilary does not jump from reference to reference, but stays close to the text that he began considering.[159] In answering questions about a verse, his first inclination is to turn to texts that bear a naturally close relation to the verse. Hilary's approach here represents a notable exception to Simonetti's statement that in Latin works written at the time of the great Trinitarian controversies, "The Scriptural passages used for doctrinal ends were normally taken out of their original context and considered in isolation, producing results sometimes quite foreign to the sense which they would have had if interpreted within their proper context."[160]

However, Hilary often develops his argument in De Trinitate in more complex ways than simple juxtaposition. He frequently argues by considering a range of references as a group, sewing them together with obvious logic and simple doctrinal statements. He answers the allegation that various signs of Christ's weakness in the garden of Gethsemane prove that Christ was not fully divine in this way because his human frailties at moments such as this indicate that he does not possess the divine attribute of impassibility.[161] In this example, he argues that all of Christ's actions were not signs of his own weakness, but to be explained by his identification with his disciples and with Christians. Thus, the angel who comforts Christ in Luke 22:43 is sent to watch over the apostles: "an angel had been sent for the protection of the Apostles, and after the Lord had

---

158. Hilary, The Trinity, 10.29, quoting John 13:31.

159. Kaiser, "The development of Johannine motifs in Hilary's doctrine of the Trinity," 237–47 notes that Hilary remains close to the text when arguing elsewhere in De Trinitate from John's Gospel.

160. Simonetti, Interpretation, 122.

161. Hilary, Trinitate, 10.40–43. Hilary also employs similar strategies against the charge that Christ lacks impassibility in his commentary on the Psalms: see Burns, A Model for the Christian Life: Hilary of Poitiers' Commentary on the Psalms, 231.

been strengthened by him in order that He might not be sad on their account, He now spoke without fear of sadness: 'Sleep on now, and take your rest,'"[162] while the fact that Christ sweated blood (Luke 22:44) is an indication of the depth of his sorrow for his followers, and a sign of his power: "He must be strengthened in the same manner in which He is sad. If He is sad for us, that is, for our sake, then He must be strengthened for our sake and for us, because He who is sad because of us and has been strengthened because of us, has been strengthened in that state in which He was sad. No one will dare attribute the sweat to weakness, for to sweat blood is even contrary to nature."[163] After these comments, Hilary explains the meaning of relevant verses from all four Gospels to support his central contention that the statements and actions that might be taken to suggest Christ's lacking full divinity (on account of his apparent earthly frailty) actually refer to his vicarious, voluntary suffering on behalf of others.[164] He concludes by neatly sewing all of the references together:

> Hence, the prayer of the Lord which John made known, the desire of the Devil which Luke mentioned, and the facts cited by Matthew and Luke—the sadness unto death, the reproach on account of the sleeping, and, again, the exhortation to sleep—leave no room for ambiguity, since by the prayer in John in which He entrusts the apostles to the Father He fully explains the cause of the sorrow and the request for the removal of the cup. The Lord does not pray that suffering be taken away from Him, but begs the Father to protect the apostles, since He is about to suffer.[165]

The reference to the fact that Christ wept in Luke 19:41 is handled similarly.[166] He considers it in the light of Christ weeping for Jerusalem (Luke 13:34) and for Lazarus (John 11:35–37), drawing elements of truth out of each reference before his conclusion: "He gives life who wept and who felt pain."[167]

---

162. Hilary, *The Trinity*, 10.40, quoting Matt 26:45.

163. Hilary, *The Trinity*, 10.41.

164. Cf. Mercer, "Suffering for Our Sake, Christ and Human Destiny in Hilary of Poitier's *De Trinitate*," 562–3.

165. Hilary, *The Trinity*, 10.43, referring to Luke 22:31–32, Matt 26:45, Mark 14:41, and John 17:6–19 respectively.

166. Hilary, *Trinitate*, 10.55–56.

167. Hilary, *The Trinity*, 10.56. He handles the references to Christ's servanthood in 10.25–26 similarly.

In all of the examples just given, the groups of verses that Hilary examines are from closely related passages, usually from the same part of Scripture. Thus, eleven out of the thirteen biblical references given by Hilary in his discussion of Christ in the garden are taken from the passion narratives of the Gospels.[168] All five references in the section on Christ's weeping are from the Gospels.[169] All of the verses quoted in the section on Christ's servanthood are drawn from the Pauline writings.[170] This is typical of Hilary's practice throughout the work. For example, towards the end of book ten, several issues are discussed at length almost exclusively in terms of Pauline references.[171] Where he considers Old Testament passages, he does so by examining them in the light of other verses from the same sections of the Old Testament. Thus, at the end of book ten, he considers a relevant quote from Deuteronomy 30:12 in view of other verses from nearby in the same book.[172] The same is true of his examination of the question of whether the Jews in the fire in Daniel 3:23 feel pain: this story is considered together with a pair of references from the same book.[173] This tendency, together with Hilary's practice when juxtaposing pairs of verses noted above, emphasizes Hilary's commitment to the natural sense of Scripture which was identified in the *In Matthaeum*.[174] He does not jump between biblical passages that are only distantly related, but argues by making obvious connections between biblical references that are located nearby in the text itself. The supplementary references that he makes seldom surprise, and the connection is usually so obvious that Hilary does not even need to explain the relationship. Hilary's tendency towards the natural sense of Scripture, and his willingness to examine verses that bear a close relationship to the text in question, would appear to contradict the view of scholars such as Newlands, who argues that, in *De Trinitate*, Hilary "usually demonstrates

---

168. Hilary, *Trinitate*, 10.38–43.

169. Hilary, *Trinitate*, 10.55–56.

170. Hilary, *Trinitate*, 10.25.

171. Hilary, *Trinitate*, 10.61–68. Ten Pauline references are made in this passage, with only one (indirect) reference from another part of the Bible, Gen 15:16, which in any case is alluded to in Rom 4:3.

172. Hilary, *Trinitate*, 10.69–70.

173. Hilary, *Trinitate*, 10.45–46. The other references are Dan 1:8–16 and 6:1–24.

174. Kaiser, "Motifs," 238 makes the related observation that in *De Trinitate*, Hilary's comments on the Holy Spirit are very closely related to those of the Gospels themselves.

the texts he uses mean what he wants by doctrinal assertion rather than by an analysis of the contents of the texts themselves."[175]

Hilary's Purpose: Theological Themes Practically Applied

This impression of Hilary's use of Scripture in *De Trinitate* is reinforced by the fact that he uses allegory only very rarely.[176] In fact, there is only one instance in the whole of book ten of the work that anything approaching allegorical exegesis is employed.[177] Although Hilary does use typological exegesis at points, he does so in the manner in which typology is used in the *In Matthaeum*, which is to make easily apparent connections between biblical events and contemporary realities.[178] Hilary's use of Scripture in such a natural way to make clear its plain meaning is intentional, as it serves his purposes: "our purpose is, by abstaining from too laborious a process . . . to make the results as accessible as possible to the reader."[179]

As this quote suggests, and as was the case with the *In Matthaeum*, Hilary's primary purpose in *De Trinitate* is to make a connection between the events of the Gospel and the contemporary reader, calling forth a response of believing faith in the true Christ of the Gospel accounts (and particularly faith in this Christ whom he points to in the Scriptures, rather than the false alternatives of his opponents).[180] He does this because he believes that this was the purpose of the Gospel writers: "let us see the reason that he has made known in the words: 'But these things are written that you may believe that Jesus is the Christ, the Son of God.' He adduced no other reason for writing the Gospel than that all might believe that Jesus Christ is the Son of God."[181] He often exhorts his readers directly to faith in Christ:

---

175. Newlands, *Christology*, 104.

176. Rousseau, "Exegete as Historian," 113.

177. Hilary, *Trinitate*, 10.61.

178. Newlands, *Christology*, 120.

179. Hilary, *Select Works*, 10.57.

180. Beckwith, *Hilary of Poitiers on the Trinity*, 192–3. See also Hilary, *De Trinitate*, 7.38.

181. Hilary, *The Trinity*, 6.41, quoting John 20:31. C.f. Kannengeisser, *Handbook*, 1002.

> It is piety not to doubt; it is justice to believe; and it is salvation to confess. Salvation consists in not being lost amid uncertainties, in not being aroused to foolish talk, in not engaging in any kind of debate about the attributes of God, in not fixing limits for His power, in not searching anew for the causes of the inscrutable mysteries, in confessing the Lord Jesus, and in believing that God raised Him from the dead. What folly it is to pass disparaging remarks about Jesus, who He is and what is His nature, since salvation knows only this, that He is the Lord![182]

This example gives a typical picture of Hilary's approach. He exhorts to true, believing, faith in Christ, and contrasts that faith with doubting unbelief, with Christology and soteriology being closely integrated in Hilary's reading of the events of the narrative.[183] For Hilary, the issue is not that Arianism is misguided faith or heretical doctrine. Rather, it consists in doubting the nature and power of Christ, and is described in the language of unbelief, rather than of heresy. He does not argue so much for the correctness of the orthodox faith, as for its demand for a response of believing faith: "salvation consists . . . in confessing the Lord Jesus."[184] He is concerned with the gospel's contemporary, practical value, in this case with its saving efficacy.

Therefore, when Hilary considers the events of the Gospels, he regards them as being primarily for "our faith and salvation." When discussing the apparently difficult passages of the passion in book ten, a central element of his argument is that those things that seem to point out Christ's "human" weakness actually occurred for the sake of contemporary Christians. He notes that these apparent signs of Christ's weakness in fact serve to emphasize the reality of his sufferings and the fact that he was suffering voluntarily in our stead, since it is not Christ who needs help even as his death approaches, but only those who would follow him.[185] As Hilary says,

---

182. Hilary, *The Trinity*, 10.70, emphasizing the need to believe that Christ has been raised from the dead, with reference to Rom 10:8–10.

183. Burns, *A Model for the Christian Life: Hilary of Poitiers' Commentary on the Psalms*, 224, observes the same kind of integration to be operative in Hilary's work on the Psalms, produced in the same period of his ministry as *De Trinitate*.

184. Hilary, *The Trinity*, 10.70.

185. Mercer, "Suffering for Our Sake, Christ and Human Destiny in Hilary of Poitier's *De Trinitate*," 541–68.

If to make us aware of His death He therefore said "God, my God, why hast thou forsaken me?" and "Father, into thy hands I commend my spirit," did He not have in mind our confession of faith when He declared that He was weak, rather than leave us in uncertainty? . . . He prayed for our sake in order that we might recognize Him as the Son, and, although the words of the petition did not bring Him any personal gain, He spoke for the benefit of our faith. Hence, He does not need any help at the moment, but we need to be instructed.[186]

As is the case in the *In Matthaeum*, Hilary tends to emphasize the need for faith from the events of the Gospels themselves and the more obvious theological realities that those events point to, rather than from obscure features of the text. Consider for example his admonition of some of his readers for their lack of faith, occasioned by the request of the thief on the cross, where he reminds his opponents that "he [the thief] begs that Christ will remember him when He comes in His Kingdom: *you* say that Christ feared as He hung dying upon the cross. The Lord promises him, 'Today you shall be with Me in Paradise'; *you* would subject Christ to Hades and fear of punishment. Your faith has the opposite expectation."[187] By contrast, Jerome's exegesis at this point is thoroughly focused on the text and lacking in any kind of practical interest or agenda; he is only concerned about the apparent discrepancy between the accounts of Matthew and Luke.[188]

The same tendency can be observed in Hilary's reflection on the sufferings of Christ before and during his confession, that "although He bears our sins, that is, while He assumes the body of our sin, He Himself does not sin. He was sent in the likeness of our sinful flesh; while He indeed bears sins in the flesh, they are our sins . . . although He was wounded, the wound was not caused by His own sin, and whatever He suffers He does not suffer for Himself."[189] Here, Hilary's homiletic concern is not as explicit as in the previous example. However, the implication that Christ's suffering was for our sake is repeated, and not to be missed.

---

186. Hilary, *The Trinity*, 10.71. Contrast this use of the quotation "why have you forsaken me?" (Matt 27:46) with Jerome's, *Math.*, IV, 1768–74, which has no practical element to it at all, only references to the Hebrew original of the quoted Psalm. The other quotation in the selection is from Luke 23:46.

187. Hilary, *Select Works*, 10.34, on Luke 23:43–44.

188. Jerome, *Math.*, IV, 1738–49.

189. Hilary, *The Trinity*, 10.47.

Typology

As in the *In Matthaeum*, typological logic plays a key role in Hilary's exegesis, particularly in allowing him to move from the events and theology of the Gospel narratives to the realities of the contemporary church and Christian. He often draws a direct connection between the events of the Gospel and contemporary realities. Observe, for example, the biting manner in which he attacks the Arians, comparing them directly with the Jews who accuse Christ in the Gospels:

> And take note that by your denial of the Son of God you have entered into partnership with the blasphemy of the Jews. They reveal the reason why they condemned Him when they declare: "And according to that law He must die, because He has made himself the Son of God." Is this not also the taunt of your own blasphemous voice in asking why He calls himself the Son who, as you assert, is only a creature? These men judge that He is worthy of death for acknowledging that He is the Son, what, pray, is your verdict when you deny that He is the Son of God? His confession is just as displeasing to the Jews as it is to you. I would like to know if your opinion is different from theirs, since your intention is not different from theirs? For, with the same godlessness you deny that He is the Son of God.[190]

Hilary also uses typology within the history of the Gospel narratives to stress his theme of faith. For example, he dwells on the fact that Christ's words about himself rapidly find fulfillment in the words of the centurion in Matthew 27:54: "The centurion of the cohort, the guardian of the cross, cries out, 'truly this was the Son of God' . . . the outcome justifies the assertion. The Lord had said, 'glorify your Son' [John 17:1] . . . so, after He was glorified, that confession touched the truth; the centurion confessed Him the true Son of God, that no believer might doubt a fact which even the servant of His persecutors could not deny."[191]

Another device that he frequently employs is to use the cross to promote faith by viewing it in its eschatological context, that is, in terms of Christ's future glory: "He hastened to the death which was to glorify him,

---

190. Hilary, *The Trinity*, 6.50, quoting John 19:7. See also Hilary, *Trinitate*, 10.67.

191. Hilary, *Select Works*, 3.11. Ambrose, *On the Christian Faith*, I, XVII, 114 (Ambrose, "*Select Works*," 219) also uses this text to raise the theme of faith, although in his case in order to attack the lack of faith of the Arians: "The centurion said, 'Truly this was the Son of God.' 'Was' said the centurion—'was *not*' says the Arian."

and after which he was to sit on the right hand of power."[192] The same eschatological focus is used to answer a contemporary Arian criticism on the cry of dereliction (Matthew 27:46): "If the contempt, the weakness, and the cross of Christ therefore are a disgrace in your eyes, you should not be unmindful of this saying: 'Nevertheless, I say to you, hereafter you shall see the Son of Man sitting at the right hand of the Power and coming with the clouds of heaven.'"[193]

At several points, he instead makes typological connections between Old and New Testament events, in order to forward his argument, such as when he compares the suffering of Christ with that of the three young men thrown into the fire in Daniel 3:19–27, asking:

> whether they experienced any pain when they were surrounded by the flames? They do not feel the flame while they are in prayer and they cannot be burnt while they are in the fire. In their case, the bodies and the fire lose their proper nature, for the former are not burnt and the latter does not burn . . . O godless heretic, you wish Christ to suffer pain from the nail that penetrates His hands and for that wound to cause Him the pain that follows from a piercing instrument. I ask why the boys did not fear the fire, and why they did not experience any pain? . . . If these boys in the ardour of their faith and in the glory of a blessed martyrdom do not know how to fear things that are to be feared, should Christ have been sad through His fear of the cross?[194]

As is the case in the *In Matthaeum*, the argument of *De Trinitate* is developed by making simple and obvious connections between the events of the Gospel narrative, basic theological ideas, and their homiletic application. Consider the following extract where Hilary discusses Christ's words "I lay down my life that I may take it up again" (John 10:17), insisting that "the facts are real, but the power behind them is a mystery . . . He lays down His life of Himself, but I ask *who* lays it down? We confess without hesitation, Christ, God the Word."[195] Here, all three elements are present and interact with one another: the events of the Gospel (Christ's factual statement about what he is about to do), a doctrinal point (Christ's status as God the Word), with a homiletic touch ("we confess . . .").

---

192. Hilary, *Select Works*, 10.49, with reference to Matt 26:64.
193. Hilary, *The Trinity*, 10.31, quoting Matt 26:64.
194. Hilary, *The Trinity*, 10.45.
195. Hilary, *Select Works*, 10.57.

Text, Theology, and Homiletics

Hilary also frequently regards the events of the Gospel and their theological significance as closely interrelated.[196] For example, he treats the miraculous cosmic events that occurred immediately after Christ's death in a similar way to that of the *In Matthaeum*:

> Then what follows? The sun does not set, but hides itself. It was not taken into a cloud, but failed to complete its ordinary course, and together with the other elements of the world shared in the experience of His death. In order that none of the heavenly works be present at this crime, they escaped from the necessity of such co-operation by what may be called self-extinction. What did the earth do? It trembled at the burden of the Lord hanging on a tree, and testified that it would not receive within itself the one who was about to die. Do not the rocks and the stones also refuse to take part? But they break asunder, fall apart, and lose their nature, and acknowledge that the tomb, hewn out of stone, cannot contain the body that is to be buried in it.[197]

Here, the elements of creation act in response to the theological story of the Gospel at that point. This close interrelationship between the events of the Gospels and the theological realities that lie behind them is also emphasized by Hilary's frequent habit of rapidly and easily moving between events and doctrinal matters.[198]

As in the *In Matthaeum*, Hilary's preference is to deal with theological themes that proceed from the events of the narrative and progress his homiletical purposes, rather than with textual concerns. This is demonstrated most clearly by one of the few examples where he does note a "critical" concern regarding the text:

> We must not, of course, overlook the fact that we find nothing in writing about the coming of the angel and the bloody sweat in very many of the Latin and Greek manuscripts. Since a doubt arises, therefore, whether these incidents are wanting in the various books or are extraneous additions (the variation in the books leaves us in uncertainty about this question), then, if heresy seeks to derive some advantage from this fact, in order to claim that He is feeble who requires the help of an angel to

---

196. Torrance, *Meaning*, 417.

197. Hilary, *The Trinity*, 3.10, with reference to Matt 27:45 and 51.

198. See, for example, his discussion of the raising of Lazarus (John 11:1–46) in Hilary, *Trinitate*, 10.56. Cf. 4.18–19; 11.7.

strengthen Him, let it bear in mind that the Creator of the angels does not need to be defended by His own creature.[199]

Here, Hilary raises an issue associated with the text itself, and refers to the fact that it is not unimportant, only to stress that the "real" issue is that the heretics should not develop the ideas that they do from the passage, for theological reasons.[200] Hilary's comments in this place also underline a point about his biblical hermeneutic. In order to read Scripture faithfully, one must read it with the same faith that Scripture points towards.[201] Faith in the "Creator of the angels" determines the correct reading of the passage in question in light of textual uncertainties, against the faithless reading of heresy which seeks to turn creaturely doubt to its own advantage.

Although *De Trinitate* is a theological treatise, and Hilary is concerned to bring out the theological story behind the Gospel references that he examines, it must be stressed that Hilary is not interested in theology for its own sake. This is seen most clearly in the fact, noted above, that he usually discusses theology for a practical purpose. In addition, it should be noted that whenever in book ten Hilary does discuss a theological topic at any length, he is quick to refer and return to the events of the passion narratives. One of the longest extended discussions of a particular such issue concerns the dialogue between Christ and the penitent thief (Luke 23:39–43). Yet even this section of the work is peppered with references to the events of the biblical narrative.[202]

In this light, the view of some scholars that Hilary's handling of texts in *De Trinitate* was dictated by his theological emphases needs some modification. From the examples just considered, it is clear that Hilary certainly did frequently interpret events directly in terms of his theological concerns. However, it must be remembered that in both the *In Matthaeum* and *De Trinitate*, the relationship was bidirectional. Hilary usually allowed the events of the text to influence which theological themes he discussed, and always related his theological statements closely to the events of the narratives. In this light, comments such as "it

---

199. Hilary, *The Trinity*, 10.41, with reference to Luke 22:43–44. An extended discussion of the fact that Jesus suffered for our sake, not his, follows.

200. See also Hilary, *Trinitate*, 9.11–12, where Hilary attempts to harmonize the theology of the evangelists, ahead of their historical or textual veracity.

201. Beckwith, *Hilary of Poitiers on the Trinity*, 185–6, 195.

202. Hilary, *Trinitate*, 10.34.

is the impossibility of the divine nature that governs Hilary's treatment of texts,"[203] must be regarded as too simplistic.

Differences Between the In Matthaeum and De Trinitate

Having examined Hilary's use of Scripture in parts of *De Trinitate*, it is apparent that there are strong similarities with his exegetical tendencies in the *In Matthaeum*. Some differences, however, are noticeable. The first is that while in the *In Matthaeum*, Hilary typically makes his homiletic concerns known indirectly and implicitly, in *De Trinitate*, he readily and frequently gives an explicit practical direction to his exposition, and often writes polemically, as was observed in most of the examples given in the section above on homiletics.[204] However, this is explained largely by the difference in nature and purpose between the two works.

Secondly, Hilary has increased the repertoire of exegetical and rhetorical techniques available to him between writing the two works. Significant here is his frequent use of juxtaposition, and his significantly wider use of word studies and wordplays. An example of the latter is found in his discussion of the text, "My soul is sorrowful unto death" ("Tristris est anima mea usque ad mortem"—Matthew 26:38), where Hilary's argument rests on the distinction that Christ said "ad mortem" ("unto death") rather than "quod mortem" ("because of death").[205] Similarly, when examining Christ's request that the cup "pass away from" himself in Matthew 26:42, he presses his point by conducting a study into other New Testament uses of variants of the term "transire" ("to pass away").[206] However, it should be noted that in both of these examples, and the majority of those in the work, Hilary's use of word studies is relatively simple, and does not lead into allegorism and the lengthy digressions that it can bring. This is possibly because in *De Trinitate* Hilary is very focused on arguing for his own readings of disputed texts, and under such circumstances we would expect him to concentrate on the

---

203. Jacobs, "Western Roots," 202.

204. Kelly, "Bible," 54 makes the related observation that when Hilary and other Latin Fathers are discussing theological issues rather than primarily engaged in exegesis, they tend to adopt more straightforward methods.

205. Hilary, *Trinitate*, 10.36.

206. Hilary, *Trinitate*, 10.42.

language, syntax, and grammar of these texts rather than offering allegorical readings which would be easier to contest.[207] Generally, Hilary uses the new techniques that he has learnt to serve his central theological and practical-polemical concerns.

Conclusions

In spite of these differences, study of *De Trinitate* reveals that Hilary's use of Scripture in the work exhibits the same predominant features as does his approach in the *In Matthaeum*. Notable in both works are the concern with the events of the Gospels rather than textual features, the tendency to monosemy, the use of typological logic, the faithfulness to the concerns/themes of the Gospel narratives, and above all the tendency to apply theological themes and ideas to contemporary realities, especially the issue of faith.

Given that these are the characteristics that stand out in both works, it must be concluded that much of the scholarship undertaken on Hilary's exegesis, surveyed at the start of this chapter, although substantially valuable for the study of other aspects of Hilary's work, does not greatly contribute to understanding his approach to interpreting the Bible in particular. While studies of Hilary's handling of specific theological themes in his works and of the antecedents of his thought, which together occupy a substantial proportion of the literature, are useful topics of study in their own right, they are of only slight usefulness to our purposes.[208] Besides the fact that they do not attempt to discover the distinctive characteristics of Hilary's exegesis, these studies make no attempt to understand Hilary's aims in writing as he does, or comprehend the concerns that motivated Hilary to write. Hilary, unlike many of his students, is not concerned with doctrinal topics for their own sake, but with encouraging faith and attacking unbelief. More significantly, this chapter has also underscored that the question of the extent to which Hilary relies on allegorical or literal interpretation is relatively less important than other lines of enquiry. Hilary only occasionally uses allegory, and where he does, it is incidental to his purposes and merely illuminates other, more important features of his work. Besides being more integral to Hilary's own exegesis, it is pre-

---

207. Such is the suggestion of Beckwith, *Hilary of Poitiers on the Trinity*, 188.

208. I am referring to studies in the vein of Newlands, *Hilary*, and Burns, *Christology* at this point.

cisely these other features—his concern with real events, his monosemy, the manner in which he uses typological logic, his strict adherence to applying the theological themes of the narrative to contemporary realities and his single-minded concern with the issue of faith—that makes Hilary's exegesis distinct from that of his contemporaries. The focus of scholarship on Hilary's use of the allegorical and literal senses detracts attention away from the salient characteristics of his exegesis that have been noted above. A better approach would be to examine his work in the light of its Latin antecedents, as some scholars have done,[209] and to place relatively less emphasis on the senses of Scripture.

---

209. E.g. Jacobs, "Western Roots," 198–200; Tevel, "Vineyard," 360, 368; Burns, *Christology*, 21–22.

4

Through the Eyes of the Evangelist
Ambrose's Expositio Evangelii Secundam Lucam

THE CASES OF JEROME and Hilary illustrate the fact that the critical factors for distinguishing among Latin exegetes lie not in the realm of the extent to which their work is allegorical or literal, but instead in terms of how they score against other criteria. Both of the authors studied so far are essentially interested in the literal sense, but willing to make substantial use of allegory when it suits their purposes, a fact which is of little value to modern scholars in distinguishing between the two interpretative approaches. However, in other respects they are quite different. While Jerome is mostly interested in the details of the text before him, Hilary is almost exclusively focused on the realities that lie behind the text. All that Hilary does is directed at driving home a particular practical-theological theme to his audience, while Jerome's work betrays relatively little unity of purpose and only slight, occasional interest in either practical or theological/doctrinal matters. Hilary avoids polysemy while Jerome is quite comfortable exploring multiple possibilities within the text.

Ambrose's *Expositio evangelii secundum Lucam* provides an opportunity to explore these issues within the context of a considerably longer and more complex primary source. As with Jerome and Hilary, Ambrose's exegesis has been viewed primarily in terms of the framework of the senses of Scripture and is regarded as heavily allegorical, as the survey of Ambrosian scholarship that follows illustrates. This chapter therefore begins by questioning whether it is fair to assess Ambrose's work as largely allegorical in the case of the selected sample of his work. His *Expositio evangelii secundum Lucam* is then evaluated in terms of the key exegetical differences which have been established between Jerome and Hilary in the previous two chapters: the extent to which Ambrose focuses on the text, the realities behind the text, or some other point of interest, his approach to polysemy and use of other passages of Scripture in his exposition, his attitude towards his audience, and his development of theological themes and ideas through his exegesis. Firstly, however, this examination must be set against past perceptions of Ambrose's exegesis.

Scholarly Conclusions

A substantial portion of the scholarship relating to Ambrose's exegesis examines it within the framework of the literal-allegorical distinction, and tends to characterize his work as heavily allegorical and best understood in terms of the Alexandrian influences acting directly and indirectly on the man himself. This is true both of analysis of his exegesis in general, and of commentary on his *Expositio evangelii secundum Lucam* in particular. Instances of the former are prominent among the major reference works relating to patristics. For example, the article on Ambrose in the *Theologische Realenzyklopädie* summarizes his exegesis by noting that "Ambrose stands in the tradition of Alexandrian theology, with very occasional forays into literal interpretation in the Antiochene style."[1] The *Encyclopaedia of Early Christianity* offers a similar summary: "[i]nfluenced by Philo and Origen, he accepted a threefold interpretation of the scriptural text (i.e. literal, moral, allegorical), and he was fond of typology."[2] In the article on "Luke" in the same publication, another contributor evaluates Ambrose's commentary in terms of its being "an amalgam of the two tendencies expressed by the schools of Antioch and Alexandria," concluding that his work is best summarized along the following lines: "Presupposing the historical and literal interpretation, he prefers symbolic and allegorical exegesis."[3] Even Kannengeisser's more recent major work on patristic interpretation approvingly quotes the old

---

1. Dassmann, "Ambrosius von Mailand," 374: "Ambrosius steht in der Tradition de altchristlich-abendländischen Theologie, was sich allerdings weniger in literarischen Abhängigkeiten äußert."

2. Swift, "Ambrose," 42. Another description along these lines can be found in McKim, *Handbook*, 11.

3. Perretto, "Luke the Evangelist," 511.

summary provided in Quasten's *Patrology* by Mara, that "[f]ollowing Philo and Origen, Ambrose accepts the triple sense of Scripture: literal, moral, and allegorical/mystical. In reality, an allegorical exegesis of a typological and moral character prevails in his works."[4] While, as we shall see, there is much truth to some of these comments, the point to note here is that even this latest of serious major works in the field has not moved very far from the old framework. In Kannengeisser's own words, "Ambrose's exegesis is entirely structured by the threefold sense of Scripture popularized by Origen."[5]

Many specialized works on Ambrose also analyze his work within the same framework and tend towards the same conclusions of strongly allegorical exegesis after the tradition of Alexandria. This was virtually the standard view among older modern accounts, such as that of de Lubac[6] and Paredi, who argues that "Ambrose's exegesis is primarily allegorical,"[7] and Malden, who goes so far as to assume that "more than any other figure he established allegorism in the West."[8] More recently, Pizzolato suggests that Ambrose's exegesis can be understood in terms of a categorization in Ambrose's mind of Scripture into different parts, which can variously be read allegorically, literally, or typologically.[9] Case studies on other parts of the Ambrosian exegetical corpus, such as de Labriolle's examination of the sermon on Psalm 118, also tend to examine his work within this framework.[10] While some scholars recognize that other factors are also important, they still prefer to interpret them within the context of the traditional approach. For example, Simonetti believes that the pastoral dimension of Ambrose's work is the most important, but

4. Kannengeisser, *Handbook*, 1046, quoting from Mara, "Ambrose of Milan, Ambrosiaster and Nicetas," 164.
5. Kannengeisser, *Handbook*, 1051.
6. Lubac, *Medieval*, 1:154.
7. Paredi, *Ambrose*, 260.
8. Malden, "St Ambrose as an Interpreter of Holy Scripture," 509–22.
9. Pizzolato, *La dottrina esegetica di sant'Ambrogio*, 328. This framework is developed from a small number of references where Ambrose could possibly be construed as dividing Scripture up in this way, one of which occurs in the selection under study here, at Ambrose, *Lucam*, 118, on how the four evangelists should be interpreted differently. However, even granting that these references mean what Pizzolato assumes, it must still be proven that this framework is actually applied consistently by Ambrose across all of his exegesis rather than only on a few occasions associated with the identified references.
10. Labroille, "Saint Ambrose et l'éxègese allegorique," 591–603.

he sets it within the context of allegory: "Alexandrian spiritual allegorism is for him congenial and easily developed along ascetic, moral and exhortatory lines."[11]

Some scholars have also placed considerable emphasis in attempting to understand Ambrose's exegesis on the basis of the brief description of his preaching in Augustine's *Confessiones*,[12] where Ambrose is said to "remove the veil of mystery and expose the spiritual meaning of things which taken literally would have seemed to teach perverse things."[13] This has led some scholars to emphasize Ambrose's use of allegorical interpretation as his main influence on later exegetes such as Augustine, suggesting that this is the salient feature of his exegesis.[14] Another proposal is that of Pasini, who argues that Ambrose normally paid little attention in his sermons to the literal sense and instead would move directly to the moral and spiritual senses, because in the context of the liturgical service he presupposed that the congregation had already heard and noted the literal significance of the text when it was read at an earlier point in the liturgy.[15]

Another, arguably more central foundation of such an understanding of Ambrose is the fact that his exegesis has traditionally been regarded as heavily dependent on the Alexandrian approach and key commentators within that tradition. Certainly, that Ambrose was quite familiar with the exegetical works of various Alexandrian authors and at times made substantial borrowings (at least indirectly, if not word-for-word) from them cannot be denied.[16] The extent of this connection is underlined by the fact that Ambrose is not only familiar with Christian Alexandrian authors, notable enough for a Latin writer, but also the fountainhead of the Alexandrian tradition, Philo. As Runia notes in his study on the use of Philo by the early church, "no church Father makes as extensive and detailed use of Philo's writings as Ambrose does."[17] Corsato argues in considerable detail that similarities between Ambrose, Cyril of Jerusalem, and Origen indicate that Ambrose drank heavily from the

---

11. Simonetti, *Interpretation*, 89.
12. Augustine, *Confessiones*, 6.4.6 (PL 32:0722).
13. E.g. Margerie, *Introduction*, 3:12.
14. Rollero, *Expositio*, 108.
15. Pasini, *Ambrose of Milan*, 203.
16. Bray, *Interpretation*, 90 and 107 summarizes the arguments for this well, concluding that the influence of Greek exegesis in Ambrose's exegesis is "prominent."
17. Runia, *Philo in Early Christian Literature: A Survey*, 292.

Alexandrian stream, and Origen in particular, even though he was not necessarily familiar with those Alexandrian authors who were his own contemporaries.[18] The extent of this influence on Ambrose's exegesis has led some scholars to suggest that Ambrose's exegesis is largely an application of Eastern, Alexandrian allegorical techniques within a Latin context. For example, Kelly posits that Ambrose, together with Hilary and others, is a representative of an "imported Alexandrian approach" in the West, in contrast to what he designates as an "authentically Latin approach."[19] While it will be argued at some length in the body of this chapter that there are more useful ways of categorizing Ambrose's exegesis with respect to its differences from other examples of Latin exegesis, it should be noted here that Ambrose's strong familiarity with Alexandrian exegesis does not entail such a conclusion. Kelly assumes that Ambrose used Alexandrian material uncritically, but this may not have been the case. Indeed, as Pizzolato's lengthy study on Ambrose's exegetical works suggests, Ambrose does not use his sources indiscriminately.[20]

Scholars commenting on Ambrose's *Expositio evangelii secundum Lucam* have tended to analyze it in similar terms to his work in general. Simonetti's summary is firmly in this mold, evaluating the work in terms of the framework of the senses of Scripture and concluding that it is largely allegorical: "His *Expositio in Lucam* (which also makes room for literal interpretation) shows his preference for allegory. Ambrose normally distinguishes between the literal, moral and mystical (spiritual) senses, but like Origen, gives greatest importance to the last."[21] Also, the reference in the prologue of the work to the three senses has led some to assume that the whole work ought to be read primarily in terms of this schema.[22] Ramsey argues in this vein, suggesting that "Ambrose discusses the literal sense of Luke, and as often as possible, then passes on to its moral and mystical senses, which he refers to respectively in the Prologue."[23] Rusch suggests that Ambrose's aim in the work is to develop a Gospel harmony, by means of allegory, and thereby explain the differences between the

---

18. Corsato, *Expositio*, 266–77.
19. Kelly, "Bible," 48.
20. Pizzolato, *Esegetica*, 335. See also: Jacob, "Reception," 690.
21. Simonetti, *Interpretation*, 89.
22. See Ambrose, *Lucam*, Prol., 2.
23. Ramsey, *Ambrose*, 60. Bellifemine also argues in the same vein, "Due ipotesti," 41–44.

four evangelists.[24] Some commentators consider that the work is less allegorical than others of Ambrose, but still evaluate it within the same familiar framework, such as Bray, who suggests that Ambrose usually followed the allegorizing tendencies of Origen, that the work on Luke "sticks more closely to the text than is usual with Ambrose."[25]

Again, a key assumption lying behind this view of Ambrose is that of Alexandrian dependence, inevitably leading to slavish imitation of the Alexandrian method. Since Jerome's day it has been recognized that the commentary owes a considerable debt to Origen.[26] Indeed, the general assumption amongst scholars has been that Ambrose's borrowings were very substantial and often word-for-word, a view widely disseminated by several influential works.[27] However, again it must be stressed that such a fact does not necessarily have to constitute the key to understanding Ambrose's own work on Luke. The possibility that Ambrose may have arranged and adapted Origen's work to suit his own distinctive purposes must be allowed for, particularly if some of the evidence suggests this possibility. While little detailed work has been done considering this matter, it is significant that Guinot briefly discusses how Ambrose's more "Western" originality is evident in how he handles some themes in the crucifixion texts. Specifically, he observes that Ambrose gives a more central role to the crucifixion accounts in his exposition of Luke than Greek Fathers typically do, and emphasizes the suffering Christ relatively more than the glorified Christ.[28] From this, and a summary consideration of other elements of Ambrose's work, Guinot argues that while Ambrose did borrow heavily from the Greeks, the themes he chooses to discuss demonstrate strong "Western" or "Roman" elements as well.[29] Likewise, Campenhausen recognizes some degree of complexity in Ambrose's work, in the form of increasing independence from Greek models over

---

24. Rusch, *Fathers*, 50.

25. Bray, *Interpretation*, 90.

26. Adkin, "Jerome on Ambrose," 13. Interestingly, Adkin argues that Jerome's criticism of Ambrose through his translation of Origen's commentary on Luke is not meant to suggest that Ambrose was a plagiarist so much as to simply show that his exegesis was inept.

27. Most notably Smalley, *Bible*, 20, and Altaner, *Patrology*, 447. The latter goes so far as to describe Ambrose as being "completely dependent" on Origen through large sections of the work.

28. Guinot, "L'exégèse," 156–7.

29. Guinot, "L'exégèse," 146.

time and growing emphasis on the practical and ethical admonition of the congregation "reaching a climax in his expositions of the Psalms and Luke's Gospel which date from the last ten years of his life."[30] Old's brief study on Ambrose's treatment of Luke 4–5 concludes that Ambrose, although borrowing substantially from Origen, consistently adds his own spin even to the material he has taken from this source, and that his practical application of such material to his audience in particular is very much his own.[31] Furthermore, the most detailed modern treatment of the matter of Origenistic dependence, that of Peuch and Hadot, casts some doubt upon the idea that Ambrose was heavily and uncritically dependent upon Origen. Instead, they conclude that he seldom quotes Origen word-for-word without alteration and adaptation, and is not really dependent upon him for exact interpretations, only for general ideas.[32] While not an overwhelming quantity of scholarship, such findings do suggest that Ambrose, in spite of his use of Origen's Gospel commentaries, may have done so with considerable independence of mind and in order to support his own distinctive purposes, and that his own works on Luke deserve to be evaluated in their own right and on their own terms, independently of any sources that he may have used.[33]

Before turning to undertake this task, however, it should also be noted that two major works have been written on Ambrose's *Expositio evangelii secundum Lucam* in the past two decades. The first of these, Celestino Corsato's, *La Expositio euangelii secundum Lucam di sant'Ambrogio* fits firmly within the tradition of scholarship described above. Corsato's argument is heavily dependent on the threefold distinction between literal/historical, moral, and allegorical/mystical senses; indeed it is the entire focus of part one of the book, which considers the rationale or hermeneutic of Ambrose's exegesis.[34] "'Historical, moral, and mystical'— these represent the three means of comprehending Scripture."[35] Corsato

30. Campenhausen, *Fathers*, 94.

31. Old, *The Reading and Preaching of the Scriptures*, 302–4.

32. Puech and Hadot, "L'Entretien d'Origène avec Heraclide et le commentaire de Saint Ambrose sur l' Évangile de Saint Luc," 204–34.

33. Certainly, widespread recognition of Ambrosian borrowing of non-Christian classical authors has not led scholars to suggest that here, as with the Christian materials he has used, Ambrose is merely an uncritical mouthpiece for his sources: Kannengeisser, *Handbook*, 1051.

34. Corsato, *Expositio*, 13–64, esp. 25–30.

35. Corsato, *Expositio*, 282: "Storico, morale e mistico—queste rappresentano i

argues that it is Ambrose's view that "the letter is the primary sense, but it is superficial: the spiritual is the sense in which God reveals his great mysteries."[36] Part two of the work is also thoroughly rooted in the traditional method. It considers how Ambrose's *Expositio* explores the truths symbolically pointed out by the biblical text, preeminently through use of the Alexandrian, allegorical method with its interest in the symbolic significance of etymologies and numbers.[37] Part three of the study examines Ambrose's sources, and concludes that he was strongly dependent on Origen's commentary on Luke for both terminology and themes (if not for direct quotations),[38] and to a lesser extent by other earlier Alexandrians,[39] but that he was probably not much influenced by contemporary Alexandrians.[40]

The second recent major work on Ambrose on Luke, Graumann's *Christus Interpres: Die Einheit von Auslegung und Verkündigung in der Lukaserklärung des Ambrosius von Mailand* has less relevance for this study. It primarily focuses on how Ambrose uses his expositions to develop and expound his Christology. In terms of how to read Ambrose on Luke, Graumann recommends—not surprisingly, given his subject matter—that the work is best understood with Christ as its guiding theological and methodological principle.[41] However, the means by which Graumann sees Ambrose reaching this conclusion are quite traditional. Ambrose's reliance on and reaction to other interpreters, particularly Origen, is seen as a key influence on his christological readings.[42] Allegory is portrayed as one of the major means by which the text is interpreted in terms of doctrines about Christ, in chapter 4.

---

tre il modo di capire le sacre Scrittura."

36. Corsato, *Expositio*, 280: "la lettera e il senso primo, ma e superficiale—lo spirito e il senso in cui Dio rivela sui misteri elevati."

37. A long section is devoted to the significances of numbers, and an even longer one to the symbolism of names, particularly of animals and plants. Corsato, *Expositio*, 73–119 and 119–75. Cf. 284.

38. Corsato, *Expositio*, 185–95.

39. By Eusebius in particular and Philo, Basil, and Didymus at a general level. Corsato, *Expositio*, 183–4.

40. Corsato, *Expositio*, 266–77. Most similarities here can be regarded as due to both authors having been influenced by Origen.

41. Graumann, *Christus Interpres*, particularly chapters 4–6.

42. Graumann, *Christus Interpres*, chapters 1 and 3. Cf. Lenox-Conyngham, "Review of: La Expositio euangelii secundum Lucam di sant' Ambrogio," 780–2.

How accurate is this view, exemplified by Corsato and Graumann, of Ambrose's exegesis? It will be argued below that other categories of thought beyond "allegorical" and "literal," such as those identified in the previous two chapters, can offer additional purchase in understanding the distinctive character of Ambrose's exegesis. However, the common contention that Ambrose's exegesis is heavily allegorical must first be examined in light of his handling of the latter chapters of Luke, and in the case of this example at least, be shown to be substantially inaccurate.

Allegory

It cannot be denied that Ambrose does make frequent use of allegorical, or "mystical" interpretation as he calls it, in his exposition of the final chapters of Luke. In the 133 verses under study here, thirty-five cases of allegorical interpretation or of related kinds of symbolism occur. This fact alone establishes that Ambrose certainly does make frequent use of allegory. However, the weight that it bears is another matter. Almost all the examples that do occur are very brief and simple.[43] By no means does allegory hold his exposition together. Indeed, whole sections pass without allegory making any appearance at all.[44] A typical example of how Ambrose uses allegory briefly and in a manner that is not integral to his exposition, is his explanation of the injunction to Mary not to touch Christ, of which he simply says "[s]urely she is justly prohibited to touch the Lord, for not in the flesh do we touch Christ, but by faith we touch Him."[45] He then continues straight on with discussing the second half of the verse, "[f]or I have not yet ascended to my Father," without reference to the allegory that has been identified.[46] Elsewhere, such brief allegories are even more disconnected from the flow of the Gospel and, more no-

---

43. Space does not permit all of the relevant instances to be listed; for some further examples beyond those discussed here, see: Ambrose, *Lucam*, X, 107, 109 and 144. The biggest exception to the rule occurs at 124–5, but even this does not extend beyond ten lines.

44. E.g. Ambrose, *Lucam*, X, 121–2; 125–7; 129–33; 146–50; 152–4; 161–2; 168–76; 180–4.

45. Ambrose, *Lucam*, X, 155, on John 20:17. Augustine, *In Ioh.*, 121.3, by contrast, interprets this verse without reference to allegory, and connects his comments more closely together.

46. This particular idea of "touching Christ" is again alluded to briefly at Ambrose, *Lucam*, X, 160.

tably, from that of Ambrose's own exposition, such as his short note on the burial of Christ: "And they bound the body of Jesus as is the custom of the Jews, not of the wicked, but in faith they bound and they placed Him in a garden [tomb], which is often compared to the Church, that has righteous trees and flowers of diverse merits."[47] The passing allegorical reference to the church does not follow directly from the fact that Christ was bound after the custom of the Jews, in faith, or from what precedes the quoted excerpt, a discussion of previous references to Joseph of Arimathea and Nicodemus. The allegory is equally incidental to the discussion which follows it, of the fact that the tomb is new and undisturbed.[48] This frequently occasional character of Ambrose's allegorizing, together with the brevity of almost all instances of allegorical interpretation, leaves Ambrose's work with a rather literal flavor.

The character of Ambrose's allegorizing in his *Expositio evangelii secundam Lucam* further reinforces this. It is almost all based on the literal sense and not disconnected from it.[49] That is to say, it relies on or assumes some kind of basic understanding of the passage that does not depend upon symbolism, but more on its "plain" meaning. Thus, even Ambrose's longest allegory, on Jesus' drinking the wine mixed with gall, is entirely based on a literal distinction within the text, that Jesus is here recorded as not drinking the mixed wine, but elsewhere is recorded as drinking unmixed wine.[50] Later, that Jesus' death was not ordinary is symbolized by the factual description of the nature of his blood. Here, the basis of the allegory is the failure of Christ's blood to congeal, "[f]or certainly in our case after the death of our bodies the blood congeals, however out of his body it is allowed to remain uncorrupted."[51] Almost all of Ambrose's allegories are based on the literal sense in this way.[52] The reason for this is that Ambrose's exegesis is heavily focused on the literal realities that lie behind the text, rather than details of the

---

47. Ambrose, *Lucam*, X, 139, on John 19:40–41.

48. Ambrose, *Lucam*, X, 140, on John 19:41.

49. Pizzolato, Esegetica, 322, and Lubac, *Medieval*, 2:59 draw a similar conclusion from other Ambrosian texts.

50. Ambrose, *Lucam*, X, 124. In Matthew's Gospel, Jesus is recorded as refusing to drink wine mixed with gall (Matt 27:34), whereas in John's Gospel, Jesus is recorded as drinking wine with no reference to gall attached (John 19:29).

51. Ambrose, *Lucam*, X, 135, on John 19:34.

52. The only clear exception being the numerological allegory at Ambrose, *Lucam*, X, 139, on Luke 2:53.

text itself. Before allegorizing, he must therefore engage with the literal meaning of the events behind the text, rather than simply jumping off into allegory from the mere presence of a key word. However, this aspect of Ambrose's exegesis will be discussed in detail later in this chapter.

Literal Exposition and Manner of Proceeding through the Text

The simplest reason why Ambrose's *Expositio evangelii secundam Lucam* is best not characterized as highly allegorical is that so much of his interpretation is purely literal, without any symbolism being developed from it. Most of Ambrose's exegesis consists of simply running through the literal details presented in the Gospel, without any allegorization.[53] Typical is the following passage on the women's discovery of the resurrection:

> Afterwards the chief priests and the assembly of the elders confirm the fact that it was night by saying to the guards: "say that His disciples came at night and stole His body while you were sleeping." For later, when they learnt from the guards [what had happened], they put out a false story. And certainly John has "early in the morning, while it was still dark," Mary Magdalene had come to John and Peter at once both proclaiming and yet still ignorant of the fact of the Resurrection which she had brought to their attention; certainly in any case, if the evening approached it would have been immediately possible for the events of the day to become known.[54]

There is nothing remarkable about this excerpt. Ambrose's aim is the rather down-to-earth goal of determining the actual timing of the events described, and he achieves it without using symbolism to digress to other matters. Similar to this example is his discussion of the number of the disciples, where he is content to identify who and how many were present at the various post-resurrection appearances, even though references to the numbers "eleven" and "twelve" would have provided Ambrose with tantalizing opportunities for allegorization.[55]

---

53. As well as the examples given below, see also Ambrose, *Lucam*, X, 129 and 175.

54. Ambrose, *Lucam*, X, 152, on Luke 24:1, with reference to Matt 28:12–13 and John 20:1.

55. Ambrose, *Lucam*, X, 183, on Luke 24:33.

The same approach is evident in how Ambrose underscores that Luke records Christ as having been buried, not by the apostles, but by Joseph and Nicodemus, two respected Jews not directly connected to the group: "Therefore the place [tomb] was built against criticism, and thus the testimony of the Jews is defeated, for if the apostles had buried Him they would surely said that He was not in the tomb, and claimed that He had been carried off."[56] His explanation for the actions of the women who attended Jesus tomb is equally simple, down-to-earth and devoid of symbolism: "the devout women stood at a distance for a long time, but, because they are devout, they watched the place diligently, in order to bring perfume and anoint Him . . . although they had steadfastness, they did not have attentiveness."[57] They remain watching for some time because they wanted to anoint his dead body, not see him rise, and therefore they are loyal but not sufficiently attentive to Christ's words.[58]

A significant proportion of Ambrose's exegesis consists of addressing difficulties which he identifies in the account. Most of these are literal difficulties, such as unexplained details and apparent contradictions between the evangelists. Furthermore, these are almost always resolved literally, through careful observation of the literal details of the text and application of clear thinking.[59] As Ambrose himself puts it, "the holy apostle taught us to look for the secret of the truth in the simplicity of the history."[60] Thus, Christ is seen to forgive Mary's initial doubting after the resurrection, at first a problem to Ambrose's mind in light of his sterner approach to Thomas, since her "doubting is allowed because she did not take [Him] to be the body of Christ due to His having taken to Himself the glory of the resurrection, so that He appeared to be different from

---

56. Ambrose, *Lucam*, X, 136, on John 19:38–42.

57. Ambrose, *Lucam*, X, 144, on Luke 23:49.

58. See also Ambrose, *Lucam*, X, 113, 153 and 169.

59. Contrary the suggestion that Ambrose "repeatedly resolves apparent contradictions through symbolism": Moorhead, *Ambrose*, 90.

60. Ambrose, *Lucam*, III, 28. Curiously, Lubac, *Medieval*, 2:83 quotes the same sentence as a clear proof of Ambrose's determination to express allegorical interpretations (he believed that all of Ambrose's allegories were developed from the literal sense). However, Ambrose here does not use any of the terms that de Lubac associates in *Medieval*, 2:25 with the allegorical sense: "Docuit enim nos Apostolus sanctus in simplicitate historiae secretum quaerere veritatis." If Ambrose were here speaking of the allegorical sense as de Lubac suggests, might we not have expected him to say "mysterium" rather than "secretum"?

Jesus."⁶¹ Given that in the post-resurrection accounts it is quite apparent that Jesus' body was changed in some way (he could live although sporting the scars of mortal wounds and was able to enter through closed doors: John 20:19–20), Ambrose's interpretation here does not ask the reader to make an extraordinary, intuitive leap to meet his own conclusion, and certainly betrays no reliance on symbolism.

A little earlier, he resolves (at least to his own satisfaction) the question of whether the women knew of Christ's resurrection at a particular point by recourse to simple logic, reasoning that "[a]ccording to John, Mary Magdalene did not know, but according to Matthew, Mary Magdalene and the other Mary did know. Surely to know before and then to not know afterwards is not possible. For if there were several Marys, there were possibly also several Magdalenes, since with the names of such people it may be the name of a place."⁶² Ambrose posits this rather doubtful historical solution even though he could presumably have advanced any number of allegorical alternatives which would have been less patently deficient.

Ambrose is also exercised by the fact that in some passages, Peter alone is described as seeing the risen Lord, and in others Peter together with various disciples. This difficulty is also resolved literally:

> For how could they speak of Peter alone seeing, if many saw Him? But just as out of the women Mary and the other Mary [Magdalene] were first, so Peter also remains the first from among the men to see. And Paul has this: "for I passed on to you that Christ died according to the Scriptures and was buried and that He rose on the third day and was seen by Peter." And therefore Mark in particular set down that directing of the women to say to "Peter and the other disciples" that the Lord has risen.⁶³

Ambrose suggests that the apparent contradiction can be resolved by recognizing that Peter was probably the first, but was followed shortly afterwards by the other male disciples. Differences appear because the various biblical writers describe this in different ways. The implication is that Paul, in mentioning Peter alone, is certainly not implying that he was the only witness, but in a sense representative, just as the two

---

61. Ambrose, *Lucam*, X, 162, on John 20:11–18. Cf. Augustine's similar treatment, *In Ioh.*, 121.5.

62. Ambrose, *Lucam*, X, 153, with reference to John 20:1–2 and Matt 28:1–9.

63. Ambrose, *Lucam*, X, 173, with reference to Luke 24:34 and Mark 16:7.

Marys were representative of all the women who Ambrose believed saw the risen Christ.[64] Mark comes closest to the truth of the matter, and so his account is given the final word by Ambrose. Again, even in this more complex example, a difficulty is resolved without recourse to allegory, even though Ambrose might have chosen to advance other, less literal explanations by developing the symbolic potential of key terms in the account such as "seeing" or "first."[65]

Typology

As well as concentrating on the literal sense, contrary to what some scholars suggest, even when Ambrose does seek out a deeper or "spiritual" meaning in the Gospel he does not necessarily resort to traditional allegory, but prefers to make use of typology, that form of spiritual exegesis which is most grounded in the historical and literal context of the narrative. In this respect he is similar to both Jerome and Hilary. Although typological connections do not occur as frequently in Ambrose as in Jerome, they are utilized often enough to form a significant part of his exposition, and he consciously seeks to connect the Old and New Testaments: "you see that the whole series of the old law was a type of the one to come."[66] One typological theme that recurs repeatedly is the idea of Christ as the second Adam.[67] Several details in the Gospel account are interpreted in the light of this concept, such as the fact that Christ was crucified "naked ... for it had been Adam's habit to live without clothes. He who conquered put down clothes ... the first man had lived in paradise in this manner, and so too the second man entered into paradise in this way."[68] Ambrose further notes that Golgotha is regarded among some Jews as the place of Adam's burial, the place of humanity's first "death" as well as where death is ended by the death of the second Adam.[69]

---

64. Cf. the example just given, Ambrose, *Lucam*, X, 153.

65. Further such examples can be found at Ambrose, *Lucam*, X, 122, 154, 179.

66. Ambrose, *Lucam*, II, 56.

67. An idea also given significant attention by Jerome, *Math.*, IV, 1679–85, on Matt 27:34.

68. Ambrose, *Lucam*, X, 110, on Luke 23:34.

69. Ambrose, *Lucam*, X, 114, with reference to Matt 27:33 and parallels. A typological connection pointedly ruled out by Jerome, *Math.*, IV, 1656–80, who, as discussed in chapter 2, believed that Adam was in fact buried at Hebron rather than at Calvary.

Similarly, Ambrose sees the prominent place given to the women in the resurrection accounts as echoing the role of Eve in the fall narrative of Genesis 3: "For just as, at the beginning, a woman was the cause of man's sin, now that man's sin is avenged [a woman], having been the first to taste death, was the first in line to see remedy of sins . . . and the fall and suffering of the womb was compensated for by her discovery of the resurrection. By the mouth of woman death had previously entered, and so by the mouth of woman was life restored."[70] Both woman's being first to know of the resurrection, and her being the first to proclaim it by her mouth, are seen to have typological relationships to details of the Genesis 3 account, that Eve tasted the forbidden fruit first, and that her words afterwards persuaded her husband to follow her example.[71] Other typological connections receive more occasional usage than these two themes from the primeval prehistory, such as the suffering of Christ being prefigured by the persecutions and martyrdoms of the Old Testament prophets.[72]

Prophecy-Fulfillment

Like Hilary, and unlike Jerome, Ambrose does not particularly stress the fulfillment of Old Testament prophecies in the Gospel account. While this may be due to the Lukan narrative offering fewer opportunities than Matthew to identify such instances, this is unlikely, firstly, because Ambrose throughout his *Expositio evangelii secundum Lucam* certainly does not focus exclusively on Luke, but devotes almost as much time to John and Matthew, both full of references to fulfilled prophecy, and secondly, because he passes over even some of the direct references in Luke without comment, such as the quotation from Hosea 10:8 at Luke 23:30.[73] Lastly, Ambrose does not seem as interested as Jerome or Hilary in the fulfillment of prophecy. Only once does he see in the contents of the Gospel eschatological prophetic significance, when the resurrection of Christ is

---

70. Ambrose, *Lucam*, X, 156, with reference to John 20:11-18. and Gen 3:6. Hilary draws exactly the same typological conclusion, *Matt.*, 33.9.

71. A further connection is made between Eve and Mary at Ambrose, *Lucam*, X, 157.

72. Ambrose, *Lucam*, 122, X, which is similar to the typology of Hilary, *Matt.*, 33.3.

73. Ambrose, *Lucam*, X, 107-9.

described as heralding the resurrection of all at the end of time.[74] The only two cases of Jesus' own words being fulfilled within the account, like eschatological prophecy and typology a common observation in Hilary, occur right at the end of his work, when he is discussing the various post-resurrection appearances of Christ. However, these instances have little impact on the whole. The first is only a passing reference to Jesus' promise that the disciples would see angels descending and ascending on him (John 1:51), which is left undeveloped.[75] In the second, Ambrose goes back to the detail of the words spoken earlier about Jesus' reappearing after death to settle otherwise problematic claims of a possible discrepancy in the fact that Jesus appeared to the disciples at a number of places as well as in Galilee as promised.[76] While, as will be seen below in the section on audience, Ambrose does frequently relate the events of the Gospel to contemporary times, he never does this by claiming that the words of the text are prophetic for the church, and only very occasionally may be considered to be drawing typological connections between Gospel events and contemporary realities.[77]

Hence Ambrose, like the other commentators considered here, and contrary to what some modern scholars hold, is quite interested in the literal sense, but will often also use allegory when it suits his purposes. In terms of differentiating his exegesis from that of other later Latin Fathers, this tells us relatively little: much the same can be said of the work of Hilary, Jerome, and as will be seen, Augustine. We must therefore examine Ambrose's exegesis in light of other factors in order to find its most distinctive features. As with Hilary and Jerome, considering the extent to which Ambrose focuses on the text, the realities behind it, or some other point of reference, yields interesting conclusions.

Realities Behind the Text

Like Hilary, Ambrose has a strong preference for studying the real events, conversations, and personalities behind the Gospel text, rather than for the text itself. Unlike Jerome, he has virtually no interest in the philological features of the text, let alone any intention of using such features to

---

74. Ambrose, *Lucam*, X, 128.
75. Ambrose, *Lucam*, X, 181.
76. Ambrose, *Lucam*, X, 182, on Matt 28:10.
77. The only example that seems to fit here is at Ambrose, *Lucam*, X, 134.

drive his exposition. In spite of his fluency in the Greek language, he makes little use of the Greek text: in the relatively lengthy section of his work on Luke under consideration here, he makes only one passing reference to the Greek version.[78] In spite of his educational background, he never discusses the grammatical construction of the verses before him.[79] Furthermore, at no point does he engage in the kind of detailed word-studies that fascinated Jerome, and as will be seen in chapters 5 and 6, Augustine.[80] The closest that he comes to such activities are a few fleeting plays on words and a small number of instances where a key common word is used to move between different passages of Scripture.[81]

The primacy of Ambrose's focus on the realities depicted by the text is apparent in all the main activities which he engages in as he relates to the text. Thus, when he wishes to make a practical point, he usually does so by holding up a person or deed in the account as an example, such as when he refers to Christ's dialogue with the penitent thief (Luke 23:39–43) as "an excellent model of conversion to strive after."[82] He neither talks about conversion to faith in Christ by means of some allegory arising from a word in the text, nor does he use the construction of the words that pass between Christ and the thief as a pretext for discussing some matter remote to the actual event of the thief asking for, and receiving, gracious consideration from Christ. Similarly, he promotes confidence in the Christian's escape from judgment by God through reference to the fact, recorded in John 20:27, that Jesus still bore the scar marks from his crucifixion in his resurrected body, underlying that the price of the Christian's freedom always stands before God the Father in the form of these wounds.[83]

When he attempts to affirm doctrinal truths, it is again to the realities described by the Lukan text that Ambrose prefers to turn. Thus, speaking of the fact that Thomas is allowed to touch the risen Christ in

---

78. Ambrose, *Lucam*, X, 151, on Luke 24:1.

79. Contra Corsato, *Expositio*, 283, who suggests, without advancing any evidence from Ambrose's works, that linguistic-grammatical instruments are one of the major means by which his exegesis goes forward.

80. In this respect the selection from Ambrose under study here does not support McLynn's contention (*Ambrose*, 238) that such features are an important part of Ambrose's exegesis.

81. Pizzolato, *Esegetica*, 334.

82. Ambrose, *Lucam*, X, 121.

83. Ambrose, *Lucam*, X, 170.

John 20:27, even though he does not beforehand believe that Christ has been truly raised, Ambrose says that this event occurs because "by his touch he was destined to teach me, just as he also taught Paul 'for this corruption must put on incorruption' ... Thomas beheld and this caused him to understand ... that this body was able to enter through the impenetrable, was invisible and yet upon entering become visible, and was able to be touched easily and yet remain difficult to understand."[84]

As is the case with Hilary, Ambrose's focus on realities rather than on the text becomes most apparent on those occasions in the selection under study where he actually does use allegory.[85] Consider, for example, his interpretation of the robe placed on Christ by the soldiers when they mocked and beat him, and the subsequent division of his garments:

> Now consider Christ's divided vestments. What are these? In Matthew, there is a single scarlet cloak, in John a purple garment, in Mark a strong purple [garment], in Luke a white vestment ... those four parts are not parts of the clothes, but to me seem to be properties of his virtue. For one [evangelist] wrote concerning [Christ's] exalted rule, another concerning His actual custom. Luke chose for you the dignity of a priestly garment ... Therefore they divided the garments of Christ, either in order to wear [themselves] or to give away. However they did not divide the tunic, surely because it represents faith, which is not the portion of several, but justly is the right of all, and being undivided it remains whole. And it is appropriately said to be "woven from above," for thus faith in Christ is [accepted to be] woven, that from the divine to humanity He descended ... therefore it is significant for our faith that it is not divided, but remained whole.[86]

This excerpt contains three interrelated allegories, intended to point respectively to the properties of Christ's virtue indicated by each evangelist, the fact that faith remains the undivided property of all, and that Christ comes as divine, "from above" down to humanity. The key point to note

---

84. Ambrose, *Lucam*, X, 168.

85. C.f. Lubac, *Medieval*, 2, 86; Jacob, "Reception," 699.

86. Ambrose, *Lucam*, X, 117–20, with reference to Matt 27:28, Mark 15:17, Luke 23:11, John 19:2 and 19:23–24. Interestingly, Augustine applies the fact that the tunic remained undivided differently, to his own context: at *In Ioh.*, 13.3 he presents this aspect of the tunic in the narrative as an image of the unity of the church, and as such this biblical reference can be taken as speaking against the Donatists who would divide it. Cf. Houghton, *Augustine's Text of John*, 345.

is that each of these three allegories is based not merely on the words of the text, but also on the three real things that the text here describes, namely, the various garments that the evangelists describe him wearing, the retaining of the tunic as an undivided whole, and the particular type of tunic that was present, specifically, one woven from the top.[87]

That Ambrose lets himself be guided by his conception of the events behind the text, rather than the actual words, is further illustrated by his allegorization of Peter's being the first to enter the tomb: "Certainly he who came without fear . . . was the first to enter, as if receiving the keys of the kingdom, so that the others might know."[88] Here, the literal fact, reported by the text, that Peter is the first, as it were, to enter through the front door of Christ's temporary home, is taken to demonstrate symbolically that he is the one who receives the keys to Christ's "house," the kingdom. It is the event of Peter's primal entrance that establishes his prime position, not some incidental detail in the text.[89]

In the course of his exposition, Ambrose frequently finds it necessary to resolve apparent difficulties in the account, such as contradictions between the descriptions of the evangelists.[90] Both of the issues that he is responding to, and his manner of resolving them, further reflect his concern with the realities behind the text. For example, he is exercised by the fact that, according to John 20:17, the risen Jesus commanded Mary Magdalene not to touch him, while according to Matthew 28:9 the women touched and worshipped him. He asks "[h]ow therefore might this mystery be resolved, except by assuming that the four evangelists probably spoke about four different occasions, so that other women [were involved] and therefore there were more appearances [than is commonly assumed]."[91] However absurd this solution may seem to the modern mind, the element to note is that Ambrose considers the problem in terms of the events described. He does not entertain other possibilities relating more to the text, such as whether one or more text may

---

87. This example, and those which follow, contradict Pizzolato's suggestion that it is the philological characteristics of words which Ambrose mostly uses for developing allegories, *Esegetica*, 333.

88. Ambrose, *Lucam*, X, 145, with reference to John 20:4–6.

89. For further examples of allegories based on the events behind the narrative, cf. Ambrose, *Lucam*, X, 137 and 152.

90. Moorhead, *Ambrose*, 78.

91. Ambrose, *Lucam*, X, 148. Contrast with Jerome's more textual treatment at *Math.*, I, 1960–8, on Matt 28:9.

be incorrect, corrupted, or have so deliberately emphasized such different features of the one event that they appear contradictory.[92]

However, Ambrose is not as single-mindedly focused on the events described by the text as Hilary is. While, as noted above, this is where his primary focus lies, and unlike Jerome he largely ignores many textual features, he does intermittently allow his exposition to be guided by the text more than by the realities it points to. On a small number of occasions he uses a key word or the writer's choice of language to develop a simple allegory. Thus, at one point he notes that the weight of herbs and spices used in Jesus' burial "is the quantity of complete faith,"[93] at another notes that Christ's death, in effecting the eclipse of the sun, points to the darkening of the eyes of the faithless,[94] and lastly, argues that the good character attributed to Joseph and Nicodemus (those who buried Jesus) is symbolic of the purity of Christ's tomb.[95]

For the most part, however, Ambrose's usage of textual features to support his exegesis comes in the form of connections between the text at hand and other passages. Consider his handling of the splitting open of the rocks at Jesus' death, recorded in Matthew 27:51, where he observes that "[t]he rocks are broken open . . . that the power of the Word might pierce through rock—the One who easily finds his way out of those rocks, just as Jeremiah prophesied, that the Lord would not grow old."[96] Here we find a double allusion: apart from the reference to the fulfillment of Jeremiah 6:16, a connection is also made to Hebrews 4:12, where the word of God is seen as piercing through all to the very heart of humanity, which Ambrose adapts to describe how the dead Christ could not be held within his rocky tomb. He then develops a third point from the passage: "O hardened hearts of rock of the Jews! The rocks were split open, but in that hour their hearts were hardened [and] . . . tombs were opened, but the Jews remain fixed in hardness in a shaken earth."[97] He treats Christ's dying words in Luke 23:46, "Into your hands, Lord, I entrust my spirit" in like fashion, urging us to "notice that He 'entrusted' His spirit, that He

92. A similar example occurs at Ambrose, *Lucam*, X, 150.

93. Ambrose, *Lucam*, X, 139, with reference to John 19:39.

94. Ambrose, *Lucam*, X, 128, on Luke 23:44–45.

95. Ambrose, *Lucam*, X, 136, on John 38:40. The three examples just given are the only instances of text-driven allegory that I can identify, apart from Ambrose, *Lucam*, X, 151.

96. Ambrose, *Lucam*, X, 128.

97. Ambrose, *Lucam*, X, 128.

entrusted and did not send. [This is] good because the spirit is a pledge, a good deposit. As it is written: 'O Timothy, guard the good deposit.'"[98] Ambrose finds another, not immediately connected passage, 1 Timothy 6:20, where the "spirit" is spoken of, that also meets his purpose of referring to the Spirit in some sense eternally proceeding from Christ (going from him to others, the Father and Timothy, but not being "sent" in the sense of departure). In both these cases, he does not rely on a simple word study or the occurrence of the same term twice in different places: Ambrose's approach is more complex than this. In the first instance, multiple elements within the relevant verse are allowed to point out almost simultaneously multiple connections elsewhere; in the second, it is both the key idea as well as the key word that forms the link.[99] In this respect, his practice differs from the more direct method preferred by Jerome, who tends to use simpler, and normally solitary, textual connections between passages.

While such uses of textual features do occur in Ambrose, it should be stressed that his primary orientation is towards the realities described in the account, as argued above. Even in the first example just listed, he bases his commentary on the actual events of the earth being shaken and the tombs being opened. This is further illustrated by the fact that even when he does use textual elements to jump to other passages, the occasion is often a "real" problem lying behind the account, such as when he responds to the fact that Christ addresses a common thief from the cross before his mother, arguing that "it is not an absurd thing if [we remember that] He came first to make sinners saved—in my view His purpose was the duty to undertake to redeem and accomplish deliverance from sins. Just as He says: 'who is my mother and my brothers?' He did not come to call the just, but sinners."[100] While the actual connection is the reference in both passages to "Christ's mother," what sends Ambrose off foraging into another part of Scripture is not the mere existence of the connection, but the need to explain what Christ has in fact done.[101]

---

98. Ambrose, *Lucam*, X, 125.

99. Another instance occurs at Ambrose, *Lucam*, X, 141, playing on the use of the term "grave."

100. Ambrose, *Lucam*, X, 131. Ambrose assumes that the conversation recorded in Luke 23:39–43 occurs before the statement made in John 19:26. The reference to "my mother and my brothers" is from Luke 8:21.

101. See also Ambrose, *Lucam*, X, 161.

Indeed, his exposition at some points makes one wonder whether such movements between passages are primarily driven by attention to textual features, as with Jerome, or by extratextual connections in Ambrose's mind, such as common ideas or useful wordplays that happen to be paralleled in sets of passages. Consider how he uses Christ's resurrection body for insight into the nature of such bodies: "For indeed this body is touched; moreover we will rise in the body; 'for it is sown a fleshy body, but it is raised a spiritual body,' and what is more the former [body] is light, while the latter is dense, because it is hardened in quality by the nature of earthly stains."[102] Although the initial connection to 1 Corinthians 15:42 is an obvious one, Ambrose's slightly neoplatonic playing upon the idea of fleshy bodies being "dense"—developed into their being hardened—is not driven by the text at all so much as his own use of a term which he has introduced into the discourse.[103]

Authorial Distinctives

However, there is another, more important and frequently occurring respect in which Ambrose's primary focus on the real events sometimes shifts elsewhere. More so than Hilary or Jerome, he is conscious of the author's intentions in compiling the Gospel text. This awareness is not of the kind that has informed much exegesis over the past two centuries, since he never doubts the divine authorship and inerrancy of the text: his concerns are quite different to those of most of the schools of textual criticism.[104] Rather, working from the assumption of a single evangelist

102. Ambrose, *Lucam*, X, 169, with reference to John 20:27.

103. Cf. the example given above re Christ's Spirit, where the term "good" is extraneously introduced by Ambrose and just happens to reinforce the connection made between the "good deposit" entrusted to Timothy and the "good" words of Christ about committing his Spirit. See also the discussion of Peter, sin, and old age in Ambrose, *Lucam*, X, 177.

104. Like virtually all other premodern exegetes, Ambrose still believes that the biblical text provides immediate and genuine access to divine truth, whether he is interpreting from the Letter or the Spirit, whether this is expressed partially through conscious authorial intention or not. The intentions of the human authors still represent divine revelation above all—they are of interest to Ambrose because of what they say about divine realities behind the human intentions. By contrast, post-eighteenth-century interest in authorial intention seeks to understand it in terms of what it reveals about human factors behind conscious authorial intentions—factors such as the author's background, bias, and unconscious cultural or personal influences. Cf. Childs, "Critical Reflections on James Barr's Understanding of the Literal and the Allegorical,"

writing each Gospel, he simply asks some of the more basic questions common to literary criticism, which may be summarized in the form, "why has this particular evangelist chosen to present the material in this way?"

Ambrose's interest in the workings of the authors is particularly apparent in his treatment of divergences and contradictions between the four Gospels. Like the other commentators examined here, he is keen to defend the veracity of the accounts.[105] However, unlike them, he moves beyond merely establishing solutions for such problems—which activity Jerome and Augustine both devote more space to, on the whole—and towards an understanding of what each evangelist was trying to achieve in writing his account in his distinctive manner. Ambrose is more interested in appreciating the cause (the narrative approach of each evangelist) rather than explaining away the symptom (divergent accounts). The following excerpt shows his mind at work in this manner:

> And since our discourse [Luke] evades this [the disciples' rejoicing on meeting the risen Christ], we may consider that according to John the apostles having believed, rejoiced, according to Luke as if unbelieving they were confuted, thereupon they received the Spirit, and in this one [Luke] they were ordered to stay in the city until [they were] clothed with power from on high. It seems to me as if the greater and more senior apostle here follows with what comes next: the latter [John] uses a historical method; whereas the former [Luke] abridges; and because the latter [John] does not want doubt to be possible about this testimony, he [stresses] that his testimony is true. For in this regard also, this is to the credit of the evangelists, the suspicion of either carelessness or of error is driven back. For although at first Luke said they did not believe, afterwards he pointed out their believing. And if at first we consider that they [the accounts] are opposed, if the above follows, things are resolved so that they agree. Therefore we consider the words to be of the same Scripture.[106]

Here, the problem that Ambrose encounters is that Luke 24: 36–49 and John 20: 19–23 appear to differ as to when the disciples actually believe, after the resurrection. However, interestingly, this is not his starting

---

3–9.

105. Cf. Ambrose, "Select Works," V, XVII, 215: "He that is true cannot make a mistake".

106. Ambrose, *Lucam*, X, 171.

point, and he does not analyze the problem primarily in terms of either reconciling the two sets of events accounted or possible problems or misunderstanding surrounding the text. Rather, the method of each writer is the key factor: John gives the whole series of events at this point, while Luke truncates his narrative. Ambrose believes that Luke writes this way deliberately and is possibly even conscious of the hole that this leaves in his narrative: "afterwards he pointed out their believing." Likewise, John's defense of his testimony at the end of his Gospel (John 20:24) is taken as deliberately supporting his narrative strategy. The result, "therefore we consider the words to be of the same Scripture," is a foundational assumption for Ambrose even though it is presented at the conclusion of Ambrose's interpretation.

Later in his exposition, Ambrose continues to be exercised by Luke's decision to present data in his account that could be seen to cast doubt upon the fact of the disciples' having believed in Christ's resurrection. Concerning the disciples' unsettled response to the appearance of Christ to them in the closed room at Luke 24:36–43, he insists that there are

> ... so many examples of virtue linked together, that we are convinced that Peter could not have doubted. It is also clear that John believed when he saw the saviour [from John 21:7] ... Why therefore does Luke discuss the fact that they were troubled? ... afterwards, although Peter had believed concerning the Resurrection, he could nevertheless be troubled when he saw that the Lord appeared unexpectedly in bodily form in a room behind bolted doors and solid walls. Luke explores details historically. One [evangelist: John] contemplates the overall purpose of events, and the other [Luke] their sequential course.[107]

Here, Ambrose partly explains the discrepancy in terms of the reality behind the account, namely Peter's understandable ability to still be troubled after he believed in the face of unexpected and startling miraculous events. However, the main focus of his attention is, again, not on Peter but on Luke and on his descriptive method. In this example, Ambrose is interested in how Luke looks at each episode in the account in terms of its historical sequence and in so doing attempts to indicate something of the complex character of Peter's faith, which can still sometimes be described as "troubled."[108] This is seen to be in contrast to the "other"

---

107. Ambrose, *Lucam*, X, 179.

108. In contrast to Augustine, where the focus in on Peter's actual relationship to Christ, rather than on how this relationship is portrayed: *Serm.*, 237.4.

evangelist, who is potentially less confusing because he is more interested in the bottom line than the precise chronological order of the details.[109]

Elsewhere, Ambrose's interest in Luke's intentions is expressed more simply, in the form of observations on what the evangelist is trying to achieve in narrating certain things. In this manner he discusses the description given by Luke of Jesus' tomb: "And well was it said to be cut into rock, for this is in support of faith."[110] He similarly notes at which points after the resurrection the evangelists list the disciples as eleven or unnumbered, observing that this is done with intent, as for example in the case of Mark, where "regarding the disciples reclining at the table, Mark writes that there were eleven of them, in order to declare that by these [eleven] all the world is to be ordered to obedience."[111] Occasionally, Ambrose also assumes that Luke has presented material in a particular order in order to meet his particular purposes, and, unlike other interpreters under study here, he does not merely see the distinctive ordering of Luke's material merely as an opportunity to harmonize the Lukan account with the others.[112] Finally, we may consider Ambrose's understanding of what Luke was doing in briefly narrating Christ's opening of the disciples' minds so that they could understand the Scriptures (Luke 24:45): "At length the disciples were disquieted, so that, according to Luke, He [Christ] uncovers their perception [of the Scriptures], in order that they might understand the things that are written. This was done at great length, al-

---

109. The idea that the four evangelists wrote in different ways in order to draw out contrasting but complementary truths about Christ and responses to him in the reader holds a particular fascination for Ambrose. For example, in the prologue to this work (*Lucam*, Prol., 4), he argues that Luke, compared to the other three evangelists, "maintained as it were a certain historical order and revealed to us more of the Lord's wondrous deeds—yet in such a way that the history in this Gospel embraces the qualities of wisdom in its entirety" (translation from Ramsey, *Ambrose*, 162). For Ambrose, the three qualities of wisdom approximate to different senses of Scripture; this quoted statement is thus not to be taken as a suggestion that Ambrose feels himself restricted to the literal sense by Luke's "historical" approach—on the contrary, he feels that the character of Luke's interest in historical order and actual deeds opens up all kinds of interpretative possibilities!

110. Ambrose, *Lucam*, X, 143, on Luke 23:53.

111. Ambrose, *Lucam*, X, 183, on Mark 16:14.

112. Ambrose, *Lucam*, X, 131 and 135, on Luke 23:36-43 and Luke 23:44 respectively. By contrast, Augustine's interest in these two passages (Augustine, *In Ioh.*, 119.2. and 117.1-2 respectively) is only in resolving the differences between the Gospel accounts by making their contradictory timings line up historically, without considering the various authorial perspectives.

though it is but succinctly written that it not be doubted."[113] At this point Ambrose's focus is neither on the text itself nor on the events behind it. In fact, he appears to be quite conscious that the text and the events it attempts to describe are disjoined, that the text cannot hope to describe the events fully and that there is therefore a world of realities apart from and beyond that contained within the text. However, this awareness does not lend itself to any modern distinctions between word and text, but to an understanding of Luke's purposes that actually supports the veracity of the text. He has not included every detail because he wishes to provide an account that is to the point and therefore credible.

The foregoing analysis suggests that, while Ambrose has a strong focus on the realities behind the text, just as Hilary does, unlike Hilary he often allows his lens to shift backwards and forwards to view the Gospels in terms of other perspectives. He will sometimes use largely textual features to move to other, relatively unconnected biblical passages, and occasionally to enable allegorization, although by no means does he do this nearly as often, nor relying on the same breadth of textual devices and tools, as Jerome does. Importantly, he often chooses as his focus a perspective largely ignored by both Hilary and Jerome, namely, the narrative intentions of the author. His strong consciousness of the evangelists' role, in addition to that of the realities which they describe and the textual elements they use to do so, is a particularly distinctive characteristic of his exegesis. Furthermore, it is a feature of his work that has tended to be obscured by scholars emphasizing that he places a heavy emphasis on the divine authorship of Scripture,[114] or even suggesting, as Corsato does, that this is foundational to understanding his exegesis.[115] Certainly, by modern standards this is the case. However, such an assessment of his work is of little value in distinguishing him from his contemporaries, the overwhelming majority of whom shared his high views on the inspiration of Scripture, without paying nearly as much attention to the intentions of the human authors as Ambrose did. This has not been sufficiently recognized by modern scholarship, which at best has typically just noted that Ambrose considers that different biblical books major on historical, moral, or allegorical themes respectively.[116]

---

113. Ambrose, *Lucam*, X, 173.

114. E.g. Vawter, *Biblical Inspiration*, 25.

115. Corsato, *Expositio*, 279. Pizzolato, *Esegetica*, 327 provides a further example of such an approach.

116. E.g. Moorhead, *Ambrose*, 83. One partial exception is Pizzolato, *Esegetica*,

Polysemy and Monosemy

One consequence of this aspect of Ambrose's exegesis is that he is less inclined towards polysemy than Augustine, although like Jerome, he is certainly aware of other interpretative possibilities. His consciousness of the authors' intentions acts as a kind of brake on the exploration of multiple interpretations. This is not to say that he does not allow for the possibility of multiple interpretations. On a small number of occasions he puts forward two meanings of the verse at hand. For example, he says that the tearing of the veil in the temple at Jesus' death means "either the separation of the two peoples or the profanation of the mysteries of the synagogue."[117] Elsewhere, he attributes two meanings to the fact that Jesus is recorded in Luke 23:36 as having drunk wine, but elsewhere refused wine mixed with gall (Matthew 27:34): he did not drink the wine mixed with gall at the cross because "it was mixed with the bitterness of they that offered it," and also because the purity of his immortal nature is not mixed with the human mortality which had soured immortality under Adam.[118] However, in the whole selection under study here, these are the only two clear examples of Ambrose setting forth more than one meaning of an element of the account. Even in these two examples, he only notes the two interpretations briefly. In the first case he simply makes the passing statement quoted above, and in the second both possibilities together merit only a few lines of comment. In neither case does he attempt to tie the two options together, assess their relative merits, indicate a preference for one over the other, or explore any potential tension between them. He just notes them in passing and moves on, so that they have little impact on the broad direction of his exposition.

This is due at least in part to an apparent belief that whatever interpretations legitimately exist normally must have some basis in the mind of the original human author. Thus, at one point in his exposition, he notes that "John as it were wove together various meanings for our faith,"[119] although without actually setting forth what the various meanings are! Unlike Augustine and Jerome, for whom the emphasis in describing multiple meanings falls upon their usefulness to the task at hand in the

---

328 and chapter 4, who goes a little further and gives some recognition to Ambrose's consciousness of different literary genres in the Bible.

117. Ambrose, *Lucam*, X, 128, on Luke 23:45.
118. Ambrose, *Lucam*, X, 125.
119. Ambrose, *Lucam*, X, 118, on John 19:23.

sermon and on the speculative abilities of the expositor, for Ambrose the original human author has a role to play in setting forth multiple meanings, in the few cases where they are noteworthy. When discussing how Luke describes the crucifixion, he notes that the other Gospels add other details, which point to different meanings within the event, reminding us that "John is not idle in pointing out more things. Matthew and Mark also wrote the following [details]."[120] The evangelists are the subjects of these two sentences, the ones who point additional things out to the reader in the laying out of their narratives, not contemporary interpreters, or even the Holy Spirit. The emphasis is on the original human author as the primary determiner of meaning. While this may not completely explain Ambrose's general avoidance of polysemy in his interpretative work, this relative emphasis on the role of the evangelist would appear to account for some restriction of the meanings that are explicitly entertained.

Throughout his commentary Ambrose displays little interest in exploring multiple meanings and possibilities in the text. Nowhere does he explicitly demonstrate awareness that other interpretations are possible, or extant in early Christianity. This is obviously not due to his ignorance of the work of other interpreters. As has been noted above, Ambrose was very familiar with the works of a number of other, mainly Greek interpreters, and often adopted their interpretations. Ambrose's relatively uncritical, monosemic approach must therefore be due to his own conscious aims in preparing his commentary. Examining his work through modern eyes, which tend to take a more strictly monosemic approach than Ambrose, can cause the reader to fail to notice that he is actually less committed to polysemy than many of his contemporaries. In this respect, Pizzolato and Corsato's emphasis on Ambrose's polysemic tendencies is an error similar to the misleading conclusions noted above in regard to the place of the human authors in Ambrose's understanding.[121] Relative to the other commentators under study here, Ambrose's strategy is focused primarily on working through the events described in the text, providing a single, satisfactory explanation for each event or detail.

---

120. Ambrose, *Lucam*, X, 129.

121 Pizzolato, *Esegetica*, 331; Corsato, *Expositio*, 281. He appears to base his conclusion on one reference in the text in which Ambrose acknowledges that multiple interpretations may be recognized in the account.

Usage of Other Parts of Scripture

Ambrose's approach to referring to other scriptural passages beyond the text at hand (besides its parallels in the other three Gospels) further underlines this point. Compared to Augustine and Jerome, his digressions to other passages are infrequent.[122] In most cases, they are fairly straightforward explorations of other references which have a substantial and obvious connection to the Gospel passage under study. For example, talking of the promise of the Spirit in Luke 24:49, he notes that

> [T]he Holy Spirit actually filled those eleven . . . even the same who was then promised. That it is not to be seen to be to the contrary, see where they are given "gifts, for some are given the speaking of wisdom, others the speaking of knowledge according to the Spirit, others faith in spiritual things, others the grace of healing, others all kind of languages" (1 Corinthians 12:7–11). For the other one [the Spirit] filled them for works, this other one who had been promised; for then the grace of forgiveness of sins is bestowed (John 20:23), in order to be seen as elevated, and this is emphasized by Christ . . . for God alone can forgive sins (Luke 5:21). Moreover Luke describes languages as a gift poured out. Certainly you then have "receive the Holy Spirit; for when you forgive sins, they are forgiven" (John 20:23). And truly in the Acts of the Apostles you have "and they were filled with the Holy Spirit and they were enabled to speak various languages even as the Spirit gave speech to them (Acts 2:4)."[123]

In this case, Ambrose is dealing with a verse that concerns the Spirit and develops his exposition by reference to three other passages that also speak primarily of the Spirit.[124] First picking up on the idea of the Spirit as a promised gift, he goes to a Pauline passage that talks of the Spirit as the giver of spiritual gifts. Ambrose then moves to a roughly parallel passage in John's Gospel, before moving, in what is probably the most obvious connection of all three, to the actual coming of the promised Spirit at Pentecost, later in Luke's account (in Acts). He has not picked up on and developed some minor detail in the text or secondary reality in Luke in order to move to other passages, but has moved from the central idea in the verse to other passages that bear directly upon the same idea.

---

122. Old, *The Reading and Preaching of the Scriptures*, 305.
123. Ambrose, *Lucam*, X, 180.
124. Like Augustine, *In Ioh.*, 121.4.

A shorter example of the same approach is found in Ambrose's discussion of the fact that Nicodemus, who with Joseph buried Jesus, "had earlier visited Jesus at night" (John 19:39), which is taken to symbolize their believing in him only at a late stage. "Either at a late hour or at night, or by whichever hour you come, you readily learn to be grateful to Jesus, because those who come later are not paid lesser wages, for both he who came at the sixth hour and he who came at the eleventh hour received the full wage."[125] Here, Ambrose attempts to determine the significance of the fact that John chooses to describe Nicodemus as the one who "had earlier visited Jesus at night." Although his initial thought may be considered a little obtuse, once he has attributed this significance to it, the passage to which he turns to develop the interpretation is an eminently obvious choice: the parable of the workers and the vineyard in Matthew 20:1–16.

Sometimes Ambrose does make quite intuitive leaps to other passages. However, such occasions are relatively rare.[126] Interestingly, when Ambrose does actually make more tenuous connections to other texts, he does not do so in a simple fashion. When speaking of the quality of John's witness on occasion of Jesus' words to him from the cross (John 19:27), he remarks that "Christ witnessed from the Cross and witnessing he marked out John, so much a worthy witness. For good witness is not for money, but of life, for it is not written with ink but with the Spirit of the Living God: 'my tongue works like the pen of a skilful writer.'"[127] This is no simple, idle connection, but the work of a highly skilled commentator. In a few brief words, Ambrose is able to meld together references from 2 Corinthians 3:3 and Psalm 45:1, and make a multifaceted connection back to his original thought: "of *life*" with "of the *Living* God" and "*written* with *ink*" with "the *pen* of a skilful *writer*."[128] Ambrose's use of other

---

125. Ambrose, *Lucam*, X, 138. Cf. Augustine, *In Ioh.*, 120.4.

126. The only other possible example apart from the two discussed is found at Ambrose, *Lucam*, X, 177, although even this case appears to be a relatively straightforward connection. In this respect, Ambrose's exegesis at least in the portion of his exposition of Luke under study here, does not have the characteristic attributed to it in general by Pisato, *Ambrose of Milan*, 213, of frequently introducing sequences of citations to other texts which would not be apparent to most readers.

127. Ambrose, *Lucam*, X, 131.

128. In this example, perhaps the aural similarity of key words may have been a supplementary connecting factor between the texts. Moorhead, *Ambrose*, 76 suggests that some of Ambrose's movements between texts were probably as a result of considering Scripture aurally.

texts in commenting on Jesus' being taken up to heaven in Luke 24:51 is equally skillful and complex:

> He also wanted to teach us in what manner we are to follow [Him] and from where we are to learn, if possible, just as it says: "If you have risen with Christ, seek things that are on high, where Christ is sitting at the right hand of God" [Colossians 3:1]. And how incredible it is that the eyes and minds of more do not believe, since it is added: "who they have taken on high, who is not on earth" [Colossians 3:1]. Therefore neither above earth, nor on earth, nor after the flesh are we to know you [Christ], for "now we do not know Christ after the flesh" [2 Corinthians 5:16]. Indeed Stephen when praying saw you at the right hand of God, not merely above the earth [Acts 7:55].[129]

Here Ambrose develops his argument by seamlessly moving between related ideas in three different passages, one of which he uses twice, both to urge seeking Christ "on high" and to observe that more ought to believe in him. He jumps from passage to passage with what seems to be little effort, like one who is well practiced in the art.

In view of Ambrose's ability to make quite intuitive and complex connections between passages when he chooses to do so, the infrequency with which he actually engages in such activities cannot be attributed to an inability to do so. Rather, it is more likely to be an intentional strategy, under which he aims to avoid utilizing this interpretative technique too often. He has chosen to focus simply on the realities described by the text at hand, for the most part giving one relatively straightforward account of the meaning of each event. Utilizing the text to jump to other passages that do not assist fairly directly in explaining the Gospel account itself, or to speculate at length about the myriad possible interpretations that might be derived from it to build up the faith, are not high priorities for Ambrose. In this light it is not really accurate, at least for his work on Luke, to suggest that "the dense and intricate chains of scriptural citations . . . alone hold together the sprawling collages of his exegetical writings."[130] On the contrary, in light of the above examples, the mostly straightforward scriptural citations used do not so much serve to hold together Ambrose's exegesis as reflect its straightforward, logical character. The events of the narrative may provide an occasion for many things, but

---

129. Ambrose, *Lucam*, X, 159-60.
130. McLynn, *Ambrose*, 237.

intuitive speculation is not one of them.[131] In this respect his approach is rather like that of Hilary. However, unlike Hilary, he does not attempt to unify his whole commentary around a single practical-theological theme, even though his work is heavily theological/doctrinal in character as well as containing elements of practical application. This can best be seen by looking at how he relates to his audience and how he makes theological points through his exposition.

Audience

Ambrose is best described as being moderately attentive to the position of his audience. While his exposition is certainly not held together by practical concerns, he is quite ready to apply the significance of the events of the account to the life of the contemporary Christian, and more so in his exposition of Luke than in his earlier works.[132] His most usual method of doing this is by holding up characters in the account as examples to follow.[133] The preeminent example is, of course, Jesus Christ. His commending his spirit to the Father "with a great voice" (Luke 23:46) means that the believer ought not be ashamed to proclaim his trust in God loudly without shame.[134] Attention is also called to his converting of the thief on the cross as "an excellent model of conversion to strive after, for the thief is swiftly released from sin and is under grace after his pleading; for the Lord always granted more than he was asked for."[135] In this example, Ambrose also shows sensitivity to the realities of living the Christian life: he is aware of the difficulties of living in a sinful world, rather than with Christ in paradise, and makes a point of noting the encouraging fact of the Lord's generosity. Christ's sympathy to those around him, particularly Mary, is also noted, so that when first meeting her after the resurrection he acts towards her in such a manner that "he immediately promotes her faith."[136] Although not an example of direct application to his audience, Ambrose's noting of this fact, together with his tendency to present Mary

---

131. Swift, "Ambrose," 42.

132. Campenhausen, *Fathers*, 94.

133. Jackson, "Ambrose of Milan as Mystagogue," 93–107 describes how Ambrose uses techniques in his mystagogic preaching similar to those found in *De Sacramentis* and *De Mysteriis*.

134. Ambrose, *Lucam*, X, 127.

135. Ambrose, *Lucam*, X, 121, on Luke 23:39–43.

136. Ambrose, *Lucam*, X, 162, on John 20:11–18.

in a sympathetic light, encourages his audience to identify with Mary and so themselves see Christ as someone keen to promote their own faith.

Peter's conduct is also set forth as exemplary in several places. Ambrose observes that Peter's "devotion is always ready and believes readily and therefore is frequently given attention to as an example of faith. Here with John [John 20:3], there alone [John 21:7], everywhere he ran quickly indeed, and was there either alone or first, not satisfied merely to hear the news second-hand, [and so] continued to observe and to seek progress in the love of the Lord, having not been satisfied to [merely] see."[137] Peter's enthusiastic devotion and eagerness to see the risen Lord is taken as indicative of his readiness to believe. Ambrose, in contrast to most Greek exegetes, therefore concludes that the evangelists present him as an example of faith.[138] To push the point home, Ambrose then lists various other occasions where he believes that the Gospel accounts note this singular eagerness of Peter to believe and follow Christ, all of which illustrate that he "was impatient with desire, passing over injury, forgetful of trials."[139] Indeed, Ambrose believes that the evangelists take a very positive view of Peter. While acknowledging that he did fail on the night of Jesus' arrest, his account of this event is almost apologetic on Peter's behalf:

> Peter, although prepared in spirit to undergo martyrdom, when he came to the trial, his determination wavered as was prophesied, for we contain the weakness of the world [together with] the virtue of heaven . . . and therefore Peter was seen to be unwilling, even though he had intended to overcome [his weakness]. And how strange would it have been if Peter had not so wished [to avoid death], when the Lord himself said: "Father, if it is possible, take this cup from me now, however, not my will but yours be done"?[140]

Peter's failure is almost excusable because Christ almost failed at the same point. It should be noted that he also subtly invites his audience to identify with Peter, to sympathize with him, through the use of the first-person plural "we" to describe human weakness. Furthermore, Ambrose assumes that Peter did not doubt at all concerning the resurrection after

---

137. Ambrose, *Lucam*, X, 174.
138. Guinot, "L'exégèse," 161–3.
139. Ambrose, *Lucam*, X, 174, on John 21:7.
140. Ambrose, *Lucam*, X, 178, on John 21:18–19, and quoting Luke 22:42.

its occurrence, because "so many examples of virtue [are] linked together, that we are convinced that Peter could not have doubted."[141] Peter is the exemplar of faith *par excellence*, and the implication is that Ambrose's audience should follow his example.

Other figures are presented as examples by Ambrose, both explicitly and implicitly.[142] The continuing singleness of Mary the mother of Jesus, implied in Jesus' having to direct John to care for her (John 19:26–27), is one such case. "At this point rich testimony to the virgin Mary is apparent. For one is not to put away a wife that one has wedded, as it is written 'what God has joined let man not separate' . . . and if we follow morals, in mourning chastity is commended."[143] After further reflection on the case of Mary, he continues, giving more explicit direction to his hearers, by noting that some Christian women "are perhaps not careful to follow [Mary's] example, are careless of the significance of Mary's overflowing desiring of Christ—they do not imitate this feeling, just like the mass of women we now hear of."[144] Another example where the significance of the Gospel events is explicitly tied to the contemporary believer occurs in the evangelist's recording that the disciples saw the risen Christ's wounds, where Ambrose notes that "it was indicated that He had appeared to His disciples and that they had seen His wounds, so that no ambiguity may be conveyed, but that we might be compelled to believe faithfully."[145] The same acts of Christ that made his resurrection unambiguously clear to the disciples also compel the reader to believe faithfully. This point is elsewhere made more explicit when he develops the theme of "touching Christ," which Ambrose takes as a metaphor for believing in him: "He who wishes to touch Christ whose members have died and risen must likewise put on a compassionate heart, not doubting what has been proclaimed to all the earth."[146]

Besides presenting figures in the account as exemplars, Ambrose also applies the meaning of the text to his audience by emphasizing that various things that are done and said are "for us," as well as for the

---

141. Ambrose, *Lucam*, X, 179. See also 175.

142. For further examples, see Ambrose, *Lucam*, X, 138 (Nicodemus) and 161 (the apparently different responses of the two Marys to Jesus).

143. Ambrose, *Lucam*, X, 133.

144. Ambrose, *Lucam*, X, 134.

145. Ambrose, *Lucam*, X, 172, on John 20:20.

146. Ambrose, *Lucam*, X, 164, on John 20:17.

disciples and the evangelist's original readers. He argues this way repeatedly with respect to the significance of Christ's passion. He begins with

> the inscription [above the Cross], which we all read. When I read the title "King of the Jews," I actually read "My kingdom is not of this world"; when I read this thing written above His head, I actually read "and God was the Word" . . . For these [details] served Jesus and today they serve, so that one ought not be undecided . . . for me, Christ clearly died with suffering . . . He was unwilling to come down for you [plural = the Jews], with the result that He suffered for me. Therefore for us Christ served; for our sake they earlier divided His garments.[147]

Ambrose repeatedly uses the first person to connect the passage to his own context, initially beginning with the singular "I" and "me" but then moving to include his audience as well: "because of us," "for us." Afterwards when discussing the fact that Christ's tunic was not divided (John 19:24), he stresses that "it is significant for *our* faith that it was not divided, but remained whole."[148] At a broader level, the very coming of Christ is to be brought home to the contemporary church, since "You [Christ] descended for us, so that we might see you with our eyes and minds, so that we might believe in you. And therefore you descended for us, so that we could follow you with our minds, whom we cannot see with our eyes."[149] He speaks in the same way concerning the coming of the promised Spirit, noting that "this is emphasized by Christ, so that *you* may believe the Spirit of Christ and that *you* may believe concerning the Spirit of God."[150] In doing so, Ambrose gives immediacy to the texts that he is preaching from.[151]

Ambrose argues in this way because he believes that the text is significant for the contemporary church as well as for the early disciples, for his hearers' faith as well as the original readers of the Gospels.[152] Thus, minor details are present in the account to "support faith."[153] Ambrose appears to regard Jesus' questioning of Peter "do you love me?" (John

---

147. Ambrose, *Lucam*, X, 115–6, on Matt 27:37–42, quoting John 18:36 and John 1:1 respectively.

148. Ambrose, *Lucam*, X, 120. Italics mine.

149. Ambrose, *Lucam*, X, 159, on John 20:17.

150. Ambrose, *Lucam*, X, 180, on John 20:22.

151. Moorhead, *Ambrose*, 97.

152. Pizzolato, *Esegetica*, 327.

153. Ambrose, *Lucam*, X, 143.

21:15–17) in this light: "He asked not so that He might learn [Peter's answer] but so that, raised up to the heavens, He might teach concerning the love that He Himself has for us, just as He suffered as our substitute."[154] He argues forcefully along similar lines with respect to the importance of Christ's wounds for contemporary Christians:

> That He might not only strengthen faith, but also stimulate devotion—because of this He chose, rather than to be in heaven, to receive wounds on our behalf, wounds that He did not wish to have removed, so that the price of our freedom might be shown to the Father. The Father, embracing the memorials of our deliverance placed Jesus at his right hand, where He still bears a scar like a crown, similar to that found on our martyrs.[155]

Here, Ambrose sees Christ's work as not only stimulating faith and devotion in general, but more specifically, he brings home its significance by stressing that his wounds were "received on *our* behalf," for "*our* freedom," pointing to "*our* deliverance." The contemporary significance of the scars is then reinforced by Ambrose's suggestion of similarity between Christ's wounds and those of "our martyrs."[156] Christ's sufferings and death, and all of the other details associated with them, have direct relevance to modern times.

Similar logic applies the significance of Christ's death to the contemporary believer, this time with reference to the wine that Jesus was offered on the cross:

> This is the wine of corruption that through Adam destroyed immortality in calamity, with the result that the human body is destroyed. And our wine, corrupted through hardness of heart, is transformed in Christ, transformed through baptism, so that we are crucified in Christ, we are transformed by repentance, so that from Him blood, the wine of heaven, will overflow to us with incorruptible purity.[157]

Here, "we" are seen as sharing in the hardening of the heart after Adam and in the transformation that follows from Christ's work, with the

---

154. Ambrose, *Lucam*, X, 175.

155. Ambrose, *Lucam*, X, 170, on John 20:27.

156. Exactly which martyrs Ambrose was speaking of at this point is unclear, although as the sermons were preached in Milan, the most probable reference is to those whose relics he had previously discovered in the city. Cf. Moorhead, *Ambrose*, 150–4 and McLynn, *Ambrose*, 209–17.

157. Ambrose, *Lucam*, X, 124, on Luke 23:36.

implied proviso that we repent and are crucified "in Christ." Ambrose uses this idea of victory "in Christ" at a number of points to stress that the meaning of the Gospel applies to his audience. He speaks in this way concerning the effects of Christ's work, reminding his audience that "In order not to conquer for only Himself but for all, He [Christ] held out His hands to draw all things to Himself, wrenching them from the bonds of death and hanging them on the yoke of faith."[158] Likewise, when describing the scene around the cross, with a number of those who faithfully followed Jesus standing nearby, he observes that "one triumph of God now makes all men triumph who are near to the Cross of the Lord."[159]

From the above discussion, it is evident that Ambrose certainly believes that the events of the Gospel are relevant to the day-to-day lives of his audience, and that he is quite willing to make this clear in the course of his exposition. However, it would be an exaggeration to say that practical application of the text to his hearers is a critical component of his exposition, along the lines of Simonetti's suggestion that Ambrose's exegesis "has chiefly pastoral interests,"[160] or Pizzolato's that "his intentions are exquisitely pastoral."[161] He does not attempt even indirectly to draw practical, contemporary applications from many of the events in the Gospel text that he discusses. Furthermore, in most of the examples noted above when he actually does relate the text in this way, he does so rather indirectly, or when he makes direct connections he typically does so very briefly often as passing remarks.[162] Instead of bluntly telling his audience what they should and should not do, he is content with holding up positive examples and other more subtle means of suggesting appropriate practical outcomes of reflection on the text. As noted above, often the contemporary significance is not made very explicit, at best being highlighted by the use of the first-person indicative rather than the second-person imperative. Furthermore, Ambrose does not seem to make much of an effort in other respects, apart from his relatively implicit practical applications, to bring home what he wants to say to his audience. At only one point in the whole of the selection under study does he make use of a contemporary example from outside the text to il-

---

158. Ambrose, *Lucam*, X, 110, on Luke 23:34.

159. Ambrose, *Lucam*, X, 109, on Luke 23:33.

160. Simonetti, *Interpretation*, 89.

161. Pizzolato, *Esegetica*, 333, quoting directly from the concluding chapter provided in English in this Italian work.

162. Cf. Pisato, *Ambrose of Milan*, 215.

lustrate his point,[163] at only one point does he seem even implicitly to acknowledge the existence of his listeners and their own possible reactions to the text.[164] In this respect he is quite similar to Jerome and Hilary, and yet very different to Augustine. However, the above survey of Ambrose's application of the text to his hearers also highlights that his approach differs from that of Hilary, for although both use similar techniques to apply the account's meaning to their hearers,[165] Ambrose's practical comments are not united by any one particular major theme. He tends to be more occasional and less systematic about this aspect of his exegesis.[166] It is therefore appropriate to consider his method as being close to that of Jerome, who also is content with merely making isolated, distinct remarks on how the text is relevant to his audience rather than repeatedly reinforcing the one central point.

From Text to Theology

Ambrose's way of moving from exegesis of the Gospel text to making theological points likewise exhibits both similarities to and differences from the other commentators considered here. Like Jerome, he tends to move from the passage at hand to discuss theological ideas for only a short period. However, unlike Jerome and like Hilary, he does so almost constantly: even though his theological remarks might be brief, his exposition is peppered with them.[167] Also like Hilary, his commentary is at times carried along by such remarks, as he uses them to explain in theological terms the reasons or background behind the events of the text. Yet unlike Hilary, and reflecting his own approach to practical matters, Ambrose is relatively unsystematic in his theological reflections on the text and does not closely tie them to any single unifying theme.[168] His explication of theological ideas through his commentary on the narrative

163. Ambrose, *Lucam*, X, 111.

164. Ambrose, *Lucam*, X, 149.

165. Interestingly, Tevel, "Vineyard," 360, develops the same conclusion about the similarity between Ambrose and Hilary in the development of moral interpretations after examining another section of the Gospel accounts.

166. McLynn, *Ambrose*, 246 argues that this is the case across his homilies in general with his admonition of the wealthy and powerful.

167. Guinot, "L'exégèse," 163–7 gives a good discussion of the doctrinal aspect of Ambrose's exegesis, complementary to the approach taken here.

168. McLynn, *Ambrose*, 239.

can therefore be summarized as brief and simple, buttressing orthodoxy, often serving to give a theological account of why events in the text occur as they do, and yet still occasional and piecemeal, rather than held together by any unity of purpose. Each of these aspects will now be considered in turn.

Firstly, Ambrose's theological comments tend to be brief, simple, and to the point, sometimes to the extent of really being just comments in passing.[169] For example, noting that Christ's clothes were removed before his crucifixion, the only reflection that Ambrose offers is that "going up to the Cross He took off his fine royal clothes, so that you may know that He is indeed a man, and it is not as if only God was fixed to the Cross."[170] The point is simple, and simply made, and yet states an important doctrinal truth: that the suffering Christ was truly human. Furthermore, the use of "you" in this example to bring the idea home to his audience further illustrates Ambrose's habit of subtly applying the text to his audience that was described above, and the fact that his doctrinal emphases are often given real, practical significance and not left as detached in a world of their own. When discussing the title above the cross, he makes a similarly succinct point about its significance, saying that "[t]he title above the Cross is fitting, for Christ's kingdom does not belong to His human body, but He holds royal power in a divine realm. The title above the Cross is fitting, because although the Lord Jesus allowed Himself to be on the Cross, the majesty of the king was shining above the Cross."[171] Here, Ambrose makes not just one brief point, but several interrelated points, briefly. In only two sentences, he is able to allude to Christ's divine nature, his royalty and rulership, the fact that he permitted himself to be crucified and was not forced to this circumstance, and that the sign declared his kingly majesty. Ambrose does not go on to prove or to develop a detailed theology of any of these ideas, or attempt to reflect their full complexity, but simply refers to each as briefly and precisely as he can, before moving on.[172]

---

169. The only exceptions, that extend for more than two or three sentences, are the still relatively straightforward and only slightly longer examples discussed below (Ambrose, *Lucam*, X, 140 and 175), and the longest of all (at seven sentences) at Ambrose, *Lucam*, X, 158.

170. Ambrose, *Lucam*, X, 108, on Luke 23:34.

171. Ambrose, *Lucam*, X, 113, on Luke 23:38. Cf. Jerome, *Math.*, IV, 1703–11, on Matt 27:37.

172. A similar example occurs at Ambrose, *Lucam*, X, 109.

In both the examples just considered, what Ambrose says is thoroughly orthodox, and implicitly denies heterodox views, notably that Christ was not fully human, or not fully divine and so moved to the cross by some external power. He does not speculate about the matter or intuitively jump to other relevant ideas or possible views, but simply states how the content of the passage supports an orthodox doctrine, and suggests that the passage likewise plainly shows the opposite view to be incorrect.[173] He appears to do so out of a desire to clearly communicate Christian doctrine to his congregation using ordinary words which they can easily understand.[174] As is the case with Hilary, neither allegorization, nor more literal interpretative methods, are regarded as instruments of doctrinal speculation.[175] However, his approach, even if simply put, is not simpleminded. In this respect his approach to theological statement is similar to his avoidance of polysemy and intuitive use of other passages, and like these other features is best regarded as an interpretative strategy rather than due to a lack of sophistication on Ambrose's part. Two further examples illustrate this point. In the first, he observes concerning the account of Jesus' burial that:

> He did not say another undisturbed tomb, but a new tomb, another tomb of Joseph. Therefore Christ did not have His own grave. Indeed this grave they prepared under the law of death; the victor of death does not have His own tomb. For what communion is there between grave and God? . . . therefore the common death of all is Christ's, and yet He was not buried with others, but He was shut up alone, for the Lord had the same flesh as all mankind. He is similar [to us], yet of a different nature: similar in that He was born of a woman, but differently conceived . . . and for Christ the death of all followed the birth of the body, but followed with singular virtue.[176]

In this example Ambrose again uses a simple detail recorded in the account to emphasize a central, simple truth about the nature of Christ: that he is different by virtue of his divinity from other humans. Even though the point is still made relatively briefly, there is evidence of a sophisticated mind at work. Ambrose is clever enough to be able to make use of the circumstance that the tomb was new and belonging to Joseph to

173. Cf. Mara, "Ambrose," 165.
174. Pasini, *Ambrose*, 216.
175. Smalley, *Bible*, 20.
176. Ambrose, *Lucam*, X, 140, on John 19:41.

argue that these facts demonstrate both the similarity and differences of Christ to other humans.[177]

Later, when discussing Jesus' asking Peter whether he loves him in John 21:15–17, Ambrose ingeniously sews together two elements in the dialogue in order to make a theological point, observing that "you have, 'Simon son of John, do you love me?' 'You know, Lord that I love you.' And Jesus says: 'care for my sheep.' For which of the others was able to acknowledge Him? And therefore because he [Peter] alone acknowledged Him out of all of them, he is placed before all; for the greatest of all is love."[178] Here, Ambrose believes that Jesus, through his uncalled-for threefold question and his apparently unconnected command, is emphasizing Peter's primacy in order to implicitly stress the primacy of love. The theological idea that is stressed ("the greatest of all is love") is a simple point lifted directly from 1 Corinthians 13:13, and Ambrose only discusses it briefly, and yet the manner in which he moves from text to idea is undeniably more complex than the simplicity of the idea or the brevity of the comment might suggest.

However, even though Ambrose sometimes evidences a sophisticated mind in setting forth theological ideas, he seldom allows himself to enter into speculative, intuitive theological reflection as he explains the text. On every occasion bar one, he restricts himself to stating the orthodox position simply and straightforwardly, noting how the text underscores it, without questioning or considering other alternatives, except perhaps to note and dismiss the view most opposite to the interpretation which he favors. The one exception to this practice ultimately also proves the rule. This can best be seen if it is quoted in full:

> Why have you not ascended, Lord Jesus? In what manner do you linger, if you have commended your spirit into the hands of the Father? Or, when were you able to go astray, if you are always in the Father and always with the Father? Indeed He said Himself "if I descend to hell, you are there; if I ascend to the highest mountain beyond the light and live in the extremities, your hands conduct me." Or how can you ascend, if you are always everywhere? Indeed, you descended as the Son of Man and not of the Father, when you were descending, you were present,

---

177. See also Ambrose, *Lucam*, X, 163.

178. Ambrose, *Lucam*, X, 175. Cf. Peter's earlier acknowledgement in Mark 8:29, before any of the other disciples, that Jesus is the Christ.

but you descended for us, so that we see you with our eyes and minds, so that we might believe in you.[179]

Here, Ambrose is provoked by Jesus' direction to not touch him because "I have not yet ascended to my Father" to reflect variously on the nature of Christ, his work, and his relationship to the Father. However, this excerpt in not really speculative in the fullest sense. Throughout, Ambrose's ruminations are based on very orthodox assumptions which have the direct support of the Gospels: "if into the hands of the Father you have commended your spirit"; "if you are always in the Father and always with the Father" and so on. Rather than engaging in theological speculation (since he does not really analyze the postulates he sets forth) he is more giving voice to the fact that he cannot really appreciate the doctrinal "givens" that he is expressing, since he cannot see how they fit into his preconceptions. However, this leads him not to doubt, to modify his views, or reflect until he finds a solution, but only to assert the central truth that he does know, namely, that regardless of the possible reasons why Christ has not yet ascended, this much is certain, that he descended for us.

His posture of asserting orthodoxy is further demonstrated by the fact that on a number of occasions in his exposition of the text he is strongly concerned to defend it not against allegations of historical or textual error, but of doctrinal inconsistency. Thus, the fact that the women are the first to receive the news that Jesus is risen, and indeed commanded to tell this to the men, must be carefully explained by Ambrose in terms that take account of Paul's comment in 1 Timothy 2:12 that he does not allow women to teach men in church, but that instead, according to 1 Corinthians 14:35, "they should ask their men at home": "Because she is sent to these men who are of her house, she therefore accepted the orders that she has been given."[180] The women are permitted to tell the men the good news because they will do so at the home of men who are in some sense their family. Ambrose's concern to doctrinally harmonize the Gospel account with the Pauline material also sets him apart from the mainstream of Greek interpretation of this passage.[181] However, the manner in which he does so is rather forced, given that 1 Corinthians permits women to ask, not to tell, at home.

---

179. Ambrose, *Lucam*, X, 158–9, on John 20:17, with reference to Luke 22:46 and John 14:9–11, and quoting Ps 139:8.

180. Ambrose, *Lucam*, X, 165, on John 20:17.

181. Guinot, "L'exégèse," 161.

The apparent conflict between Jesus' command to the women not to touch him because he has not yet ascended (John 20:17), and his permitting of Thomas to touch him before his ascension (John 20:27), must also be explained not only in terms of the simple contradiction in directions given, but also in theological terms, given that Ambrose regards "touching Christ" as a metaphor for believing in him and commands the women not to touch him because as yet they do not truly believe. "How can it be that Thomas, who until this point had not believed, nevertheless touched Christ? But he is seen to have doubted not the Resurrection of the Lord, but rather concerning the nature of the Resurrection, and it was right for him to teach me."[182] Ambrose feels that he must primarily address the theological difficulty raised by Thomas' being allowed to touch Christ while the women were not, and his solution is a theological one, namely, that he may do so because his doubt was of a lesser kind than that of the women.[183]

Ambrose addresses such questions in his exposition because, like Hilary, he believes that the events in the text occur to demonstrate theological truths. This is seen most clearly in the fact that he often takes time to explain the account in terms of what is occurring theologically. Such is the case with Jesus' response to Mary's tears, where "Jesus says: 'woman, why do you weep?' (John 20:15). It is as if he says: 'God does not need your tears, but demands faith.'"[184] Ambrose notes both what Jesus actually says, and the theological reason behind his actual words. What is happening in the minds of the characters can also explain their actions, such as when "the mother of Christ (while the sheep were fleeing) stood before the cross and her eyes beheld the atoning wounds of the Son, for she expected not death but worldly deliverance."[185]

Such observations are not very different from examples found in Hilary. Where Ambrose is distinctive, however, is in his attributing such theological background information specifically to the evangelist, rather than merely noting that it is present in the text. This is in accord with his greater awareness of the role of the human authors, discussed above. Thus, Ambrose does not merely observe that Christ said to the thief that he would be with him that day in paradise (Luke 23:43), but, further, that

---

182. Ambrose, *Lucam*, X, 168.

183. A further example occurs at Ambrose, *Lucam*, X, 139. Cf. Augustine, *In Ioh.*, 121.3, who argues similarly.

184. Ambrose, *Lucam*, X, 161.

185. Ambrose, *Lucam*, X, 132, on John 19:25–26.

"Luke made it clear that the thief was set free by the intercession of the priest's gift of grace and a demand that forbearance be bestowed on the persecuting Jews."[186] He explains what Christ was actually doing in making his declaration to the thief, and notes that it is *Luke* who makes this apparent in his account. It is possible to argue that this reference to Luke has no reference to Luke's actual, conscious intentions, and that the point made is a meaning intended by the Holy Spirit and not the evangelist. However, the fact that Ambrose chooses to use the terminology "Luke made it clear" ("Lucas autem conpetere evidentur adseruit") in place of other, more passive alternatives suggests that he most likely has in view here a Luke who is conscious of what meaning he intends.[187] Later, that this forgiveness of the thief is accomplished by Christ, before Mary is addressed by Christ (John 19:26), is likewise seen in terms of Luke's narrative intentions.[188]

Ambrose also differs from Hilary in that his theological commentary on the events in the narrative is not closely united by any one particular theme. While he does tend to give a fair amount of attention to christological issues, as the foregoing examples illustrate, he also addresses a range of other unrelated matters at points. Seldom does one issue connect to the next that emerges in Ambrose's exposition. Furthermore, Hilary's consistent tying-in of his theme of believing faith to practical implication is only patchily echoed in Ambrose, who as seen above sometimes chooses to relate his theological comments to practical matters, but at other points does not. Ambrose's aims in moving from text to theology are therefore closer to Jerome's than those of Hilary.

Conclusions

Overall, Ambrose's exegesis, at least in the selection under study here, can best be summarized as being more complex than that of Jerome or Hilary, occupying a middle position between them on the majority of the factors considered. Like Hilary, he is primarily interested in the realities behind

---

186. Ambrose, *Lucam*, 129.

187. Contrast with Ambrose, *Lucam*, X, 115, 116, 128, where Ambrose, intending to speak of a meaning which Luke would not have been conscious of uses other means of describing the Gospel text ("of the Holy Spirit"; "the Spirit of God"; "therefore it is indicated through this").

188. Ambrose, *Lucam*, X, 131. Cf. Ambrose, *Lucam*, X, 163. See n.100 on how Ambrose treats the temporal relationship between John 19:26 and Luke 23:43.

the text, but certainly not completely disinterested in the text, and he is distinct from both Hilary and Jerome in his explorations of the intentions of the human author. Like Hilary, he tends not to be polysemic in his own practice, but like Jerome, is very comfortable with polysemy in principle and occasionally in practice. He is more attentive to his audience than Jerome, but less so than Hilary. Ambrose is more interested in developing theological ideas from his text than Jerome, but less focused on promoting any one such idea than Hilary. As a whole, his exegesis tends to share the occasional and unsystematic character of Jerome's. Most importantly, in spite of minor differences in how all three writers use allegory and typology, Ambrose's exegesis at this point can best be described in similar terms to Jerome's and Hilary's. All three are primarily interested in the literal sense, while retaining a substantial place for allegorical interpretation, and some significant role for typology. Ambrose's *Expositio evangelii secundum Lucam* therefore reinforces the contention of this study that other factors than how allegorical or literal their interpretations might be are of greater use to modern scholars in articulating in what respects Latin exegetes really do differ from one another.

5

Augustine and the Senses of Scripture
In Iohannis Evangelium and Sermones De Tempore

Scholarly Conclusions

THE EXEGETICAL METHOD OF Augustine's *In Iohannis evangelium* (Tractates on John) has frequently been described by scholars in terms of literal, spiritual, allegorical interpretation, and the related theory of the senses of Scripture. Most often, this comes in the form of the view that allegory is central to Augustine's work. For example, Carroll claims that it was "on allegory that his [Augustine's interpretation] rested."[1] Likewise, Altaner is of the opinion that Augustine prefers "the allegorical-mystical sense, especially in his homilies,"[2] as is Simonetti: "In his work on John's gospel, Augustine turns readily to allegorical interpretation."[3] Allied to this is the view that "[i]n his exegetical practice there is little that is original: he is, in the end, an heir of the Alexandrian tradition."[4] Teske has examined the place of allegory in Augustine in a number of articles,

---

1. Carroll, *Preaching*, 192. See also Cameron, "Figurative Exegesis," 75; Hall, *Readings*, 119, 122.

2. Altaner, *Patrology*, 509, where his work on John is given as an example of this.

3. Simonetti, *Interpretation*, 107.

4. Norris, "Augustine and the Close of the Ancient Period of Interpretation," especially 406.

and concluded that allegory is the key to understanding his exegesis, specifically allegorical interpretation that is based on an anthropology by which humanity is divided into the "spirituals," who are able to perceive the divine truth, and the "animals," who are not.[5] This view is based on a solitary reference to a passage at the start of the *In Iohannis evangelium*.[6] However, Teske does recognize that it is anachronistic to conclude from this that Augustine had a fully developed theory of the spiritual sense of Scripture; for him it was merely a useful way for the interpreter to read Scripture.[7]

Some scholars have differed from this view. Comeau's monograph (1930) on Augustine's interpretation of the Fourth Gospel contrasts with the majority of more recent studies in arguing that Augustine placed the highest importance on literal interpretation and based his exegesis on this rather than on the spiritual sense.[8] This opinion has also been put forward more recently by Bray[9] and Scalise.[10] In so far as the question of the relative importance of the literal and figurative senses is one worth answering, this study supports this minority opinion. However, the main point to note is that the view of Comeau and Bray does not differ from that of the others noted above at the most critical juncture. They both still view Augustine's work within the same framework of literal and allegorical interpretation. Comeau's book gives this issue the central place in his analysis.[11] Although Bray's analysis is briefer, he also operates within the same, familiar framework, and summarizes Augustine's works on the Gospel by saying that "Augustine generally tackled problems from a literalistic point of view, though he also frequently lapsed into allegory."[12]

---

5. Teske, "Spirituals and Spiritual Interpretation in Augustine," 65–81. See also Teske, "Criteria for Figurative Interpretation in St. Augustine," 109–19.

6. Teske, "Spirituals and Spiritual Interpretation in Augustine," 66.

7. Teske, "Spirituals and Spiritual Interpretation in Augustine," 75.

8. Comeau, *Saint Augustin: Exégète du Quatrième Evangile*, 92.

9. Bray, *Interpretation*, 93.

10. Scalise, "The 'Sensus Literalis': A Hermeneutical Key to Biblical Exegesis." *Scottish Journal of Theology* 42 (1989) 45–65. He argues from Augustine's suggestion that there is little in the obscure parts of Scripture (those parts which need to be interpreted allegorically) which is not found plainly stated elsewhere in the Bible, in *Doctrina*, 2.6.8 (*CCSL* 32:10–11).

11. Comeau, *Augustin*, chapters 3–6 and 9–10 are devoted to determining which sense is the more important, and how they are both used by Augustine.

12. Bray, *Interpretation*, 93.

Several scholars portray Augustine's work as standing somewhere between these two alternatives. Smalley argues that "[i]n his exegesis St. Augustine tries to steer a middle course between literal and allegorical exposition."[13] Similarly, de Margerie's view is that Augustine avoids the extremes of "Origen's allegorism and converges with the outlook of the more moderate representatives of the Alexandrian school . . . who reject universal allegorism."[14] Scalise concludes that his work has a "joint literal-and-figurative status,"[15] to some extent echoing the older verdict of de Lubac that "Augustine, who is just as much an 'allegorist' as Origen, is not less indissolubly the great theoretician . . . of history."[16] Although more attentive to some of the subtleties of Augustine's exegesis, such opinions are one of a kind with the more extreme views surveyed above in attempting to explain Augustine's approach to allegory in terms of where he fits into the allegorical-literal spectrum and categories more appropriate to the thought world of Greek exegesis.

Some other scholars, who have studied the *In Iohannis evangelium* for reasons other than a desire to determine whether Augustine prefers the literal or the spiritual sense, tend to operate within the same framework. Norris's examination of the theology of the work examines the work within the framework of how Augustine relates the literal and the spiritual senses, and attempts to relate his love for allegorical exegesis to trends in his theology.[17] Weissman's introduction to the *In Iohannis evangelium*, after noting matters of occasion, date, background, and theological themes, discusses his hermeneutic solely in terms of how he relates the literal and spiritual senses.[18]

---

13. Smalley, *Bible*, 24. See also Jeanrond, *Hermeneutics*, 22.

14. Margerie, *Exegesis*, 3:34; A similar problem exists with Berrouard, "Augustin," 338. The former work is to be regarded as the weakest of the author's four volumes on the history of exegesis, according to Oort's excellent recent overview of major works in the field: Oort, "Interpretation," 94.

15. Scalise, "Sensus," 52.

16. Lubac, *Medieval*, 2:213.

17. Norris, "The Theological Structure of Augustine's Exegesis in the *Tractatus in Euangelium Ioannis*," 385–93.

18. Weismann, "Introducción," 57–59. In addition to the works above, we might add brief discussions within more general treatments of Augustine's exegesis. A prominent example is Williams's chapter within the most recent edition of the *Cambridge Companion to Augustine*, which while devoting attention to other aspects of Augustine's exegesis, devotes substantial attention to discussing Augustine's work in relation to the senses of Scripture (see pages 312, 315, 319, 323–6), and describes the tractates

The other prominent feature of the body of scholarship on Augustine's exegetical works is an interest in what they have to say about his theological views. An example of this is Hardy's book-length study on how the *In Iohannis evangelium* bears upon Augustine's theology of revelation.[19] This work is primarily interested in Augustine's theology of John rather than in how he interprets the text. Such analysis as this, while valuable for better understanding Augustine's theology as a whole, is of little assistance in terms of describing the character of his exegesis. In the case of Hardy's work, its usefulness to our purpose is further limited by the fact that he is more interested in making connections between Augustine and modern thinkers than in making comparisons with Augustine's contemporaries. Kilmartin's article on tractate 27 is chiefly interested in what light this tractate bears on Augustine's views on the Eucharist and the question of sacramental realism.[20] Poque's study of Augustine's usage of imagery focuses on how particular theological motifs are developed in his works, with the *In Iohannis evangelium* in any event receiving only cursory attention.[21] Old's brief examination of the tractates on John 1–6 evaluates his approach in terms of how Augustine understands the relationship between Christ's divinity and "believing" in John.[22]

Studies on the *Sermones*, like those on the *In Iohannis evangelium*, have also tended to focus on where they fit into the literal-spiritual paradigm and what they reveal about Augustine's theology in preference to other matters,[23] although the quantity of material that has been written specifically on the *Sermones* is substantially less than that on the *In Iohannis evangelium*. However, that which there is tends to utilize the same familiar categories to understand his exegesis. For example, Car-

---

on John as being "a masterful blend of literal and allegorical exegesis," 312.

19. Hardy, *Actualité de la révélation divine: une étude des "Tractatus in Iohannis Euangelium" de Saint Augustin*.

20. Kilmartin, "Tractate 27," 162–79.

21. Poque, *Le langage symbolique dans la prédication d'Augustin d'Hippone*. The section on the *In Iohannis evangelium* is found on pp. 233–39. The same is true of TeSelle, *Augustine the Theologian*, which although frequently referring to the tractates, also has little interest in Augustine's exegesis. An exception to the rule is Drobner, "Grammatical Exegesis and Christology in St. Augustine," 49–63, who examines the relationship between a part of Augustine's theology and his exegetical method. However, this article draws most of its examples from parts of Augustine's works other than the *In Iohannis evangelium*, and draws no firm conclusions.

22. Old, *The Reading and Preaching of the Scriptures*, 350–8.

23. For example, Albaric, "A Eucharistic Catechesis," 253–64, on sermon 227.

roll's treatment of the *Sermones*, like that of the *In Iohannis evangelium*, examines them primarily in terms of how Augustine uses the different senses of Scripture.[24] Tevel is keenly interested in the relationship between the various senses of Scripture in the *Sermones*.[25]

Having established that a large portion of the scholarship on Augustine's exegesis is not greatly different from that relating to our first three interpreters in the strong emphasis it places on the framework of the literal and spiritual senses of Scripture, we will first turn to consider how helpful that framework is for the task of describing Augustine's exegesis and whether we might draw the same conclusions concerning it as we have for the other three interpreters. This is the topic of the present chapter. It begins by examining Augustine's manner of progressing through the "letter" of the text, and then his use of allegory and its circumstances, purpose and relative importance within his work. Much the same conclusion is apparent as was evident for Jerome, Hilary, and Ambrose: Augustine's exegesis is fundamentally literal, but incorporates some use of allegory within this overall picture. The chapter then moves on to describe how Augustine's use of allegory helps us to see other significant features of his exegesis beyond the extent to which he does or does not use allegory. Specifically, it highlights for us his preference, like that of Hilary and in contradistinction to that of Jerome, for realities behind the text rather than philological details within it. Augustine's use of typology and prophecy-fulfillment is also considered, which provides helpful points of comparison with our other three interpreters. We then turn in the following chapter to discuss other features of Augustine's work beyond the framework of the senses of Scripture, such as his free-ranging style of exegesis, his polysemy, pastoral concern for his hearers, and his development of theological themes and doctrinal truths from his exegesis, all of which provide more assistance to modern scholars than the traditional framework is able to in highlighting how Augustine differs from the other authors in our sample.

Progressing through the Letter of the Text

Augustine's manner of progressing through his text for the day in both *In Iohannis* and the *Sermones* reveals an approach to exegesis which is

24. Carroll, *Preaching*, 189.
25. Tevel, "Vineyard," 360, on sermons 49 and 87.

fundamentally literal, albeit with some use of allegory along the way. Although as we shall see his concerns consistently range well beyond the compass of the narrative itself, he does not allow anything that is of particular interest to distract him for long from the actual events of the Gospel account. He is always conscious of the need to return to the narrative itself,[26] an awareness that is illustrated by his remarks at the end of an excursus into the apparent discrepancy between the evangelists on the time of Christ's crucifixion: "Now after these matters have been briefly expounded, let us return to the narrative of John the Evangelist,"[27] which is precisely what he does. This is because, for all of its intuitive character and its frequent digressions, Augustine's exegesis is still anchored in the Gospel, and progresses through it in an orderly manner, even if he remains less close to the text than do other commentators, notably Jerome. In fact, much of his exegesis is basic, literal discussion of the plain meaning of the account, or founded on simple analysis of its facts. Neat, straightforward explanations of the events of the Gospel are more frequent than complicated, winding allegorical ones, and are the usual springboards for digressions onto theological themes and practical matters.[28] Even when Augustine encounters difficulties in the text, it would be a mistake to assume that his reflexive response is to turn to allegory. In fact, a much more common reaction is to develop a straightforward explanation, based on the literal facts of the text.

Thus, Augustine's comments on particular verses often consist exclusively of obvious points on the text. Sometimes, he virtually paraphrases what the passage says, as is the case for the first part of his exegesis of the fact that the soldiers cast lots for Christ's tunic in John 19:24, so that they would not have to cut it: "And so it is apparent that in the other garments they had equal parts so that it was not necessary to cast lots, but in that one they could not have had individual parts unless it were cut so that they would uselessly take pieces of it."[29] When dealing with the Jews' attempt to get Pilate to execute Jesus by saying "If you release this man, you are not Caesar's friend" (John 19:12), Augustine simply makes the implicit assumption of the Jews' words explicit, observing "they thought that they were forcing Pilate to suffer greater fear, by terrifying him about

26. Old, *The Reading and Preaching of the Scriptures*, 349, 353.

27. Augustine, *Tractates*, 117.2, on Mark 15:25 and John 19:14. All subsequent translations of passages from the *In Iohannis evangelium* are from this source.

28. Cf. Milewski, "Augustine's 124 Tractates on the Gospel of John," 77.

29. Augustine, *In Ioh.*, 118.2.

Caesar, so that he might slay Christ."[30] Equally simple are Augustine's comments on Jesus' words when appearing to the disciples shortly after his resurrection, "And when he had said this, he showed them his hands and side," "For nails had pierced His hands, a spear had opened His side. And here the traces of the wounds were preserved for healing the hearts of doubters."[31] Augustine merely reminded his audience of the basic events related earlier in the narrative, that Jesus' hands and side had been pierced, before making a point, obvious in light of the Thomas dialogue that follows immediately after, about the significance of the scars being visible.

A frequent starting point for Augustine as he turns to discuss a verse is a fact clearly and literally present in the text, that enables him to make a brief theological point without having to jump through too many intellectual hoops. An example of this is his exegesis of the Jews' unwillingness in John 18:28 to enter into Pilate's palace on the evening of Christ's arrest, according to John so that they might not be defiled before the Passover:

> For they had begun to celebrate the days of unleavened bread, and on these days it was a defilement for them to enter the dwelling of a foreigner. O ungodly blindness! They would be defiled, of course, by a foreign dwelling place and would not be defiled by their own crime! They were afraid to be defiled by the praetorium of a foreign judge and were not afraid [to be defiled] by the blood of an innocent brother.[32]

Here, Augustine takes a basic fact made explicit by the Gospel, that the Jews were afraid of being defiled, and uses a sense of irony to take a straightforward step and imply their guilt in the matter of Christ's death.[33]

A further example is found in Augustine's words on the Jews' clamoring for Christ's death before Pilate, that "you [the Jews] kill an innocent

---

30. Augustine, *In Ioh.*, 116.7. Shortly afterwards, at *In Ioh.*, 116.9, when he comments on the Jews' subsequent words to Pilate in John 19:15, that "we have no king but Caesar," Augustine returns to this point, and in doing so provides a further illustration of his preference to argue with relatively simple logic.

31. Augustine, *In Ioh.*, 121.4, on Luke 24:40.

32. Augustine, *In Ioh.*, 114.2.

33. In this example, and several others that occur elsewhere in our discussion of Augustine, the matter of Augustine's perspective on the Jews is raised—a subject with substantial literature of its own. See Fredricksen, "Excaecati Occulta Justitia Dei: Augustine on Jews and Judaism," 299–324. Although not intending to supply an overview of the state of scholarship, this article provides a helpful entry point to the topic.

man. But unless this happened, the true Pasch would not happen. But the shadow of truth was held onto by the erring Jews; and by the wondrous dispensation of divine wisdom, through deceitful men the truth of this same shadow was fulfilled."[34] Augustine here makes his point through a relatively simple irony, without the aid of an allegory or complex theological reasoning. Augustine often uses irony and paradoxical juxtapositions of plain features of the passage with theological realities in this way to display truths in sharp relief. A similar example, where he deals with the Jews' demand in John 19:7 that "according to the Law He must die because He made himself the Son of God" further illustrates this: "And yet to neither [this nor the claim to be king of the Jews] had Jesus falsely asserted His rightful possession, but both are true; He both is the only-begotten Son of God, and He was appointed king by him over Sion."[35]

Augustine's preferred starting point in his exegesis, the glue that holds the disparate elements together as he shifts from point to point, is not deep theological reflection or detailed allegorical commentary. Rather, it is simple comments on and questions of the plain, literal meaning of the text.[36] More often than not, he commences his exposition of a sentence or incident by going over the basic facts contained therein, as with the beginning of the account of the discovery of Christ's resurrection in John 20:1–3, where Augustine notes that

> ... we heard and we witnessed with the eyes of faith the attitude of a devoted woman toward the Lord Jesus. She was seeking Jesus, however, she was as yet looking for the corpse of a dead man, and she was loving Him as if he were only a good teacher. Because she saw the stone rolled away from the tomb, she believed that the body which she was seeking had been taken away, and she reported the sad news to the disciples. Two of them ran ahead ...[37]

Augustine repeats the obvious facts from the account, and yet he does much more than that. He embellishes them somewhat, in order to take his audience closer to the situation (for example, the "devoted woman" and the "sad news") and then weaves in simple interpretative comments as he proceeds, such as his reference to Mary loving Jesus as merely a

---

34. Augustine, *In Ioh.*, 115.5, on John 18:38.
35. Augustine, *In Ioh.*, 116.3.
36. Augustine, *Serm.*, 245.1 is similar to the example given here.
37. Augustine, *Sermons*, 244.1.

good teacher. What immediately follows in this sermon is further illustrative of the essentially straightforward manner in which Augustine proceeds. After noting that Peter and John run to the tomb, fail to find the body, and then "believe," he asks the obvious question "But what did they believe?"—and answers:

> What they ought not to have believed. Therefore, when you heard the words: "and they believed," perhaps you thought that they believed what they should believe, that is, that the Lord had risen from the dead. They did not believe this, but rather what the woman had announced. Indeed, so that you may know that they believed this, the Evangelist adds directly: "for as yet they did not understand the Scripture, that He must rise from the dead."[38]

He moves forward by asking a simple question that arises naturally from the text, answering it directly, and then supporting his answer with a straightforward appeal to the text.

Often, Augustine will begin a series of comments by identifying an apparent difficulty or something that seems a little absurd in the passage. Most commonly, his next step is not to resolve the difficulty by utilizing allegory or to utilize the apparent absurdity of the letter as an opportunity to read the text symbolically, but to deal with the problem by simple recourse to common sense or the biblical context.[39] This is the case in his discussion of the fact that John was recorded as entering into Christ's empty tomb, that he believed, and of the verse that follows:

> Here, some, paying little attention, suppose that John believed this, that Jesus arose; but what follows does not indicate this. For what does that which He immediately added on mean? "For as yet they knew not the Scripture that he must rise again from the dead." Therefore, He did not believe that He rose again, since He did not know that He must rise again. What, therefore, did he see? He saw, of course, the empty sepulchre and He believed what the woman had said, that He was taken from the sepulchre.[40]

---

38. Augustine, *Sermons*, 244.1, on John 20:3–8.

39. In addition to the examples given below, see also Augustine, *In Ioh.*, 117.1, 118.3 and 122.2.

40. Augustine, *In Ioh.*, 120.9, on John 20:8–9.

Here, Augustine chooses to resolve a potentially difficult issue, that of exactly what John did "believe" upon seeing the empty tomb, by arguing directly from what follows in the next verse. In the light of examples such as this, one must be careful about conclusions such as the statement that "Augustine pays little attention to context."[41]

Augustine deals similarly with the objection that Jesus says of Thomas "because you have seen me, you have believed" (John 20:29) when Thomas's sense of touch was relevant, rather than his seeing: "he does not say, 'you have touched me,' but, 'you have seen me,' because in a certain way the sight is the generic sense. For it is commonly named also by the other four senses, as when we say: 'hear, and see how well it sounds, sniff, and see how well it smells . . .' Consequently, here too the Lord Himself says, 'Put in your fingers here and see my hands' [John 20:27]."[42] Augustine explains a peculiarity in the text, which is more likely to be a concern to a child than to a theologian, by reference not to an allegory or a word study, but to a commonplace. Augustine also applies a relatively straightforward solution to the question of why Jesus asks Peter three times "do you love me more than these?" by suggesting, not an elaborate allegory based on the number "three," but that "a triple confession is paid back to the triple denial [by Peter, on the night of Christ's arrest] so that his tongue may not give less service to love than to fear."[43] Not long before in the same account, Peter had denied Christ three times; hence, it was only right that he acknowledge him the same number of times in order to compensate. Augustine's frequent use of obvious and plain meanings suggest that the view exemplified by Bonner of "Augustine's willingness to . . . expound it [the text] in a manner which appears to be mere fantasy"[44] is not an entirely accurate one in the context of his exegesis of John.

Augustine does not reflexively turn to allegory as soon as common sense begins to appear unconvincing or absurd, as some scholars have suggested he tends to do.[45] Rather, on occasions in his discussions of the

---

41. Lienhard, "Reading," 18.
42. Augustine, *In Ioh.*, 121.5.
43. Augustine, *In Ioh.*, 123.5, on John 21:15–17.
44. Bonner, "Augustine," 547.
45. E.g. Hall, *Reading*, 122; Scalise, "Sensus," 53. These two scholars, like many before them, have made this claim based on certain statements made by Augustine in *De Doctrina Christiana* 3.5.9 and 3.10.14 (*PL* 34:0068–0069 and 0071) and *Confessiones* 6.4.6 and 6.5.8 (*PL* 32:0722–23). In the former work, Augustine stresses that one

Gospel texts, he is willing to push literal solutions to difficulties in the narrative as far as credibility will stretch. When dealing with John's statement (21:14) about the disciples meeting Jesus at the side of the lake that "This is now the third time that Jesus was manifested to his disciples after He had risen from the dead," when there appear to have been more than three occasions, Ambrose explains, rather questionably, that "we ought to refer this not to the appearances themselves but to the days (that is, on the first day when he arose, and eight days afterwards when the disciple Thomas saw and believed, and this day . . .) for on that very first day He was not seen once . . . but his manifestation must be numbered according to days, so that this is the third."[46]

Another favorite device that Augustine uses to help give a clear explanation of the meaning of a verse is to ask and answer a question that might naturally occur to a reader of the narrative, and to proceed from there.[47] This is how he handles the fact that the disciples were recorded as having returned to fishing after Jesus' death:

> It is usually asked about this fishing of the disciples, why Peter and the sons of Zebedee returned to that which they were before they were called by the Lord . . . Why is it then that now, as if leaving behind the apostleship, they become what they were and seek again what they had put aside . . . the answer must be given that they were not forbidden to seek necessary subsistence by their art, a licit and permissible one of course, while maintaining the integrity of their apostleship, if at any time they did not have anything else on which to live.[48]

---

must be careful to avoid taking figurative expressions literally, and that the criterion for distinguishing whether it is appropriate to read a text according to the letter or the spiritual sense is whether or not that text can be literally read as supporting right behavior or true belief. In the *Confessiones*, Augustine describes how Ambrose helped him to esteem the Christian Scriptures by assisting him to see that certain passages which appeared absurd when read literally could in fact reveal profound mysteries when read allegorically. While these references might support the claims of Hall, Scalise, and others, it does not necessarily follow that Augustine's exegetical practices are consistent with his theoretical statements on the subject. To the extent that these scholars are correct in their readings of the *Confessiones* and *De Doctrina Christiana*, it would appear that Augustine's practice in the *In Iohannis evangelium* and the *Sermones* is not consistent with the principles laid down in the former pair of works, as the following examples suggest.

46. Augustine, *In Ioh.*, 123.3.

47. For further examples of this tendency, see also Augustine, *In Ioh.*, 114.4 and 124.6.

48. Augustine, *In Ioh.*, 122.1–3, on John 21:3. He goes on to defend this position,

Augustine handles John's comment in 21:12 that "No one dared to ask him, 'Who are you?' knowing it was the Lord" on the disciples' encounter with Jesus after their fishing expedition with a similarly inquisitive technique: "If indeed they knew, what need was there for them to ask? But if there was no need, why is it said 'they did not dare,' as if there were need, but by some fear they would not dare? The meaning, therefore is this: so great was the evidence of the truth by which Jesus appeared to those disciples that none of them dared not only to deny but even to doubt. For if anyone doubted, of course he ought to ask."[49] In both these examples, Augustine does not raise a question in order to answer it by recourse to allegory or abstract theologizing, but by applying common sense to the recorded events and context of the passage, that is, by discussing the literal sense of the text.

Augustine uses this interrogative method of asking simple questions that arise directly from the literal sense of the passage in the *Sermones* as well as in the *In Iohannis* in order to lead into his interpretative work, whether that work remains concerned with simple or more complex matters. For example, in Augustine's discussion of Christ's repeated question to Peter, "do you love me?," he comments that Peter "answered Him from the heart. If Peter answered from the heart, why was the Lord who could see into hearts asking the question? As a matter of fact even Peter himself was surprised, and as he was well aware that Jesus knew the answer, it was with a certain weariness that he heard Him asking the question . . . [Peter gave] the answer, 'I love you Lord, as you know.'"[50] Augustine does not merely ask an obvious question of the text, but one that is raised by the text itself, in the person of Peter. Although the answer he gives in this case relies on symbolism somewhat (that Christ is forcing Peter to express his devotion three times to make up for his three denials earlier) the point remains that Augustine's entry point into the passage is a simple question that is formed from the plain meaning of the text rather than some obscure detail.

When Augustine does progress beyond simple or brief comments to more complex matters, he frequently uses reasoning at a literal level as his primary tool, in preference to allegory or abstracted philosophical reasoning. This can be seen in his longer discussion of why Jesus forbade

---

with reference to Paul's working with his own hands (1 Cor 4:12).

49. Augustine, *In Ioh.*, 123.1.

50. Augustine, *Sermons*, 253.1, on John 21:15–17.

Mary to touch him after his resurrection, "for I have not yet ascended to my Father":

> What is this? If, standing on earth, He is not touched, how would He, sitting in heaven, be touched by men? Now certainly before He ascended, He offered himself to His disciples to be touched... But who would be so ridiculous as to say that He did indeed wish himself to be touched by his disciples, but did not wish [to be touched] by women except when He had ascended to the Father? But even one who wanted to would not be left in such a state of unreason. For one also reads that women had touched Jesus, after the Resurrection.[51]

It is only after proceeding to sort through possible meanings in this manner for some time that he gives an allegorical explanation, of shorter length than the preceding literal discussion.[52] Note also Augustine's disparaging reference to being "left in such a state of unreason," another pointer to the value that he purports to place on reason and his disdain for its absence. Elsewhere, the fact that a possible meaning for a text is not logical provides Augustine with sufficient cause to dismiss it out of hand: "I do not see how that can be understood in this context," is the quick dismissal given to the very plausible idea that Christ's death on the cross is what is meant by the words "what death He [Christ] would die."[53]

Allegory?

Even in places where Augustine does appear to be interpreting allegorically, this is not necessarily the case. One must not assume the presence of allegorical interpretation wherever Augustine uses certain key words such as "signify" or "symbol."[54] Elsewhere in his own works, in the *Liber de Utilitate Credendi*, Augustine suggests that the literal sense includes certain figures of speech and analogies, which are distinct from

---

51. Augustine, *In Ioh.*, 121.3, on John 20:17. Ambrose, *Lucam*, X, 162 argues from a similarly literal basis.

52. TeSelle, *Augustine*, 176 provides a brief discussion of Augustine's interpretation of this account.

53. Augustine, *In Ioh.*, 114.5, on John 18:32.

54. As well as varying degrees of abstraction which might create the impression of allegory, contemporary scholarship recognizes that patristic authors distinguished a metaphorical use of the literal sense: Kannengeisser, *Handbook*, 173.

the "allegorical" sense which he also calls "non ad litteram."[55] As an example, consider the commentary on Mary's statement in John 20:13 to the "gardener" that "they have taken away my Lord and I know not where they have laid Him": "[Mary], calling Lord the dead body of her Lord, from the whole signifying the part, just as we all confess that Jesus Christ, the Only Son of God, our Lord . . . has nevertheless been crucified and buried, although only His flesh was buried."[56] Here, Augustine's primary purpose is not to uncover a "deeper" or "hidden" meaning in the text, but to clarify exactly what Mary meant, literally, and in doing so make the more sophisticated, doctrinal point that Christ's entombment entailed only the burial of his flesh, not his whole being.[57]

Similarly, care must be taken to avoid treating every instance where some modern readers might think that Augustine avoids the plain meaning of the passage as allegorical. A relevant example here are his words on Christ's prediction to Peter in John 21:18–19 that "'When you are old, you will stretch forth your hands and another will gird you and lead you where you would not.' For he [Jesus] said this to him [Peter], signifying by what death he would glorify God":

> That you [Peter] may come to this, "another will gird you and will lead," not where you would, but "where you would not." First he said what would happen and then how it would happen. For not crucified, but definitely about to be crucified, he was led where he would not, for crucified, he went not where he would not, but rather where he would. For indeed loosed from the body, he wished to be with Christ, but if it were possible, he ardently desired eternal life apart from the distress of death.[58]

Here Augustine places the emphasis on the (presumed) fact that Peter in a sense wanted to be crucified, where the plain meaning of the passage appears to be saying the opposite. However, the basis for his oblique exegesis here is not allegorical symbolism, but an assumption about Peter's attitude towards being crucified.

Elsewhere, Augustine's exegesis contains elements of allegorical interpretation, but is not therefore necessarily allegorical in essence. One

---

55. Augustine, *De utilitate credendi*, III, 5 (PL 42:0068–0069).

56. Augustine, *In Ioh.*, 121.1.

57. See Augustine, *In Ioh.*, 121.4 for a similar example, on the nature of Christ's resurrection body.

58. Augustine, *In Ioh.*, 123.5.

example where allegorical elements are present, but where it would be unreasonable to describe the whole tenor as allegorical, is found in Augustine's discussion of the fact that Christ told Peter to "follow me," while making an enigmatic statement about the possibility of John's remaining until he came again (John 21:19–23). Augustine explains that Christ is referring to two different lives that the believer lives before God, and that Christ's words to each of Peter and John symbolize one of these two lives by stating that "the Church knows two lives, preached and commended by Divinity to her, of which one exists in faith, the other in direct vision; one in the time of sojourning abroad, the other in an eternity of dwelling ... this [first life] has been signified by the Apostle Peter, that other by John."[59] Augustine here clearly begins his exegesis with allegorical symbolism, by stating that the two apostles symbolize different realities. However, what follows is better described as a more figurative, oblique form of the literal sense, rather than allegorical, although it is in part an extension of the allegorical identifications just noted:

> The former is wholly spent here up to the end of this world and finds its end there; the latter is put off to be completed after the end of this world, but it does not have an end in the world to come ... And this can be said more clearly as follows: Let perfected action follow me, shaped by the example of my passion, but let contemplation remain imperfect till I come, to be perfected when I come. For the goodly plenitude of patience, reaching even to death, follows Christ; however, the plenitude of knowledge remains till Christ comes, then to be made manifest.[60]

By the end of this excerpt, Augustine has largely left his original allegory behind, and is concentrating on the point that he is making about the Christian life. His statement that "this can be said more clearly as ..." would seem obviously untrue in light of what follows to most readers or listeners, a fact which underlines that the obtuseness of the passage is more due to its dealing with difficult concepts than its relatively simple allegorical assumptions. It is therefore argued that in Augustine's exegesis, the use of the literal meaning and reason is more significant than allegorical interpretation. This is further reinforced when we turn to consider Augustine's practice when he does use allegory.

---

59. Augustine, *In Ioh.*, 124.5.
60. Augustine, *In Ioh.*, 124.5.

Any attempt to understand Augustine's exegesis as primarily "allegorical" in comparison with that of other Western commentators fails to grasp the entire breadth of Augustine's own purposes in commenting on the biblical text. It also fails to appreciate the limited extent of the role that allegory plays in his exegesis. That allegorical interpretation frequently occurs in Augustine's exegesis cannot be denied, nor can the fact that he utilizes this type of interpretation a little more often than Jerome and Hilary. However, this does not mean that it is central to his exegesis, at least in the texts under study here. Augustine does not see himself proceeding through the text in order to develop largely allegorical interpretations. Rather in the *In Iohannis evangelium* and the *Sermones*, allegory is seen as a luxury that one might engage in to gain pious insights helpful to the faith additional to those already gained from more straightforward modes of interpretation. Consider, for example his comments on the clothes in the tomb of the risen Christ: "Do we suppose that these things signify nothing? In no way would I suppose this. But we are hastening on to other things on which we are compelled to linger by necessity of some question or obscurity. For these things which are obvious in themselves, to ask what each one signifies is indeed a holy delight, but for those at leisure —which we are not."[61] Here, allegorical interpretation is regarded as an optional extra.[62] Certainly, allegorical meaning is there and is useful to Augustine's exegesis, but is not an essential element of his exposition of the passage.

Thus, while Augustine does use allegory in his exegesis of the Gospels, it is not the chief tool of his exegesis. In fact, when allegorical interpretation does occur, it is usually restrained. Easily the longest passage of allegorical exegesis in the *In Iohannis evangelium* is found where Augustine deals with Christ's post-resurrection appearance to his disciples in John 21:12–19, which includes the well-known allegory on the number of 153 fish.[63] It is noteworthy that of the thirteen tractates under consideration, this is the only one in which allegorical exegesis makes up over half of the tractate, and in which allegory could be in any sense said to predominate. However, even in this case, the allegorical meanings of

---

61. Augustine, *In Ioh.*, 120.8, on John 20:5–7. A similar comment is made shortly afterwards, in 120.9.

62. As it is in Ambrose's discussion of the tomb, *Lucam*, X, 143.

63. Augustine, *In Ioh.*, 122. This is a topic which Augustine addresses several times in his corpus, including at length in his *De Diversis Quaestionibus* as well as in the *Sermones* as discussed presently.

details in the passage are only given after a lengthy discussion of the plain meaning of the passage and various mundane and obvious issues that arise naturally from the text.[64] Augustine does not simply launch into frenzied allegorizing of an eclectic collection of details from the text, but proceeds by methodically working through the literal facts of the passage, prior to engaging in the "luxury" of allegorical interpretation. Furthermore, the allegorizing that does occur is not disconnected from the basic literal facts of the passage: "For it must be believed that He imposed on them the need by which they were compelled to go fishing for no other reason except His wanting to exhibit the planned miracle, so that at the same time He might feed the preachers of His Gospel and augment the Gospel itself with respect to so great a mystery [*sacramentum*] that He would reveal from the number of fishes."[65] The opportunity for the miracle, and for the allegorizing that follows from it, is brought about by a very earthly set of circumstances that also led to the disciples being fed!

The lengthiest example of allegorical interpretation in the *Sermones* also deals with the matter of the 153 fish. Although different at points from his treatment in the *In Iohannis evangelium*, it does not substantially support the case for allegory being central to Augustine's exegesis, either. The primary purpose of the allegory in the *Sermones* appears to be practical.[66] He begins his commentary similarly to his more succinct analysis of the same passage in *In Iohannis evangelium*, but much of his time is taken up with moral exhortation: he finds the number ten and the Law early in his speculations, and devotes the rest of the sermon to urging his congregation to obey the commandments. The fact that it was allegorical interpretation that allowed him to take this line is of no special importance to him, as he doesn't feel the need to spell out all of the numerological details of the allegory, even telling his hearers that "[t]here's no need now to count them all, count it for yourselves."[67] Augustine's use of allegory more often than not has a down-to-earth, practical purpose. It is not concerned primarily with obscure mysteries and fine doctrinal points,[68] or as the primary means of accessing the transcendent God.[69]

---

64. Augustine, *In Ioh.*, 122.1–5 contains no allegorical tendencies whatsoever.
65. Augustine, *In Ioh.*, 122.4.
66. Augustine, *Sermons*, 248.4–5.
67. Augustine, *Sermons*, 248.5.
68. For example, see also Augustine, *Serm.*, 243.2, 249.3 and 250.3.
69. Kenney, *Contemplation and Classical Christianity: A Study in Augustine*, 164.

Even in the few places where Augustine does allegorize at greater length, it would appear as if his purpose is not to engage in allegorical interpretation for its own sake.

However, beyond these two longer examples, in almost all of the other instances where Augustine allegorizes, he does so briefly, simply, and most frequently bases his comments on the literal facts of the text. He seldom takes more time about allegorizing than he has to; his most common use of allegory is when he makes passing comments like "as for the blood and water which His side, pierced with the lance, poured forth upon the earth, without a doubt they represent the sacraments by which the Church was formed, as Eve was formed from the side of the sleeping Adam."[70] Elsewhere, he comments that "the fact that the soldiers took His garments after they had divided them into four parts signified that His sacraments would penetrate into all four parts of the world."[71] Such brief allegorical comments are littered throughout his sermons. However, the point to note is not that Augustine's sermons are therefore essentially allegorical in character, but that whenever Augustine does allegorize, it is typically briefly, in passing and without much ostentation, with little interest in comprehensive allegorization.[72] Allegory is therefore relatively incidental to his work. In both of the examples just given, Augustine moves on immediately after the quoted portion to consider the next verse in the text. In neither case does he pause to digress at length or justify his use of the allegory, instead, he simply states what he sees as the allegorical significance of the verse and then returns to the passage.

Typically, in the *In Iohannis* and *Sermones*, Augustine entertains an allegorical meaning only briefly before returning to the predominant non-allegorical modes of interpretation. A simple case of this occurs in his discussion of the fact that according to John 19:41, Jesus was laid in a new, empty tomb. Augustine briefly (in one sentence only) draws a connection between the nature of the tomb and the fact that Mary's womb was that of a virgin, before returning to make at greater length the more basic point that the burial was hurried.[73] Likewise, when Augustine in-

---

70. Augustine, *Sermons*, 218.14, on John 19:34. Cf. Hilary, *Tractatus Mysteriorum*, 1.3, who argues along similar lines with respect to the same incident.

71. Augustine, *In Ioh.*, 218.9, on John 19:23. Cf. Houghton, *Augustine's Text of John*, 345.

72. Cf. Muller, "Iohannis euangelium tractatus CXXIV, In," 717.

73. Augustine, *In Ioh.*, 120.5. Jerome, *Math.*, IV, 1881–8 treats the new tomb in a very similar manner, very briefly drawing a connection between it and Mary's womb

vokes the reference (Isaiah 53:7; Acts 8:32) to the biblical symbolism of Christ as a lamb in handling the trial of Jesus before Pilate, he does not develop the allegory at all, but states that the symbolism is there that we may rightly understand Christ's literal actions before Pilate, since "the comparison with a lamb was given for this purpose, that in his silence He be held not guilty, but innocent. Therefore, when He was being judged, wherever he did not open his mouth, as a lamb He did not open it, that is not as one who had a bad conscience but as the gentle One."[74]

Furthermore, the possibility of overreliance on an allegorical approach was clearly a real one for Augustine. For example, when discussing the fact that the disciples did not understand that Christ had to rise from the dead, Augustine also appears to criticize the disciples for being too willing to understand Jesus' promises to rise allegorically: "And for this reason when they heard it from the Lord himself, although it was stated very openly, from their normal experience of hearing parables from Him, they did not understand and believed that He signified something else."[75] In this light, views such as that of Simonetti, that "[i]n his work on John's Gospel, Augustine turns readily to allegorical interpretation,"[76] could be modified.

In the light of Augustine's heavy reliance on the literal sense and interpretative techniques associated with it in the texts under study here, and the fact that allegory does not exercise a dominant function within his exegesis even when it does feature, the tendency in some scholarship to characterize Augustine's exegesis as primarily allegorical needs to be corrected. It is a little exaggerated to suggest, as Brown does, that for Augustine the Bible is written "in an intricate code ... it was a communication that was intrinsically so far above the pitch of human minds, that to be made available to our senses at all, this 'Word' had to be communicated by means of an intricate game of 'signs.'"[77] Certainly, Augustine does at times regard Scripture's meaning as being hidden, and semiotic ideas are an important part of his thought. But that does not mean that it is critical to his exegesis, which is actually much more frequently dependent on plain simple meanings that can be readily understood

---

before moving back to discuss literal aspects of the text at considerably greater length.

74. Augustine, *In Ioh.*, 116.4, on John 19:9–10.
75. Augustine, *In Ioh.*, 120.9, on John 20:9.
76. Simonetti, *Interpretation*, 107.
77. Brown, *Augustine*, 252.

by his audience. It is thus unhelpful to argue as Carroll does that "[o]n allegory his [Augustine's interpretation] rested."[78] Likewise, Altaner's view that Augustine prefers "the allegorical-mystical sense, especially in his homilies,"[79] where his work on John's Gospel is given as an example, would benefit from some moderation.[80]

Furthermore, comments such as "[i]n his exegesis St. Augustine tries to steer a middle course between literal and allegorical exposition,"[81] that understand Augustine's exegesis in terms of where it sits on an allegorical-literal spectrum are also not quite accurate with respect to the texts studied here, as Augustine's exegesis is fundamentally "literal," and incorporates a range of other elements unrelated to this distinction. Similarly, de Margerie's view that Augustine "goes beyond the limits of Origen's allegorism and converges with the outlook of the more moderate representatives of the Alexandrian school . . . who reject universal allegorism,"[82] while containing some truth, is flawed in that it tries to explain Augustine's approach to allegory in terms of where he fits into the thought world of Greek exegesis. As will be further explored below, Augustine's use of allegory cannot be explained in terms of categories like this. Finally, it should be emphasized that Augustine's primary emphasis on "literal" interpretative features such as reason and the apparent meaning, as seen above, means much more than any allegorical meanings being based on the literal. Where Augustine's reliance on allegory is downplayed by scholars, it is usually in this sense of being based on the literal meaning, rather than being small in general, as the forgoing suggests it should be.[83] Having thus established our case that the literal meaning, and not allegory is central to Augustine's exegesis in the *In Iohannis* and *Sermones*, it would appear that in terms of the senses if Scripture, Augustine's work is relatively similar to that of our other inter-

78. Carroll, *Preaching*, 192.

79. Altaner, *Patrology*, 509.

80. Likewise the assertion of Cameron, *Christ Meets Me Everywhere*, 284, that Augustine in his later works retains the same very strong interest in allegorical interpretation that he demonstrated prior to 400. Cameron suggests that readers of Augustine who deny this do so on the basis of his theological treatises: whereas the analysis conducted here on the basis of the *Tractates* and *Sermones* rather than a theological treatise does in fact still call Cameron's view into question.

81. Smalley, *Bible*, 24. See also Jeanrond, *Hermeneutics*, 22.

82. Margerie, *Exegesis*, 3:34; A similar problem exists with Berrouard, "L'Exegese," 338.

83. E.g. Harrison, *Beauty*, 90; Lubac, *Medieval*, 2:47, 52.

preters in being fundamentally literal, without being necessarily averse to introducing some allegory if doing so suits his purposes. His exegesis of the Gospels differs not in kind but only in degree from that of Jerome and Hilary, and then only a little, in using allegory somewhat more frequently overall than they do. It is therefore apparent that factors beyond the extent to which Augustine's exegesis is "literal" or "allegorical" should be explored if we wish to draw sharp contrasts between his work and that of his contemporaries. Some of those which have been investigated for our other three interpreters shall be discussed in the next chapter. For the present, however, it is worthwhile examining how Augustine does use allegory somewhat further, as his allegories provide some of the more obvious illustrations for a crucial distinguishing feature of his exegesis, his concern with the real words and events described by the Gospel rather than with the philological features of the text.

Realities Behind the Text

A key characteristic of Augustine's exegesis, and a point at which his approach differs significantly from that of other exegetes, particularly Jerome, is his being more interested in the realities that lie behind the Gospel account than the text itself.[84] Augustine concentrates on the significance of the historical events and words contained in the narrative much more than on philological issues and features of the text such as variations between manuscripts, the meaning of the Greek version, the histories of words in the text, or literary details, all of which barely rate a mention, let alone detailed discussion.[85] When Augustine does allegorize, he prefers to develop his allegory from something in the history behind the text, rather than from some textual detail.[86] In this respect, his practice in the *In Iohannis* and *Sermones* reflects the statement that he makes in *De Trinitate*, that "where the apostle calls something 'allegory,' he finds it in the fact and not in the words,"[87] and also his understanding of figurative signs (*signa translata*) in *De Doctrina Christiana*—these

---

84. As well as being evident in how he uses allegory, it has also been suggested that Augustine's manner of handling of discrepancies between the evangelists also implies a focus on realities rather than texts: De Jonge, "Augustine on the Interrelations of the Gospels," 2416.

85. Bonner, "Augustine," 546–7.

86. Markus, *Signs*, 5, 10 sets forward a similar idea to the point made here.

87. Augustine, *De Trinitate*, XV, 9 (*CCSL* 50A:27–28).

Augustine regards as resting on a connection between the *thing* usually meant by the chosen word (rather than merely the word itself), and that which is being referred to figuratively.[88]

Thus, for example, Augustine's allegorical interpretation of the division of Christ's clothing in John 19:23 into four parts representing the four parts of the church is based upon the historical fact present in the account that Christ's garments were divided into four parts.[89] The allegory is not developed from a study of a key word or interesting phrase, or a peculiarity in the Greek version, or a grammatical feature in the Latin. By contrast, Jerome's interpretation of the relevant verse rests on the reference which Matthew 27:35 connects it to in Psalm 22:18, and the use of the terms "divide" and "garments" in this part of the Old Testament.[90] Furthermore, it should be noted that Augustine's allegory is preceded by a lengthy, literal explanation of the passage, not of features of the text, but of the details of the division of Christ's clothing.[91] It is upon this foundation that the allegory is built.

Augustine frequently allegorizes not one reality within the text, but a series.[92] This is the case in his discussion of John 19:28:

> Afterwards Jesus, knowing that all things were accomplished . . . says, "I thirst." Now there was a vessel set there full of vinegar around [a stalk of] hyssop, they raised it to His lips: he said, "I thirst," as though he were to say, "In doing this you have fallen short; give what you are." For indeed the Jews themselves were the vinegar, deteriorating from the wine of the Patriarchs and Prophets, and, as it were, filled from a full vessel, from the iniquity of this world, having their heart like a sponge, deceitful, so to speak, in its cavernous and tortuous hiding-places. But the hyssop around which they put the sponge full of vinegar, because it is a lowly herb and purges the breast, we take appropriately as

---

88. Augustine, *Doctrina*, 2.10.15 (*PL* 34:0042). In the example he gives here, the connection is between the animal designated by the sign "ox" and one of the evangelists.

89. Augustine, *In Ioh.*, 118.4.

90. Jerome, *Math.*, IV, 1695–8 only makes word-based connections to other texts from this episode (Matt 27:35).

91. Augustine, *In Ioh.*, 118.2–3.

92. In addition to the examples given below, see also Augustine, *In Ioh.*, 121.3 and 118.5.

the lowliness of Christ which they surrounded and thought they had come round to thwarting.[93]

Here, various words and events within the text, namely, Jesus' statement "I thirst," the vinegar, the full vessel, the sponge and the hyssop are all in turn allegorized briefly in order to make a series of theological points.

Augustine proceeds similarly when describing what happened when the disciples cast their fishing nets into the water after Christ's resurrection:

> Here He [Jesus] says, "Cast the net on the right side of the ship," so that he might signify those who were standing at the right, the good only. There [the last time the disciples went fishing] the net was broken, signifying schisms, but here, because then at that point, in that perfect peace of the saints there will be no schisms, it was a matter of consequence to the Evangelist to say, "and although they were so vast . . . the net was not broken," as though He looked back at that occasion where it was broken and in comparison with that evil commended this good.[94]

In this example, Augustine compares the historical facts of two fishing trips of Christ's disciples, supported by a brief allusion to the discussion of the sheep and the goats in Matthew 25:34, and develops his allegorical interpretations from there.[95]

Even where a philological detail in the text is significant in the development of an allegory, Augustine's exegesis is still strongly linked to the realities of the narrative. Thus, although Augustine begins allegorizing on Jesus' wounding in the side when on the cross by noting that John 19:34 says that the spear "opened" his side rather than "pierced" or "wounded" him, he develops the allegory through reference to details of the realities of the account, noting that "here the second Adam, his head bowed, slept on the cross in order that from there might be found for him a wife—that one who flowed from the side of the One sleeping [i.e. the Church]."[96] Here, the similarities between the account of the creation of Eve and Christ's death are connected symbolically, in a manner that is

---

93. Augustine, *In Ioh.*, 119.4.

94. Augustine, *In Ioh.*, 122.7, on John 21:6 and Luke 5:4–11. Augustine continues for some length in this vein, comparing the literal details of the two fishing expeditions and allegorizing from the comparisons.

95. See also his related discussion of the same passage at *Serm.*, 249.1.

96. Augustine, *In Ioh.*, 120.2.

partly allegorical and partly typological.⁹⁷ In this respect, the example is similar to the case of the fishing expedition, in that its symbolism was based on a comparison with an earlier biblical event.

An examination of Augustine's use of allegory in the *Sermones* also yields the same conclusions reached from the *In Iohannis* about his preference for the real events and characters behind the text ahead of text-based features in the narrative. This is true of simple allegories on a single detail in the account, such as when Augustine, commenting on Mary's mistaking Christ for a gardener, notes that Christ is "the gardener who sows a grain of mustard seed . . . [which] looks small, nothing less noteworthy to the sight, but nothing stronger to the taste. And what does it signify but the very great fervour and inner strength of faith in the Church?"⁹⁸ Augustine does not proceed to discuss the biblical usage or etymological history of the terms "gardener" or mustard seed," but makes his point by drawing on the qualities of the mustard seed itself.

Augustine draws similarly on the qualities of the things discussed in the text when he allegorizes on certain details of the drink given to Christ as he hung on the cross:

> . . . instead of the sweetness of faith, they gave him the vinegar of faithlessness, and that in a sponge. They are indeed comparable to a sponge, a thing not solid but swollen; not open with the straight access of confession, but hollow with the tortuous twists and turns of treachery. It's true that drink also contained hyssop, which is a lowly herb, said to have been an extremely strong root with which to cling to the rock. There were some, that is to say, among the people, for whom this dark deed was kept as a means of humbling their souls by their repudiation of it later on, and their repentance.⁹⁹

Augustine commences and further develops his allegory, and makes a sequence of points from it, by noting one physical characteristic after another about the props that form part of the crucifixion scene, the vinegar, sponge, and hyssop.¹⁰⁰ Augustine believes that every detail in the text can

---

97. On Augustine's blurring of the line between allegory and typology, see Markus, *Signs*, 11.

98. Augustine, *Sermons*, 246.3, on John 20:15, with reference to the man who plants a mustard seed in Matt 13:31 and Luke 13:19, and also to that faith which is as small as a mustard seed (Matt 17:20 and Mark 4:31).

99. Augustine, *Sermons*, 218.11, on John 19:29.

100. A further example of a sequence of allegorized details is found at Augustine,

potentially have some significance, but his emphasis is very much on the details of realities that lie behind the text, such as events and people, as the following quote illustrates: "it may rightly be assumed that by every single deed that was carried out and recorded about His passion, He also wished to signify something."[101] Christ speaks not through the Greek original or literary details, but through real events.

Augustine's preference for analysing the realities that lie behind the text rather than the text itself is not only seen in how he allegorizes, but throughout his exegesis in the *In Iohannis* and *Sermones* in general. Augustine's practice here is related to a tendency that Rogers and McKim observe in passing, that "Augustine . . . focussed on the meaning expressed, not the mechanics of expression."[102] Consider, for example, Augustine's comment on Jesus breathing on the disciples and saying in John 20:22, "Receive the Holy Spirit," that "By His breathing [on them] He signified that the Holy Spirit is not the Spirit of the Father alone, but also of Him."[103] Here, it is Christ's breathing that points to a doctrinal truth, in this case the idea of the Spirit proceeding from both the Father and the Son that would later lead to the "filioque" controversy. Even when words are considered more important, it is the actual words of Jesus or the other actors in the narrative that receive attention, rather than some philological aspect of the text, and even then, the events can perform the same function as the words of the characters, to instruct and inform. For example, in a discussion of how church leaders are to be shepherds of God's people, Augustine's main point is developed from Jesus' example, rather than from his words, which is seen as teaching others how they should act.[104]

These tendencies are further underlined by Augustine's being quite conscious of the distinction between exegesis of the text, and of the realities it describes.[105] When comparing the disciples' fishing after the resurrection (John 21:3–14) with the fishing done in the parable in Matthew 13:47–49, he comments, "that parable consists in its words [only], not stemming from an actual event. But in this passage the Lord signified

---

Serm., 248.2.

101. Augustine, *Sermons*, 218.1.

102. Rogers and McKim, *The Authority and Interpretation of the Bible*, 29.

103. Augustine, *In Ioh.*, 121.4.

104. Augustine, *In Ioh.*, 123.5, on John 21:15–17.

105. A consciousness also briefly noted by Bernard's study on books 11–13 of the *Confessiones*, "The Rhetoric of God in the Figurative Exegesis of Augustine," 99.

by an actual event how the Church will be at the end of the world."[106] Here, Augustine explicitly makes the point that Jesus' intended meaning is based on an "actual event," and shows that he is aware of the possibility that Scripture may elsewhere signify meanings through its words only. Likewise, when discussing John 20:3-4, "Peter, therefore, went out, and that other disciple, and they came to the sepulchre. Now they both ran together and that other disciple did out run Peter and came first to the sepulchre," Augustine shows his awareness of the distinction between text and reality, although more obliquely than in the previous example: "Here one ought to observe and approve the restatement, how the text returned to that to which it had passed over, and yet this was added on as though it followed. For when [the Evangelist] had already said, 'they came to the sepulchre,' he went back to relate how they came and he said, 'Now they both ran together,' etc."[107] Here, Augustine makes the point that the order in which events are described in the Gospel is different to the order in which they actually happened, and in doing so further demonstrates his awareness of the distinction between text and reality. In light of this awareness, it is all the more noteworthy that Augustine has a strong preference for explaining the text in terms of the real events and words that it reports.

At a number of points Augustine does pursue text-based issues. Certainly, we must not think that he is incapable of doing so, when in fact his rhetorical training would have given him most of the necessary skills—apart from the same level of fluency in Greek and Hebrew, of course—to pursue a similar exegetical approach to Jerome, for example.[108] However, it appears that he simply chooses not to study the Gospel in this manner, and that in the majority of these cases where he does show a philological inclination, his apparent concern with the text is largely incidental to his non-textual purposes. A relevant example is found in Augustine's discussion of the post-resurrection appearance to Thomas, and speculation as to whether the disciples actually did touch Jesus, given that Jesus had said

106. Augustine, *In Ioh.*, 122.7.
107. Augustine, *In Ioh.*, 120.7.
108. Augustine begins to describe such skills at *Doctrina*, 3.29.40 (PL 34:0080), before stopping and suggesting that they can easily be learnt from any grammarian—the implication is that Augustine was well acquainted with such matters and could have easily dominated his exegesis with them, or that he feels readily able to access them if he so desired. For a recent treatment of Augustine's use of his rhetorical training in his work, cf. Schäublin, "The Contribution of Rhetorics to Christian Hermeneutics," 149-63 in Kannengeisser, *Handbook*, 153-6.

to Thomas "touch and see" (John 20:27), whereas he had forbidden Mary to touch him outside the tomb (John 20:17):

> It can be said, though, that the disciples did not dare to touch, although He offered himself to be touched; for it was not written, "and Thomas touched him." But whether by looking only or also by touching he saw and believed, that which follows foretells and commends more the faith of the Gentiles, "Blessed are they who have not seen and have believed." He used verbs of the past tense as That One who knew in His own predestining as already done what would be done.[109]

Here, what was *not* written in the text is taken as the starting point for a discussion about the events that lay behind it. However, Augustine does not go on to consider the textual issue, but a practical one: that the event commends faith, whether Thomas touched Jesus or not. Note also the passing reference to the use of the past tense, which although superficially is a textual concern, is turned to underline Christ's predestining of events, which points to his divinity.[110]

Elsewhere, when discussing Mary's statement to the gardener "They have taken my Lord from the sepulchre," Augustine makes a rare reference to the Greek, in this case, to the fact that several Greek codices have a slightly different rendering of the verse.[111] However, Augustine does not discuss this point beyond noting it, before he moves on to the next verse. Unusually for him, he does not even take the opportunity to use the variation to digress onto doctrinal or practical matters.

Sometimes, Augustine notes a subtle point in the wording of the text in the course of his exegesis, an apparently "textual" concern. However, when he does this, it is seldom the case that his primary concern is textual. More often than not, the textual point is only used in passing to support other, non-textual interests. For example, when discussing Jesus' words to Pilate that "My kingdom is not of this world," Augustine notes that "consequently, here too He does not say, 'My kingdom is not in this world,' but 'is not of this world.'"[112] However, he makes this brief point only at the end of his (rather lengthier) discussion of the idea that Chris-

---

109. Augustine, *In Ioh.*, 121.5.

110. Cf. Houghon, *Augustine's Text of John*, 351.

111. Augustine, *In Ioh.*, 120.6, on John 20:13.

112. Augustine, *In Ioh.*, 115.2, on John 18:36. Cf. Augustine, *Retractiones*, I, 3 (*CCSL* 57:19–20).

tians are to be "in" the world, even though his kingdom is not "of" it. The textual point does not form the basis of his discussion but is really just an incidental footnote to it that is not developed in any way.[113]

When commenting on John 19:39, "And there came Nicodemus, who at first had come to Jesus by night, bringing a mixture of myrrh and aloes" in the account of Jesus' burial, Augustine makes an apparently textual remark on how the verse is to be read:

> This must not be so punctuated that we say, "At first bringing a mixture of myrrh," but that the phrase "at first" belongs to the prior clause. For Nicodemus had come to Jesus by night at first—an event which the same John narrated in the earlier pasts of his Gospel. Here, therefore, it must be understood that Nicodemus came not only then, but that subsequently he had come frequently in order that by hearing he might become a disciple.[114]

Here, the textual remark on how the passage is to be punctuated is not the primary determinant of meaning. Instead, Augustine's views on how the clauses of the quotation are to be read are determined by his understanding of the historical facts of Nicodemus's part in the Gospel account. Augustine reminds his audience that Nicodemus had come to Jesus for the first time earlier in the Gospel, and that therefore Nicodemus's coming now with a mixture of myrrh, therefore, was not Nicodemus's first coming to Jesus. These factual details, and not the question of punctuation, dictate Augustine's understanding of the passage, and assist him to make the further, factual, deduction that Nicodemus must have frequently come to Jesus in order to become a disciple.

Typology

When making connections between the passage at hand and other parts of Scripture, Augustine most often links passages using typological logic, drawing historical connections between real events, rather than

---

113. Another relevant example is found in Augustine, *In Ioh.*, 122.9.

114. Augustine, *In Ioh.*, 120.4. "Non ita distinguendum est, ut dicamus: 'primum ferens mixturam myrrhae'; sed ut quod dictum est: 'primum,' ad superiorem sensum pertineat. Venerat enim Nicodemus ad Iesum nocte primum, quod idem Iohannes narrauit in prioribus euangelii sui partibus. Hic ergo intellegendem est ad Iesum, non tunc solum, sed tunc primum uenisse Nicodemum; uentitasse autem postea ut fieret audiendo discipulus."

philological methods such as linking two passages on the grounds that a key word is present in both.[115] An example of Old–New Testament typological interpretation is found in the following comments on Christ's resurrection: "Circumcision typified the stripping off of the carnal life on the eighth day through the resurrection of Christ. For the seventh day of the week is completed by the Sabbath. On the Sabbath, the seventh day being the day of the Sabbath, the Lord lay in the tomb. He arose on the eighth day; and His Resurrection renews us. Therefore, by rising on the eighth day He circumcises us."[116] In this excerpt, Augustine establishes a typological relationship between Christ's resurrection and two key Old Testament concepts, circumcision and the Sabbath, and then relates them forward to the contemporary Christian.[117]

In addition, Augustine frequently links the events of the passage at hand to various Old Testament passages through use of the prophecy-fulfillment motif,[118] which also connects passages typologically by drawing a real historical (and thence a theological) comparison between them.[119] In this respect his exegesis is like that of Jerome. Thus, Augustine says concerning Jesus' silence before Pilate when asked about his claiming to be the Son of God, "that prophecy which been spoken previously about him was not spoken in vain: 'As a lamb before his shearer was without voice, so he opened not His mouth'—now, not surprisingly, He does not answer those questioning [Him]."[120] As with his discussion of allegorical material, Augustine's comments on fulfillment of prophecy are typically brief notes. Sometimes this is because the evangelist has already done Augustine's work for him in noting that a particular event fulfilled prophecy, as in the case of the casting lots for Jesus' clothing, where Augustine does little more than draw attention to the note in the text "that the Scripture might be fulfilled, saying . . ."[121] Other examples of Augustine's belaboring

115. Cf. Augustine, *In Ioh.*, 28.9.

116. Augustine, *Liturgical*, 231.2, on Matt 28:1.

117. Another example of Old–New Testament typology is found at Augustine, *Serm.*, 232.2.

118. His relatively strong interest in the fulfillment of prophecy may reflect earlier trends in North African exegetical tradition. A brief discussion of this aspect of North African tradition is given in Froehlich, *Biblical Interpretation in the Early Church*, 26.

119. Vawter, *Inspiration*, 34 on Augustine on fulfillment of prophecy, as linked to his view of the infallibility of Scripture.

120. Augustine, *In Ioh.*, 116.4, on John 19:9 as the fulfillment of Isa 53:7.

121. Augustine, *In Ioh.*, 118.2, on John 19:24.

a point on the fulfillment of prophecy already made in the text of John are found in his comments on the fact that not a bone of Jesus' body was broken (John 19:36), and on his being given vinegar to drink shortly before his death (John 19:28–29).[122] However, this is also true where no signal comment is made in the passage, and even where the connection made is a little indirect, as is the case with his observations on the fact that Christ was crucified between two thieves: "And in regard to this a prophecy had been given in advance and had said, 'And He was counted among the wicked.'"[123] Augustine's willingness to make such connections in the area of typology and prophecy-fulfillment (normally without further reference or development into allegory), indicates that this was a distinct element of significant and positive importance within his exegetical practice. His emphasis in this regard runs against the suggestion of Cameron, that typology was relatively unimportant to Augustine (even if he used the terminology at times), and "the most primitive form of figurative reading and [which] ever needed completion in allegory." [124]

Sometimes, a connection is made between two New Testament events, as is the case with the example of the disciples' two fishing expeditions, noted above, where the similarity between the two events is taken as a hint that they both refer to the church.[125] In this example, the difference between what the two similar events signified is explained by the fact that they happened at different points in sacred history: "that one was performed before, but this one after the Lord's Resurrection."[126] The two events are linked, and properly understood, not just theologically but also historically. A similar approach is at work when Augustine devotes considerable attention, in his discussion on the Jews' urging Pilate to execute Jesus, to the exact meaning of the note in John 19:32, that "[t]his

---

122. Augustine, *In Ioh.*, 120.3 and 119.4 respectively.

123. Augustine, *In Ioh.*, 117.3, on John 19:18. Cameron, *Christ Meets Me Everywhere*, 269–71 makes the point from some of Augustine's earlier works that Augustine does not require exact duplicates when making connections between Old and New Testament passages, but frequently prefers to work simply with a degree of conceptual similarity.

124. Cameron, *Christ Meets Me Everywhere*, 17.

125. Augustine, *In Ioh.*, 122.7, comparing Luke 5:4–11 and John 21:3–11. Augustine also compares these two passages to the same effect at *Serm.*, 248.1–2. A further example of typology within the scope of New Testament history is in Augustine, *Serm.*, 253.1. See also Carroll, *Preaching*, 189.

126. Augustine, *In Ioh.*, 122.7.

happened so that the words Jesus had spoken indicating the kind of death He was going to die would be fulfilled."[127]

A good example of the creation of a historical link between events in the Gospel and contemporary realities is Augustine's use of the disciples' recognition of Christ when he breaks the bread after his resurrection (Luke 24:30–31) by asking "where did the Lord wish to be recognized? In the breaking of bread. We're alright, nothing to worry about; we break bread, and we recognize the Lord. It was for our sakes that He didn't want to be recognized anywhere but there, because we weren't going to see Him in the flesh, and yet we were going to eat His flesh."[128] Augustine does not refer the incident back to where we might expect, to when Christ last broke bread with His disciples in the upper room, but gives the event described a greater immediacy by referring it forward to the contemporary church practice of sharing in the Lord's Supper.[129] However, it should be noted that Augustine does not draw such typological connections between events in the Gospels and events and practices in the life of the contemporary church very often. As we shall see in the section in the next chapter on "Audience," he is very interested in drawing practical applications for his congregation from the Gospels. However, he seldom accomplishes this by identifying specific, historical connections between events and practices. Instead, he prefers to rely on taking the theological principles present in the text and adapting these principles for contemporary application, or by using characters in the Gospels as generally applicable exemplars for Christians.

Conclusions

An examination of Augustine's usage of literal and allegorical forms of exegesis reveals that his practice in interpreting the crucifixion and resurrection accounts is not substantially different from that of the other three exegetes considered here. In general terms, he sits alongside Jerome, Hilary, and Ambrose in being primarily driven by a concern for the literal sense, while still exhibiting significant interest in the allegorical. To the extent that he does engage in spiritual exegesis, like our other authors his preference is for typology rather than other kinds of allegory. The

---

127. Augustine, *In Ioh.*, 114.5.
128. Augustine, *Sermons*, 235.3.
129. C.f. Kremen, *Imagination*, 63, who identifies several related examples.

most significant facet of his interpretative method revealed by a study of his use of literal and allegorical readings, however, is his penchant for highlighting realities rather than philological characteristics of the text. In this respect he is closer to Hilary's and Ambrose's practice than that of Jerome. That said, there is considerably more that can be said about Augustine's exegesis than this. An investigation of where he sits in terms of some of the other criteria applied to the work of Jerome, Hilary, and Ambrose, along with some additional perspectives on his work, is helpful in distinguishing it from that of his contemporaries. These matters are the subject of our next chapter.

6

A Wide-Angle Lens
Distinguishing Features of Augustine's Exegesis

Wide-Ranging Interests

THE KEY FEATURE THAT distinguishes Augustine's Gospel exegesis from that of the other three writers under study is that he ranges more widely in his concerns than any of them in terms of what he attempts to do with his exegesis. For Augustine, no particular issue or even broad area of interest dominates. As he moves through the passage, he is interested variously in theological speculation, discussing particular doctrinal issues, untangling obscurities in the narrative, developing allegorical interpretations, identifying multiple meanings, bringing practical issues to bear on his audience, and at other times dazzling with rhetoric. While all these characteristics are notable features of Augustine's exegesis, and in some cases serve to distinguish his methods from those of others, not one of them can be said to dominate his exegesis in the same way that concern for the theological narrative is central to Hilary's exposition, or textualism to Jerome's. This chapter will examine in turn Augustine's free-ranging use of other biblical passages, his tendency towards polysemy, concern for his audience, his interest in the inner workings of the human heart and mind, and the manner in which he explores theological themes through his exegesis. While in most of these areas Augustine's exegesis will be shown to differ significantly from that of the other three it is important to remember throughout that it is also distinguished by the very fact that Augustine is concerned with such a wide array of different matters. His exegesis consists essentially in digging many and diverse gems from all aspects of the passage.

An Intuitive Love of Tangents

One aspect of Augustine's exegesis that quickly becomes obvious to the reader is its highly intuitive, tangential character.[1] Although he does proceed through the text in an orderly and sequential manner, as we shall see, Augustine's work is often characterized by brief digressions, and the occasional longer excursion, away from the Gospel narrative and onto matters only obliquely connected, or not related at all to it. He is always alert to concepts distantly related to the material before him.

Nowhere is this more apparent than in his tendency to jump freely to other parts of Scripture, tangentially using his intuition to make use of texts that at first sight might seem to bear little relation to the Gospel account. Sometimes, his use of other material is surprising, as when he quotes the title of Psalms 56 and 57, "Do not destroy the inscription of the title" in connection with Pilate's insistence to the Jews that "What I have written, I have written" (John 19:22), even though the Psalms in question are not particularly messianic in content: "Did not some hidden voice chant to Pilate in a certain (if one can say it) shouting silence what so long before was prophesied in the written text of the Psalm . . . look, he does not destroy the inscription of the title, what he has written, he has written."[2] Although the Psalm title in its own right can be readily applied to Pilate's decision, its original context hardly suggests this use; there is no natural connection between the two passages except for Augustine's immediate purposes. A similar example is found in Augustine's musings on the Apostle John taking Mary as "his own" mother while Jesus hung on the cross: "But in what sense did John take the mother of the Lord to be 'his own'? For he was one of those who said to Him, 'Look, we have put aside all things and have followed you.' But there too he heard: 'Whoever has put aside these things for me will receive in this world a

1. E.g. Muldowney's Introduction to Augustine, *Serm*, xv, or Williams, "Hermeneutics and Reading Scripture," 313–5.
2. Augustine, *In Ioh.*, 117.5. Ps 57 and 58 in modern English Bibles. This contrasts with Jerome's more predictable treatment of the same verse in Matthew (27:37), *Math.*, IV, 1703–11.

hundred times as much.' Therefore that disciple had a hundredfold more things than he had put aside to which he might take the mother of Him who had bestowed these things."[3] Here, Augustine jumps unexpectedly to another passage, apparently because the text at hand raised a question for him that would not have occurred to others: how could John look after Mary materially if he had given up all his material possessions?[4] Once on this topic, Augustine jumps again to another passage in order to further develop his question, this time in Acts, although now that he is talking about the poverty of the early believers, his selection of text is somewhat more predictable: "But the blessed John had received a hundredfold in that society where no one claimed anything as his own, but all things were common to them, as was written in the Acts of the Apostles... How, therefore, did the disciple and servant take the mother of his Master and Lord to his own where no one claimed anything as his own?"[5] Augustine's solution to his question is as driven by his intuitive mind as the question itself, in that it is ingenious, does not draw on the Gospel passage for support, yet is attractively simple and plausible: "Therefore he took her to his own—not to his own properties (none of which he possessed on his own), but took upon himself those official duties which by special dispensation it was his care to carry out for her."[6]

The same tendency is apparent in Augustine's exegesis in the *Sermones*. For example, when discussing the Gospel of Luke's account of the post-resurrection meeting of the disciples and Christ on the road to Emmaus in sermon 239, Augustine develops the theme of Christ as a wayfarer wandering upon the earth and uses this as an opportunity to introduce another biblical wayfarer, Elijah. He returns to the Gospel account at hand by noting that the Lord used the ravens to feed Elijah and would therefore have fed Christ irrespective of whether he had later eaten ("broken bread") with the disciples.[7]

Elsewhere, Augustine rapidly jumps across several passages as his intuitive mind draws connections between the text before him and other texts drawn from all over the Bible to support particular ideas and

3. Augustine, *In Ioh.*, 119.3, on John 19:26–27.

4. Ambrose, *Lucam*, X, 133 discusses this verse in detail, but this question does not occur to him.

5. Augustine, *In Ioh.*, 119.3, with reference to Acts 2:44–45 and 4:32.

6. Augustine, *In Ioh.*, 119.3.

7. Augustine, *Serm.*, 239.2–4, on Luke 24:13–35 and with reference to 1 Kgs 17:4–6. Another example here is found in Augustine, *Serm.*, 232.3.

insights. Augustine was a master of the art of intertextual criticism, analyzing one scriptural text in terms of others.[8] This is certainly true of his answer to Pilate's question, "Are you a king, then?," where the concluding part of Christ's answer reads, "for this I came into the world, that I give testimony to the truth. Everyone who is of the truth hears my voice." Augustine's treatment of this short excerpt ranges over six references from elsewhere in Scripture:

> Because "not all men have faith" [1 Thess. 3.2], He added and said "everyone who is of the truth hears my voice." He listens, of course, with the inner ears, that is, he listens to my voice, and this would mean just the same as if he were to say "believe me." And so, when Christ gives testimony to the truth, undoubtedly He gives testimony to himself; for indeed it is His word, "I am the truth" [John 14.6], and in another place he said, "I give testimony of myself" [John 8.18]. But by His words, "Everyone who is of the truth hears my voice," He has commended the grace by which he calls "according to the purpose." And about this purpose the Apostle says, "we know that to those who love God all things work together for the good of these who have been called according to the purpose of God" [Rom 8.28] ... And this has been put more clearly elsewhere, as follows: "Labour with the gospel according to the strength of God who saves and calls us, not according to our works but according to his purpose and grace" [1 Tim. 1.8–9]. ... But not all are those to whom it is granted from Truth Itself that they hear the truth, that is, listen to the truth and believe in the truth, with no merits preceding, beyond doubt, lest grace not be grace [Rom 11.6].[9]

In this example, Augustine refers to passages elsewhere in the Gospel of John, as well as from three of Paul's letters, jumping in a kind of exegetical hopscotch from one passage to the next as he notes a particular idea in each passage that causes him to move briefly to another topic and passage, then to another, and so on.[10] Typically, Augustine's use of other scriptural passages is more wide ranging than that of the other commentators

---

8. Van Fleteren, "Augustine's Principles of Biblical Exegesis, De Doctrina Christiana Aside: Miscellaneous Observations," 109–30.

9. Augustine, *In Ioh.*, 115.4, on John 18:37.

10. A similar example is found at Augustine, *In Ioh.*, 122.9, where Augustine jumps in turn to three verses outside the passage he is commenting on, and also at 120.2, where three Old Testament references are noted. Cf. Berrouard, "Exégèse," 332.

considered here.¹¹ Where Hilary leaves the Gospel account, he typically does so in order to spend some time in another (single) book or portion of Scripture, rather than jumping across many different portions as Augustine does. Jerome tends to depend upon favorite types of biblical literature, notably the Old Testament prophets, at the expense of other parts of the Bible, when he draws on other references.

When Augustine deals with the Gospel, other relevant biblical passages are at his fingertips, ready to be referred to in a passing array as required, as is the case with Augustine's rhetorical response to the Jews' comments to Pilate about Christ in John 18:30 that "If He were not a malefactor, we would not have delivered Him up to you," where he suggests "[l]et those be questioned and give answers who were freed from unclean spirits, the sick who were healed, the lepers who were cleansed, the deaf who hear, the dumb who speak, the blind who see, the dead who rise again, and, that which surpasses all, the foolish who are become wise—[let these say] whether Jesus is a malefactor."¹² Another striking example of Augustine's random use of other parts of the Bible is found in an encouragement towards the end of one of his sermons to reflect Christ's risen glory by "living well":

> But what is living a good life? "Savour the things that are above, not those that are on earth" [Col 3:2]. As long as "you are earth, it is into earth that you shall go" [Gen 3:19]; as long as you go on licking the dust of the earth—it is by loving earth, of course, that you lick the dust of the earth—you are also turned into the enemy of the one about whom the psalm says, "And his enemies shall lick the dust" [Ps 72:9]. What were you? Children of men. What are you? Children of God. "Children of men, how long with a heavy heart? Why do you love futility, and seek after lies?"¹³

Augustine continues for some length after this in a similar vein. Here we see him at his most random and intuitive, almost skating from reference to disparate reference, linked only by a single, vaguely related concept.¹⁴

Sometimes the connections which he draws, while having some form of exegetical or theological logic to them, effectively give the

11. Berrouard, "Exégèse," 327.

12. Augustine, *In Ioh.*, 114.3. Addition to text inserted by translator.

13. Augustine, *Sermons*, 231.4. Also of interest is the surprising route by which Augustine gets to this point in this sermon from the passage: see also 231.3.

14. Cf. also Augustine, *In Ioh.*, 117.3.

passages chosen quite a different meaning or slant to what they mean in their own individual context. For example, when dealing with the sign on Christ's cross, Augustine makes the point that it was written in Greek and Latin as well as in Hebrew in order to emphasize the subjugation of the Gentiles as well as the Jews to Christ. This is because: "'The law,' as it says, after all, 'will go forth from Zion, and the word of the Lord from Jerusalem' [Is 2:3]. I mean, who are the people who say in the psalm, 'He has subjected peoples to us, and nations under our feet' [Ps 47:3], but those of whom the apostle says, 'If the nations have shared in their spiritual goods, they ought at least to attend to their needs with material goods' [Rom 15:27]?"[15] Although it seems reasonable to apply the passage from Isaiah to the Christian age in general, it would seem to be applied more readily and obviously to the proclamation of the gospel or to the spread of the Christian Church than to Christ's eschatological subduing of the nations. Likewise, while the second reference from Psalm 47:3 does encapsulate the idea of the subjugation of the Gentiles, it seems something of a leap to move from their being put under the feet of the Jews in Old Testament times to their being under the rule of Christ, whom the Jews have just demanded be crucified. While the final reference from Romans 15:27 does make sense in terms of the internal logic of Augustine's exegesis, it is an unusual choice to use in supporting the meaning of the term "people" in the Psalms. This is because the passage from Romans is making a very different point about Jew-Gentile relations, and is a completely different part of the Bible which might be expected to use particular terms very differently to the Psalms in any case.

So broad-ranging is Augustine's reach that even extra-biblical material that might be related to the Gospel is confidently utilized, as in Augustine's handling of the question raised by John 21:22–23 of whether the Apostle John would remain alive until Christ returns.[16] Here, Augustine mentions the stirring of the dust at John's supposed burial site and "the story—which is found in certain writings, although doubtful—that he [John] . . . was buried while sleeping, and so he remains until Christ should come, and he makes known his life by the heaving of the dust . . . that this dust is stirred by the breath of the one at rest."[17]

---

15. Augustine, *Sermons*, 218.6, on John 19:19–20.
16. See also the reference to John's marital status at Augustine, *In Ioh.*, 124.7.
17. Augustine, *In Ioh.*, 124.2. Addition to text mine.

Augustine's intuitive, tangential manner of doing exegesis is also illustrated by his often-repeated habit of digressing in order to resolve questions or answer problems that he sees in the account, but that would not occur to most commentators in any age, let alone the three others studied here.[18] An example is his discussion of John 21:12, "And none of those reclining dared to ask him, 'Who are you?' knowing that it was the Lord," which is added as a comment when the disciples eat breakfast with the resurrected Christ: "If therefore, they knew, what need was there for them to ask? But if there was not need, why was it said 'they did not dare,' as if there were need but by some fear they would not dare?"[19] Augustine's solution to the dilemma is quite clever, but it is hardly necessary, as most would not have even asked the question in the first place: "so great was the evidence of the truth by which Jesus appeared to those disciples that none of them dared not only to deny but even to doubt. For if anyone doubted, of course he ought to ask. So therefore it was . . . as if it were said 'No one dared to doubt that it was He.'"[20] When developing an allegory on the soldiers' casting of lots for Christ's clothing, Augustine pauses for a moment to defend the allegory from a peculiar potential charge, insisting that "no one say that these things did not signify something good for the reason that they were done by evil men."[21] While Augustine's recognition of this possible objection is not surprising when one bears in mind his conclusions about the validity of the sacraments irrespective of the priest who dispenses them—and his probable belief that it was pastorally necessary to affirm these conclusions—it is a highly unusual point on which to defend his allegory, particularly as it is the only point on which a defense is given. However, it is typical of Augustine's mind, to be thinking further afield than other interpreters.[22]

---

18. In addition to the examples given here, see also Augustine, *In Ioh.*, 124.4 and 5. See also Lienhard, "Reading the Bible and Learning to Read: The Influence of Education on St. Augustine's Exegesis," 7–25, where Augustine's use of a questioning technique in general is related to his comments in *De Magistro*.

19. Augustine, *In Ioh.*, 123.1.

20. Augustine, *In Ioh.*, 123.1.

21. Augustine, *In Ioh.*, 18.5.

22. C.f. Hilary, *Matt.*, 33.4, who interprets the casting of the lots allegorically, but is apparently unaware of this or of other such possibilities.

An Intuitive Love of Insightful Questions

The extent to which Augustine's intuitive tendencies take him on journeys far away from the text at hand is sometimes illustrated by the fact that he spends time raising and dealing with issues that are themselves a response to issues distant from the text that Augustine is discussing. When commenting on the discussion at the end of John's Gospel in which Peter repeatedly says that he loves Christ, and Christ makes the enigmatic statement about John remaining until he returns, Augustine engages in a lengthy analysis of the questions of why Christ loved John more than Peter, and why Peter loved Christ more than John.[23] The fact that Augustine automatically assumes that both of these statements are true, and devotes his attention to determining instead the question of "why" is in itself remarkable. But he continues even further, taking matters another step by emphasizing that he does not want his conclusions about the differences between the two apostles overemphasized: "Nevertheless, let no one separate these distinguished apostles," and discusses this matter at length, in its own right.[24] Augustine devotes significant time and effort to discount a possible incorrectly drawn implication of something he says, when the original point, let alone the caveat, is hardly likely to occur to most other commentators, let alone a North African congregation.[25] Another example here is found in his comments on John's statement (21:25) about other things that Jesus did that are not in his account, for "the world, I think, would not contain the books that should be written," that "one must not believe that the world could not contain [them] in spatial location. For how could things be written in it if it would not bear them to be written? But perhaps they could not be comprehended by the capacity of the readers."[26] The discussion of this latter possibility continues for some time, before Augustine gives the obvious reply to these

---

23. Augustine, *In Ioh.*, 124.4–6, on John 21:15–23. Note the contrast with Ambrose's much simpler analysis, *Lucam*, X, 175. Augustine's interest in this question is all the more notable given that the key Latin phrase "plus his" ("more than these") which leads to the question being raised is not even present in the most early Latin translations of John: and yet Augustine discusses the question at length regardless. On the presence of this phrase in Augustine's text, see Houghton, *Augustine's Text of John*, 130.

24. Augustine, *In Ioh.*, 124.7.

25. Lawless, "Rhetoric," 53–67.

26. Augustine, *In Ioh.*, 124.8.

complex possibilities, that "this method of speaking teachers ... call by a Greek name hyperbole."[27]

This tendency to ask questions of the text that others might not ask, let alone answer in the imaginative fashion that Augustine does, is also apparent in the *Sermones*. For example, consider his discussion of the fact that Christ ate with the disciples after his resurrection: "If the corruption of the body will not remain in the Resurrection, why did the Lord Christ eat? You have read the statement that He ate; did you read that He was hungry? The fact that He ate was a manifestation of power, not of need."[28] The question is not particularly surprising given Augustine's Manichean background, but the answer, though simple, jumps off in a different direction. The question and the discussion that precedes it are quite philosophical in tone, but having set up the audience for an answer in this vein, Augustine deals with the issue by simply referring to the context (the absence of mention of Christ's hunger) and by making a straightforward point.

An Intuitive Love for Examining Alternatives

Augustine's intuitive style of exegesis is also seen in his tendency to make points about the passage by stating that what is to be understood is "not this, but that."[29] He is aware of other possibilities as he interprets the passage, often quite distant from the meaning that he prefers or dwells primarily upon, even if he dismisses those possibilities altogether.[30] Sometimes, his point is made by directly stating that the evangelist "did not say this, but that," as is the case with his commentary on the words of John 18:37, that "Everyone who is of the truth hears my voice":

> But not all are those to whom it is granted [by God] ... that they hear the truth, that is, listen to the truth and believe in the truth, with no merits preceding ... lest grace not be grace. For

---

27. Augustine, *In Ioh.*, 124.8.

28. Augustine, *Liturgical*, 242.2, with reference to Luke 24:42–43. On the nature of Christ's resurrection body, Augustine's view here, as elsewhere, is that such a body is still *able* to eat, although it does not *need* to. Cf. *De civitate dei*, XIII, 23.

29. In addition to the examples given below, see also Augustine, *In Ioh.*, 116.9, 120.2, 121.5, 123.5, 124.5.

30. De Lubac regards such instances as examples of "Disputation," which he defines as distinguishing between truth and falsehood within one's own mind: *Medieval*, 1:52.

if He had said "Everyone who hears my voice is of the truth," it might be thought that a person was said to be of the truth for the reason that he obeys the truth. But He did not say this, but said "Everyone who is of the truth hears my voice." And he is not therefore of the truth that hears, but he hears for the reason that he is of the truth.[31]

Jesus' answer to Pilate in John 19:11 that "he who has delivered me to you has the greater sin" is dealt with similarly: "The truthful Teacher does not say, 'he who delivered me up to you' himself has sin, as though that man [i.e., Pilate] did not have it; but he says, 'has the greater sin,' so that he might understand that he also has [sin]."[32]

In other examples, Augustine makes a simple point about what the meaning is not, as in the fact that lots were cast for Christ's clothing: "'The soldiers, therefore, when they had crucified Him, took His garments (and they made four parts, to every soldier a part) and His tunic'—one must understand 'they took' so that this is the sense: they took His garments and they made four parts, to every soldier a part; they also took the tunic. And He has spoken so in order that we may understand that for the other garments no lot was cast."[33] Here, Augustine is careful to stress that the reader must not understand that lots were cast for all of the garments, but only for the tunic.[34] This stands in contrast to Ambrose's interpretation of the same incident, in which the possibility of another interpretation is not even considered.[35]

Elsewhere, Augustine is concerned not so much with the possibility of a simple misunderstanding of the text as an almost opposite problem of reading too much into it, as with the 153 fishes caught by the disciples after Christ's resurrection: "In that fishing the number of fishes is not expressed as though there occurs what was foretold by the prophet, 'I have declared and I have spoken; they are multiplied above number.' But here they are not an unspecified 'above number,' but there is a definite number, one hundred and fifty-three; and an accounting of this number must now be rendered."[36] While Augustine is not afraid to advance sev-

---

31. Augustine, *In Ioh.*, 115.4. Translation slightly amended.
32. Augustine, *In Ioh.*, 116.5.
33. Augustine, *In Ioh.*, 118.2, on John 19:23–24.
34. See also Augustine, *In Ioh.*, 120.1 for a similarly simple and yet less obvious example.
35. Ambrose, *Lucam*, X, 115–6.
36. Augustine, *In Ioh.*, 122.7, on John 21:11. Quotation is from Ps 39:6.

eral valid interpretations of this miraculous catch of fish, as the ensuing commentary attests, he is still anxious to ensure that particular improper interpretations of it are not made, in this case through the misapplication of an Old Testament reference.[37] Of course, it is interesting to note that the reference chosen is quite obscure and unlikely to have occurred to many apart from the intuitive Augustine.

This concern to note other possible interpretations, and to ensure that improper alternatives are not accepted, is also prominent in the *Sermones*. Sometimes this is seen simply in the straightforward dismissal of one possible interpretation with a statement like "I do not want you to believe this" before the preferred meaning is given.[38] Elsewhere he is much stronger, conscious of possibilities that he wants to warn against. This is the case with the first option that he considers as a potential explanation for the fact that the resurrected Christ allows the disciples but not the women to touch him, that "perhaps someone who lacks wisdom has declared; 'Before He ascended to His Father, men could touch him; but women could do so only when He had ascended to the Father.' That is an absurd thought and a perverse opinion."[39] In the *Sermones* he often also makes statements of the pattern, already noted in the *In Iohannis*, "the Evangelist does not mean this, but that."[40] Augustine's tendency to examine multiple alternative meanings, ranging from the probable to the highly speculative, provides further evidence of his intuitive cast of mind and style of exegesis.[41]

Polysemy

Related to Augustine's habit of identifying and addressing potential incorrect readings of the text is a strong tendency towards recognizing multiple meanings in it, which we will refer to here as polysemy.[42]

---

37. The very specificity of the number restricts what interpretations are possibly valid, because in Augustine's view there are appropriate ways of interpreting numbers that the exegete should not be ignorant of: Cf. Augustine, *Doctrina*, 2.16.25 (*PL* 34:0048).

38. Augustine, *Liturgical*, 237.4.

39. Augustine, *Liturgical*, 244.2, on John 20:17.

40. For example, Augustine, *Serm.*, 246.5.

41. Harrison, *Beauty*, 69 notes this tendency, and suggests that it may reflect Stoic-Cynic philosophical influences on Augustine. Cf. Mohrmann, "Augustin," 92–93.

42. Augustine elsewhere explicitly discusses and defends the practice of polysemy,

However, it should be noted that this tendency is more marked in the *In Iohannis* than in the *Sermones*, and that Augustine's more heavily polysemic approach in the former work is one of the key points of distinction between it and the latter.[43] Both the intuitive and polysemic nature of Augustine's exegesis underline the point made at the outset of this chapter that his work is very wide ranging and diverse, not dwelling on one particular area or theme. This is also a key area of differentiation between Augustine, and Jerome and Hilary, for whom the possibility of multiple meanings being present in the text would be unthinkable.

By contrast, Augustine frequently advances two or more meanings that he regards as valid, sometimes without even expressing a preference for one.[44] For example, Augustine gives his audience two quite detailed alternative interpretations of the disciples' miraculous catch of 153 fish in John 21:11. After explaining at great length and with much gusto the significance of the number of 153 fish as being made up of ten (signifying the law) and seven (signifying the Spirit) which together make seventeen, significantly because the sum of all numbers from one to seventeen adds up to 153, Augustine gives another allegorical significance to the number:

> And this number also contains the number fifty-three times, and in addition three itself, in regard to the mystery of the Trinity. Now the number fifty is completed when seven has been multiplied by seven and by the addition of one; for seven times seven

---

most famously in *Confessiones*, 12.18.27–12.32.43 (*PL* 32:0835–0844) and *Doctrina*, 3.25.36–28.39 (*PL* 34:0079–0080). A small number of scholars have recently questioned whether Augustine in these passages really intended to support a plurality of meanings: Norris, "Augustine," 398. However, this seems difficult to square with some statements of Augustine's that seem to be fairly clearly speaking in favor of it, e.g. in *Doctrina*, 3.27.38 (*PL* 34:0080), cf. Andrews, "Why Theological Hermeneutics Needs Rhetoric," 195–7; also Cameron, *Christ Meets Me Everywhere*, 274–7 is a recent example of recognition of Augustine's engagement in polysemic exegesis, in this case with reference to Augustine's reading of the Old Testament prophetic literature, albeit in Cameron's perspective with an emphasis on teaching readers habits of seeing multiple possibilities in the text with a view to building up their capacity for intertextual reading across the biblical canon. Another recent positive recognition—and supportive affirmation—of the practice in Augustine is given by Harrison, "Augustine," 689–90.

43. In fact, it is arguable that at only one point in the sermons under consideration here, his discussion of the question of why Christ forbids the women to touch him but encourages the disciples to do so (Augustine, *Serm.*, 244.2–3, on John 20:17), does Augustine engage in full-blown polysemy at any length, and posit multiple possible meanings, of which he allows several to stand as viable.

44. Augustine's tendency towards polysemy briefly discussed by Leinhard, "Reading," 21 in terms of the supposed dialectical quality of his mind.

becomes forty-nine. And one is added so that thereby it may be signified that He is the one who is designated by seven . . . and we know that after the Ascension of the Lord the Holy Spirit was sent on the fiftieth day.[45]

It should be noted in relation to this example that the two interpretations given do not directly contradict each other. Although they are quite different, they both point to essential biblical truths and facts, and in this way buttress his emphasis on the authority of Scripture, rather than detracting from it.[46] Augustine doesn't just believe that the authors of the texts were inspired "one fine day," but that the sacred books were and remain inspired, and for him this means that every day they are capable of supporting fresh meanings that edify.[47] This is true of most instances of Augustine's polysemy: to some extent, his multiple interpretations are complementary in that they all support the same collection of harmonious orthodox doctrines.[48]

Another example of this point is his handling of the question of how the fact that Pilate and his soldiers crucified Christ (and their implied liability) could be reconciled with the evangelist's statements that the Jews bore the entirety of the guilt for the same crime: "But what follows . . . can be referred to the soldiers . . . for afterwards it is more clearly said, that 'the soldiers, when they crucified Him.' Although, even if the Evangelist attributes all of it to the Jews, he does it rightly."[49] In this case, Augustine's point is that both understandings of the passage are true, in that both the soldiers and the Jews bear a heavy responsibility for the crucifixion of Christ.

Sometimes, Augustine does not engage in full-blown polysemy as such, but does display a keen awareness of different possible explanations for events in the text at the literal level, giving the lie to the claims of some scholars that such a tendency to polysemy is driven by a supposed preference for allegorization.[50] An example here is his handling of Mary's looking twice into the tomb of the resurrected Christ: "What, therefore,

---

45. Augustine, *In Ioh.*, 122.8.

46. On this last possibility, see Markus, *Signs*, 9.

47. Lubac, *Medieval*, 1:81–82. Naturally, de Lubac argues that these multiple meanings are generated and supported by the structure of the senses of Scripture.

48. Bonner, "Augustine," 547 and 555.

49. Augustine, *In Ioh.*, 116.9, on John 19:15. The reference to the soldiers' subsequent crucifixion of Christ occurs at 19:18.

50. E.g. Jacobs, "Reception," 698.

does it mean that this woman, while she was weeping, stooped down and looked into the sepulchre again? Can it be that, because she was grieving exceedingly, she thought that ready belief ought not to be given either her own or their eyes? Or rather was her decision to look produced in her mind by a divine impulse?"[51] Augustine is quite comfortable with setting forward two possible explanations for an event in the narrative, and does not appear to feel any pressure to resolve the matter by carefully weighing each option and identifying one rather than the other. He is not concerned that the question is left hanging, and just moves on to his next point immediately after the section quoted. Presumably he is content to move on because he feels as if he has done his job by advancing two plausible explanations for something in the text, when prior to his intervention, his audience would have had no explanations at all.[52]

Understanding his exegesis in this way helps to make sense of passages such as Augustine's resolution of the evangelists' giving of different times for the crucifixion of Christ.[53] The two possibilities given here are mutually exclusive. The first potential explanation of the discrepancy argues that Jesus was crucified according to John at the sixth hour but according to Mark at the third hour because "at the third hour the Lord was crucified by the tongues of the Jews, at the sixth hour by the hands of the soldiers."[54] The alternative explanation argues that Christ was not crucified at the sixth hour, but at the third (as in Mark), "For John does not say 'now it was the sixth hour of the day,' . . . but he says 'Now it was the parasceve of the Pasch about the sixth hour.'"[55] He then uses this subtle distinction to argue that even according to John, Christ was crucified at the third hour of the day, as Mark says. Even where the choice is quite stark, Augustine does not prefer one explanation to the other, but comments, "of these two solutions to this difficult question, let each one

51. Augustine, *In Ioh.*, 121.1, on John 20:11.

52. A similar example is found at Augustine, *In Ioh.*, 124.1, on Jesus instructions to Peter to "follow me."

53. For an assessment of Augustine's approach to discrepancies between the evangelists, see de Jonge, "Interrelations," 2409–16.

54. Augustine, *In Ioh.*, 117.1, referring to Mark 15:25 and John 19:14. While the latter reference is not speaking about the time when Christ was crucified, but the time at which he was sentenced, a difficulty similar to that identified by Augustine still remains to be resolved: otherwise Christ would be crucified before he is sentenced! Such details lead Houghton to observe, not without reason, that Augustine's approach to resolving this discrepancy is rather contrived: *Augustine's Text of John*, 55.

55. Augustine, *In Ioh.*, 117.2.

choose which he will. But he will better judge which he should choose who has read the arguments wrought with most painstaking effort in *On the Harmony of the Gospels*. But if even other solutions to it can be found, the consistency of the gospel truth will be more abundantly defended against the capricious criticism of an unbelieving and ungodly vanity."[56] We see here that Augustine is not particularly concerned which interpretation people prefer, provided that they are aware of all of the relevant arguments. More significantly, Augustine actually regards the proliferation of meanings as something to be welcomed, not for the sake of intellectual curiosity, but for the practical purpose of defending the gospel and explicating the full message of Scripture; Augustine finds so much in so many texts of Scripture because he expects to do so, because he is so confident in the Holy Spirit's inspiration of the texts for the benefit of the church.[57] This is the key to explaining why Augustine is quite comfortable with positing multiple meanings without having to prefer one to the other: interpretations of a passage are primarily meant to be helpful for his audience in building up their faith in Christ, rather than a definitive, exclusive statement of truth.[58] As Brown comments, for Augustine "the first question he must ask is not 'what,' but 'why.'"[59] It is to Augustine's interest in the impact of Scripture on people practically to which attention is now turned.

Concern for Audience

A notable feature of Augustine's exegesis in the *In Iohannis* and *Sermones* is his strong pastoral concern for his audience.[60] In particular, he frequently applies what he sees as relevant points from the text to his hearers

---

56. Augustine, *In Ioh.*, 117.2.
57. Williams, "Hermeneutics and Reading Scripture," 313.
58. Cf. Lubac, *Medieval*, 2:81.
59. Brown, *Augustine*, 253. Cf. Margerie, 3, *Exegesis*, 34.
60. As noted by some students of his work in general, and occasionally of the *In Iohannis evangelium* in particular. A recent example of the latter is the short comment on this feature made by Balás and Bingham, "Books," 346. However, these authors and most others who make such observations seldom pass beyond briefly noting Augustine's concern in general for his audience, to his active application of the text to his hearers, the focus of the following discussion. Other similar instances of this lack of penetration include Carroll, *Preaching*, 195–6 and Lawless, "Preacher," 23.

at a practical level.⁶¹ Often, this homiletical focus appears driven by a belief that the text, or at least parts of it, was written for the benefit of the contemporary Christian, and could—and should—therefore be applied directly to his audience.⁶² Consider, for example, his comments on Pilate's question "Are you the king of the Jews?" and Christ's counterquestion:

> The Lord of course knew both what He Himself asked and what that man would answer, but nevertheless He wanted it to be said, not that He might know himself but that what He wanted us to know might be written down . . . He wanted to show from that man's answer that this had been levelled against him before that man by the Jews as a charge, making clear to us "the thoughts of men," which he knew.⁶³

Note the repeated emphasis on "us": Christ said what he did with people like Augustine's audience in mind. This use of the first-person plural, common across the *Sermones* and *In Iohannis evangelium* as a whole, gives his preaching an almost conversational tone, as Augustine sidles up alongside his congregation.⁶⁴ We find him speaking similarly in his response to the disciples' eventual recognition that Christ had risen when he broke bread with them (Luke 24:30–31), when he urges "Let us believe in Christ crucified, but let us also believe in Him who rose again on the third day. This is the faith which distinguishes us from others, from pagans and Jews; namely, the faith by which we believe that Christ rose

---

61. Overall, while this is true of both his works as the following pages indicate, one gains the impression that Augustine tends to do this a little more in the *Sermones* than in the *In Iohannis evangelium*. Why is this so? Both works were, in the main, preached to similar audiences, North African cathedral congregations, so neither the medium nor the nature of the audiences would have been the decisive factor. More significant is the fact that the *In Iohannis evangelium* was a series of sermons on the one text (the Gospel of John) produced in order while the sequence of most of the *Sermones* under consideration here was determined by the Christian calendar. Augustine may have had more incentive to concentrate on exegetical and theological issues and themes raised by the text of John (rather than on more practical matters one or more steps removed from the text) when he was preaching on that text in regular sequence than when each sermon was drawn from a different biblical author to the one before.

62. Andrews, "Why Theological Hermeneutics Needs Rhetoric," 193.

63. Augustine, *In Ioh.*, 115.1, on John 18:33–34.

64. Carroll, *Preaching*, 194. That the first-person plural is still relatively common in tractates 55–124, along with some of the other quite immediate and oral features taken below, lends support to the suggestion that they were originally preached sermons rather than beginning life dictated to a secretary: Milweski, "Augustine's 124 Tractates in the Gospel of John," 71–75.

again from the dead."⁶⁵ Here, Augustine does not just make the point that might have been made naturally from the text about the necessity of believing that Christ has risen, but also brings it a step closer to his audience by stressing in the first-person plural that faith in the risen Christ is what distinguishes "*us*" (Christians) from others.

For Augustine, the Gospel directly addresses the life of today's Christian to an extent that is not the case for Jerome or Ambrose. A highly developed example of this appears in his exegesis of the discussion in John 21:19–25 between Jesus, Peter, and John on the future of these two apostles. The command to Peter to "follow me" is used to suggest that the Christian should love Christ in the present, while John's remaining until Christ comes as the "disciple whom Jesus loved" points to the fact that the Christian is preserved for heaven by Christ's love:

> For His words "I will have him to remain till I come" must not be understood in such a way as if he said "to remain behind," but "to wait," because what is signified by him [John] will be fulfilled, not now, of course, but when Christ comes. However, what is signified by this man [Peter] to whom it was said, "Do you follow me?" should be done now, and should not remain as something awaited [in the future] . . . therefore let Peter love Him so that we may be delivered from this mortality; let John be loved by Him so that we may be preserved in that immortality.⁶⁶

Peter and John symbolize different aspects of the Christian life that each Christian can directly identify with.⁶⁷

The same belief that the words of the Gospel were written to address contemporary concerns directly, prompting and supporting the faith of believers in his own time, is found in Augustine's comments on John 19:40, "[t]hey took the body of Jesus and bound it in linen cloths, with the spices, as the manner of the Jews is to bury," where he observes that "it does not seem to me that the Evangelist intended to say 'as the manner of the Jews is to bury' without a purpose, for indeed, if I am not mistaken,

65. Augustine, *Liturgical*, 234.3.

66. Augustine, *In Ioh.*, 124.5. Augustine's treatment of this passage is in contrast to that of Ambrose, *Lucam*, X, 175, who, rather than focusing equally on the complementary truths embodied by Peter and John as Augustine does, prefers to concentrate mostly on Peter. While Ambrose stresses the idea of love, he does so in a more abstract fashion and applies his words less directly to his hearers.

67. Furthermore, if Augustine's comments in *De civitate dei*, XIV, 7 are a good guide, it would appear that he regards the idea of love as a very broad concept, descriptive of a wide range of dispositions, actions, and contexts.

he thus advised that in duties of this sort that are performed for the dead, the custom of each nation ought to be preserved."[68] Here, a minor detail in the text is seen as having significance for a contemporary practicality of life, such is his faith in the power of the biblical text to shape and direct its Christian readers. Details of this kind in a passage can also have significance for the life of the church, as is the case in Augustine's discussion of the shape of the cross: "What is, as all know, the sign of Christ except the cross of Christ? And unless this sign should be applied either to the foreheads of those believing or to the very water by which they are regenerated, or to the oil with which they are anointed, or to the sacrifice with which they are nourished, none of these things are done by the proper rite."[69] Here, a historical reality described by the text is connected to the present day used to make a practical, liturgical point.[70]

For Augustine, everything that is described in the Gospel is included for a reason, specifically, a reason with contemporary relevance.[71] As he says of Jesus' command to the disciples in John 21:6 to let down their fishing nets in the Sea of Tiberias, "the Lord would never have given this command unless He wished to indicate something which it would be of benefit for *us* to know."[72] Augustine, is firmly of the view that Scripture is something graciously given to Christians and the church from above and outside of themselves, and so must be presented and explained to people, with practical applications following on from this as an important step.[73] We therefore often find him unpacking and addressing the text directly to his audience or his own age, and on this basis deriving subsequent practical points from it. As Augustine says succinctly in one of the *Sermones*, "Behold, the Gospel speaks to us!"[74] Thus, he argues at the beginning of a sermon on Christ's sufferings that

> ... in these sufferings which He endured from his enemies our Lord has deigned to give us an example of patience, for our ultimate salvation and for practical use in living this life ... in

68. Augustine, *In Ioh.*, 120.4.
69. Augustine, *In Ioh.*, 118.5, on John 19:23.
70. Cf. Sanlon, *Augustine's Theology of Preaching*, 142–3.
71. C.f. Lubac, *Medieval*, 2:142, who sees Augustine's omnipresent interest in speaking about "charity" from the text as an incipient form of the sense of Scripture that was to develop into the thoughts of later writers as the "tropological."
72. Augustine, *Liturgical*, 248.1 (emphasis mine).
73. Cf. Andrews, "Why Theological Hermeneutics Needs Rhetoric," 193.
74. Augustine, *Liturgical*, 137.2.

> the first place, He gave us as a sign of patience the fact that He, having been given up to be crucified, carried His own cross, and, by thus going before us, He showed those desirous of following him what they ought to do.[75]

Occasionally, Augustine refers his comments about the events in the Gospel to his contemporaries outside the church rather than those in it. For example, when discussing the fact that the risen Christ had a real body, he directs the following remarks against the Manichean heretics:

> You, as well as the disciples, have made a mistake; now be corrected along with the disciples. I grant you that it is human to err. You think Christ is a spirit. Peter, too, thought this, and the others who thought that they saw a spirit. But they did not remain in their mistake, although you know for a fact that this false idea had been in their minds. The Physician [Christ] did not leave them in this state.[76]

Augustine makes his point here by placing the heretics in the same category as the disciples before they fully believed, and argues from the implication that the heretics should make the same transition to orthodox belief that the disciples did centuries earlier. What happened in biblical times is therefore made all the more vividly relevant in Augustine's day.

At points, Augustine indicates his belief that events in the Gospel account are written with a pedagogical purpose in mind.[77] One case of this is found in his comments on Jesus' establishment of a mother-son relationship between John and Mary while he hung on the cross, that "A passage of moral import is, therefore, inserted. He does what He advises ought to be done, and by his example the Good Teacher instructed His own that care should be accorded by dutiful children to their parents, as though that wooden cross, where were fixed the members of Him who was dying, was also the chair of the master who was teaching."[78] Note the emphasis here on Christ as teacher, who teaches his followers how to live by his own words.[79]

Augustine's assumptions about the fundamental applicability of the Gospel to the contemporary Christian lead him to address readily and

---

75. Augustine, *Sermons*, 218.1–2, on John 19:17–18.
76. Augustine, *Sermons*, 237.4, on Luke 24:37–39.
77. Harrison, *Beauty*, 44.
78. Augustine, *In Ioh.*, 119.2, on John 19:26–27.
79. See also the stress on Christ as teacher in Augustine, *In Ioh.*, 121.3.

frequently practical comments to his audience. Sometimes, these comments are made quite directly. Thus, when discussing Peter's repeated answer to Jesus' repeated question, "do you love me more than these?," Augustine dwells on Peter's strength of belief in the risen Lord, and urges his audience towards the same degree of faith by reminding them that "it is now our situation that we should not fear the death of this life, because by the Lord's rising an example of another life has gone before us."[80] Likewise, when dealing with Jesus' death, Augustine moves easily from the nature of that death to its implications for the attitude of his audience: "Who departs from a place when he wants to as he departed from life when he wanted to? How great a power of this must be hoped for or feared, when someone considers that so great a power was evident when He died?"[81] Even more simple is Augustine's emphatic statement on the evangelist's words in John 21:24, "And he who saw it has given testimony, and he knows that he says the truth that you also may believe," that "He did not say 'that you also may know' but 'that you may believe.'"[82]

Augustine's pastoral interest in his congregation's practical habits of living is also seen in the following excerpt where he is criticizing penitents whose "former evil life is dead" for not being truly repentant: "I examine penitents and I find them living badly. How are they repenting of what they are doing? If they are repentant, let them not commit these sins... I address you who are called penitents without being so. I speak to you. What shall I say to you? Shall I praise you? No, in this I do not praise you; on the contrary, I groan and lament."[83] Here we see the depth of Augustine's concern for his congregation. He is so determined that they not sin that he addresses them personally, "I," as if from the heart and in strongly emotional terms. In this passage we also can clearly see Augustine's strong understanding of sin, particularly the critical importance of Christians struggling against the old sinful nature persistently and in their actions as well as their intentions. In expounding Scripture, Augustine believes that as a preacher or an interpreter, he is to enable Scripture to speak as God's voice, a word from outside of fallen human life, against the corrupt human nature and its habits: the preacher-interpreter is a

---

80. Augustine, *In Ioh.*, 123.4, on John 21:15–17. Ambrose's comments on the same dialogue are noticeably less oriented towards his congregation: *Lucam*, X, 175.

81. Augustine, *In Ioh.*, 119.6, on John 19:30.

82. Augustine, *In Ioh.*, 120.3.

83. Augustine, *Liturgical*, 232.8.

conduit for the challenging and transforming grace of God, which produces and promotes godliness.[84]

Augustine wants to encourage his hearers towards having rightly-formed Christian beliefs. We see this concern for rightly-informed faith present in the practical conclusion to his allegorizing of the women and disciples' "touching" of the risen Christ as believing in him: "They didn't touch Him well, because they didn't believe well. Do you want to touch well? Understand Christ where He is co-eternal with the Father, and you've touched Him. But if you just think He's a man, and think nothing further, then for you He has not yet ascended to the Father."[85]

Elsewhere in the texts under study, Augustine makes statements about contemporary realities that are likely to be of relevance to his audience indirectly, by implication. An example of this is found in Augustine's discussion of the dialogue before Pilate, where he stresses that it should not be doubted that Christ is a king, since "he is both the onlybegotten Son of God, and he was appointed king by him over Sion, his holy mountain, and both would now be revealed if he did not prefer to be as patient as he was powerful."[86] Here Augustine directly answers the obvious implicit question: if Christ is king, why does he not show forth his power before Pilate, or before his enemies of the present time? It should be noted in passing that the focus in the past two selections from Augustine has been on faith or belief in Christ, in contrast to some of the other selections that have focused more on the theme of love. Augustine's practical focus is quite broad in its content, and not directed by a single theme or idea. In this regard, the impression gained from his actual exegesis is different to that gained by some scholars from his more formal statements on biblical interpretation, such as de Margerie: "It was probably in 397, when he wrote *De Doctrina Christiana*, that Augustine first expressed clearly the fundamental principle which was to govern his entire exegetical undertaking, that charity is the soul and aim of all Scripture."[87] In the context of the sample of Augustine's exegetical writings under consideration here at least, it would appear that this assessment is a little exaggerated.

Augustine's concern to earth what he is saying practically in contemporary experience is so strong that he does not just frequently make

---

84. Andrews, "Why Theological Hermeneutics Needs Rhetoric," 194, cf. 198–9.
85. Augustine, *Sermons*, 243.2, on John 20:7.
86. Augustine, *In Ioh.*, 116.3, on John 19:7.
87. Margerie, *Exegesis*, 3:20.

brief remarks applying what he is saying to his audience, but also on occasions allows this concern to predominate in his exposition. For example, sermon 219 commences with a practical point and finishes not long afterwards having hardly digressed onto other matters.[88] The rather longer sermon 231 commences with a brief discussion of some doctrinal issues related to the resurrection account in Mark which are applied quite directly to the contemporary Christian:

> Now the Resurrection of our Lord Jesus Christ is the new life of those who believe in Jesus. And this is the mysterious meaning of his passion and resurrection, which you certainly ought to know about and live up to . . . What punishment did He release us from? The one that was our due after this life. So He was crucified in order to demonstrate on the cross the downfall of our old self, and He rose again in order to demonstrate in His own life the newness of our life.[89]

Note Augustine's repeated use of the first-person plural, "us . . . our . . . our," discussed earlier, emphasizing the relevance of the point to the audience and his solidarity with them. Shortly after this excerpt, the sermon moves onto a succession of practical points directed at the audience and seldom moves far from them for the remaining three fifths of the sermon.[90] The most obvious example of an entire exposition being dominated by practical concerns in the *In Iohannis evangelium* is found in tractate 123, where Augustine deals with Christ's repeated command to Peter in John 21:15–17 to "feed my sheep," almost half of which is devoted to developing and reinforcing the point that church leaders, "those who feed Christ's sheep," must imitate Christ, and act lovingly and selflessly, even to the point of being prepared to die for those under their care.[91] By contrast, Ambrose does not at all discuss the command to feed the sheep in terms of its contemporary relevance, preferring to concentrate on its

---

88. Augustine, *Serm.*, 219. This may possibly have been due to Augustine's particular concerns in relation to the participants in the Easter Vigil, to whom the sermon would have been preached: Sanlon, *Augustine's Theology of Preaching*, 141.

89. Augustine, *Sermons*, 231.2, on Mark 16:1.

90. Augustine, *Serm.*, 231.3–5.

91. Houghton, *Augustine's Text of John*, 75, suggests that Augustine adds immediacy to this text by replacing "Simon Iohannis" (which appeared in most Latin biblical texts of the period) with the more personal "Petre"—which would add to the sense of directness with which the text speaks to the congregation.

significance for Peter at that point in John's narrative.[92] Here is an excerpt from this example:

> Therefore, let those who feed Christ's sheep not be "lovers of themselves," that they may feed them not as their own but as His, and may not wish to acquire their own gains from them, as "lovers of money," or to be their lords, as "haughty," or to glory over honours which they take from them as "proud," . . . But if the Good Shepherd who laid down His life for His sheep has made so many martyrs for himself from these sheep, how much more ought they to strive for truth even to death and even to blood against sin, they to whom He entrusts His sheep to be fed?[93]

Two important points, which illustrate the manner in which Augustine handles practical matters in his expositions, should be noted from this passage. The first is that Augustine normally relates his practical points to the passage at hand. Even in the foregoing example, where Augustine dwells on a particular concern at some length, he repeatedly returns to what he sees as the key phrases in the Gospel passage, "Do you love me?" and "feed my sheep." He also notes the context of the passage as following soon after Christ's death, and develops his argument accordingly.[94] Although Augustine may at times be predominantly concerned with various practical points, these points are not idle speculation, but always have some reference back to the Gospel. The second feature to note in the example just considered is Augustine's ability to develop his argument further by drawing in references from other parts of the Bible, in this case from various of Paul's writings.[95] In this example, the majority of the quotations from Paul are presented in a free-flowing, rhetorical sequence, describing how the "shepherds" should not act, that adds to the homiletical drive of Augustine's words.[96]

---

92. Ambrose, *Lucam*, X, 175.

93. Augustine, *In Ioh.*, 123.5.

94. In the material surrounding the excerpt quoted, he notes a further two times that the context of the passage is the death of Christ, Augustine, *In Ioh.*, 123.5.

95. Augustine, *In Ioh.*, 123.5. Specifically, from Phil 3:21 and 23, 2 Tim 3:1–5, 1 Tim 1:7, and 2 Cor 5:4. Another example of Augustine's ability to buttress his practical conclusions with references to other parts of the Bible is found in *Serm.*, 239.4.

96. In relation to examples such as this from Augustine, an observation of Kannengeisser's is apt: "rhetorical culture and familiarity with scripture . . . for Augustine, these two streams were consciously joined together": *Handbook*, 1149.

Augustine's belief that the Scriptures are "for us" and the concomitant importance that he places on practically applying them to his congregation is further illustrated by the various features which he includes in his sermons in order to aid the task of listening to and personally appropriating their content.[97] Firstly, Augustine is careful to give his audience "signposts" as to where he is going in his expositions, and why. For example, he concludes a sermon on the resurrection from John's Gospel with the following explanation: "That's as far as the Gospel reading went relating to the Lord's resurrection, as written by the evangelist John, and that must now be enough for a sermon; for the good reason that there are other readings to be read from the same Gospel of John about the Lord's resurrection. Nobody, you see, told more stories about His resurrection than John; which is why it can't all be read on one day."[98] Here, Augustine has not just thought out his preaching program and the rationale behind it, but has explained the same to his congregation, using the first person plural "our" to emphasize that they are traveling through the Gospels together. Augustine gives such signposts for the material covered within expositions as well as across them. For example, he commences a sermon on John 20:19–31 with an overview of the basics of what has happened in the Gospel account leading up to and including his text for the day, explaining that "there was no need for me to mention these facts to you, but only for you to note them. However, it was fitting for me to mention them, by reason of the scant intelligence of certain persons and the excessive negligence of others, so that you may understand, not only what you have heard, but also from what portion of Scripture that which you have heard was read to you."[99] Augustine wants to be sure that all of his hearers are aware of the basic background to what he is speaking about, even those of "scant intelligence" and "excessive negligence!" In a similar vein of pastoral sensitivity, Augustine is prepared to arrange things in order to prevent people's faith being unsettled. The following discussion of whether all four passion accounts should be read from each of the evangelists in turn from year to year is instructive:

> The resurrection of our Lord Jesus Christ was recounted today as well . . . these seven or eight days give us space for the

---

97. He underlines the importance of this at points in *De Doctrina Christiana*, e.g. at 3.7.7 and 4.10.25.

98. Augustine, *Sermons*, 246.6, on John 20:18. Another similar example occurs in *Sermons*, 243.1.

99. Augustine, *Liturgical*, 247.1.

> Resurrection of the Lord to be recounted according to all the evangelists; while His passion, being read on one day only, is customarily read just according to Matthew. Once upon a time I wanted the passion too to be read according to all the evangelists on successive years. It happened; people didn't hear what they were used to, and were upset. Those, however, who love the divine literature, and are not willing always to remain uneducated, know all of them and diligently study them all. But, "as God has allotted each the measure of faith" [Rom 2:3], so each makes progress.[100]

Augustine works hard to make sure that his audience understands what he is saying.[101] For all of their speculative, roaming intellectualizing, Augustine's expositions are still intended to be consumed by the average Christian.[102] Although intelligent and well educated, he is not afraid to come down to the level of his audience. Thus, when asking rhetorical questions in order to show the nature of faith, he pointedly refers to examples within the everyday experience of the congregation: "I am asking about things ordinary and familiar—give me an explanation as to why the seed of so great a tree as the fig tree is so small that it can hardly be seen, and why the lowly gourd produces such a large seed . . . There is no need of mentioning many examples; no one offers an explanation of daily happenings; yet you demand of me an explanation about miracles."[103]

At other points, Augustine similarly underlines for his congregation the fact that a truth in the passage bears upon contemporary realities by speaking with considerable rhetorical flourish, such as in his declamation on Christ's statement in John 18:36 that his kingdom is not of this world:

> Therefore, hear, Jews and Gentiles! Hear, circumcision! Hear, uncircumcision! Hear all earthly kingdoms! I obstruct not your dominion of this world. Do not fear with the most groundless fear with which the elder Herod, when the birth of Christ was reported, became terrified and slew so many infants . . . "My kingdom," He says "is not of this world." What more do you want? Come to the kingdom which is not of this world; come by believing and do not vent your rage out of fear of Him.[104]

100. Augustine, *Sermons*, 232.1.
101. Murray, *Preaching*, 501.
102. In addition to the example given below, see also Augustine, *In Ioh.*, 122.3.
103. Augustine, *Liturgical*, 247.2. In addition to the example given here, see also *Serm.*, 234.3.
104. Augustine, *In Ioh.*, 115.2. Ambrose, *Lucam*, X, 115–6 makes the same

More than that, Augustine uses a range of rhetorical devices in order to drive home the practical relevance of his exegesis,[105] notwithstanding his criticisms elsewhere of reliance on rhetoric in preaching.[106] As Brown says, "the Latin language has been fused, has caught alight, in the almost-daily flame of Augustine's sermons."[107] One such device particularly favored by Augustine is to speak in contrasting parallelisms that address his audience for added emphasis, such as is found in his comments on Jesus' carrying his own cross:

> A grand spectacle! But if ungodliness should watch, a grand ridiculous absurdity! If godliness [should watch], a grand mystery! But if ungodliness [should watch], a grand demonstration of shame! If godliness [should watch], a grand fortification of faith! If ungodliness should watch, it laughs that in the place of the rod of royal power the king carries the wooden cross of punishment. If godliness should watch, it sees the king bearing the wooden cross for Himself to be fastened on, which He was going to fasten even on the foreheads of kings, He who would be scorned in the eyes of the ungodly in the very matter in which the hearts of the saints would glory.[108]

In this example, Augustine develops a parallelism around the great divide between the godly and ungodly, but earths it in the different practical responses of the two groups to the cross and in doing so clearly implies what the attitude of his audience should be.[109] A similar case occurs in the *Sermones*, when Augustine discusses the statement of the disciples who had unknowingly talked with Jesus on the Emmaus Road in Luke 24:32 that their hearts had been "burning" within them as they had spoken with Jesus. Augustine uses a stark counterpoint to alert his audience to the importance of godly behavior: "Burn, in order not to burn with the

---

theological point about the nature of Christ's kingdom, but does not apply it to his audience as Augustine does.

105. Old, *The Reading and Preaching of the Scriptures*, 355.

106. E.g. *Doctrina*, 2.31.48 (*PL* 34:0058). However, occasionally his attitude is more tolerant, e.g. *Confessiones*, 1.13.20–1.20.31 (*PL* 32:0670–0676). A detailed discussion of how Augustine uses classical rhetorical devices in his preaching can be found in Murray, "Preaching, Scripture and Visual Imagery in Antiquity," 481–503.

107. Brown, *Augustine*, 257. For similar, more extensive examples of the traditional approach to rhetoric in Augustine's exegesis, see Carroll, *Preaching*, 167–73; Harrison, *Beauty*, 68–70; and Lawless, "Rhetoric," 53–66.

108. Augustine, *In Ioh.*, 117.3, on John 19:17.

109. See also the related parallelism at the end of Augustine, *In Ioh.*, 117.

fire the demons are going to burn with. Be on fire with the ardour of charity, in order to differentiate yourselves from demons."[110] Here, the idea "to burn" is cleverly used as a common element in both sides of the contrast, and yet it is the type of fire involved that distinguishes the demons and the faithful Christian.

Another device often used by Augustine to emphasize what he is saying is repetition, such as when he tells his congregation that "before God I rend my garments in fear lest I be rebuked for not having spoken thus. I am performing my duty; I seek results from you; I wish to get joy, not money, from your good works . . . My riches are nothing unless your hope is in Christ. My joy, my solace, and even my breathing-in of dangers during these trials are nothing unless your life is good."[111] Note the repeated appeals from the first person, "I," and "My," designed to stir the congregation to action. He speaks similarly when urging the congregation to emulate Peter's faith in the resurrected Christ, encouraging them that "just as we are set apart by faith, let us be distinguished by our morals; let us be distinguished by our works; let us be enkindled by the fire of charity."[112] Here, the repeated emphasis is on Augustine's identification with the congregation, "let us," to promote his desired objectives.

Elsewhere, Augustine prefers to bring his interpretations closer to his audience by asking rhetorical questions,[113] as he does at one point in his discussion of the nature of Christ's resurrected body:

> What do you think, O Catholic? What do you think, O faithful spouse? What can you think except what you have learned from Him? . . . What, then, do you say? You have learned that Christ is the Word, and that He has a human body and soul. What have you learned about the Word? "In the beginning was the Word, and the Word was with God and the Word was God." What have you learned about His human soul? "And bowing His head, he gave up his Spirit."[114]

At points, his commentary takes on a passionate, devotional strain designed to stir the emotions of his audience, such as in these concluding reflections on Christ's death: "Here the second Adam, His head bowed,

---

110. Augustine, *Sermons*, 234.3.
111. Augustine, *Liturgical*, 232.8.
112. Augustine, *Liturgical*, 234.3, on John 21:7.
113. Old, *The Reading and Preaching of the Scriptures*, 355.
114. Augustine, *Sermons*, 238.2, quoting John 1:1 and 19:30.

slept on the cross in order that from there might be found for Him a wife—that one who flowed from the side of the one sleeping. O death from which the dead live again! What is cleaner than this blood? What is more healthful than this wound?"[115] In this example, Augustine mingles the typology of the "new Adam" concept with almost poetic language about the benefit of Christ's death for his people. Elsewhere, Augustine can be seen encouraging his audience, such as when commenting on the breakfast that Christ prepared for his disciples after he had risen that "for those who believe, hope, love and participation in great happiness is shown by this breakfast."[116]

Having examined Augustine's strong concern for his audience, it is apparent that Augustine substantially differs from Jerome and Ambrose at this point.[117] While Augustine frequently and reflexively applies the events of the Gospel to his audience and often uses various other devices to bring those events closer to the understanding of the contemporary Christian, Jerome only occasionally takes up homiletical interests, usually at the end of his expositions if at all. Augustine's approach is also different to Hilary's. While both share a strong homiletical focus, Augustine does not have the same burning concern with one particular issue throughout the *In Iohannis evangelium* or *Sermones*, that Hilary does with engendering faith. Rather, Augustine in making points of practical importance ranges much more widely than Hilary does, covering a diverse collection of matters relevant to Christian living, from general attitudes to the details of specific practices. Augustine is also much more direct in relating what he is saying to his audience. He frequently gives

---

115. Augustine, *In Ioh.*, 120.2, on John 19:34; cf. Houghton, *Augustine's Text of John*, 345, on Augustine's emphasis on *aperuit* in this place to achieve the connections to other biblical texts which he intends. More generally, Augustine's ability to identify with his audience's emotions is noted by Brown, *Augustine*, 251.

116. Augustine, *In Ioh.*, 123.2. Interestingly, when Augustine speaks of hope in the *In Iohannis evangelium*, it is the resurrection of Christ (in the past) alone which is in view: the hope of heaven and judgment is seldom in view. Cf. Shippee, "Paradoxes of Now and Not Yet: The Separation between the Church and the Kingdom in John Chrysostom, Theodore, and Augustine," 112–4. Shippee suggests that this tendency in Augustine's works is driven by a low level of confidence in the future throughout most of his career, which meant that he looked to the past more than the future for guidance.

117. Simonetti, *Interpretation*, 104 also notes this as a key distinction between Augustine and Jerome, and Wright between Augustine and Jerome: Wright, "Augustine, His Exegesis and Hermeneutics," 721.

direct practical instructions, whereas Hilary is more frequently content to let what he is saying imply the necessity for living faith.

The Workings of the Human Heart

Another area of interest for Augustine, related to his keen concern with practical application, that features much more prominently in his interpretation of the crucifixion and resurrection narratives than in those of the other writers under study is his interest in the internal workings of the heart.[118] This is an expression of his concern with human interiority which has been much commented on in relation to his anthropology and parts of his corpus more generally.[119] Often, this comes in the form of comments on the emotions and motives of the Christian, as in tractate 123, where Augustine, discussing the role of the "shepherds" of Christ's people, examines their potential sins in internal terms:

> For these vices and ones like them, whether they all happen to one person or some rule over some persons, sprout from that root where men are "lovers of themselves." And this vice must be especially guarded against by those who feed Christ's sheep that they may not seek the things that are their own . . . And the love of Him in that man who feeds His sheep ought to grow to

---

118. In addition to the passages discussed in what follows, for clear examples of this, see also Augustine, *Serm.*, 234.2, 236.3, 239.4.

119. In contemporary literature, Phillip Cary's (2000) *Augustine and the Inner Self* is a well-known example, in which this aspect of Augustine's thought is argued to be largely an expression of the formative influence of Neoplatonism on his thought. A more specialized work is Coleen Hoffman Gowans's *The Identity of the True Believer in the Sermons of Augustine of Hippo* (1998), which examines Augustine's anthropology as evidenced in his *Sermones*, concluding that with respect to anthropological identity at least, for Augustine the heart (*cor*) is central. More recently (2014), Peter Sanlon's *Augustine's Theology of Preaching* is a thorough and insightful study of Augustine's *Sermones* and *De Doctrina Christiana* which argues that Augustine's theological conception of his preaching is best understood as structured around his ideas of interiority and temporality (the latter defined by Sanlon, 86, as "the successive flow and teleological development of God's plan for creation from beginning to consummation"). A full discussion of Sanlon's thesis is beyond the scope of this study; his excellent work is commended to readers interested in exploring the concept of interiority in Augustine further, while noting that this author would not regard temporality as being quite as central to Augustine's program of biblical interpretation and preaching as Sanlon does (although as the discussion of the related concept of typology above indicates, it clearly has some significant role within Augustine's approach).

so great a spiritual ardour that it conquers even the natural fear of death.[120]

While it was not uncommon for writers in Augustine's time to comment on matters such as the importance of biblically-shaped virtue in Christian leaders and the mortification of sin in the same persons, the nature of Augustine's comments is noteworthy, given that none of our other three writers speak from such an internalized perspective. Nonetheless, Augustine's tendency here is to some extent simply an extension of his concern with practical matters.

However, there is more to Augustine's "internal" focus than this aspect of his application of his exegesis to his contemporary audience. His concern with feelings and motives becomes more obvious when we consider his frequent interest in these matters in his discussions of the people in the Gospel. The most prominent example here is his repeated discussion in the *In Iohannis evangelium* of the inner workings of Pilate's mind and heart. The first such comment is made on Pilate's question "What is truth?" (John 18:38) and the small, almost unnoticed detail that Pilate apparently did not wait to hear the answer to his own question:

> I believe that when Pilate had said, "what is truth?," there had immediately come into his mind the custom of the Jews whereby one man was usually released to them at the Pasch, and therefore he did not wait for Jesus to answer him as to what the truth is, so that there might not be a delay once he had recalled the practice by which He could be released to them.[121]

Here, a small fact stimulates Augustine's thinking on what exactly went through Pilate's mind at a critical point in time.[122] However, while Augustine's discussion of Pilate's inner workings begins with a small point, it immediately moves on to discuss much more significant things: "Nonetheless it could not be wrested from his heart that Jesus was the king of

---

120. Augustine, *In Ioh.*, 123.5, on John 21:17. Cf. Ambrose, *Lucam*, X, 175, who concentrates solely on the external words and actions of the actors at this point in John's account. Augustine's comments here may be directed against the Donatists, given his handling of the verse on some other occasions: cf. Houghton, *Augustine's Text of John*, 360.

121. Augustine, *In Ioh.*, 115.5.

122. In contrast to the discussions of the same scene from Matt 27:37 in Hilary, *Matt.*, 33.1, and Jerome, *Math.*, IV, 1703-11.

the Jews, about which Truth Itself . . . fixed this notion there, and on the title."[123]

In the tractate that follows, Augustine gives a reason for Christ's scourging (neither Jerome nor Hilary does) that, although obvious, is also significantly at the internal level of self-interested motives: "Pilate should not be believed to have done this for another reason except that the Jews, glutted with the injurious treatment of him, might think it sufficient for them and cease from their constant savage raging for His death."[124] Shortly afterwards, Augustine speaks about Pilate's motives in the light of Christ's words "You would not have any power against me unless it were given you from above" (John 19:11), observing that "indeed that man [Herod] delivered me up to your power, feeling ill-will, but you are going to exercise the same power against me, feeling fear. Indeed a man ought not slay a man from being afraid; nevertheless, it is much more evil to do it from being jealous than from being afraid."[125] Here, the probable motives of the various actors are seen to indicate their relative guilt. Subsequently, when Augustine deals with Pilate's question of the Jews in John 19:15, "shall I crucify your king?," he views it as part of a struggle in which Pilate and the Jews are trying to manipulate one another's emotions: "He still tries to overcome the fear that they forced him to suffer concerning Caesar, wishing to break them because of the disgrace to them, by saying, 'Shall I crucify your king?' as he could not assuage them with the disgrace to Christ; but he is soon defeated by fear [of Caesar]."[126] As with some of the other examples noted, here again we see Augustine's interest in the inner workings of the human heart primarily concentrating on the illumination of human sin. Augustine's interest in the sinful inclinations, musings, and motivations of the inner person, which we see further developed in several of the additional examples given below, highlights that his concern with these matters is not so much for the sake of persons "finding God" within themselves, but strictly anthropological, and within that focus, arguably with a hamartiological center.[127]

According to Augustine, what is going on inside the various actors in the narrative is just as important as the external realities, if not more

---

123. Augustine, *In Ioh.*, 115.5.

124. Augustine, *In Ioh.*, 116.1, on John 19:1.

125. Augustine, *In Ioh.*, 116.5.

126. Augustine, *In Ioh.*, 116.8.

127. Contrary to proposals such as Kenney's, *Contemplation and Classical Christianity*, 164.

so, and is the measure against which people's sin shall be assessed. When discussing the soldiers' taking of Christ's garments, he argues for the Jews' guilt rather than the soldiers' by noting that "What the Jews wished was done; not by themselves, but by the soldiers who carried out Pilate's orders, [and] upon his judgement, crucified Jesus. And yet if their wills, if their plottings, if their effort . . . [are what] we reflect upon, undoubtedly the Jews crucified Him more."[128]

Augustine's interest in people's emotions and motives extends beyond those of Pilate and the Jews.[129] Another example is Augustine's explanation for Mary's remaining at the tomb when the others had left:

> For although the men returned, a stronger feeling of affection held the women fixed in the same place. And the eyes that had sought for the Lord and had not found Him were now full with tears, grieving more that He had been taken away from the sepulchre than that He had been slain on the cross, since not even a memorial-place was left behind of so great a teacher.[130]

Shortly afterwards, Augustine continues by commenting on Mary's explanation to the "gardener" that she does not know where Christ has been taken, that "this was the greater cause for grief, because she did not know where to go for consoling her grief."[131] Thus, Mary's emotional world forms a significant part of the account of Mary at the tomb for Augustine. Elsewhere, internal motivations are important to Augustine's exposition, such as when he begins a discussion of why Jesus chose the disciples he did with the observation that "the Lord Jesus . . . did not begin with generals or senators, but with fishermen. For, if they had enjoyed any honours before their selection, they would have dared to attribute the Lord's choice to themselves, not to the grace of God."[132] Augustine explicates an aspect of the Gospel account by referring to the internal workings of the heart, or in this case, the potential workings of the apostles' collective egos.

---

128. Augustine, *In Ioh.*, 118.1, on John 19:23.

129. See also Augustine's analysis of the post-resurrection discussion between Christ and Peter in John 21:15–19, where Peter is commanded to look after Christ's sheep and asked whether he loves Him, in Augustine, *Serm.*, 253.2.

130. Augustine, *In Ioh.*, 121.1, on John 20:11.

131. Augustine, *In Ioh.*, on John 20:13.

132. Augustine, *Liturgical*, 250.1, with reference to John 21:2–3.

Augustine is so interested in internal factors because his understanding of human nature begins with the internal rather than the external person. When an allegory on the 153 fish caught by the disciples after Christ's resurrection (John 21:11) leads Augustine into a discussion of the ten commandments, he makes the following revealing statement: "He who says 'thou shalt not covet' directs His blows at internal sins; He strikes at the interior; it is concupiscence that perpetrates the deed."[133] Augustine's comments here do not just reveal a consciousness of the distinction between internal and external, but also that it is the internal sin (concupiscence) that is the root of the symptomatic external one (deed).[134]

All of these examples serve to underline Augustine's concern with internal factors. Although this concern does not appear particularly significant to the modern mind, which is used to living in a world heavily influenced by psychological study of all kinds of internal phenomena, it is important not to miss it in Augustine, as it is a key factor that distinguishes his work from that of many of his contemporaries.[135]

From Text to Theology

Another prominent feature of Augustine's exegesis is his strong interest in broader theological themes and questions, as opposed to purely exegetical concerns. He frequently sees the data present in the Gospel narrative as being present for a theological reason.[136] Thus, that Jesus said to his disciples "Whose sins you shall remit, they are remitted them; and whose you shall retain, they are retained" immediately after he had breathed on them and said "receive the Holy Spirit" is seen as having theological significance, since "the love of God which is poured forth in our hearts by the Holy Spirit [Rom 5:5] dismisses the sins of those who participate in it, but it retains [the sins] of those who do not participate in it. Therefore, after He said, 'Receive the Holy Spirit,' immediately he added this about

---

133. Augustine, *Liturgical*, 250.3.

134. The subject of Augustine's views on sin is a very substantial one; for a brief introduction, see Wetzel, "Sin," 800–802.

135. Other examples of Augustine's emphasis on emotions and motives are found at Augustine, *In Ioh.*, 121.4 (the disciples) and 123.5 (Christ himself).

136. Balás and Bingham, "Books," 346.

the remission and retention of sins."[137] The fact that these two different comments of Jesus sit side-by-side is not coincidental, but points to a work of the Holy Spirit through the church.[138]

Augustine's facility with theological matters is also demonstrated by the fact that he readily makes frequent references to doctrinal truths or issues in a familiar, almost offhand way. Thus, he starts tractate 120 with the following words: "After the Lord Jesus, when all the things which He foreknew had to be completed before His death had occurred, delivered over His spirit when He wanted to, let us see from the Evangelist's narration what followed next."[139] Not content to merely state that Jesus gave up his life when he had done everything that he came to do, Augustine notes in passing two points, namely, that Christ had foreknowledge of what he had to do before he died, and that he could give up his Spirit "when He wanted to," two points that he had discussed at greater length when commenting on earlier sections of the crucifixion narrative.[140] Minor details in the narrative often sometimes elicit such brief doctrinal comments from Augustine, as is the case when discussing Mary's statement to the angels, "they have taken away my Lord" (John 20:13), he notes that she is "calling Lord the dead body of her Lord, from the whole signifying the part, just as we all confess that Jesus Christ, the only Son of God, our Lord—that which, of course, is at the same time both the Word and soul and flesh—has nevertheless been crucified and buried, although only His flesh was buried."[141] This observation is longer than the previous one, but its place in Augustine's exegesis is the same. It is a passing remark about a theological matter that bears no direct relation to what comes before or after (he is discussing Mary's grief at the disappearance of the body on either side of the excerpt) but is mentioned simply because Augustine has had occasion to mention it, as something of interest to him.

---

137. Augustine, *In Ioh.*, 121.4, on John 20:22. Jerome's comments, while having a theological flavor, are much less developed: *Math.*, IV, 2001–6, on Matt 28:19.

138. A similar example can be found in Augustine, *In Ioh.*, 115.1 (on John 18:33–36).

139. Augustine, *In Ioh.*, 120.1, with reference to John 19:30.

140. Augustine, *In Ioh.*, 119.4 for the former; 119.6 for the latter.

141. Augustine, *In Ioh.*, 121.1. By contrast, Jerome, *Math.*, IV, 1915–35 (on Matt 28:2), does not draw attention to this detail, or make the theological points that Augustine does. Augustine's comment that only Christ's flesh was buried is taken up and given theological significance in *De civitate dei*, XIV, 2, where it is asserted that Christ also had a human soul, which never went into the tomb of death.

The nature of these passing comments underline the fact that Augustine has a strong interest in broader theological themes and doctrinal matters: typically, they are not belabored, but the confident statements of an exegete who is thoroughly familiar with the theological issues and concepts that he is referring to. Consider, for example, the following passing christological reference: "For He who was hidden as God appeared as man; He who appeared suffered these things and He who was hidden, the very same One, organized all these things."[142] In this case, Augustine is sufficiently familiar with the doctrinal matter as to be able to perform a little wordplay with the idea of "hidden" versus "apparent." In another example, when Augustine is commenting on the Jews' accusation that Jesus called himself the Son of God, he briefly emphasizes that the accusation is true, and develops it further to make a punchy point about the underlying theological reason why Jesus' lordship is not immediately made apparent: "He both is the only-begotten Son of God, and He was appointed king by him over Sion, his holy mountain, and both would now be revealed if He did not prefer to be as patient as he was powerful."[143]

On occasions, Augustine allegorizes in order to refer to doctrinal truths; indeed, the majority of his allegories draw out such ideas. Sometimes, these allegorical references are also brief, passing ones, as in the case of this comment on the "lot," at the end of the discussion on the casting of lots for Christ's clothing, where he highlights the character of God's grace as an unmerited gift which issues from God's will alone: "in the lot, moreover, what has been commended except the grace of God? For indeed in this way it comes to all, since the lot pleased all, because in unity the grace of God also comes to all; and when the lot is cast, one yields not to the person or merits of anyone but to the judgement of God."[144] On a small number of occasions, Augustine also uses an allegory at length to discuss various theological issues. The best example here is his commentary on the cross, where he discusses its three dimensions in some detail.[145]

As he progresses through the passage at hand, Augustine tends to be more interested in what the text says about theological themes than

142. Augustine, *In Ioh.*, 119.4, on John 19:28.
143. Augustine, *In Ioh.*, 16.3, on John 19:7.
144. Augustine, *In Ioh.*, 118.4, on John 19:24.
145. Augustine, *In Ioh.*, 118.5, on John 19:25. The other major example of relevance here is his allegorization of the disciples' post-resurrection fishing trip (John 21:1–14) in *In Ioh.*, 122.7–9.

in features intrinsic to the text itself, as is the case with Jerome. This is illustrated by how he compares the accounts of the different Gospels.[146] Consider how Augustine handles the fact that Mark said that Christ was crucified at the third hour, while John has him crucified at the sixth hour:

> Because the Jews tried to transfer the crime of Christ's killing from themselves to Pilate and his soldiers, for this reason Mark, refraining from mentioning the hour at which Christ was crucified by the soldiers, which was the sixth hour, instead recalled and intentionally wrote the third hour, the hour at which they would have cried out before Pilate, "Crucify, crucify," so that not only those men are found to have crucified Jesus, that is the soldiers who hung Him on the cross at the sixth hour, but also the Jews who at the third hour cried out that He be crucified.[147]

Augustine does not attempt to reconcile the difference in times through reference to textual factors, but uses the fact that there is a discrepancy to emphasize a general concept that he wishes to assert as true, namely that both the Jews and the Romans are responsible for Christ's death.[148] Another example is this excerpt from Augustine's discussion of the fact that Christ allows John to repeatedly refer to himself as "the disciple whom Jesus loved": "His [Christ's] purpose, I believe, was to commend more highly in this way the divine excellence of this Gospel."[149] The superiority of John's Gospel is not seen in the fact that it is more historically accurate, more detailed, or better written, but in Christ's love of John.

Augustine believes that every minute element in the text has theological meaning and does not fail to point this out. This is certainly the case when discussing the details of the crucifixion when he argues that "it may rightly be assumed that by every single deed that was carried out and recorded about His passion, He also wished to signify something,"[150] and goes on to briefly list the significance of ten events in the account, a selection of which are given here to illustrate:

> By the fact that two others were crucified with Him, one on either side, he indicated that some would suffer to their advantage

---

146. Compare with Jerome, *Math.*, IV, 1768–74, on Matt 27:46.

147. Augustine, *In Ioh.*, 117.1, comparing Mark 15:25 and John 19:14.

148. By contrast, Jerome resolves similar difficulties in a more text-based fashion, with less regard for theological themes, e.g. Jerome, *Math.*, IV, 1657–62 and 1740–5.

149. Augustine, *In Ioh.*, 119.2, on John 19:26.

150. Augustine, *Sermons*, 218.1.

> and others, to their disadvantage . . . the title placed upon His cross, bearing the inscription, "The King of the Jews," indicated that, even by killing Him, they were not able to prevent their having as King Him who would render to them according to their works . . . Because the title was written in three languages, the announcement was made that He would rule not only over the Jews, but also over the Gentiles.[151]

That Augustine discusses so many aspects of the passage in terms of their significance should not be allowed to disguise the fact that no individual point receives more than a few sentences worth of his attention. He effortlessly moves from idea to idea, but his aim is not to enter into in-depth discussion so much as to briefly point out the importance of what he encounters in the text. Also, the variety of different ideas discussed in the example just quoted serves to underline that he is not using the text to support the proclamation of one particular doctrine, as is the case with Hilary.

Although theological matters are of substantial interest to Augustine, and he frequently refers to them in the course of his exposition, several disclaimers should be noted. Firstly, Augustine's commentary is not a theological narrative, in the sense that Hilary's is. Augustine's objective is not merely to progress through the Gospel and point out those doctrinal truths and general theological themes that he believes the narrative was largely written to illustrate.[152] He refers to such issues and themes as they arise and interest him, alongside any other matters, such as moral or practical ones, that he thinks are interesting or relevant to his audience. As stated at the outset of this chapter, his exegesis is best characterized as a wide-angle lens, in that he delights in digging many and diverse gems from all aspects of the passage. In addition, he does not focus around one particular idea, as Hilary does with faith, and use it to give his exegesis a unified, common purpose. Rather, as we have seen in the example just discussed from sermon 218, Augustine discusses a very diverse range of matters, without necessarily connecting them to each other or to the overall flow of his argument. Sometimes these comments are incidental to the flow of the narrative, as when Augustine notes that the reading for the day was from Mark and proceeds to make a brief doctrinal point about the status and divine appointment of the Gospel writers out of this fact: "Mark merited that arrangement, in spite of the fact that, like Luke,

---

151. Augustine, *Liturgical*, 218.3–6, on John 19:17–20.
152. Cf. Cameron, *Christ Meets Me Everywhere*, 12.

he was not one of the twelve Apostles . . . For the Holy Spirit willed to choose for the writing of the Gospel two who were not from those who made up the Twelve, so that it might not be thought that the grace of evangelisation had come only to the Apostles and that in them the fountain of grace had dried up."[153] Augustine moves first to the fact that the reading did not come from one of the Twelve, and from there to giving a reason why Mark and Luke are in the canon which implies something of practical worth, namely that the "grace of evangelisation" had not ended with the apostles. As we have seen, Jerome and Ambrose also frequently distinguish between the different evangelists. However, the kinds of distinctions they draw are quite different to Augustine's, Jerome preferring to discuss differences intrinsic to the text, while Ambrose might discuss the authors, but more from the point of view of their different perspectives on the text than from the Holy Spirit's choice of authors in order to make a tangential theological point.

Secondly, Augustine's interest in theological matters does not mean that he is concerned to discuss particular doctrines in detail, or to become immersed in the theological-philosophical debates that characterized much Greek exegesis of his era.[154] As described above, most of the theological discussion that occurs in Augustine's commentary consists of brief, passing remarks.[155] Although he frequently digresses onto such matters, he seldom digresses at any great detail, and where he does, it is usually because he has jumped between several doctrines rather than just examining any one at length.[156] Where he does deal in more abstract concepts, such ideas are usually rooted in mundane realities, as is the

153. Augustine, *Liturgical*, 239.1.

154. Carroll, *Preaching*, 194.

155. However, it should be observed here that a noticeable difference between *In Iohannis* and the *Sermones* is that while Augustine very rarely discusses theological issues at length in the *In Iohannis*, in the *Sermones* he does so a little more frequently. In particular, some of the *Sermones* are essentially homilies on particular doctrines. Of the sermons under study here, those that fall into this category are sermon 233, which is devoted to a discussion of the nature of salvation loosely based around the resurrection account in Mark, and sermon 238, which is concerned to defend the reality of Christ's physical body from Luke 24:38–47. However, apart from these examples most of Augustine's theological commentary is brief. Unless he devotes an entire sermon to a particular theological topic, his pattern is the same as in *In Iohannis*, where short, sharp comments are the rule.

156. There is only one particularly lengthy example even of Augustine digressing onto theology in order to examine multiple theological ideas: the lengthy allegory on the post-resurrection fishing expedition and 153 fish in *In Ioh.*, 122.7–9.

case in this reflective excerpt where Christ's words to Mary from the cross and his much less kind words at the wedding in Cana are discussed in the context of Christ's two natures: "Then [at Cana], therefore, as He was about to perform divine deeds, He rebuffed as though unknown the mother, not of His divinity, but of His weakness; but now, enduring human sufferings, with human affection He commended her from whom He had been made man. For then He who had created Mary was making himself known by power, but now that to which Mary had given birth was hanging on a cross."[157] As was the case with most of the examples of Augustine's theologizing considered above, Augustine here is explaining the events of the Gospel in terms of the doctrinal realities that define those events, and not engaging in theological speculation in splendid isolation. Augustine is more interested in how doctrines are applied and worked out in the events of the Gospel, rather than in these doctrines in their own right. For example, consider his words on John 20:21, "As the Father has sent me, I also send you" where he reminds his congregation that "we know the Son is equal with the Father, but here we recognize the words of the Mediator. For indeed He shows himself in the middle by saying, 'He me, I also you.'"[158] Here, Augustine is more interested in Christ's function than in his ontological nature.[159] The key point for him is that Christ mediates between God and people in a particular situation; he does not take the opportunity to discuss the more theoretical matter of Christ's innate equality with the Father.

Generally speaking, Augustine prefers to make brief, even pithy theological comments rather than to digress at length. One example is in his exegesis of a scene at the crucifixion where Augustine observes "That on the cross He knew His mother, and entrusted Her to the beloved disciple, aptly indicated His human affection at the time when He was dying as a man . . . You see, He had not received from Mary the power He had in His divinity, as He had received from Mary what was hanging on the cross."[160] Here, in a few brief words, Augustine manages to allude not only to what the passage says about Christ's humanity but also the fact that Christ did not gain his divinity from Mary and that in dying

157. Augustine, *In Ioh.*, 119.1, on John 19:26–27, and with reference to John 2:4.
158. Augustine, *In Ioh.*, 121.4.
159. Similar to a point made by Stefano, "Lordship over Weakness: Christ's Graced Humanity as Locus of Divine Power in Augustine's Tractates on the Gospel of John," 1–19.
160. Augustine, *Sermons*, 218.10, on John 19:26–27.

he took away her sin. The effect is the same in the case of Augustine's commentary on John 20:17, "I ascend to My Father and your Father, to My God and your God," where Augustine asks, "Why does He not say: 'To our Father and our God,' instead of making the distinction: 'to My Father and your Father'? 'My Father' because I am His only Son; 'your Father' by grace, not by nature. 'My Father' because I have always been His Son; 'your Father' because I have chosen you."[161] In these examples and in many others, Augustine demonstrates a cleverness and easiness about his handling of doctrinal themes that shows him to be in full command of such matters as well as always thinking about them at one level or another.

Thirdly and lastly, Augustine does not theologize as an end in itself, but is careful to relate his theology in a straightforward manner to his audience. Consider how he handles the potentially difficult question of why Christ came to die in the following excerpt:

> Dying, I mean, was not Christ's due. Where death came from—if we look for its origin, the father of death is sin. You see, if there had never been any sin, nobody would ever have died. The first man received God's law, that is God's commandment, with the condition that if he kept it he would live, if he broke it he would die. He didn't believe he would die, and so he did the thing he would die from ... So it is as bound to this condition of death, to these laws of hell, that every human being is born; with the exception, though, of that human being who became man in order that mankind might not perish ... who did not die for any fault, but shared the punishment with us and did not share the fault ... By sharing with us the punishment without any fault, He released us from both fault and punishment.[162]

Augustine discusses the question at hand not just by trotting out some catechistic formula, but by putting forward his own view, with his characteristic emphasis on original sin. However, he does not indulge himself to the point of excluding his audience. In fact, his remarks are quite simple and straightforward. He uses no doctrinal or philosophical terms ("sin" is as difficult as his vocabulary gets), and is careful to argue in short, simple steps, making clear where he is going. He is careful to spell out things, such as in what sense he is using the phrase "God's law."

---

161. Augustine, *Liturgical*, 246.5.
162. Augustine, *Sermons*, 231.2, on Mark 16:1.

Related to this concern for his hearers is the fact that Augustine frequently gives his theological musings a practical focus. Thus, after equating touching the resurrected Christ —something the women at the tomb were not permitted to do—with faith in him, Augustine attacks contemporary heresy at a doctrinal level.

> Let the Arian step forward; first though let the Photinian step forward. We answer the Photinian thus: "Do not touch; what's the meaning of do not touch?" Do not believe in that way; for you, Christ has not yet ascended to the Father. Let the Arian step forward. "I," he says, "believe that Christ is God, but God junior." Neither for you has He ascended to the Father. When He ascends to the Father, extend yourself, in order to touch Him; stretch out, touch God.[163]

Augustine continues for some time in the same manner holding his imaginary dialogue with the heretics and various details of their views. What is noticeable about this example is not just his ready application of his theological ideas, but the skillfully rhetorical manner in which he brings them home to his contemporaries.[164]

Similarly, Augustine defends the veracity of Christ's resurrection with a clever mix of doctrine, analysis of the workings of the human mind, and apologetic:

> In carnal man the habit of perception is the sole guide of understanding; what they are accustomed to see, that they believe; what they are not accustomed to see, they do not believe. On account of that habit, God works miracles because He is God. Indeed, there are greater miracles in the fact that so many men are born each day who did not exist before than in the fact that a few who did exist have risen again, yet those miracles have not been grasped by consideration, but have been underestimated by reason of their repetition.[165]

In this case, Augustine's theological assumptions are combined with clever insight into human nature and then shaped and presented so that the resurrection is placed on the same level (or a better one) as something as common as childbirth.[166]

---

163. Augustine, *Sermons*, 244.4, on John 20:17.
164. A similar example is found at Augustine, *Serm.*, 235.1.
165. Augustine, *Sermons*, 242.1, on Luke 24:42-43.
166. O'Collins, "Augustine on the Resurrection," 65-75.

Conclusions

In light of the selections from his work studied here, Augustine's exegesis can be summed up as a process of casting a wide-angle lens over the text before him: all manner of insights whether they be pastoral, psychological, doctrinal, typological, literal, or allegorical are captured within its gaze. In both the *In Iohannis* and the *Sermones*, Augustine can be seen using a range of tools, ideas, and exegetical methods to create a richly varied interpretative tapestry. He freely applies other parts of Scripture, theological musings, insights into the human heart, and typology in order to bring forth from the text those things that he believes that his audience need to see through his "lens." Robert Markus's comments on Augustine's exegesis of the *Literal Commentary on Genesis* comes closest among the views of recent commentators on Augustine to describing what is occurring as he interprets Scripture: he is "concerned with discovering the truth about a number of things related to the texts he is commenting on, rather than the truth about what was meant by their author."[167] That said, Augustine does even more than Markus describes here. Besides also occasionally being interested in the truth about what was meant by the biblical authors, he is also strongly concerned to bring the truths that he discovers to his audience so as to benefit their faith. However, in doing so he is not unrestrained in his ranging over a wide variety of topics, as he does stay relatively close to the narrative itself and is focused on utilizing the realities that lie behind the text rather than the text itself. In this light, to do full justice to the entire breadth and richness of Augustine's exegesis, it is necessary to give relatively more attention than some scholars have done in the past to other factors beyond the senses of Scripture. Some such other factors are also of substantial relevance. His relatively random manner of proceeding through the text, his manner of incorporating theological themes and doctrinal truths into his exposition, his strong interest in the human heart, his polysemic tendencies, and his focus on the realities behind the text are all significant features of his work which can add much in the way of understanding Augustine's exegesis to the traditionally favored enquiry as to the extent to which he uses allegorical interpretative methods. In addition, it is precisely the characteristics of his exegesis that have been highlighted as significant in this chapter that serve best to distinguish Augustine's work from that of his contemporaries. By contrast, the question of his usage of allegori-

---

167. Markus, *Signs*, 36.

cal versus literal interpretation is in this regard at least of only minor assistance, since roughly the same conclusions are reached regarding Augustine's exegesis as for the other three writers studied here: his approach is essentially literal, whilst still utilizing allegory on occasions.

7

Conclusions: Interpretation Then and Now

HAVING CONSIDERED OUR SEVERAL examples of Latin exegesis from the late patristic period, a number of clear themes have emerged. The first concerns the relative utility to modern scholars of the senses of Scripture framework and the related categories of "literal," allegorical," and "spiritual" interpretation. It has become clear that this framework is not the only useful tool for either distinguishing between the different exegetical strategies of the Latin Fathers, or helpfully describing the exegesis of any of them individually. When attempting to identify important or distinctive elements in the exegesis of Jerome, Hilary, Ambrose, or Augustine in the particular case of the Gospels, there are other features worthy of substantial attention alongside the extent of their use of allegorical or literal methods of interpretation. This study has proposed that a helpful alternative approach, which can be used as a complement to discussions of the senses of Scripture, is to consider what type of "lens" each interpreter uses to study the text—where is the primary focus of each writer? At what distance from the reader? Jerome's eyes are firmly focused on the text of Scripture itself; Hilary's just as firmly on the realities and events that lie behind the text. Ambrose tends to focus more on the author who stands before the text, arranging it and the events that it refers to. Augustine's approach is best described as being that of a wide-angle or perhaps a multifocal lens, as he ranges more widely than the other three exegetes in his efforts at bringing to light varied gems for his audience through a substantial array of interpretative methods.

The traditional framework, although very valuable in its description of an important part of the way in which the Fathers saw their own exegesis, has two substantial and related limitations. The first is that a strong focus on how relatively literal or spiritual a patristic interpreter is can lead to other key features of their work being obscured or neglected, such as the characteristics which have been highlighted in our four authors in this study. The second is that it does not readily facilitate the description of some substantial differences—perhaps the most notable and important differences—between the chosen exegetical methods of the different commentators. In some cases, such as for the four major later Latin interpreters discussed here, it can lead to comparisons which are at best bland and at worst fail to present any meaningful and significant points of differentiation between contemporaneous commentators. Regarding our four authors from late antiquity studied above, in the area of literalism and allegory they have much in common, with the differences between them being relatively small, and less substantial with respect to other key characteristics of their work that have been identified. All four can be said to place primary emphasis on the literal sense but are comfortable employing allegory when it suits their purposes. In terms of their regard for the literal sense as foundational and their small to moderate use of allegory, all of our case studies are in the same range. To the extent that they do engage in spiritual interpretation, all prefer typology of one kind or another to other kinds of non-literal interpretation. Certainly, there are some minor differences hidden within this generalization. For example, Jerome's use of allegory is best described as occasional whereas the other three exegetes use it a little more often than he does, and the kinds of typology which are preferred differ somewhat from commentator to commentator. The general picture, however, is substantially the same. In fact, this study has repeatedly found that the only significant differences between how the four exegetes use allegory simply express and reflect the other differences of "lens focus" described above. For Jerome, where allegory appears it is used to express and support his close observations and adherence to the text. Where Hilary interprets allegorically, he treats the spiritual readings given as integral, monosemic elements of the story: as actual parts of the theological story pointed to by realities described by the text. For Ambrose, allegories are normally utilized to highlight authorial intentions built upon historical realities lying behind the text, for the purpose of making connections between the text and relevant theological truths. In Augustine's case, allegory tends to appear as a means of making intuitive intertextual and theological connections, and applications to his audience. That is to say, the differences in the use of spiritual interpretation among our four exegetes tend to appear where other differences between them exist: and to disappear or at least become relatively small at other times. It is therefore suggested that the alternative categories identified through this study are more powerful means of differentiating between the exegetical strategies of the later Latin Fathers.

This study has proposed that the most significant of the alternative categories identified is the primary "lens focus" of each author. This is because, as stated above, it is the various foci of the different exegetes that both provides the most substantial point of difference between them, and best describes what each of them sees his exposition as attempting to do. Thus, Jerome's aim in his commentary can best be summed up as attempting to explain the text to his readers, whereas for Hilary it is to articulate the significance of the realities behind the text for his audience. Ambrose's fundamental aim is to get across the intentions of the evangelist in writing the Gospel, and that of Augustine is to advance the truths that he believes his congregation needs to hear by utilizing whatever methods will best achieve this for each particular passage.

In addition to this, the preceding analysis had identified several other factors that usefully highlight differences in the interpretative strategies of the four examples considered. These factors are not quite as important as the "lens focus," as they do not always directly speak to the principal aims of the writer in question in the same way that the question of focus does. However, they do still act as useful means of describing each exegete's approach, even if the writer in question was not particularly conscious that his work displayed such characteristics. Chiefly, they are of value for comparative purposes, because taken together, they provide a valuable list of points at which different Latin exegetes tend to be substantially distinct from one another.

Thus, whether each writer tended towards a polysemic approach or not was largely irrelevant to his actual purposes, but as we have seen, polysemy could be a powerful tool for an interpreter such as Augustine to use in the achievement of his aims. It also represents a major point of difference between the methodology of Augustine, and that of Jerome and Ambrose, who allow for the possibility of polysemy but tend to avoid using it in practice. It makes for an even sharper distinction between Augustine and Hilary, since the latter not only avoids it altogether, but also has such a focused approach to his exegesis that the very possibility of there being more than one interpretation of the text—particularly one other than that which Hilary has expounded—seems impossible. Likewise, our four exegetes' different manner of proceeding through the passage at hand is more of a tool that is used to serve their purposes than an end in itself, but it is also a point of significant difference between them. In this case, the chosen criterion divides our case studies evenly down the middle: Jerome and Hilary are quite ordered in how they predictably move from one verse to the next, whereas Ambrose and Augustine, although still reasonably ordered, are relatively eclectic.[1] A similar result obtains if we consider the extent to which each interpreter ranges widely in his choice of comments on whichever verse he is commenting on. However, in this case the teams line up a little differently, as it is Jerome and Ambrose who are the more eclectic, and Hilary and Augustine who tend to be more ordered and focused.

The practice of drawing attention to instances of prophecy-fulfillment is quite prominent in Augustine and Jerome, but very rare in Hilary and Ambrose. While we might expect interest in prophecy-fulfillment to go hand in hand with use or disuse of typology, this is not necessarily the case. In terms of applying typological logic to make connections between the passage and contemporary realities, Jerome and Hilary do use this kind of logic from time to time, whereas Ambrose and Augustine prefer not to. The complement of this pattern is the fact that Augustine and particularly Ambrose are more willing to apply intrabiblical typology to their texts. Lastly, the place of practical application in each example is also a useful means of differentiation. Although this indicator is open to the charge that it is influenced by the audience to whom the work is addressed, the results do not necessarily indicate this. For example, Hilary's and Jerome's commentaries were both produced as written, probably for a select audience, and yet are at opposite poles in this regard—the main purpose of Hilary's commentary is to encourage faith and belief, whereas Jerome's practical advice, although not infrequent, is marginal to his aims. Both Ambrose and Augustine's works consisted of sermons preached to cathedral congregations—although Ambrose's listeners would have been

1. To this conclusion it might be replied that one would expect the pair of preachers to be more eclectic than the pair of written commentators. However, the force of this objection is blunted when it is recalled that Jerome's "written" commentary was dictated at high speed to a secretary, while most of Augustine's sermons from the *In Iohannis evangelium* under study here were likely to have been prepared beforehand—also dictated to a secretary. Given the speed at which Jerome composed his work it may in fact have been more of a "live" performance than Augustine's.

better educated on average—and yet we find Augustine placing considerably more emphasis on the practical application of his exposition than Ambrose. It would therefore appear that the degree to which each exegete addresses his audience does tell us something about their approach, and not just about their audience.

We have concluded that the traditional framework applied to the exegesis of the later Latin Fathers should receive somewhat less attention in the future than it has done in the past, relative to alternative approaches. In the case of Gospel interpretation at least, there are other approaches that can add substantially to the picture of the Fathers' work provided by the senses of Scripture, and are of more use to modern students in distinguishing between their different strategies. However, for the validity of the identified categories to become firmly established across the whole field of exegesis, it will be necessary for them to be tested against commentaries on other parts of the Bible. Furthermore, as we noted in the introduction, case studies taken from patristic works on the Old Testament rather than the New might be expected to encourage the retention of a more substantial place for the senses of Scripture framework than this project has suggested. It has also been observed that the senses of Scripture should retain an important place in discussions of Latin patristic exegesis because it is a framework that is consciously present in the works of the Fathers themselves. That said, on the basis of this study, it appears that there are definite limits to this framework's usefulness in describing the full scope of the characteristic exegetical approaches of the Fathers. These limits have become apparent through consideration of how the Fathers treat with a part of the biblical corpus which both they and we today would regard as of particular importance, namely the Gospels. For this reason, the conclusion drawn from this project would still need to be reckoned with, and included in future accounts of Latin exegesis, even if analyses of examples of Old Testament exegesis from the same writers resulted in a different conclusion. Our case study therefore highlights the fact that there is some need for other frameworks and categories to be identified and applied. The apparent relative unimportance of the senses of Scripture in the examples considered has made it possible to so identify and apply some alternatives with a degree of clarity which might not have been possible had examples from the Old Testament been considered instead. In particular, the points of distinction that have been identified, particularly the "lens" used by various interpreters, would seem to have substantial value for improving our understanding of at least some parts of the corpus of Latin exegesis.

It should be noted that these distinguishing features which have been discussed in relation to our four authors are for the most part consciously held aims and categories of Jerome, Hilary, Ambrose, and Augustine themselves, rather than modern conceptual impositions upon their work. Many of the activities which we have discussed above would reasonably be assumed to relate to conscious interpretative decisions for most interpreters. Certainly, the choice to make points of application to one's particular audience would fit in this category, as would a decision to advance only one or more than one interpretation of a text. As we have seen, our authors will sometimes explicitly ponder or point out certain decisions they have made with respect to the differentiating categories which we have identified, such as when discussing the fulfillment of prophecy, typological connections, and the value or otherwise of additional, alternative interpretations.[2] It might be argued that some of the distinguishing features of their exegetical methods could have been at least partially habitual, the result of having imbibed certain assumptions about connections between individual texts (typologically or prophetically) or reflexive turns to allegory at certain moments in the reading process. However, in response it should be remembered that the four authors all wrote in the same language, were roughly contemporaneous interpreters of Scripture (and in relation to the Gospels, were discussing closely overlapping parts of Scripture), and in three out of four cases would have been aware of the general exegetical practices of at least some of the other members of the quartet, as well as other interpreters of the time. They would have known of contemporary alternative exegetical approaches to their own on the key points of difference which we have noted above, in relation to the "lens focus" and other matters. Yet they still chose to read the Bible in ways that were quite distinct from one another—and consistently so. This suggests that both the deliberative and the more habituated aspects of their respective interpretative methods were selected from a range of options which were "live" for them at the time—even if some of their more habitual practices were selected and shaped by the authors prior to the actual composition of the works considered here.

2. Many examples exist above; to point to but one feature within one author, on Augustine's conscious use of polysemy, see: Augustine, *In Ioh.*, 117.2 and Augustine, *In Ioh.*, 116.9, as well as *Confessiones*, 12.18.27–12.32.43 and *Doctrina*, 3.25.36–28.39.

Modern readers are certainly capable of overlaying their own perspectives and prejudices across works of patristic exegesis. One basic form is the tendency in some Christian contexts to use the traditional framework of the senses of Scripture to divide exegetical works of the period and their authors into the "good" and the "bad," with the former comprising those examples which are relatively literal in flavor and the latter those which are more heavily allegorical. Likewise, the spiritual exegesis of the period might be conveniently divided into the "positive" typological kind and the more "negative" allegorical type. As we have seen, the exegesis of early Christian authors involved far more than a series of decisions to utilize or not utilize allegorical techniques of interpretation. Very often such considerations were irrelevant to both their aims and their methods, and instead other objectives and hermeneutical questions appear to have frequently occupied their minds, with at least some of these other foci being of at least as much importance to their work as the senses of Scripture. Therefore, modern readers would do well to note that far more was going on for the interpreters of late antiquity than a mechanical application of rules of allegory or literalism to the text, even in works where we might still grant a substantial role to the senses of Scripture. In addition, it is worth remembering that for some authors, their forays into spiritual interpretation were in fact motivated to a great extent by a high doctrine of Scripture, driven by concerns which still motivate more conservative evangelical readers today for example. Specifically, they were often motivated to allegorize out of a desire to assert and to demonstrate the unity of all Scripture, a belief that all of the Scriptures are written for Christian readers "today," and a conviction that all elements and details in the text are worthy of close attention as inspired by God and potentially relevant to the contemporary reader in any era. In at least three of the four interpreters considered here (Jerome being the possible and partial exception) there is also a strong commitment to Scripture as a deeply theological document, rather than merely as an interesting historical text. As a result, the exegete is seen to bear the great responsibility for walking readers through the theological story told by the text at hand within the context of the unified canon of Scripture and the truths of Christian doctrine which lay beneath it. As we consider these fundamental convictions of later Latin Fathers regarding how Christians ought to read Scripture, we repeatedly see aims and concerns present which reflect positive values held by biblical interpreters in other times: and which can serve to helpfully affirm and remind us today of these values.

Other modern readers, and modern habits of reading, can produce understandings of patristic exegesis which are problematic in different ways. For example, it is sometimes suggested that the patristic authors call us back to a pre-Enlightenment way of reading Scripture, assisting us to look behind and beyond both the chimera of the perfect historical text of fundamentalism and the unhealthy obsession of liberal criticism with uncovering the true intentions of the author.[3] Patristic exegesis is in this sense assumed to model an approach that is superior to all of the more popular methods of the past 250 years, often with one or another practice being identified as both central to the approach of early Christian authors, as well as being the key to transforming the biblical reading habits of late modernity. For Bushur, the relevant feature is the liturgical setting and community context of reading the Bible in the ancient world.[4] While we might agree that these elements do have some importance, at least for certain works, our study underlines that there is considerable diversity among key authors in late antiquity on this score. Certainly, we have seen plenty of evidence for a strong concern with the immediate community context of Augustine's exegesis, and in the case of his *Sermones* at least the liturgical setting is also quite significant on occasions. By contrast however, Jerome betrays very little interest as he writes in either matters of liturgical setting or any communal dimension (real or potential) to his exegesis. The liturgical context appears to shape Ambrose's work to some degree, however much of the time his exegesis presents as a relatively solitary exercise in which awareness of community is largely absent. Conversely, liturgical setting or background is of little relevance to Hilary, even as the community context does hold some relevance for his work.

Likewise, understanding patristic exegesis as a kind of ancient prefiguring of contemporary reader-response or community-reception theories is problematic, and not clearly supported by the results of this case study. Cameron argues that Augustine "and other ancient interpreters asked not how Scriptures were *composed*, but how they were to be *received*."[5] In seeking to avoid the supposed pitfalls of modernist historical reconstructionism, the risk with such an approach is that it falls

---

3. Bushur, "Patristic Exegesis," 198–9.
4. Bushur, "Patristic Exegesis," 199.
5. Cameron, *Christ Meets Me Everywhere*, 16.

into the opposite error of imposing a postmodern set of assumptions onto the patristic works.[6] To take the example of Cameron's claims regarding Augustine, we observe that while Augustine indeed is very interested in the *In Iohannis* and *Sermones* with how his audience grasps and responds to the text, there is much more that ought to be added. In particular, Cameron appears to be setting up a false dichotomy between composition and reception which Augustine himself would not recognize. As we have seen, Augustine considers that the biblical text is "written for us," whoever is reading or hearing it contemporaneously—yet he also strongly emphasizes the role of the Holy Spirit in so composing and shaping the text through the human authors that it reaches into the hearts and lives of hearers centuries later. For Augustine, composition and reception are tightly bound together. The hermeneutic of some of his fellow interpreters from late antiquity is even less amenable to such postmodern concerns. Ambrose, as we have seen, is very concerned with historical human authorial intentions, while Jerome is not very interested in reader reception in the sense that Augustine is, let alone Cameron.

While it is important for modern readers to exercise caution when seeking to understand the exegetical works of late antiquity using twenty-first century paradigms and categories, it is certainly possible—and a valuable exercise—to read ancient interpreters to generate a greater degree of self-awareness as we engage in exegesis today. Just as modern approaches and methods cannot simply be overlaid across ancient exegesis, so too the methods of late antiquity should not be simplistically imported as determinative for understanding modern interpretative activity. However, reflecting upon our own modern exegetical practices in light of the work of the patristic authors can assist us to be more conscious of the methodological choices that we ourselves make, of other alternatives which may exist, and of the risks and pitfalls involved with certain practices. In this way, some of the distinctions and issues highlighted by this study's identification of the different "lens foci" of our four interpreters are reflected in a broad sense in exegetical options and methods chosen and practiced today. In the early twenty-first century, some exegetes write with a strong focus on the text and its intrinsically *textual* features and more technical details, in a way that is analogous to while not equivalent with Jerome's practice. Where readers of the Bible today practice modern equivalents of this exegesis, they would be well served by utilizing Jerome's work as a

---

6. Cf. Cameron, *Christ Meets Me Everywhere*, 14–15.

mirror to their own, to highlight the obvious advantages of this approach alongside the risks it can carry, of sometimes missing as Jerome did the realities behind the textual details or the theological story to which they point. Moving to a different kind of method, the rise of the "theological interpretation" movement of recent years mirrors, again not exactly, Hilary's and to an extent Augustine's emphases on telling Scripture's theological story in a way that is relevant to the doctrinal and practical concerns of the interpreter's audience. Hilary's and Augustine's approach also serves to heighten awareness of the strengths and the potential downsides of this kind of method, the latter including the temptation to develop quite sophisticated theological stories which might in fact be undermined by details on the text which have been passed over or missed altogether. Others today, like Ambrose, remain keenly interested in the intentions of the human authors of Scripture, although unlike Ambrose often with a significant focus on editorial activity and final canonical form. Ambrose's example points us to both the level of insight into and from the Scriptures which can be gained from this type of interpretative focus, as well as the necessarily speculative nature of the task (to some degree) and the caution with which conclusions about human authorial intention must be made. Some commentators choose to have a strongly multifocal approach, as Augustine did, where no single technique or simple objective predominates in reading the text. Such an approach to reading Scripture, now as then, we can see from the case of Augustine promises much in its capacity to relate Scripture on a broad front to doctrinal convictions and the Christian life, while at the same time relying more heavily than alternatives on the judgement, prudence, and insight of the interpreter. As we have seen, it can therefore readily yield rich and applicable insights which are well-grounded in wider theological considerations, but also easily slip into merely showcasing the interests and idiosyncrasies of the commentator.

There is much that contemporary interpretative practice, at least in some modern Christian contexts, has in common with key elements of the exegesis of late antiquity as identified in this study. Most more conservative interpreters would, like the commentators considered here, have a significant place for highlighting the fulfillment of biblical prophecy. However, when it comes to the related area of typology, the degree of emphasis and the type of approach employed continues to vary considerably among interpreters even within the same subsection of Christianity (evangelicalism for example), as it did for the four late-antique interpreters. The degree to which modern commentators seek to apply their exegetical insights to their intended audience, and also the extent to which their readership is explicitly in view, also varies considerably. We might observe that many of these variations today are due to the sharp distinction which can exist between different genres of contemporary commentary: technical commentaries would be expected to address their audiences quite differently to commentaries designed for preachers, for example. That said, the same is true of Hilary and Augustine, each of whom produced two quite different works concentrating on the gospel texts (intended for different audiences of differing capabilities)—this is not merely a twenty-first century consideration, and as we have seen there are consistent habits and trends in both Augustine's and Hilary's handling of the question of relationship to their audience. Also, modern commentators still do need to make decisions regarding how much to write with their primary readership and context in mind, and how much contemporary application to include relative to other matters. The advent of a global audience for modern commentaries arguably makes such decisions more difficult, and means it is more difficult to speak to one's readers with a high degree of specificity. However, we must remember that the late Roman world was not so different to our own on this point: it was quite a diverse context, with cities such as Milan, Poitiers, and Hippo each containing multiple different kinds of Christian readership, as well as varying considerably from each other in terms of their local Christian culture. Commentators both ancient and modern do make and need to make decisions in areas such as how to address their audience, and often the decisions made can be surprising. For instance, in this study the one commentary addressed to a single, specific reader—Jerome's work on Matthew—is the one example out of the six examined which has the least explicit recognition of the intended audience and the least time devoted to personal application.

One particular contemporary issue brought into focus by the distinctions made between our four interpreters in this study, is the question of whether interpreters ought to assume that the biblical text before them admits of only one meaning, or potentially several: the matter of monosemy and polysemy. For centuries Protestantism tended to read Scripture with the assumption that any text had only a single meaning, with a few special exceptions such as where typology and prophecies and their fulfillment were in view, or a very rare example of allegory such as Galatians 4:21–31. This posture originated in the Reformation's reaction against the practices of medieval exegesis, with its strong tendency towards multiple interpretations and frequent recourse to quadruple senses of Scripture to support this. It was further reinforced by the theological debates of the post-Reformation period, and subsequently by the Enlightenment's emphasis on the virtues of clarity and simplicity in communication. However, in the late twentieth and early twenty-first centuries, the idea that biblical texts might appropriately be read in more than one way has again gained significant traction in some circles. Reader-response theories push in the direction of polysemy, some more strongly than others. The rise of postmodern approaches to reading Scripture, and the more pluralistic context of modern interpretation in general, have both acted as forces encouraging the decline of the idea that the biblical text ordinarily holds a single clear meaning, as opposed to multiple meanings for different readers or distinct subsections within the church. One sign among many of this shift has been the increasingly common assumption that different subgroups within the local church, or even whole continents, need their own commentaries and Bible study notes. Related late-modern emphases, such as the emphasis on reading the biblical texts "as literature," and the renewed emphasis on the importance of reading Scripture from the perspective of one's own particular community, can also—but not necessarily or always—promote polysemic and pluralistic understandings of the task of interpretation.

In this context, those who are supportive of the Reformers' approach for example, need to consider how they might respond. Valuing different perspectives on the Scriptures from diverse parts of the church and engaging deeply with alternative interpretations of any biblical text are beneficial for any reader of the Bible and for the church as a whole. Such biblical reading habits can enrich the understanding of the text by highlighting otherwise overlooked or underemphasized features and assist in applying the text appropriately to others or to new situations. They can even strengthen monosemic approaches, by helping to identify and discard more dubious interpretations. However, stressing these benefits at the expense of other interpretative values could in time lead a reader or a church to tip over into polysemy. Likewise, a recognition that different audiences will, and indeed ought to, apply the text in somewhat distinctive ways is important as well as appropriate. However, this not the same thing as saying that the text possesses or should admit of multiple meanings, although an overemphasis on contextualizing and personalizing application can sometimes engender pressure towards full-blown polysemy over time. In an increasingly pluralistic age, and in the context of an increasingly pluralistic Christianity, polysemy will tend to be the most attractive route for many churches and individuals.

In this light, those who hold to classical Protestant assumptions about the reading of Scripture (and their equivalents in other branches of Christianity), need to present the case for this alternative in a form which is persuasive in pluralistic times, as well as formulating responses to more polysemic tendencies and practices. This might begin by asking whether there are any criteria, such as those applied by Augustine in his own time to his own practice, which might at least shape and discipline polysemy in directions which allow Scripture to interpret itself and for Scripture to generate the principles by which it is interpreted. However, for those committed to a more monosemic understanding of reading the Bible, the models of Jerome, Hilary, and Ambrose appear best, and provide the most valuable resources identified in this study on the question of polysemy and monosemy, even if not in relation to other aspects of exegetical method. Jerome and Ambrose both model the presentation of a single meaning of the text, while being aware of and generous towards other interpretations which support orthodoxy and godliness. Hilary promotes reading the text as a single narrative which articulates a divinely-authored theological story, which is both the proper focus of faith and supportive of it. All three commentators seek to locate a single meaning or story line in the text which is respectful of the text and its divine author, while allowing for catholicity in the reading and application of the text, a capacity to learn from the wider Christian community, and an appropriate epistemic humility on the part of fallible human readers. At the same time, they avoid allowing the existence of a diversity of extant interpretations within the church to be translated into the assumption that the text itself is inherently diverse, or intended to produce diverse or potentially contradictory readings.

Taking into account all of these considerations, it is apparent that there is much that can be gained by reading and reflecting upon the exegetical work of the later Latin Fathers. Their interpretative habits are not simply, or even primarily, characterized by the presence or absence of allegorical exegesis. Their aims and methods incorporate a range of other important elements and points of differentiation, which continue to reflect key issues of importance to biblical interpreters today. Jerome, Hilary, Ambrose, and Augustine understood the task of reading and applying Scripture to be a matter of the utmost importance, worthy of careful thought, to which they all devoted substantial attention over many years. We who today regard this work with the same seriousness should expect to gain much by reading them.

Bibliography

Primary Sources

Ambrose. *De Abraham*. Edited by Jacques-Paul Migne. *PL* 14.
———. *Expositio evangelii secundam Lucam*. Edited by Marcus Adriaen. *CCSL* 14.
———. "Select Works and Letters." In *Nicene and Post-Nicene Fathers: Second Series* 10. Translated by Henry De Romestin et al. New York: Christian Literature, 1896.
Augustine. *The City of God*. Translated by Henry Bettenson. London: Pelican, 1972.
———. *Confessiones*. Edited by Jacques-Paul Migne. *PL* 32.
———. *De civitate dei*. Edited by Bernhard Dombart and Alfons Kalb. *CCSL* 47–48.
———. *De doctrina christiana*. Edited by Jacques-Paul Migne. *PL* 34.
———. *De Trinitate*. Edited by William J. Mountain. *CCSL* 50, 50A.
———. *De utilitate credendi*. Edited by Jacques-Paul Migne. *PL* 42.
———. *In Iohannis evangelium*. Edited by Radobus Willems. *CCSL* 34–36.
———. *On Christian Doctrine*. Translated by Durant W. Robertson, Jr. Upper Saddle River, NJ: Prentice-Hall, 1958.
———. *Retractionum*. Edited by Almut Mutzenbecher. *CCSL* 57.
———. *Sermones de tempore*. Edited by Jacques-Paul Migne. *PL* 38.
———. *Sermons on the Liturgical Seasons*. Translated by Mary S. Muldowney. *FOC* 38, 59. New York: The Fathers of the Church, 1958–59.
———. *Sermons. The Works of Saint Augustine: A Translation for the 21st Century*, III/6–7. Translated by Edmund Hill. New Rochelle, NY: Augustinian Heritage Institute, 1993.
———. *Tractates on the Gospel of John, 55–111 and 112–24*. Translated by John W. Rettig. *FOC* 90, 92. Washington, DC: The Catholic University of America, 1994–95.
Hilary. *Commentary on Matthew*. Translated by Daniel H. Williams. *FOC* 125. Washington, DC: The Catholic University of America, 2012.
———. *De Trinitate*. Edited by Pierre Smulders. *CCSL* 62, 62A.
———. *Select Works, Nicene and Post-Nicene Fathers: Second Series* 9. Translated by Edward W. Watson and Leighton Pullan. New York: Charles Scribner's Sons, 1899.
———. *Sur Matthieu*, 2. Edited by Jean Doignon. Paris: Les Éditions du Cerf, 1979.
———. *The Trinity*. Translated by Stephen McKenna. *FOC* 25. New York: The Fathers of the Church, 1954.
———. *Traité des Mystères*. Edited by Jean-Paul Brisson. 2nd ed. Paris: Les Éditions du Cerf, 1967.
———. *Tractatus super Psalmos*. Edited by Jean Doignon. *CCSL* 61A.

Jerome. *Commentarii in prophetas minors.* Edited by Marcus Adriaen. *CCSL* 76.
———. *Commentarioli in psalmos.* Edited by Germain Morin. *CCSL* 72.
———. *Commentariorum in Matheum.* Edited by David Hurst and Marcus Adriaen. *CCSL* 77.
———. *Commentary on Matthew.* Translated by Thomas P. Scheck. *FOC* 117. Washington, DC: The Catholic University of America, 2008.
———. *De viris illustribus.* Edited by Jacques-Paul Migne. *PL* 23.
———. *Epistolae.* Edited by Jacques-Paul Migne. *PL* 22.
———. *In Amos.* Edited by Jacques-Paul Migne. *PL* 25.
———. *Liber Hebraicarum Quaestionum in Genesim.* Edited by Jacques-Paul Migne. *PL* 23.
Origen. *Commentary on John, Ante-Nicene Fathers,* 9. Translated and edited by Allan Menzies. New York: Christian Literature, 1896.

Secondary Sources

Adkin, Neil. "An Echo of Hilary of Poitiers in Jerome." *Museum Helveticum* 53 (1996) 56–60.
———. "Jerome on Ambrose: The Preface to the Translation of Origen's Homilies on Luke." *Revue Bénédictine* 107 (1997) 5–14.
Aland, Barbara, and Joël Delobel, eds. *New Testament Textual Criticism, Exegesis and Church History: A Discussion of Methods.* Kampen: Kok Pharos, 1994.
Albaric, Michel. "A Eucharistic Catechesis." In *Saint Augustine and the Bible,* edited by Anne-Marie Bonnardiere, 253–64. Translated by Pamela Bright, with several additional articles added in English. Notre Dame, IN: University of Notre Dame Press, 1999.
Albright, William F., and Christopher S. Mann. *Matthew,* 26, *The Anchor Bible,* Doubleday, New York, NY, 1971.
Allen, Pauline, and Wendy Mayer. "Computer and Homily: Accessing the Everyday Life of Early Christians." *VChr* 47 (1993) 260–80.
———. "Through a Bishop's Eyes: Towards a Definition of Pastoral Care in Late Antiquity." *Aug* 47, no. 2 (2000) 345–98.
Altaner, Berthold. *Patrology.* Translated by Hilda C. Graef. Edinburgh: Nelson, 1960.
Amersfoort, J. Van. "Some Influences of the Diatessaron of Tatian on the Gospel Text of Hilary of Poitiers." *SP* 15 (1984) 200–205.
Andrews, James. "Why Theological Hermeneutics Needs Rhetoric: Augustine's *De Doctrina Christiana.*" *International Journal of Systematic Theology* 12, no. 2 (2010) 184–200.
Ayres, Lewis. Review of Kannengeisser, Charles, *Handbook of Patristic Exegesis,* 2 vols. Leiden: Brill, 2004. *JECS* 13, no. 4 (2005) 532–6.
Babcock, William S. "Augustine's Interpretation of Romans." *AugSt* 10 (1979) 55–74.
Baker, Matthew, ed. *What Is the Bible? The Patristic Doctrine of Scripture.* Minneapolis: Fortress, 2016.
Balás, David L., and D. Jeffrey Bingham. "Patristic Exegesis of the Books of the Bible." In *Handbook of Patristic Exegesis,* 1. Edited by Charles Kannengeisser, 271–375. Leiden: Brill, 2004.

Bammel, Caroline P. "Augustine, Origen and the Exegesis of St Paul." *Aug* 32 (1992) 341–68.

———. "Pauline Exegesis, Manichaeism and Philosophy in the Early Augustine." In *Christian Faith and Greek Philosophy in Late Antiquity*, edited by L. R. Wickham and C. P. Bammel, 3–25. Leiden: Brill, 1993.

———. "Rufinus' Translation of Origen's Commentary on Romans and the Pelagian Controversy." In *Antichita Altoadriatiche 39, storia ed esegesi in Rufino di Concordia*, edited by A. Scotta, 131–42. Udine: Arti Grafiche Friulane, 1992.

Barnard, Leslie W. "To Allegorise or Not to Allegorise?" *Studia Theologica* 36 (1982) 1–10.

Barr, James. "The Literal, the Allegorical, and Modern Biblical Scholarship." *Journal for the Study of the Old Testament* 44 (1989) 3–17.

Beckwith, Carl L. *Hilary of Poitiers on the Trinity: From De Fide to De Trinitate*. Oxford: Oxford University Press, 2008.

———. "Photinian Opponents in Hilary of Poitier's *Commentarium in Matthaeum*." *Journal of Ecclesiastical History* 58, no. 4 (2007) 611–27.

Bellifemine, Marta. "Due ipotesti ilariani nell'*Expositio evangelii secundum Lucam* di Ambrogio." *Auctores Nostri* 1 (2004) 31–52.

Bellinzoni, Arthur J. "The Gospel of Matthew in the Second Century." *The Second Century* 9 (1992) 197–258.

Bernard, Robert W. "The Rhetoric of God in the Figurative Exegesis of Augustine." In *Biblical Hermeneutics in Historical Perspective*, edited by M. S. Burrows et al., 88–99. Grand Rapids: Eerdmans, 1991.

Berrouard, Marie-François. *Introduction aux homilies de saint Augustin sur l'Evangile de saint Jean*. Paris: Institut d'études augustiniennes, 2004.

———. "Les Tractatus LV–CXXIV dictée à partir de Novembre 419." *Bibliothèque Augustinienne* 74A (1988) 9–52.

———. "L'exégèse de saint Augustin predicateur du quatrième Evangile." *Freiburger Zeitschrift für Philosophie und Theologie* 34 (1987) 311–38.

Blamires, Henry. *A History of Literary Criticism*. Basingstoke: Macmillan, 1991.

Bonnardiere, Anne-Marie. "Augustine, Minister of the Word of God." In *Saint Augustine and the Bible*, edited by Anne-Marie Bonnardiere, 22–64. Translated by Pamela Bright, with several additional articles added in English. Notre Dame, IN: University of Notre Dame Press, 1999.

———. "Did Augustine Use Jerome's Vulgate?" In *Saint Augustine and the Bible*, edited by Anne-Marie Bonnardiere, 245–51. Translated by Pamela Bright, with several additional articles added in English. Notre Dame, IN: University of Notre Dame Press, 1999.

———. *Recherches de chronologie augustinienne*. Paris: Études augustiniennes, 1965.

Bonner, Gerald. *Augustine: Life and Controversies*. 2nd ed. London: SCM, 1963.

———. "Augustine as Biblical Scholar." In *CHB 1*, edited by Peter R. Ackroyd and Christopher F. Evans, 542–62. Cambridge: Cambridge University Press, 1970.

Borresen, Kari E. "Augustin, interprété du dogme de la résurrection: Quelques aspects de son anthropologie dualiste." *Studia Theologica* 23 (1969) 141–55.

Bray, Gerald. *Biblical Interpretation Past and Present*. Leicester: InterVarsity, 1996.

Brennecke, Hans C. "Hilarius von Poitiers." In *ThR* 15, edited by Gerhard Müller et al., 315–22. Berlin: W. de Gruyter, 1986.

Bright, Pamela. "Biblical Ambiguity in African Exegesis." In *De Doctrina Christiana: A Classic of Western Culture*, edited by Duane W. H. Arnold and Pamela Bright, 25–32. Notre Dame, IN: University of Notre Dame Press, 1995.

Bromiley, Geoffrey W. "The Church Fathers and Holy Scripture." In *Scripture and Truth*, edited by Donald Carson and John Woodbridge, 199–224. Grand Rapids, MI: Zondervan, 1983.

———. *Historical Theology*. Edinburgh: T. & T. Clark, 1978.

Brown, Dennis. "Jerome and the Vulgate." In *A History of Biblical Interpretation*, 1, *The Ancient Period*, edited by A. J. Hauser and D. F. Watson, 355–79. Grand Rapids, MI: Eerdmans, 2003.

———. *Vir Trilinguis: A Study in the Biblical Exegesis of Saint Jerome*. Kampen: Kok Pharos, 1992.

Brown, Peter. *Augustine of Hippo: A Biography*. New edition with epilogue. London: Faber and Faber, 2000.

Bühler, Pierre. "Hermeneutics." In *The Oxford Companion to Christian Thought*, edited by Adrian Hastings et al., 295. Oxford: Oxford University Press, 2000.

Burns, Paul C. *The Christology in Hilary of Poitiers' Commentary on Matthew*. Rome: Institutum Patristicum Augustinianum, 1981.

———. *A Model for the Christian Life: Hilary of Poitiers' Commentary on the Psalms*. Washington, DC: Catholic University of America, 2012.

Bushur, James G. "Patristic Exegesis: Reading Scripture in the Eucharistic Gathering." *Concordia Theological Quarterly* 3–4 (2010) 195–208.

Cameron, John. "The Rabbinic Vulgate?" In *Jerome of Stridon: His Life, Writings and Legacy*, edited by Andrew Cain and Josef Lössl, 117–130. Farnham, England and Burlington, VT: Ashgate, 2009.

Cameron, Michael. *Christ Meets Me Everywhere: Augustine's Early Figurative Exegesis*. Oxford: Oxford University Press, 2012.

———. "The Christological Substructure of Augustine's Figurative Exegesis." In *Saint Augustine and the Bible*, edited by Anne-Marie Bonnardiere, 75–97. Translated by Pamela Bright, with several additional articles in English. Notre Dame, IN: University of Notre Dame Press, 1999.

———. Medieval Exegesis. Volume 1: The Four Senses of Scripture/Spiritual Exegesis and the Church in the Theology of Henri de Lubac. *Anglican Theological Review* 82, no. 1 (Winter 2000) 91–2.

———. "Transfiguration: Christology and the Roots of Figurative Exegesis in St. Augustine." *SP* 33 (1996) 40–47. Papers Presented at the Twelfth International Conference on Patristic Studies.

Campenhausen, Hans Von. *The Fathers of the Latin Church*. Translated by M. Hoffmann. London: A & C Black, 1964.

Canellis, Aline. "L'*In Zachariam* de Jérôme et la Tradition Alexandrine." In *Jerome of Stridon: His Life, Writings and Legacy*, edited by Andrew Cain and Josef Lössl, 153–62. Farnham, England and Burlington, VT: Ashgate, 2009.

Carroll, Thomas K. *Preaching the Word: The Message of the Fathers of the Church*, 11. Wilmington, DE: Michael Glazier, 1984.

Cary, Phillip. *Augustine's Invention of the Christian Self: The Legacy of a Christian Neoplatonist*. Oxford: Oxford University Press, 2000.

Cassidy, Eoin G. "Augustine's Exegesis of the First Epistle of John." In *Scriptural Interpretation in the Fathers*, edited by T. Finan and V. Twomey, 201–21. Dublin: Four Courts, 1995.
Cavadini, John C. "The Sweetness of the Word: Salvation and Rhetoric in Augustine's *De Doctrina Christiana*." In *De Doctrina Christiana: A Classic of Western Culture*, edited by Duane W. H. Arnold and Pamela Bright, 164–78. Notre Dame, IN: University of Notre Dame Press, 1995.
Chadwick, Henry. *Augustine*. Oxford: Oxford University Press, 1986.
Childs, Brevard S. "Critical Reflections on James Barr's Understanding of the Literal and the Allegorical." *Journal for the Study of the Old Testament* 46 (1990) 3–9.
Clancy, Finbarr G. "The Cross in Augustine's *Tractatus in Iohannem*." *SP* 33 (1995) 55–62. Papers Presented at the Twelfth International Conference on Patristic Studies.
Colish, Marcia L. *The Mirror of Language: A Study in the Medieval Theory of Knowledge*. New Haven, CT: Yale University Press, 1968.
Comeau, Marie. *Saint Augustin: Exégète du Quatrième Evangile*. 3rd ed. Paris: Beauchesne, 1930.
Corsato, Celestino. *La Expositio euangelii secundum Lucam di sant'Ambrogio: Ermeneutica, simbologia, fonti*. Rome: Institutum Patristicum Augustinianum, 1993.
Courcelle, Pierre. *Late Latin Writers and Their Greek Sources*. Translated by H. E. Wedeck. Cambridge, MA: Harvard University Press, 1969.
Courtray, Régis. "La Figure des Duex Larrons chez Jérôme." In *Jerome of Stridon: His Life, Writings and Legacy*, edited by Andrew Cain and Josef Lössl, 105–16. Farnham, England and Burlington, VT: Ashgate, 2009.
Cross, Frank L., and Livingstone, Elizabeth A., eds. *The Oxford Dictionary of the Christian Church*. 3rd ed. London: Oxford University Press, 1997.
Crouzel, Henri. "La distinction de la 'typologie' et de l'"allegorie."" *Bulletin de Littérature Ecclésiastique* 65 (Suppl.) (1964) 161–74.
Cuddon, J. E. *The Penguin Dictionary of Literary Terms and Literary Theory*. 4th ed. Revised by C. E. Preston. London: Penguin, 1998.
Cummings, John T. "St Jerome as Translator and as Exegete." *SP* 12 (1975) 279–82.
Cunningham, Lawrence S. "Medieval Exegesis by Henri de Lubac." Translated by Marc Sebanc." *Commonweal* 126, no. 6 (9 April 1999) 28–29.
Dassmann, Ernst. "Ambrosius von Mailand." In *ThR*, edited by Gerhard Müller et al., 362–86. Berlin: W. de Gruyter, 1978.
Davidson, Ivor J. "Pastoral Theology at the End of the Fourth Century: Ambrose and Jerome." *SP* 33 (1995) 295–301. Papers Presented at the Twelfth International Conference on Patristic Studies.
De Jonge, Henk J. "Augustine on the Interrelations of the Gospels." In *The Four Gospels*, 3, edited by F. Van Segbroek et al., 2409–17. Leuven: Leuven University Press, 1992.
Dekkers, Eligius. *Clavis Patrum Latinorum*. 3rd ed. Steenbrugis: Brepols, 1995.
Dewart, Joanne M. "Augustine's Developing Use of the Cross." *AugSt* 15 (1984) 15–33.
Dockery, David S. *Biblical Interpretation Then and Now*. Grand Rapids, MI: Baker, 1992.
Doignon, Jean. "Deux approches de la résurrection dans l'exégèse d'Hilaire de Poitiers." *Recherches de Théologie Ancienne et Médiévale* 56 (1987) 5–12.

———. *Hilaire de Poitiers avant l'Exilé, Recherches sur la naissance, l'enseignement et l'épreuve d'une foi épiscopale en Gaule au milieu du IV siècle*. Paris: Études Ausustiniennes, 1971.

———. "La connexion du spirituel et du charnel dans la méthodologie exégétique d'Hilaire de Poitiers. A propos d'un texte malmené d'*In psalmum* 1, 17." *Vetera Christianorum* 30 (1993) 259–66.

———. "L'éxégèse d'Hilaire de Poitiers." In *Le monde latin antique et la Bible*, edited by Jacques Fontaine and Charles Pietri, 508–20. Paris: Beauchesne, 1985.

Doyle, G. Wright. "Augustine's Sermonic Method." *Westminster Theological Journal* 39 (1976–77) 213–38.

Driscoll, Jeremy. "The Transfiguration in Hilary of Poitiers' Commentary on Matthew." *Aug* 24 (1984) 395–420.

Drobner, Hubertus R. "Grammatical Exegesis and Christology in St. Augustine." *SP* 18, no. 4 (1987) 49–63.

Dudden, Frederick H. *The Life and Times of St Ambrose*. Oxford: Clarendon, 1935.

Edwards, Mark. "Figurative Readings: Their Scope and Justification." In *The New Cambridge History of the Bible: From the Beginnings to 600*, edited by James Carleton Paget and Joachim Schaper, 714–33. Cambridge: Cambridge University Press, 2013.

Elliot, Mark W. "Exegetical Genres in the Patristic Era." In *The New Cambridge History of the Bible: From the Beginnings to 600*, edited by James Carleton Paget and Joachim Schaper, 775–97. Cambridge: Cambridge University Press, 2013.

Ellis, E. Earle. *Prophecy and Hermeneutic in Early Christianity*. Tübingen: Mohr-Siebeck, 1978.

Farkasfalvy, Denis. "Interpretation of the Bible." In *Encyclopaedia of Early Christianity*, edited by Everett Ferguson, 466–69. 2nd ed. New York: Garland, 1997.

Finan, Thomas. "St Augustine on the 'mira profundatis' of Scripture." In *Scriptural Interpretation in the Fathers*, edited by Thomas Finan and Vincent Twomey, 174–99. Dublin: Four Courts, 1995.

Fitzgerald, Allan. "Ambrose and Augustine: *Confessio* as *initium iustitiae*." *Aug* 40, no. 1 (2000) 173–86.

———. "Johannis evangelium tractatus." In *Augustine Through the Ages: An Encyclopaedia*, edited by Allan D. Fitzgerald, 474–5. Grand Rapids, MI: Eerdmans, 1999.

Fitzmyer, Joseph A. *The Gospel According to Luke (X–XXIV)*, 28A, *The Anchor Bible*. New York: Doubleday, 1985.

Fleteren, Frederick Van. "Augustine's Principles of Biblical Exegesis, De Doctrina Christiana Aside: Miscellaneous Observations." *AugSt* 27, no. 2 (1996) 109–30.

———. "Per Speculum et in aenigmate: 1 Corinthians 13:12 in the Writings of St. Augustine." *AugSt* 23 (1992) 69–102.

Fredricksen, Paula. "Excaecati Occulta Justitia Dei: Augustine on Jews and Judaism." *JECS* 3, no. 3 (1995) 299–324.

———. "Vile Bodies: Paul and Augustine on the Resurrection of the Flesh." In *Biblical Hermeneutics in Historical Perspective*, edited by M. S. Burrows and P. Rorem, 5–87. Grand Rapids, MI: Eerdmans, 1991.

Freeman, Curtis W. "Figure and History: A Contemporary Reassessment of Augustine's Hermeneutic." In *Augustine: Presbyter Factus Sum*, edited by Joseph T. Lienhard et al., 320–48. New York: Peter Lang, 1993.

Froehlich, Karlfried, ed. *Biblical Interpretation in the Early Church*. Philadelphia, PA: Fortress, 1984.
Gasque, W. Ward and William S. LaSor, eds. *Scripture, Tradition, and Interpretation*. Grand Rapids, MI: Eerdmans, 1978.
Goldsworthy, Graeme. *According to Plan: The Unfolding Revelation of God in the Bible*. Leicester: InterVarsity, 1991.
Gorday, Peter. *Principles of Patristic Exegesis: Romans 9–11 in Origen, John Chrysostom, and Augustine*. Lewiston, NY: Edwin Mellen, 1983.
Gowans, Coleen Hoffman. *The Identity of the True Believer in the Sermons of Augustine of Hippo: A Dimension of His Christian Anthropology*. NY: Edwin Mellen, 1998.
Grant, Robert M. *The Letter and the Spirit*. London: SPCK, 1957.
———. *A Short History of the Interpretation of the Bible*. 2nd ed. London: Adam and Charles Black, 1965.
Graumann, Thomas. *Christus Interpres: Die Einheit von Auslegung und Verkundigung in der Lukaserklarung des Ambrosius von Mailand*. Berlin: De Gruyter, 1994.
Graves, Michael. "'Judaizing' Christian Interpretations of the Prophets as Seen by Saint Jerome." *VigChr* 61, no. 2 (2007) 142–56.
Griboment, Jean. "The Translations. Jerome and Rufinus." In *Patrology*, 4, *The Golden Age of Latin Patristic Literature*, edited by Johannes Quasten, 195–254. Translated by Placid Solari. Westminster, MD: Christian Classics, 1986.
Guinot, Jean-Noël. "L'exégèse ambrosienne des apparitions pascales (Lc. 24)." *Aug* 40, no. 1 (2000) 145–72.
Hagendahl, Harald. "Jerome and the Latin Classics." *VChr* 28 (1974) 216–27.
Hall, Christopher A. *Reading Scripture with the Church Fathers*. Downers Grove, IL: IVP, 1998.
Hardy, Richard P. *Actualité de la révélation divine: une étude des "Tractatus in Iohannis Euangelium" de Saint Augustin*. Paris: Beauchesne, 1974.
———. "The Incarnation and Revelation in Augustine's *Tractatus in Iohannis Evangelium*." Église et Théologie 3 (1972) 193–220.
Harrison, Carol. "Augustine." In *The New Cambridge History of the Bible: From the Beginnings to 600*, edited by James Carleton Paget and Joachim Schaper, 676–96. Cambridge: Cambridge University Press, 2013.
———. *Beauty and Revelation in the Thought of Saint Augustine*. Oxford: Clarendon, 1992.
Hartmann, Louis N. "St. Jerome as an Exegete." In *A Monument to Saint Jerome: Essays on Some Aspects of His Life, Works, and Influence*, edited by Francis X. Murphy, 35–83. New York: Sheed and Ward, 1952.
Hastings, Adrian. "Theology." In *The Oxford Companion to Christian Thought*, edited by Adrian Hastings et al., 700–702. Oxford: Oxford University Press, 2000.
Hayward, C. T. R. *Jerome's Hebrew Questions on Genesis: Translated with an Introduction and Commentary*. Oxford: Clarendon, 1995.
Heimann, David F. "The Polemical Application of Scripture in St. Jerome." *SP* 12 (1975) 309–16.
Hollingworth, Miles. *Saint Augustine of Hippo: An Intellectual Biography*. London: Bloomsbury, 2013.
Horbury, William. "Jews and Christians on the Bible: Demarcation and Convergence 325–451." In *Christliche Exegese zwischen Nicaea und Chalcedon*, edited by Johannes van Oort and Ulrich Wickert, 72–102. Kampen: Kok Pharos, 1992.

Hoskyns, Edwyn C. *The Fourth Gospel*. 2nd ed. London: Faber and Faber, 1947.
Houghton, Hugh A. G. *Augustine's Text of John*. Oxford: Oxford University Press, 2008.
Hughes, Kevin L. "The Fourfold Sense: de Lubac, Blondel, and Contemporary Theology." *Heythrop Journal* 42 (2001) 451–62.
Irvine, Martin. *The Making of Textual Culture: Grammatical and Literary Theory, 350–1100*. Cambridge: Cambridge University Press, 1994.
Jackson, Pamela. "Ambrose of Milan as Mystagogue." *AugSt* 20 (1989) 93–107.
Jacob, Christoph. "The Reception of the Origenist Tradition in Latin Exegesis." In *Hebrew Bible/Old Testament: The History of Its Interpretation, 1, From the Beginnings to the Middle Ages (Until 1300), Part 1: Antiquity*, edited by Magne Sæbø, 682–700. Göttingen: Vandenhoeck & Ruprech, 1996.
Jacobs, J. W. "The Western Roots of the Christology of St Hilary of Poitiers: A Heritage of Textual Interpretation." *SP* 13 (1976) 198–203.
Jay, Pierre. "Jerome et la pratique de l'exégèse." In *Le monde latin antique et la Bible*, edited by Jacques Fontaine, and Charles Pietri, 524–41. Paris: Beauchesne, 1985.
———. *L'exégèse de saint Jérôme sur Isaïe d'après son Commentary sur Isaïe*. Paris: Études augustiniennes, 1985.
———. "S. Jerome et le triple sens de l'ecriture." *REAug* 26 (1980) 214–27.
Jeanrond, Werner G. *Theological Hermeneutics: Development and Significance*. Basingstoke: MacMillan, 1991.
Kaiser, Christopher. "The development of Johannine motifs in Hilary's doctrine of the Trinity." *Scottish Journal of Theology* 29 (1976) 237–47.
Kamesar, Adam. "Jerome." In *The New Cambridge History of the Bible: From the Beginnings to 600*, edited by James Carleton Paget and Joachim Schaper, 653–75. Cambridge: Cambridge University Press, 2013.
———. *Jerome, Greek Scholarship, and the Hebrew Bible: A Study of the* Quaestiones Hebraicae in Genesim. Oxford: Clarendon, 1993.
Kannengeisser, Charles. *Handbook of Patristic Exegesis*. 2 vols. Leiden: Brill, 2004.
———. "A Key for the Future of Patristics: The 'Senses' of Scripture." In *In Dominico Eloquio: In Lordly Eloquence*, edited by P. M. Blowers, et al., 90–107. Grand Rapids, MI: Eerdmans, 2002.
Kato, Teppai. "Jerome's Understanding of Old Testament Quotations in the New Testament." *VigChr* 67, no. 3 (2013) 289–315.
Kelly, John N. D. "The Bible and the Latin Fathers." In *The Church's Use of the Bible Past and Present*, edited by D. E. Nineham, 41–55. London: SPCK, 1963.
———. *Early Christian Doctrines*. 5th ed. London: A & C Black, 1977.
———. *Jerome: His Life, Writings, and Controversies*. London: Duckworth, 1975.
Kenney, John Peter. *Contemplation and Classical Christianity: A Study in Augustine*. Oxford Early Christian Studies. Oxford: Oxford University Press, 2013.
Kieffer, Rene. "Jerome: His Exegesis and Hermeneutics." In *Hebrew Bible/Old Testament: The History of Its Interpretation, 1, From the Beginnings to the Middle Ages (Until 1300), Part 1: Antiquity*, edited by Magne Sæbø, 663–81. Göttingen: Vandenhoeck & Ruprech, 1996.
Kilmartin, Edward J. "Augustine's Tractate 27 and Sacramental Realism." In *Preaching in the Patristic Age: Studies in Honour of Walter J. Burghardt*, edited by D. G. Hunter, 162–79. New York: Paulist, 1989.
Kirwan, Christopher. *Augustine*. 2nd ed. London: Routledge, 1991.

Kremen, Kathryn R. *The Imagination of the Resurrection*. Cranberry, NJ: Associated University Presses, 1972.
Kugel, James L., and Rowan A. Greer. *Early Biblical Interpretation*. Philadelphia, PA: Westminster, 1986.
Kunzelmann, Adalberto. "Die Chronologie der Sermones des Hl. Augustinus." *Miscellanea Agostiniana* 2 (1931) 417–520.
Labriolle, Pierre de. *History and Literature of Latin Christianity: From Tertullian to Boethius*. Translated by H. Wilson. London: Routledge & Kegan Paul, 1924.
———. "Saint Ambrose et l'exégèse allegorique." In *Die Eschatologie des heiligen Ambrosius*, edited by J. E. Niederhuber, 591–603. Paderborn: Josef Kössel, 1907.
Lancel, Serge. *St. Augustine*. Translated by A. Nevill. London: SCM Press, 2002.
Lardet, Pierre. "Jerome exégète: une cohérence insoupçonnée." *REAug* 36 (1990) 300–307.
Lawless, George. "Augustine of Hippo as Preacher." In *Saint Augustine the Bishop: A Book of Essays*, edited by C. Kleinhenz and F. Le Moine, 13–31. New York: Garland, 1994.
———. "Augustine's Use of Rhetoric in His Interpretation of John 21:19–23." *AugSt* 23 (1992) 53–67.
———. "Preaching." In *Augustine through the Ages: An Encyclopaedia*, edited by A. D. Fitzgerald, 675–77. Grand Rapids, MI: Eerdmans, 1999.
Lenox-Conyngham, Andrew. "Review of: La Expositio euangelii secundum Lucam di sant' Ambrogio." *JTS* 50:2 (1999) 780–82.
Lienhard, Joseph T. "Reading the Bible and Learning to Read: The Influence of Education on St. Augustine's Exegesis." *AugSt* 27, no. 1 (1996) 7–25.
Lössl, Josef. "A Shift in Patristic Exegesis: Hebrew Clarity and Historical Verity in Augustine, Jerome, Julian of Aeclanum and Theodore of Mopsuestia." *AugSt* 32, no. 2 (2001) 157–75.
Loughlin, James F. "St. Ambrose." In *Catholic Encyclopedia*. New York: Encyclopedia, 1913. http://www.newadvent.org/cathen/01383c.htm.
Louth, Andrew. "Typology." In *The Oxford Companion to Christian Thought*, edited by Adrian Hastings et al., 727–29. Oxford: Oxford University Press, 2000.
Lubac, Henri de. *Exégèse médiévale: Les quatre sens de l'Écriture*. Part 1: T1 and 2. Paris: Aubier, 1959, 1961. English Translation: *Medieval Exegesis: The Four Senses of Scripture*. Translated by Marc Sebanc (volume 1) and Edward M. Macierowski (volume 2). Edinburgh and Grand Rapids, MI: T. & T. Clark and Eerdmans, 1998, 2000.
Luz, Ulrich. *Matthew in History: Interpretation, Influence and Effects*. Minneapolis: Fortress, 1994.
Madec, Goulven. "Les Christ des païens d'après le *De consensu euangelistarum* de saint Augustin." *RAug* 26 (1992) 2–67.
Madigan, Kevin. "Christus Nesciens? Was Christ Ignorant of the Day of Judgment? Arian and Orthodox Interpretation of Mark 13:32 in the Ancient Latin West." *Harvard Theological Review* (July 2003) 1–23.
Malden, Richard. H. "St Ambrose as an Interpreter of Holy Scripture." *JTS* 16 (1915) 509–22.
Mara, Maria G. "Ambrose of Milan, Ambrosiaster and Nicetas." In *Patrology, 4, The Golden Age of Latin Patristic Literature*, edited by Johannes Quasten, 144–94. Translated by Placid Solari. Westminster, MD: Christian Classics, 1986.

Margerie, Bertrand de. *An Introduction to the History of Exegesis, 2, The Latin Fathers*. Translated by Pierre de Fontnouvelle. Petersham, MA: St Bede's, 1995.

———. *An Introduction to the History of Exegesis, 3, St. Augustine*. Translated by Pierre de Fontnouvelle. Petersham, MA: St Bede's, 1991.

Markus, Robert A. *Signs and Meanings: World and Text in Ancient Christianity*. Liverpool: Liverpool University Press, 1996.

Marrou, Henri-Irénée. *Saint Augustin et la fin de la culture antique*. Paris: Éditions E. de Boccard, 1958.

McDermott, William C. "Saint Jerome and Pagan Greek Literature." *VChr* 36 (1982) 372–82.

McLynn, Neil B. *Ambrose of Milan: Church and Court in a Christian Capital*. Berkeley, CA: University of California Press, 1994.

McKim, Donald K., ed. *Historical Handbook of Major Biblical Interpreters*. Downers Grove, IL: InterVarsity, 1998.

McPartlan, Paul. "de Lubac, Henri." In *The Oxford Companion to Christian Thought*, edited by Adrian Hastings et al., 157. Oxford: Oxford University Press, 2000.

McWilliam, Joanne. "The Study of Augustine's Christology in the Twentieth Century." In *Augustine: From Rhetor to Theologian*, edited by Joanne McWilliam, 184–95. West Waterloo: Wilfrid Laurier University Press, 1992.

———. "Weaving the Strands Together: A Decade in Augustine's Eucharistic Theology." *Augustiniana* 14 (1991) 497–506.

Megivern, James J. *Bible Interpretation*. Wilmington, DE: McGrath, 1978.

Mercer, Jarred. "Suffering for Our Sake, Christ and Human Destiny in Hilary of Poitier's De Trinitate." *JECS* 22, no. 4 (2014) 541–568.

Metzger, Bruce M. "The Practice of Textual Criticism among the Church Fathers." *SP* 12 (1975) 340–9.

Milewski, Douglas. "Augustine's 124 Tractates on the Gospel of John." *Augustinian Studies* 33 (2002) 61–77.

Mohrmann, Christine. "Saint Augustin Prédicateur." *La Maison Dieu* 39 (1954) 83–96.

Moorhead, John. *Ambrose: Church and Society in the Late Roman World*. London: Longman, 1999.

———. "Cooking a Kid in its Mother's Milk: Patristic Exegesis of an Old Testament Command." *Aug* 37 (1997) 261–71.

———. "Hearers and Readers of Christian Latin Texts in Late Antiquity." In *Studies in Latin Literature and Roman History*, 14, edited by Carl Deroux, 479–99. Brussels: Latomus, 2008.

Muller, Hildegund. "Iohannis euangelium tractatus CXXIV, In." *Aug-Lex* 3 (2004–2010) 704–30.

———. "Theory and Practice of Preaching: Augustine, *De doctrina christiana* and *Enarrationes in psalmos*." *SP* 38 (1999) 233–7.

Muncey, Raymond W. *The New Testament Text of St Ambrose*. Cambridge: Cambridge University Press, 1959.

Murray, Mary C. "Preaching, Scripture and Visual Imagery in Antiquity." *Christianesimo Nella Storia* 14 (1993) 481–503.

Nassif, Bradley. "The 'Spiritual Exegesis' of Scripture: The School of Antioch Revisited." *Anglican Theological Review* 73 (1993) 437–70.

Nautin, Pierre. "Hieronymus." In *ThR*, edited by Gerhard Müller, 306. Berlin: W. de Gruyter, 1986.

Newlands, George M. *Hilary of Poitiers: A Study in Theological Method*. Bern: Peter Lang, 1978.
Newman, Hillel I. "How Should We Measure Jerome's Hebrew Competence?" In *Jerome of Stridon: His Life, Writings and Legacy*, edited by Andrew Cain and Josef Lössl, 131–140. Farnham, England and Burlington, VT: Ashgate, 2009.
Norris, John M. "The Theological Structure of Augustine's Exegesis in the *Tractatus in Euangelium Ioannis*." In *Augustine: Presbyter Factus Sum*, edited by Joseph T. Lienhard et al., 385–93. New York: Peter Lang, 1993.
Norris, Richard A., Jr. "Augustine and the Close of the Ancient Period of Interpretation." In *A History of Biblical Interpretation, 1, The Ancient Period*, edited by Alan J. Hauser and Duane F. Watson, 380–408. Grand Rapids, MI: Eerdmans, 2003.
Oberhelman, Steven M., ed. *Rhetoric and Homiletics in Fourth Century Christian Literature*. Atlanta, GA: Scholars, 1991.
O'Collins, Gerald. "Augustine on the Resurrection." In *Saint Augustine the Bishop: A Book of Essays*, edited by Fannie LeMoine and Christopher Kleinhenz, 65–75. New York: Garland, 1994.
O'Keefe, John J. Review of Young, Frances M. *Biblical Exegesis and the Formation of Christian Culture*. Cambridge: Cambridge University Press, 1997. *JECS* 7, no. 2 (1999) 310–2.
Old, Hughes Oliphant. *The Reading and Preaching of the Scriptures in the Worship of the Christian Church*, 2. Grand Rapids, MI: Eerdmans, 1998.
O'Meara, John J. "Augustine and Neoplatonism." *RAug* 1 (1958) 91–111.
Oort, Johannes Van. "Biblical Interpretation in the Patristic Era, A 'Handbook of Patristic Exegesis' and Some Other Recent Books and Related Projects." *VChr* 60, no. 1 (2006) 80–103.
Paredi, Angelo. *Saint Ambrose: His Life and Times*. Translated by M. Joseph Costelloe. Notre Dame, IN: University of Notre Dame Press, 1964.
Pasini, Cesare. *Ambrose of Milan: Deeds and Thought of a Bishop*. Translated by Robert L. Grant. New York: St Pauls, 2013.
Pelikan, Jaroslav. *The Emergence of the Catholic Tradition (100–600)*. Chicago, IL: The University of Chicago Press, 1971.
———. *The Shape of Death: Life, Death, and Immortality in the Early Fathers*. New York: Abingdon, 1961.
Penna, Angelo. *Principi e carattere dell' esegesi di S. Gerolamo*. Roma: Pontificio Instituto Biblico, 1950.
Perkins, Pheme. *Resurrection: New Testament Witness and Contemporary Reflection*. London: Cassell, 1984.
Perretto, Elio. "Luke the Evangelist." In *The Encyclopedia of the Early Church*, edited by Angelo Di Berardino, 509–11. Translated by Adrian Walford, 1. Cambridge: James Clarke, 1992.
Pizzolato, Luigi F. *La dottrina esegetica di sant'Ambrogio*. Milan: Vita e Pensiero, 1978.
Pollmann, Karla. "Augustine's Hermeneutics as a Universal Discipline!?" In *Augustine and the Disciplines: From Cassiciacum to Confessions*, edited by Karla Pollmann and Mark Vessey, 206–31. Oxford: Oxford University Press, 2005.
Pontet, Maurice. *L'Exégèse de S. Augustin*. Paris: Aubier, 1945.
Pope, Hugh. "St. Augustine's Tractatus in Iohannem: A Neglected Classic." *The American Ecclesiastical Review* 49 (1913) 161–72.

Poque, Suzanne. *Le langage symbolique dans la prédication d'Augustin d'Hippone.* Paris: Études Augustiniennes, 1984.
Puech, Henri-Charles and Hadot, Pierre. "L'Entretien d'Origène avec Heraclide et le commentaire de Saint Ambrose sur l' Évangile de Saint Luc." *VChr* 13 (1959) 204–34.
Ramsey, Boniface. *Ambrose.* Routledge, London, 1997.
Rebenich, Stefan. *Jerome.* London and New York: Routledge, 2002.
Reijners, Gerardus Q. *The Terminology of the Holy Cross in Early Christian Literature.* Nijemegen: Dekker and Van de Vegt, 1965.
Rogers, Jack B., and McKim, Donald K. *The Authority and Interpretation of the Bible.* San Francisco, CA: Harper and Row, 1979.
Rollero, Piero. *La "Expositio evangelii secundum Lucam" di Ambrogio come fonte della esegesi agostiniana.* Torino: Universita di Torino, 1958.
Rousseau, Philip. "The Exegete as Historian: Hilary of Poitiers' Commentary on Matthew." In *History and Historians in Late Antiquity*, edited by Brian Croke and Alanna M. Emmett, 107–15. Sydney: Pergamon, 1983.
Runia, David T. *Philo in Early Christian Literature: A Survey.* Minneapolis: Fortress, 1993.
Rusch, William G. *The Later Latin Fathers.* London: Duckworth, 1977.
Sanlon, Peter T. *Augustine's Theology of Preaching.* Minneapolis: Fortress, 2014.
Satterlee, Craig A. *Ambrose of Milan's Method of Mystagogical Preaching.* Minneapolis: Liturgical, 2002.
Savon, Hervé. *Saint Ambroise devant L'exégèse de Philon le Juif.* Paris: Études Augustiniennes, 1977.
Scalise, Charles S. "The 'Sensus Literalis': A Hermeneutical Key to Biblical Exegesis." *Scottish Journal of Theology* 42 (1989) 45–65.
Schatkin, Margaret. "The Influence of Origen upon St. Jerome's Commentary on Galatians." *VChr* 24 (1970) 49–58.
Schäublin, Christoph. "The Contribution of Rhetorics to Christian Hermeneutics." In *Handbook of Patristic Exegesis*, 1, edited by Charles Kannengeisser, 149–63. Leiden: Brill, 2004.
Scheck, Thomas P., ed., trans. "Introduction." In *Commentary on Matthew*, 24–30. FOC 117.
Schlinder, Alfred. "Augustin." In *ThR*, 4, edited by Gerhard Müller, 646–98. Berlin: W. de Gruyter, 1979.
Schmidt, Margot. *Typus, Symbol, Allegorie.* Regensburg: Verlag Friedrich Pustet, 1982.
Schnackenburg, Rudolf. *The Gospel According to St John*, 1. Translated by Kevin Smyth. New York: Herder and Herder, 1965.
Scott, T. Kermit. *Augustine: His Thought in Context.* New York: Paulist, 1995.
Shippee, Arthur Bradford. "Paradoxes of Now and Not Yet: The Separation between the Church and the Kingdom in John Chrysostom, Theodore, and Augustine." In *Reading in Christian Communities: Essays on Interpretation in the Early Church*, edited by Charles. A. Bobertz and David Brakke, 106–23. Notre Dame, IN: University of Notre Dame Press, 2002.
Simonetti, Manlio. *Biblical Interpretation in the Early Church: An Historical Introduction to Patristic Exegesis.* Edinburgh: T. & T. Clark, 1994.

---. "Exegesis, Patristic." In *The Encyclopedia of the Early Church*, edited by Angelo Di Berardino, 309–11. Translated by Adrian Walford, 1. Cambridge: James Clarke, 1992.

---. "Hilary of Poitiers and the Arian Crisis in the West: Polemicists and Heretics." In *Patrology, 4, The Golden Age of Latin Patristic Literature*, edited by Johannes Quasten, 33–143. Translated by Placid Solari. Westminster, MD: Christian Classics, 1986.

---. "Note sul commento a Matteo di Ilario di Poitiers." *Vetera Christianorum* 1 (1964) 35–64.

Smalley, Beryl. *The Study of the Bible in the Middle Ages*. Oxford: Basil Blackwell, 1952.

Snare, Gerald. "The Practice of Glossing in Late Antiquity and the Renaissance." *Studies in Philology* 94, no. 4 (1995) 439–59.

Souter, Alexander. *The Earliest Latin Commentaries of St. Paul*. Oxford: Clarendon, 1927.

Sparks, Hedley F. D. "Jerome as Biblical Scholar." In *CHB*, 1, edited by Peter R. Ackroyd and Christopher F. Evans, 510–40. Cambridge: Cambridge University Press, 1970.

Spijker, Ineke v'ant. "Introduction." In *The Multiple Meaning of Scripture: The Role of Exegesis in Early-Christian and Medieval Culture*, edited by Ineke v'ant Spijker, 1–14. Leiden: Brill, 2009.

Stefano, Frances. "Lordship over Weakness: Christ's Graced Humanity as Locus of Divine Power in Augustine's Tractates on the Gospel of John." *AugSt* 16 (1985) 1–19.

Stock, Brian. *Augustine the Reader: Meditation, Self-Knowledge and the Ethics of Interpretation*. Cambridge, MA: Harvard University Press, 1996.

Studer, Basil. "L'esegesi patristica, un incontro con Cristo. Osservazioni sull'esegesi dei padri latini." *Aug* 40, no. 2 (2000) 321–44.

Swift, Louis J. "Ambrose." In *Encyclopaedia of Early Christianity*, edited by Everett Ferguson, 41–44. 2nd ed. New York: Garland, 1997.

Taylor, Vincent. *The Gospel According to St Mark*. 2nd ed. London: Macmillan, 1966.

TeSelle, Eugene. *Augustine the Theologian*. London: Burns and Oates, 1970.

---. "Serpent, Eve, and Adam: Augustine and the Exegetical Tradition." In *Augustine: Presbyter Factus Sum*, edited by Joseph T. Lienhard et al., 350–83. New York: Peter Lang, 1993.

Teske, Roland J. "Criteria for Figurative Interpretation in St. Augustine." In *De Doctrina Christiana: A Classic of Western Culture*, edited by Duane W. H. Arnold and Pamela Bright, 109–19. Notre Dame, IN: University of Notre Dame Press, 1995.

---. "Spirituals and Spiritual Interpretation in Augustine." *AugSt* 15 (1984) 65–81.

Tevel, Johannes M. "The Labourers in the Vineyard: The Exegesis of Matthew 20:1–7 in the Early Church." *VChr* 46 (1992) 356–80.

Tilley, Maureen A. *The Bible in Christian North Africa: The Donatist World*. Minneapolis: Fortress, 1997.

Torrance, Thomas F. *Divine Meaning: Studies in Patristic Hermeneutics*. Edinburgh: T. & T. Clark, 1995.

Trigg, Joseph W. *The Message of the Fathers of the Church, 9, Biblical Interpretation*. Wilmington, DE: Michael Glazier, 1988.

Vawter, Bruce. *Biblical Inspiration*. London: Hutchinson, 1972.

Vessey, Mark. "Conference and Confession: Literary Pragmatics in Augustine's *Apologia contra Hieronymum*." *JECS* 1 (1993) 175–213.

———. "The Great Conference: Augustine and His Fellow Readers." In *Saint Augustine and the Bible*, edited by Anne-Marie Bonnardiere, 57–69. Translated by Pamela Bright, with several additional articles added in English. Notre Dame, IN: University of Notre Dame Press, 1999.

Weismann, Francisco. "Introducción a la Lectura e Interpretación de los *Tractatus in Iohannis Evangelium* de San Augustin." *Stromata* 15 (1987) 51–69.

Wiesen, David S. *St Jerome as a Satirist: A Study in Latin Thought and Letters*. Ithaca, NY: Cornell University Press, 1964.

Wetzel, James R. "Sin." In *Augustine through the Ages: An Encyclopedia*, edited by Allan D. Fitzgerald et al., 800–802. Grand Rapids, MI: Eerdmans, 1999.

Wille, Wilhelm. "*Studien zum Matthäuskommentar des Hilarius von Poitiers*." PhD diss., Universität Hamburg, 1969.

Williams, Daniel H. *Ambrose of Milan and the End of the Nicene-Arian Conflicts*. Oxford: Clarendon, 1995.

———. "Defining Orthodoxy in Hilary of Poitiers' Commentariorum In Matthaeum." *JECS* 9, no. 2 (2001) 151–71.

Williams, Megan H. *The Monk and the Book: Jerome and the Making of Christian Scholarship*. Chicago: University of Chicago Press, 2008.

Williams, Thomas. "Biblical Interpretation." In *The Cambridge Companion to Augustine*, edited by Eleanore Stump and Norman Kretzmann, 59–70. Cambridge: Cambridge University Press, 2001.

Williams, Thomas. "Hermeneutics and Reading Scripture." In *The Cambridge Companion to Augustine*, edited by David V. Meconi and Eleonore Stump, 311–27. 2nd ed. Cambridge: Cambridge University Press, 2014.

Woollcombe, Kenneth J. and Geoffrey W. H. Lampe. *Essays on Typology*. London: SCM, 1957.

Wright, David F. "Augustine, His Exegesis and Hermeneutics." In *Hebrew Bible/Old Testament: The History of Its Interpretation, 1, From the Beginnings to the Middle Ages (Until 1300), Part 1: Antiquity*, edited by Magne Sæbø, 701–30. Göttingen: Vandenhoeck & Ruprech, 1996.

———. "The Manuscripts of St. Augustine's *Tractatus in Euangelium Iohannis*: A Preliminary Survey and Check-list." *RAug* 8 (1972) 55–143.

Young, Frances M. *Biblical Exegesis and the Formation of Christian Culture*. Cambridge: Cambridge University Press, 1997.

———. "The Rhetorical Schools and Their Influence on Patristic Exegesis." In *The Making of Orthodoxy: Essays in Honour of Henry Chadwick*, edited by Rowan Williams, 183–97. Cambridge: Cambridge University Press, 1989.

———. "Traditions of Exegesis." In *The New Cambridge History of the Bible: From the Beginnings to 600*, edited by James Carleton Paget and Joachim Schaper, 734–51. Cambridge: Cambridge University Press, 2013.

www.ingramcontent.com/pod-product-compliance
Lightning Source LLC
Chambersburg PA
CBHW071244230426
43668CB00011B/1579